At the Edge of Empire

Terek Cossack trick riding (*dzhigitovka*)

At the Edge of Empire

The Terek Cossacks and the North Caucasus Frontier, 1700–1860

Thomas M. Barrett

Westview Press

A Member of the Perseus Books Group

Copyright © 1999 by Westview Press, A Member of the Perseus Books Group

Published in 1999 in the United States of America by Westview Press, 5500 Central Avenue, Boulder, Colorado 80301-2877, and in the United Kingdom by Westview Press, 12 Hid's Copse Road, Cumnor Hill, Oxford OX2 9JJ

A CIP catalog record for this book is available from the Library of Congress.
ISBN 0-8133-3671-6

The paper used in this publication meets the requirements of the American National Standard for Permanence of Paper for Printed Library Materials Z39.48-1984.

10   9   8   7   6   5   4   3   2   1

For Liisa, Frontier Companion

Contents

Illustrations

Acknowledgments

Several organizations provided support for research for this work. I spent an enjoyable year in Finland on a Fulbright grant, researching in the Slavonic Library of the University of Helsinki. IREX provided support for eight months of research in Moscow. ACTR provided a two-month grant for research in St. Petersburg and the Kennan Institute for Advanced Russian Studies granted me a short-term research award to spend one month at the Library of Congress. I am deeply grateful to all of these organizations. Thanks also go to the Social Science Research Council for sponsoring a workshop on "Rethinking Russian History," which gave me the occasion to formulate some of the questions that I address in the following study.

The staff of the Slavonic Library in Finland was extremely helpful—I can think of few more congenial places to work. I am much indebted to the staff of the Russian State Military History Archive in Moscow for directing me to particularly useful material and for their tireless and good-natured assistance. I am also grateful to the staffs of the Library of Congress, the Russian State Library, the Russian National Library, and the Russian State Historical Archive.

Ed Lazzerini and Dan Brower, and the other participants of the "Russia's Orient" conference at the University of California, Berkeley, read an earlier version of Chapter 6 and provided many useful suggestions. Thanks especially to Ed and Dan for leading a stimulating conference and helping to revitalize Russian imperial studies. John McNeill contributed much to Chapter 4. Willard Sunderland and Chris Adams offered stimulating insight on a version of Chapter 7. Marcus Rediker has been a model teacher, scholar, and guide; I am indebted to him for his interest and support. Al Rieber also gave warm encouragement at an early stage of this project. Richard Stites inspired me as an imaginative and generous historian (and person). I first began to research the history of the North Caucasus in David Goldfrank's foreign policy seminar at Georgetown University. Both Richard and David have been good teachers and friends and have helped me understand the intellectual and creative possibilities of history. Thanks also to Catherine Evtukhov for her useful suggestions and to Pam Hicks for cheerfully and skillfully guiding the desktop publishing process.

A deep debt of gratitude also goes out to many friends who provided fellowship, intellectual nourishment, and good cheer, and who made life quite enjoyable in Finland, Moscow, and Vladikavkaz: Marja-Liisa Ravantti, Jukka Ravantti, Jakub Lapatka, Vera Medvedeva, Alia Gavrilova, Dima Oleinikov, David Schimmelpenninck van der Oye, and Tatiana Filippova. I am in particular gratitude to Liudmila Gatagova for her kindness and generosity and to S. B. Gatagov, Z. Z. Gatagova, Alan Gatagov, and M. M. Bliev for their warmth and hospitality in Vladikavkaz.

Finally, I wish to acknowledge those who have been the most helpful and supportive, without whom this work would not have been possible: A. Lee Barrett, Mary Barrett, Mary Anne Decker, Dick Franzén, Edie Franzén, and most of all Liisa Franzén, to whom this work is dedicated.

I gratefully acknowledge the permission to reprint the following. The map on page xiv and parts of Chapter 6 originally appeared in Daniel R. Brower and Edward J. Lazzerini, eds., *Russia's Orient: Imperial Borderlands and Peoples, 1700-1917* (Bloomington & Indianapolis: Indiana University Press, 1997), 100, 227-48. Parts of Chapter 1 originally appeared as "Lines of Uncertainty: The Frontiers of the North Caucasus," *Slavic Review* 54, no. 3 (Fall 1995): 578-601. Thanks to the American Association for the Advancement of Slavic Studies for permission to reprint. Chapter 4 originally appeared in *Environment and History* 5, no. 1 (1999).

Thomas M. Barrett

Illustration 1 A Cossack woman in Chervlennaia stanitsa
(drawing from an album by P.I. Chelishchev)

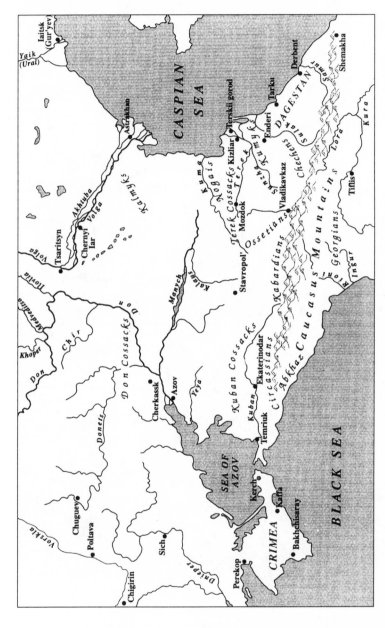

Illustration 2 Crimea, the Caucasus, and southern Russia. *Source*: Daniel R. Brower and Edward J. Lazzerini, eds., *Russia's Orient: Imperial Borderlands and Peoples, 1700-1917* (Bloomington & Indianapolis: Indiana University Press, 1997)

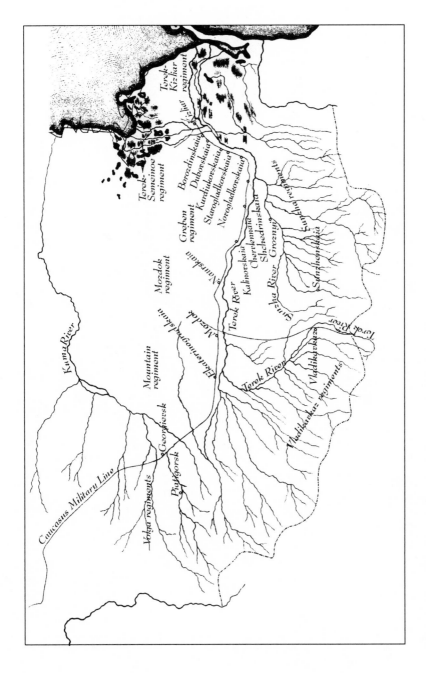

Illustration 3 Select Terek Cossack villages and towns circa 1860

At the Edge of Empire

1

Introduction:
Frontier History and Methodology

The left side of the Terek and the right side of the Kuban, and the Cossack stanitsas of the [Caucasus] line regiments positioned in a row along them, are in some kind of transitional state: it is not Russia, but it's not Asia either. At each step you see the Kabardian hat, Kubachi pistol, Chechen sword, and wiry mountain horse; but at each step also a Russian woman, Slavic face, familiar speech with a mixture of Russian words, husks of nuts and seeds on the streets, and cockroaches in the hut.
—I. Slivitskii, *Kavkaz*, 18 September 1848

A fortress is a stone thrown on the field: wind and water will wear it away; but a stanitsa is a plant, which imbibes from the soil with its roots and little by little envelops over and covers the entire field.
—Mountaineer saying

Location, in Cossack history, is everything. In the nineteenth century Cossacks became a legal order or estate, but even before that the privileges and duties of the numerous hosts positioned across the vast empire were roughly the same, in law; in practice, the value of the privileges and the burden of the duties were largely determined by where Cossacks lived. All Cossacks sent detachments to fight alongside the regular army on distant battlefields and performed a variety of escort and guard duties; all Cossacks received in exchange for these and other services, land, local self-government, freedom from direct taxation, and salaries. Service for land and a large degree of local autonomy—this system allowed the state to supply the army with tough warriors on the cheap, since Cossacks provided for, and outfit and equipped, themselves with bounty brought in by the land. The quality of that land obviously helped determine how well this aspect of the Cossack system worked. But there was a twin function of cossackdom that was also deeply rooted in the land. The state used Cossacks to colonize the Russian frontier, secure new territories, integrate local economies, and spread Russian civilization in Siberia, the lower Volga, Central Asia, and the North Caucasus. The societies, economies, environments, and peoples that Cossacks encountered along these frontiers contributed to the success or failure of this mission.

Nowhere was a Cossack more Cossack, trying to fulfill all of these functions, than in the North Caucasus. In many regions of the empire, the frontier duties of Cossacks ceased to be necessary by the eighteenth and nineteenth centuries; as soon as Cossack lands became well integrated into the Russian empire, cossackdom there became anachronistic. What is the purpose of having fortified lines when the border has shifted hundreds of miles away, frontier militias when there is no one to fight, scouts when there is nothing to scout, and economic colonizers when the region has already been colonized? The Terek Cossacks of the North Caucasus are particularly important in understanding cossackdom in the Russian empire because they were so very Cossack in every sense.

All Cossacks faced a tension between the demands of service and the needs of settlement—the more time they spent fighting meant less time for tending often-precarious home economies. For the Terek Cossacks, that tension was stretched nearly to the breaking point because of the vital role they played in the creation of empire. They lived on a turbulent frontier, where the Russian empire was in the process of a protracted and difficult expansion, where the mountain people of the North Caucasus resisted ferociously, and where the conflict took on the trappings of a Christian-Muslim religious war. Although the state pulled all Cossacks into active service, Siberian or Ural Cossacks, for example, never faced a prolonged, widespread military threat from the indigenous population and Don Cossacks by the eighteenth century faced no local threat at all. In the North Caucasus, Cossacks actively built empire through settlement and military service. What made their job particularly difficult was the fact that their land was poor, labor scarce, and enemies strong. In the process of negotiating between the demands of the state and the needs of their communities, Terek Cossacks created a frontier society that reflected some of the strengths and weaknesses of the Russian empire.

The backdrop for this story is the Russian conquest of the North Caucasus, one of the most costly and protracted military expansions of the empire, and one that was unrivaled in the creation of modern Russian national identity. As the story goes, the Russian state began pushing to the south with the conquest of Kazan and Astrakhan in the sixteenth century and forts were established in the North Caucasus soon thereafter. Large-scale warfare began with Peter I's Persian campaign (1722) and a series of wars with Persia and the Ottoman empire on Caucasian lands ensued throughout the eighteenth and nineteenth centuries. The military line crept south into the North Caucasus, beginning with the Kizliar-Mozdok Line (1769), and fortress after fortress advanced Russian forces further into the mountains. After the completion of the Caucasus

Military Line in 1832, the Black Sea Coastal Line was raised to the west, cutting off the peoples of the Caucasus from the Black Sea and contact with Turkey. The native peoples resisted the Russian encroachment with guerilla warfare and major conflagrations, culminating in Shamil's holy war (1834-1859). When the Circassian resistance was finally defeated in 1864, the conquest of the North Caucasus was complete and the region became a pacified colony of the Russian empire.

The western historiography of that conquest has greatly advanced in this century, but the history of Russia and the North Caucasus remains essentially military history—the frontier is represented as a fault line of war, conflict, and religious division where Cossacks and mountain people stand on opposite sides of the divide, glaring at each other with hostile intent.[1] As the following study will show, the Russian advance through the North Caucasus was much more than a military conquest: it was also a frontier process involving the in- and out-migration of large numbers of people, the settlement and creation of new communities, and the abandonment of old ones. And, as on all frontiers, borders were crossed and allegiances shifted continually by Russians and Ukrainians, by mountain peoples, by Armenians and Georgians. To understand the Russian annexation of the North Caucasus, we must look behind the military lines, to the movements of peoples, the settlements and communities, the transformation of the landscape, and the interactions of neighbors, not just in war but in everyday life.

Russian and Soviet historians of the North Caucasus sometimes were more interested than their western counterparts in exploring behind the military lines, but usually for rather narrow reasons. Pre-revolutionary historiography focused on the military conquest of the region, and discussed administration, resettlement policy, and the use of native peoples only as they facilitated Russian expansion. D. I. Romanovskii's *Kavkaz i Kavkazskaia voina*, for example, does delve into Russian settlement of the North Caucasus, but as a projection of Russian power which was bringing the "triumph of civilization over stubborn barbarity." The leading military historian of Russia in the Caucasus was V. A. Potto; as a general he was most interested in depicting the glory of Russian arms and used terms such as "the Chechen mutiny" and "the Kabardian revolt" to describe what he felt was illegitimate resistance to Russian rule. His was a heroic history of military triumph:

> There, hundreds of people courageously withstood the thousands and either triumphed or died down to the last person; there a general, in a word, was prompted to heroic deeds and gave an example of heroic death to his soldiers; there a soldier, with a touchingly simple consciousness, gave his life for the common cause, not suspecting that he performed anything unusual.[2]

Soviet historians studied the peoples of the North Caucasus for their own sake and developed national histories to represent many of the ethnic groups there. The tendency was either to downplay destruction by the Russian military or to portray it as fending off the real enemies of the Caucasus (Persia, the Ottoman empire, the Crimean khanate) or as a part of an oppressive, but ultimately progressive, tsarist "colonial politics" that brought the North Caucasus into the timetable of history.[3] There are plenty of Soviet studies of migration and ethnic mixing in the North Caucasus, of the development of the regional economy, of cities, and of Cossacks. In these, grandiose claims are often made about the closeness and mutual influence of Russians and mountain peoples, but with no real examination of frontier life with all of its complexity, tensions, and violence. Only bits and pieces are extracted that inevitably add up to *sblizhenie* ("drawing together") and *druzhba narodov* ("the friendship of peoples").[4]

If Soviet historians tended to define Russian frontiers as zones of *sblizhenie*, western historians either have seen them as colonies or borders or have not seen them at all. Compared to their apparently inexhaustible fascination with the American West, historians have been hesitant to explore Russian frontiers. The few attempts to cast Russian history in terms of an expanding frontier have foundered on an overly metahistorical, Turnerian approach, more concerned with the spirit of the state than life at the edge, and backed up by little supporting research. All of Russian history is presented as frontier history, beginning with Kiev and ending with Siberia, with little distinction between the different periods of Russian migration and always omitting the Caucasus (and usually the lower and middle Volga). Or, the Russian frontier is simply equated with the American one: Kazan becomes St. Louis, the conquest of Novgorod is likened to the acquisition of Ohio from Britain, and the conquest of Ukraine is Russia's Louisiana Purchase.[5] A few historians have been more restrained in their approach but still make a quick leap from Kazan to Siberia, ignoring the fact that colonization moved south well before it moved east, and that the lower Volga was as non-Russian as Siberia until the late eighteenth century.[6] Similarly, major works on migration, colonization, and frontier society focus mostly on Siberia, or on the steppe frontier and the settlement of Ukraine and the Crimea. It is usually forgotten that these migrations were part of a larger and more diverse process (and that the steppe extends to the foothills of the Caucasus).[7]

Extremely valuable recent work has been done on the non-Russian edge of the expanding frontier and it is partly due to these studies that historians of Russia no longer flirt with Turner's notion of the frontier as an engine of progress.[8] But they too depict the transformation of Ukrainian, Crimean, Volga, and Siberian borderlands into Russian regions more as a political process than as a social one. Our understanding is limited mostly to conquest (war and administration), while the "constructive" aspects of Russian colonization (the creation of new social identities, ethnic relations, landscapes, regional economies, and material cultures) have yet to be explored. Or, the social history focuses exclusively on the "losers" and their repression, resistance, extinction, and emigration.

The type of frontier history appropriate for the North Caucasus, and for other Russian frontiers as well, should draw upon developments in the historiography of the American frontier in the last twenty years. The Turnerian type of frontier history that was so inappropriate to Russia has finally been abandoned, with its free white settlers moving west to "vacant" lands and gloriously creating American individualism and democracy in the process. In its place, historians are writing about a more complicated process, involving people of various colors and nations, environmental manipulation, cultural mixing, social stratification, and grand myth-making.[9] The following study has been especially influenced by the new American frontier histories that have sought to depict the mutual influences between Native Americans and colonists. Daniel H. Usner, Jr.'s *Indians, Settlers, & Slaves in a Frontier Exchange Economy* has encouraged me to examine the creative role of local trade on the frontier, where enemies often become trading partners for practical reasons. Richard White's *The Middle Ground* inspired me to discover a North Caucasus that was something more than conquest and resistance, as he puts it, "the place in between: in between cultures, peoples, and in between empires and the nonstate world of the villages."[10]

The specific focus of this study is the Terek Cossacks, frontier settlers along the Terek River of the North Caucasus who became servants of the Russian state, warriors, and occasional brigands and deserters. The traditional narrative of Cossack history has been how they gradually lost their wild freedom and became servitors and subjects of the Russian empire, how the meaning of "Cossack" transforms from the original Turkish *Qazaq* ("a free, independent person, adventurer, vagabond") to a particular Russian legal estate with well-defined privileges and obligations. Cossack historiography has focused either on the original freedom of the Cossacks and their early rebellions against Russia or on the encroachment of a bureaucratic state that gradually restricted their traditional liberties.[11] In many respects, though, the period in between is the most interesting, for it was then that Cossacks and military-governmental officials had to work out a mutually tolerable relationship that fell between independence and subservience. It was then that Cossacks became somewhat ambivalent servants to the Russian state and when the Russian state became a somewhat ambivalent patron of the semi-independent warrior communities of Cossacks. Both sides had to give, perhaps nowhere more so than in the North Caucasus.

The central tension in modern Cossack history has been the conflict between the twin purpose of Cossack conquest and Cossack colonization, between military service and the needs of their communities. An exploration of that tension is central to this work. In the North Caucasus, Cossacks created and defended the Caucasus Military Line and this was essential to the conquest of the region. As settlers, though, Cossacks and mountain people transversed the military line whose porousness was essential to the Cossack communities. So on the one hand, Cossacks were to participate in a military-economic blockade to channel trade through official trading posts and make the mountain people economically dependent on Russia. As settlers, though, Cossacks needed free flowing trade, and took every opportunity to subvert the quarantine measures. Cossacks participated in campaigns to push threatening Chechens further south into the mountains. As settlers, their communities suffered from the resulting cutoff of the firewood and grain trade. The demands of conquest forced Cossacks to spend a good part of their lives manning watchtowers and patrolling for invaders. The demands of their labor-starved economies forced them to shirk military service to attend to their farms and livestock. Cossacks helped cut down forests to create military highways to facilitate the movement of troops; many more trees fell to provide building and heating material for the new Cossack villages popping up along the Terek. The resulting deforestation and flooding had disastrous effects on the same villages. Cossacks took part in a holy war of Christianity versus Islam, when the mountain leader Shamil managed to rally his people under the banner of jihad. Cossack communities, though, often practiced Old Belief, which made their main religious opponent the Orthodox church.

In practice, the state was mostly concerned about military service and often pushed the Cossacks to their limit in order to keep the military lines fully staffed. And the commanders were largely successful; Cossacks never deserted en masse, they fought with élan, they probably identified with Russia more than the mountain people. They played an essential role in the military conquest. But that is only half of the story.

In practice, Cossacks were often affected the most by the facts of settlement. The weakness of the Russian state in the North Caucasus allowed Cossacks to maintain a large degree of independence; the weakness of the Russian economy made them dependent on native economies and labor power; the particularity of the local environment encouraged them to adopt native material culture. While Russian power expanded, Russian civilization contracted; the North Caucasus was pulled into the empire, but at the same time the Terek Cossacks were pulled into the North Caucasus. If we take seriously Russia's aspiration to be a civilizing, western empire, then both sides of this history need to be told. And the imperial mission failed as much as it succeeded.

The North Caucasus, and no doubt many other far-flung corners of the empire, experienced a very different type of development than the Russian center. The estate system was very weak, there was almost no serfdom, and little manorial agriculture. Those who ended up settling in the North Caucasus found a new and challenging environment, their numbers were small compared to the natives, and their local economy was far away from the supplies and demands of internal Russia. With the center so distant, and the central aspects of Russian society so weak, a flow of influence from the North Caucasus washed these shores, bringing great ethnic and religious diversity, and a frontier culture and economy extremely different from that of the heartland. The position of women, for example, was considerably stronger than in the interior of Russia, belying the oft-stated supposition that Cossack society was extremely patriarchal and misogynist.

Since "frontier" has become such a loaded word, especially in the American context, perhaps it would be more suitable to borrow the concept of edges from ecology. Edge habitats are transition zones between two different ecosystems such as grassland and forest and are the locus of great biological diversity. In human terms, we can say that edges are zones of great cultural complexity, interchange, and creativity. Part of the purpose of this study is to describe one such edge and to give places like it their due in national histories.

Historiography has concentrated on how the edge contracted into military lines and lines of ethnic typecasting. The resurrected Cossack and North Caucasian history in the new Russia so far has chosen to remember mostly these divisions.[12] The history of the Russian conquest and the native resistance has been pressed into use by both sides in the contemporary Russo-Chechen conflict, often at the expense of truth. All cultures resurrect that history which is most useful to them, so it is natural—and unfortunate—that a nineteenth century war would be recreated to expedite a twentieth century war.

But human experience comprises more than borders, conquest, and expansion. Any study of empire at the edge should also be conscious of interstices, fluidity, uncertainty, "middle grounds," and countervailing forces. To write only state history, to write narrow national history is to obscure this and to lose an important part of the human experience and one that has great relevance to our future.

Russian historiography has been a history without edges, so much so that there is not even a general word for métis, or a person of mixed blood, in the contemporary Russian language. I hope that the following will be a small first step in rectifying that, not to ignore conquest, but to remember that there are other usable histories also.[13]

The experience of the Terek Cossacks is also important because it stands so apart from the Cossack myth. Like cowboys in the United States, gauchos in Argentina, and many other frontier social groups who became national icons, by the end of the nineteenth century Cossacks represented the soul of Russian national identity. They were, according to the myth, deeply Russian in spirit if not ethnicity (strong, spontaneous, Russophone, Orthodox), Christian warriors for the tsar, intrepid scouts and explorers, the vanguard of Russification, conquering wilderness, alien enemies, and alien cultures alike.[14] The history of the Terek Cossacks shows how shallow that myth was—many were neither Russian nor Orthodox, they were more losers than victors in their struggle with the "wilderness," they fought mostly for themselves and their sense of honor rather than for an empire or a tsar, and they were far from being agents of Russian civilization.

The goal of the following study, then, is twofold: to reinterpret part of the history of Russia and the North Caucasus as a frontier encounter and to reorient Cossack history towards the social and cultural world of a heretofore neglected group, the Terek Cossacks.

Notes

1. John F. Baddeley, *The Russian Conquest of the Caucasus* (London: Longmans, Green and Co., 1908); W. E. D. Allen and Paul Muratoff, *Caucasian Battlefields* (Cambridge: Cambridge University Press, 1953); Marie Bennigsen Broxup, ed., *The North Caucasus Barrier* (New York: St. Martin's Press, 1992); Moshe Gammer, *Muslim Resistance to the Tsar: Shamil and the Conquest of Chechnia and Daghestan* (London: Frank Cass, 1994).

See also the following works on the image of the Caucasus in Russian literature and society, a subject more of the center than the frontier: Uwe Halbach, "Die Bergvölker (*gorcy*) als Gegner und Opfer: Der Kaukasus in der Wahrnehmung Russlands," in *Kleine Völker in der Geschichte Osteuropas*, eds. Manfred Alexander, Frank Kämpfer, and Andreas Kappeler (Stuttgart: Franz Steiner Verlag, 1991), 52-65; Thomas M. Barrett, "The Remaking of the Lion of Dagestan: Shamil in Captivity," *Russian Review* 53 (July 1994), 353-66; Susan Layton, *Russian Literature and Empire: Conquest of the Caucasus from Pushkin to Tolstoy* (Cambridge: Cambridge University Press, 1994).

2. D. I. Romanovskii, *Kavkaz i Kavkazskaia voina* (St. Petersburg: Tipografiia Tovarishchestva "Obshchestvennaia pol'za," 1860), 48, 361. V. A. Potto, *Kavkazskaia voina v otdel'nykh ocherkakh, epizodakh, legendakh i biografiiakh*, 5 vols. (St. Petersburg: Tipografiia R. Golike, 1885-1891), 1: 3; and *Utverzhdenie russkogo vladychestva na Kavkaze*, 3 vols. (Tiflis: Tipografiia Ia.K. Libermana, 1901-1904).

3. For example, S. K. Bushuev, ed., *Istoriia Severo-Osetinskoi ASSR* (Moscow: Izdatel'stvo Akademii nauk SSSR, 1959); G. D. Daniialov, ed., *Istoriia Dagestana*, 3 vols. (Moscow: Nauka, 1967-1969); T. K. Kumykov, ed., *Istoriia Kabardino-Balkarskoi ASSR s drevneishikh vremen do nashikh dnei*, 2 vols. (Moscow: Nauka, 1967); N. A. Smirnov, *Politika Rossii na Kavkaze v XVI-XVII vv.* (Moscow: Izdatel'stvo sotsial'no-ekonomicheskoi literatury, 1958); N. S. Kiniapina, M. M. Bliev, and V. V. Degoev, *Kavkaz i Srednaia Aziia vo vneshnei politike Rossii. Vtoraia polovina XVIII-80e gody XIXv.* (Moscow: Izdatel'stvo Moskovskogo universiteta, 1984).

4. The best general Soviet histories are B. B. Piotrovskii, ed., *Istoriia narodov Severnogo Kavkaza s drevneishikh vremen do kontsa XVIII v.* (Moscow: Nauka, 1988) and A. L. Narochnitskii, ed., *Istoriia narodov Severnogo Kavkaza konets XVIIIv.-1917 g.* (Moscow: Nauka, 1988). Two bibliographies are M. M. Miansarov, *Bibliographia Caucasica et Transcaucasica* (St. Petersburg: Tipografiia O. I. Baksta i Gogenfel'den i komp., 1874-1876); Moshe Gammer, "Shamil and the Murid Movement, 1830-1859: An Attempt at a Comprehensive Bibliography," *Central Asian Survey* 10, no. 1/2 (1991): 189-247.

5. Joseph L. Wieczynski, *The Russian Frontier* (Charlottesville: University Press of Virginia, 1976); George V. Lantzeff and Richard A. Pierce, *Eastward to Empire: Exploration*

and Conquest on the Russian Open Frontier to 1750 (Montreal: McGill-Queen's University Press, 1973); Roger Dow, "Prostor: A Geopolitical Study of Russia and the United States," *Russian Review* 1, no. 1 (November 1941): 7-8. Even a recent article by Denis Shaw uses Turner's frontier. See Judith Pallot and Denis J. P. Shaw, *Landscape and Settlement in Romanov Russia, 1613-1917* (Oxford: Clarendon Press, 1990), 13-32.

John P. LeDonne's *The Russian Empire and the World, 1700-1917* (New York, Oxford: Oxford University Press, 1997), a history of foreign policy and imperial conquest, uses a concept of core areas and frontiers borrowed from Owen Lattimore. This is state history with a vengeance. The personalities and groups who created the Russian empire, though, are absent.

6. Donald W. Treadgold, "Russian Expansion in the Light of Turner's Study of the American Frontier," *Agricultural History* 26, no. 4 (October 1952): 147-52; A. Lobanov-Rostovsky, "Russian Expansion in the Far East in the Light of the Turner Hypothesis," in *The Frontier in Perspective*, ed. Walker D. Wyman and Clifton B. Kroeber (Madison: University of Wisconsin Press, 1957), 79-94. Intensive settlement in the lower Volga did not begin until the 1780s. See V. M. Kabuzan, *Narody Rossii v XVIII veke. Chislennost' i etnicheskii sostav* (Moscow: Nauka, 1990), 90.

7. Donald W. Treadgold, *The Great Siberian Migration* (Princeton: Princeton University Press, 1957); Raymond Fisher, *The Russian Fur Trade, 1550-1700* (Berkeley: University of California Press, 1943); Terrence E. Armstrong, *Russian Settlement in the North* (Cambridge: Cambridge University Press, 1965); William H. McNeill, *Europe's Steppe Frontier, 1500-1800* (Chicago: University of Chicago Press, 1964); E. I. Druzhinina, *Severnoe prichernomor'e v 1775-1780 gg.* (Moscow: Izdatel'stvo Akademii nauk SSЗR, 1959); N. D. Polons'ka-Vasylenko, "The Settlement of the Southern Ukraine (1750-1775)," *The Annals of the Ukrainian Academy of Arts and Sciences in the U.S.*, 4-5 (Summer-Fall 1953); D. L. Bagalei, *Materialy dlia istorii kolonizatsii i byta stepnoi okrainy Moskovskogo gosudarstva v XVI-XVII stolety*, 2 vols. (Khar'kov: Tipografiia K. P. Schasni, 1890).

One of the few works on a non-Siberian frontier is Michael Khodarkovsky's *Where Two Worlds Met: The Russian State and the Kalmyk Nomads, 1600-1771* (Ithaca: Cornell University Press, 1992). While mostly interested in Kalmyk society and relations with the Russian state, Khodarkovsky briefly discusses (pp. 308-35) Russian colonization along the Volga and the resulting clashes with Kalmyks. Two other classic exceptions are Boris Nolde, *La Formation de l'Empire russe*, 2 vols. (Paris: Institut d'Etudes slaves, 1952-53) and Andreas Kappeler, *Russlands erste Nationalitäten. Das Zarenreich und die Völker der Mittleren Wolga vom 16. bis 19 Jahrhundert* (Cologne: Bohlau, 1982).

Willard Sunderland has also done excellent work on Siberian and non-Siberian frontiers. See "An Empire of Peasants: Empire-Building, Interethnic Interaction, and Ethnic Stereotyping in the Rural World of the Russian Empire, 1800-1850s," in Jane Burbank and David L. Ransel, eds., *Imperial Russia: New Histories for the Empire* (Bloomington: Indiana University Press, 1998), 174-98.

8. Alan Fisher, *The Crimean Tatars* (Stanford: Hoover Institution Press, 1978); Azade-Ayşe Rorlich, *The Volga Tatars* (Stanford: Hoover Institution Press, 1986); Zenon H. Kohut, *Russian Centralism and Ukrainian Autonomy* (Cambridge, Mass.: Harvard University Press for the Harvard Ukrainian Research Institute, 1988); James Forsyth, *A History of the Peoples of Siberia: Russia's North Asian Colony, 1581-1990* (Cambridge: Cambridge University Press, 1992).

9. For reviews of recent American frontier history see William Cronon, George Miles, and Jay Gitlin, eds., *Under an Open Sky: Rethinking America's Western Past* (New York: W. W. Norton, 1992); Patricia Nelson Limerick, Clyde A. Milner II, and Charles E. Rankin, eds., *Trails: Towards a New Western History* (Lawrence: University of Kansas Press, 1991).

10. Daniel H. Usner, Jr., *Indians, Settlers, and Slaves in a Frontier Exchange Economy: The Lower Mississippi Valley Before 1783* (Chapel Hill: University of North Carolina Press for the Institute of Early American History and Culture, 1992); Richard White, *The Middle Ground: Indians, Empires, and Republics in the Great Lakes Region, 1650-1815* (New York: Cambridge University Press, 1991), x. For more on the frontier conceptualization of the North Caucasus see Thomas M. Barrett, "Lines of Uncertainty: The Frontiers of the North Caucasus," *Slavic Review* 54, no. 3 (Fall 1995), 578-601.

11. See, for example, Robert H. McNeal, *Tsar and Cossack, 1855-1914* (New York: St. Martin's Press, 1987); Paul Avrich, *Russian Rebels 1600-1800* (New York: W. W. Norton & Co., 1972); Philip Longworth, *The Cossacks* (New York: Holt, Rinehart and Winston, 1969); Gunter Stökl, *Die Enstehung des Kosakentums* (Munich: Isar Verlag, 1952).

The standard histories of the Terek Cossacks are V. A. Potto, *Dva veka Terskago kazachestva (1577-1801)*, 2 vols. (Vladikavkaz: Elektropechatnia tipografiia Terskago oblastnago pravleniia, 1912); I. V. Bentkovskii, *Grebentsy* (Moscow: Russkaia topolitografiia, 1889); I. D. Popko, *Terskie kazaki so starodavnikh vremen. Istoricheskii ocherk* (St. Petersburg: Tipografiia Departamenta udelov, 1880); G. A. Tkachëv, *Stanitsa Chervlennaia. Istoricheskii ocherk* (Vladikavkaz: Elektropechatnia tipografiia Terskago oblastnago pravleniia, 1912); L. B. Zasedateleva, *Terskie kazaki* (Moscow: Izdatel'stvo Moskovskogo universiteta, 1974); I. L. Omel'chenko, *Terskoe kazachestvo* (Vladikavkaz: "Ir," 1991).

12. Some old, triumphal, reductionistic histories such as Potto's *Kavkazskaia voina* have been reprinted. Cossacks, and Cossack historians, are busy resurrecting the minutiae of their host structure and military paraphernalia. The occasional new Cossack histories have been extremely derivative of nineteenth-century secondary sources, which means triumphal and nationalistic. A. M. and V. M. Gdenko's *Za drugi svoia ili vsë o kazachestve* (Moscow: Mezhdunarodnyi fond slavianskoi pis'mennosti i kul'tury, 1993), for example, does not even mention that "our friends" in the North Caucasus happened to be largely Old Believer (i.e., not Orthodox warriors), and that some were in fact Muslims.

V. A. Potto, *Kavkazskaia voina* (Stavropol': "Kavkazskii krai," 1994), 5 vols.; V. K. Shenk, *Kazach'i voiska* (St. Petersburg: Imperatorskaia glavnaia kvartira, 1912; repr. n.p.: Aktsionernoe obshchestvo "Dobral'," 1992); Iu. Galushko, *Kazach'i voiska Rossii* (Moscow: Informatsionno-izdatel'skoe agenstvo "Russkii mir," 1993); Oleg Agafonov, *Kazach'i voiska Rossiiskoi imperii* (Moscow: AOZG "Epokha," izdatel'stvo "Russkaia kniga; Kaliningrad: GIPP "Iantarnyi skaz," 1995). The most prrofessional and hopeful of the new histories are M. M. Bliev and V. V. Degoev, *Kavkazskaia voina* (Moscow: "Roset," 1994) and L. S. Gatagova, *Pravitel'stvennaia politika i narodnoe obrazovanie na Kavkaze v XIX v.* (Moscow: Izdatel'skii tsentr "Rossiia molodaia," 1993).

13. There were regional words indicating quite specific interethnic mixes. *"Boldyr"* was mostly used for animal crossbreeds, but it also could mean a Russian-Kalmyk in Astrakhan; a Russian-Buriat or a Russian-Tungus in Siberia; a Russian-Tatar, Russian-Mongol, or Russian-"Chud" in Orenburg; a Russian-Samoed in Arkhangelsk; and so on. Dal' says that this was the most general word for métis. It is, however, an extremely rare word in modern Russian and does not appear in most contemporary dictionaries. Vladimir Dal',

Tolkovyi slovar' zhivogo velikorusskogo iazyka (St. Petersburg-Moscow: Tovarishchestva M. O. Vol'f, 1903; repr. Moscow: Izdatel'skaia gruppa "Progress" "Univers," 1994), 1:268-69.

14. The Cossack myth pervaded high literature, history, folk culture, and mass culture. On literature see Judith Deutsch Kornblatt, *The Cossack Hero in Russian Literature: A Study in Cultural Mythology* (Madison: University of Wisconsin Press, 1992). For nineteenth century historiography, see *Kazachestvo: bibliograficheskii ukazatel'* (Moscow: Rossiiskaia akademiia nauk institut etnologii i antropologii imeni N. N. Miklukho-Maklaia, 1995). For a brief discussion of the songs and legends associated with Yermak, "the conqueror of Siberia," see Terence Armstrong, ed., *Yermak's Campaign in Siberia*, The Hakluyt Society, second series, no. 146 (London: The Hakluyt Society, 1975), 13-18. For some examples of the Cossack myth in mass culture, see the excerpts from Nikolai Polevoi's *Ermak Timofeich*, Nikolai Zriakhov's *The Battle of the Russians with the Kabardians*, and *The Heroic Feat of the Don Cossack Kuzma Firsovich Kriuchkov* in James von Geldern and Louise McReynolds, eds., *Entertaining Tsarist Russia* (Bloomington: Indiana University Press, 1998).

2

The Origins of the Terek Cossacks

I grant you, our dear Cossacks,
The river, rapid and free,
Terek, son of the Mountain,
From the very ridge
To the blue sea.

—Ivan the Terrible in Terek Cossack song

There are Cossacks who don't receive state salaries, but there are no Cossacks who
don't fill their bellies.

—Ossetian saying

The groups of settlers that coalesced into the Terek Cossacks of the early eighteenth century came to the North Caucasus from various places at various times. They were formally enrolled in Russian service only in 1720, after two centuries of an independent and rather obscure existence in the region. There are few things we can say about their origins with great certainty and their early historiography is as much legend as fact. Historians of the Cossacks have claimed that they descended from Novgorod river pirates of the fourteenth century (*ushkuiniki*), from Riazan' Cossacks fleeing south in the sixteenth century after Muscovy's absorption of their princedom, or from migrating Volga or Don Cossacks of the sixteenth century. There is no solid documentary evidence to support any of these claims.[1] What is certain is that there were people, usually called "free Cossacks," living under the mountain ridge (*greben'*, hence their name Greben Cossacks) along the left bank of the Sunzha River and along the banks of the Terek in the mid-sixteenth century who occasionally provided their services to the fledgling Russian forts of the Terek region. The first mention in Russian documents of Cossack villages in the North Caucasus is in 1563; the first document awarding them a salary dates from 1623.[2]

The Terek Cossacks themselves were similarly divided about their ultimate origins. Nineteenth century songs and folklore tell of Cossacks living as outlaws in the mountains, intermarrying with native people, and finally being forgiven by Ivan IV and allowed to resettle north to "Russian" land. Oral tradition sometimes began their genealogy with Yermak's Cossacks (the "conquerors of Siberia") in the sixteenth century. According to stories of old-timers recorded in 1856, a Cossack Andrei split off from Yermak, headed south, and settled beyond the Terek in the Kumyk lands, founding Andreevskaia derevnia ("Andrei's village"), which they connected to "Endirei," a Kumyk village. Another variant held that Yermak himself settled in the North Caucasus before moving on to Siberia. But in 1881, ataman Svistunovyi claimed instead that they were "free birds" from Riazan.'[3]

Why would these Slavic warriors of the plains move all the way to the rugged mountains and settle amidst the Caucasian tribes? The Cossack myth has the pilgrims reaching the bank of the Terek, pausing to notice that "this is the end of the Russian land," and after a fierce debate moving on and settling beyond the Terek where the soil was rich and the water, trees, and game plentiful. And they declared, "the land is free here, but we will see Russia at our threshold."[4] Strange that they would abandon their beloved homeland in the first place.

Cossack legend and historiography alike cloud the few known facts about the nature of Cossack settlement in the North Caucasus by fixing on a Great Russian essence and clinging to mytho-historical ties to a Russian homeland. Although Cossack historians do not ignore the ethnic mixing of the early Terek Cossacks, their links with the native peoples of the North Caucasus are minimized and claims to Russian origins maximized, often in quite fanciful ways. I. Abozin, writing in *Voennyi sbornik* in 1862, vigorously refuted the suggestion that the most important fact of Terek Cossack origin was their intermixing with the native peoples of the Caucasus. Instead, he tied them to the same Cossack Andrei, who supposedly came from the village of Grebna on the Don. They were named Greben Cossacks, then, because they came from the Don, not because they were Caucasus mountain Cossacks; while he reluctantly admitted that some moved to the mountains, he insisted that they always dreamed about returning to Russia, north of the Terek. I. V. Bentkovskii similarly claimed they were Cossacks from the Greben mountains of the Don, probably resettled by Andrei. However, he realized that it was impossible to ignore how unusual it was that Cossacks, who always based themselves by large navigable rivers, crossed over the Terek and settled in the mountains. The best he could do was to suggest that they just kept going, not knowing what lay ahead. (Since the mountain chain is visible from the Terek, they certainly knew that forbidding mountains were on their path; the "natural" place of settlement would have been the fertile river valley.)[5]

This line of thinking led to even more outrageous origin myths, such as that of I. A. Rodionov, the famous Don Cossack monarchist, novelist, and publicist. As he wrote in his 1914 *Tikhii Don*, the Don Cossack Andrei and his flotilla sailed about for an entire summer on the Caspian Sea, attacking and plundering Persian merchant ships and Muslim towns along the coast. They got so carried away that they failed to notice the bad weather of autumn approaching and loaded down with booty, could not make it back to the Volga in time. So, they landed on an unknown bank with the Caucasus mountains in sight, pitched their tents, and wintered over. They took a fancy to this new land and the next spring sent messengers to the Don, inviting new crowds of colonists.[6]

The Andrei story seems to originate with captain Johann-Gustav Gerber's 1728 description of the village of Endirei; Tatishchev evidently picked it up and published it in his *Istoriia Rossiiskaia*. P. L. Iudin was the first to refute it, showing that there is no documentary evidence of any village of Andrei in the North Caucasus or of any ataman Andrei settling there. It is apparently only a folk toponym, of which there are an unusually large number for the Kumyk village Endirei. Recent research has unearthed a total of fourteen such fanciful etymologies for Endirei, including Andrei the Don Cossack; a Russian hunter Andrei; Andrei the Armenian; the name of a Kumyk prince of the Shamkhal of Tarku; Kumyk words meaning "harvest moon" (because they had to harvest at night to avoid attacks of Mongols); the Khazar capital, Semender; and an ancient Turkish wording meaning border.[7]

There is also one dissenting origin story from the mid-nineteenth century. An anonymous, self-educated Cossack sergeant (*uriadnik*), published an article in *Voennyi sbornik* (the article that Abozin so angrily rejected), based partly on local archival research and stories of old-timers. According to him, the Terek Cossacks came from "foreigners" (*inorodtsy*)—Russian migrants, Kuban princes, Circassians, "Okochenskii Tatars" (probably Chechens or Ingush), and Georgians—who came together in brigand gangs.[8]

Eighteenth-century sources, more reliable then nineteenth-century oral tradition or Cossack myth-making, concur with this Cossack sergeant and usually mention the diverse origins of the Terek Cossacks. Gerber reported in 1728 that the Greben Cossacks descended from fugitive Russians and Cossacks. But he also mentioned other neighboring communities that complicate the "ethnogenesis" of the Terek Cossacks: Terek Tatars who converted to Christianity and joined the Terek Cossacks; Stavropol' Tatars, who were Christian, spoke Russian, and worked as Cossacks; and the village of the Dagestanians and Kumyks of Andrei (Endirei), which was established by fugitive Russians, Cossacks, and Tatars who lived by thieving. According to Gerber, confessional differences were also somewhat murky—he claimed that "fifty to seventy years earlier" all of the "mountain Circassians" of upper Kabarda were Orthodox; there were also some Christian "mountain Circassians" and Christian Lower Kabardian Circassians who lived along the Terek.[9]

Alexander Rigelman, in 1778, wrote that the Terek Cossacks came from the

Volga and were supplemented by refugees from various Cossack rebel and bandit groups, and *strel'tsy* (musketeer) fugitives. According to local Cossacks with whom he spoke, they lived on the ridges in Kabarda, and in the Kumyk lands, and married captives and other women from various places. The 1767 "instructions" of the Greben Cossack representatives for Catherine the Great's Legislative Commission concurred that their ancestors lived along the mountain ridges south of the Terek, along the Sunzha River. The Kizliar host, according to their "instructions," descended from converted mountain people. A report by inspector general Knorring, who was in the North Caucasus in 1799, stated that their ancestors came to the Terek at an unknown time from various places and were Kuban people, Tatars, Circassians and other mountain people, Poles, Don Cossacks, and Georgians.[10] Johann Anton Güldenstädt, professor of natural history at the Imperial Academy, visited Kizliar in the early 1770s and reported that the Cossacks there all descended from "Tatars" and "Circassians."[11] Many roads and many bloodlines—Slavic and Caucasian—led to the Cossack villages of the North Caucasus.

The type of ethnic cleansing of messy frontier history that Rodionov and many others writing about the Terek Cossacks engaged in was not unusual in the late nineteenth century, in Russia or elsewhere. Willard Sunderland has shown, for example, how Russians in the late imperial period writing about Siberian colonization could not accept nativization and held on to the long-standing faith, despite ample evidence to the contrary, that Russification would ultimately triumph over Iakutization. At the same time, half a world away, nationalist Argentineans musing about the origin of the gauchos often stressed their supposed Spanish—or Arabic—roots and minimized their mestizo heritage. In North America, Frederick Jackson Turner, fearful of the distortion of American national identity by the contemporary wave of European immigration flooding the Eastern seaboard, turned West to embrace the purifying simplicity of an Anglo-Americanized frontier. In all of these cases, a sanitized, less culturally threatening version of frontier history helped to shore up national identities during a period of rapid social change. A paler frontier was romanticized as the actual frontier faded from sight.[12]

Of course the search for the ultimate origins of Cossacks in the North Caucasus is futile, misdirected, and more indicative of Cossack nationalism of the nineteenth century than of any genuine beginnings. Although the source base is extremely fragmentary, it is probably incorrect to visualize the history of settlement in the North Caucasus in terms of some "pure native" region being visited by an original Slavic migration in the sixteenth century. From the first days of recorded history, the southern steppe, lower Volga, Black Sea, and North Caucasus had been an area of opposition and intermingling between Slavs, Turkic and Iranian peoples, and Caucasians. Kasogians (Circassians) and Iasians (Alans; Ossetians) figure in the Russian *Primary Chronicle*—Sviatoslav I conquered both in the tenth century; Mstislav conquered the

Kasogians, who then fought with his troops, in the eleventh century; and Rostislav again conquered the Kasogians in 1066. Avar helmets (of Dagestan) appear in the twelfth-century *Tale of the Host of Igor*.[13] Also, Rus' princes engaged in a series of dynastic marriages with the Iasians.

Toponyms and ethnonyms also reveal a long heritage of interaction. Cherkassk, the capital of the Don Cossacks from the mid-seventeenth century, derives from the word "Circassian" and many think it was originally a Circassian settlement. Indeed, there are many Circassian toponyms in southern Russia and Ukraine. The word "Cossack" itself is most likely of Turkish origin, along with many other general Cossack words such as *esaul* (Cossack captain), *kinzhal* (dagger), *kosh* (camp), *nagaika* (whip), *papakha* (sheepskin cap), *sharovary* (wide trousers), and perhaps *ataman* and *gaidamak* (haydamak).[14]

The essentially hybrid nature of cossackdom and the heritage of Slavic-Caucasian-Turco-Tatar-Persian intermingling helps explain why it is so difficult to make definitive statements about the early Cossack settlements in the North Caucasus. Vinogradov and Magomadova claim that the region between the Terek and the Sunzha was so well known in the sixteenth century because of the continual march of embassies between Muscovy and Georgia that Cossack villages would have been noticed and recorded. (By Cossack they mean, of course, predominantly Slavic free settlements.)[15] But what would have made them stand out to the traveler as particularly "Cossack" villages? There was no Cossack estate yet. In sixteenth-century Russian usage "Cossack" meant simply a hired worker, a farm laborer at a peasant farm, or a person without a determined occupation and permanent place of residence.[16] Denominational difference would have been difficult to detect casually since this was before the Chechen, Ingush, and Kabardian lands were Islamicized and there is no evidence of any Cossack churches there before the eighteenth century. Ethnic difference would have been hard to delineate at least because of local intermarriage and at most because of the long interrelations between Slavs and natives. As late as the nineteenth century, travelers and even Russian peasants in the North Caucasus had a difficult time distinguishing between Terek Cossacks and native mountain people, because of their similarity in dress and appearance. Such villages also would have been easy to miss; some of the Cossack villages recorded in the mid-seventeenth century had only twenty to thirty-five residents.[17]

For a traveler from the Ottoman lands such as Evliya Çelebi in the seventeenth century, identifying "Cossacks" was easier because of a more expansive definition: free brigands from the north. But Slavic settlers were far from being the only stateless plunderers in the North Caucasus. And Çelebi himself expressed a confusion over who was who when he reports that "once, either two tribes of Turkmen or a tribe of Muscovite Cossacks" attacked Gilian.[18]

Probably the most reliable marker would have been "political" alignment or paid service to Russian frontier forts. But, at that time, Cossacks in the North

Caucasus were at best only casual servitors of the Russian state and there were as many natives in Russian service as Slavs, so this was no fail-safe test. The languages of the North Caucasus do not clarify much either: "Cossack" could mean "a free settler from the south Russian steppe," but it also meant "free peasant" or "peasant," "hired worker," "migratory warrior," "brigand," "Kazakh," "hero," or "fine fellow."[19] In Chechen, the word for Russians ("gIazakhi") literally means "Cossacks" (in the sense of free Cossacks) and the word for Cossacks ("gIalagIazki") literally means "town Cossacks" (or Cossack servitors). So they defined Cossacks as servitors, but called Russians "free Cossacks"! In Kumyk, "Cossack" means "a henchman [*oruzhenosets*] of a feudal lord" or "a military servitor."[20]

The oral tradition of the North Caucasus also points to a long-standing mixing between Cossacks and natives, Russians and Caucasians. The Circassians in the nineteenth century had a legend that the Kabardians of the thirteenth century pastured their livestock and set up camps all the way to Riazan'. Magomet-bek Atazhukin, a Kabardian delegate in St. Petersburg in 1732, claimed that his ancestors were all Christians of the Greek faith from Ukraine who moved to the Kuma River and settled in the Piatigorsk canyon and came to be called the Piatigorsk Circassians. The Kabardians later forcibly converted them to Islam.[21] Chechen legends of the mid-nineteenth century say that the early Russians settled in Chechnia, that Russian carts ascended the mountains (a sign of settled life), and that in those days "a Russian was made father of the country." The Kumyks claimed that a Cossack named Konstantin, or Koste in the shortened Kumyk version, founded their village of Kostek. He was later joined by Muslim fishermen who converted him to Islam. Supposedly, his descendants, named Balaev, still lived there in the late nineteenth century.[22]

So we must recognize that the line between "Cossack" and "native" in the North Caucasus was blurred from the start by a middle continuum of, on the one side, Slavs who fully entered into the fabric of the mountain societies and disappeared from the sources and, on the other side, natives who served the Russian forts, received salaries and provisions from Muscovy, and were called Cossacks. The definition of a Cossack began to be clarified only with the resettling of the so-called Greben Cossacks to the north side of the Terek in the early eighteenth century and their enrollment under the authority of the War College. Then there was an ironclad official criterion of what a Terek Cossack was—a settler-servitor of the Russian state in the North Caucasus. But this did not erase the free-flowing population of both natives and Slavs on the margins of the officially recognized Cossack villages.

Of course the problem of early Cossack identity is a general one in Cossack history, since Cossacks were a functional or occupational group rather than an ethnic, legal, national, political, or religious community. The original Turkish meaning of *Qazaq*—"a free, independent person, adventurer, vagabond"—

captures this best. "Cossacks" arose only in relation to a separate state power or powers. They were the stateless people who came into being in the interstices between states, in our case between Muscovy/Russia, Iran, and the Ottoman empire. They were defined by what they were not—servitors or subjects.

In the sixteenth and seventeenth centuries, the Cossacks of the North Caucasus occasionally derived their livelihood from the Muscovite state, but the bulk of the references to them have to do with their independence, piracy, plundering, and highway robbery. Muscovy/Russia had to win over the Terek Cossacks, just as it had to win over natives of the North Caucasus to pledge their allegiance to the tsar and work as servitors in the fledgling forts of the region. And by no means were the Cossacks easier to win over.

Up until the eighteenth century, the Russian presence in the North Caucasus was limited to two forts on the lower Terek River. The first fort, Sunzhenskii Ostrog, was built soon after Ivan IV's conquest of Astrakhan in 1556. After receiving an embassy of Kabardian princes in 1557 and marrying a Kabardian princess in 1561, Ivan IV built Sunzhenskii Ostrog in 1567 on the right bank of the Terek, at the influx of the Sunzha River. Not much is known about this fort, except that it was relocated several times and then abandoned because of pressure from the Ottoman empire. Its placement, some ninety miles inland, was indefensible, and suggests considerable native influence regarding location.[23]

The second fort lasted, in one shape or another, over a century. Terskii Gorod was founded in 1588 at the mouth of the Terek—a more defensible and accessible location. The first Russian fort to have any noticeable impact on North Caucasus economy and society, it existed until Peter I closed it down in 1722. Terskii Gorod was important primarily as a staging and receiving point for diplomatic missions (especially to and from Georgia), as a border post and trade center,[24] and as a recruiting point for attracting mountain people and Cossacks to state service.

The projection of Muscovite power into the North Caucasus was limited by Ottoman and Crimean pretensions in the region, by the Shamkhal of Tarku in Dagestan, and by the jumble of tribes and peoples that frustrated "cooptation" strategy. The political situation in the North Caucasus was incredibly fluid during this period, and it would remain so for centuries to come. While Muscovy was pushing south, the Ottomans were marching east: in the sixteenth century, the Turks built several forts along the eastern coast of the Black Sea, including Sukhum and Anapa and they mounted an unsuccessful campaign against Astrakhan in 1569. Like Muscovy, the Ottoman empire also sought to build allegiances among the mountain people; both sides focused attention on the Kabardians, who subsequently split into pro-Muscovite and pro-Ottoman camps.[25]

As Chantal Lemercier-Quelquejay has made clear, cooptation of elites was extremely difficult in the North Caucasus because of the fragmented nature of political power. When two Kabardian princes, Temriuk and Siboq, offered their "submission" to Muscovy in 1557, they were not binding Kabarda to Russia, but rather were hoping to receive protection against local enemies, most probably the Shamkhal of Tarku and the Crimean Tatars. They were not charismatic princes in the manner of the Chingizids—they were not khans who could bring the rest of the Kabardians along in their alliance with Moscow. They were not even princes in the Muscovite sense, but only clan chiefs. After 1563, then, Kabarda was split between a pro-Muscovite camp led by Temriuk and a pro-Ottoman, pro-Crimean camp led by his rivals.[26]

The first substantial Muscovite military operation in the region was against the Shamkhal of Tarku in Dagestan, one of the most important states in the Caucasus. After the cooptation strategy failed there too, Prince I. A. Khorostinin launched an attack against Tarku in 1594 and was routed, with perhaps 3,000 of his forces killed. In 1604, Muscovy tried again with a force of some 10,000, and this time managed to take the capital before they were surrounded and massacred. Despite these summary failures and a minimal presence in the Caucasus, by 1594 tsar Fedor, in the exaggerated Muscovite manner, had assumed the title of "sovereign of the Iberian lands, of Georgian tsars, and of the Kabardian lands and Circassian and mountain princes."[27]

This, then, was the political context in which Terskii Gorod was planted and in which the first Cossack settlements evolved a relationship with the Muscovite state. Terskii Gorod had a negligible military presence, but it did provide a focus for trade and for state service, and by the late seventeenth century it was a lively, diverse town with a population of perhaps 20,000.[28] Lying at the extremity of Muscovite power, it was chronically short of servitors and populated more by natives than by Cossacks, and was more a transit point for diplomatic missions than an effective foothold for Muscovite expansion in the North Caucasus (although the two aims cannot be neatly separated).[29] But the *voevoda* (town governor) did have to cultivate good relations with surrounding tribes to ensure the safety of missions, and to do so he largely relied on natives in Muscovite service and on Cossacks.

There were four native quarters in Terskii Gorod. Tatarskaia sloboda was the "Tatar quarter," where mountain people who were indiscriminately labeled "Tatars" lived. Novokreshchenskaia sloboda ("the quarter of the newly baptized") comprised mountain people who had converted to Christianity. The princes Cherkasskii and their retainers lived in Cherkasskaia sloboda. These Cherkasskiis descended from pro-Muscovite Kabardian princes who settled in Terskii Gorod in the 1590s, converted to Christianity, and received the name Cherkasskii, meaning "the Circassian." They came to have great power in Terskii Gorod and became prominent servitors, merchants, and noblemen in the North Caucasus and Astrakhan. The Okotskaia quarter was settled by emigrants from Chechen and/or Ingush lands who became known in Russian sources as Okoki, Okochane, or Akkintsy. They became servitors and worked often as translators, couriers, and escorts for embassies.[30] In function, these native servitors were indistinguishable from Cossacks and in time they in fact became enrolled as Cossacks.[31] Some of those who settled in Terskii Gorod were fugitives: in 1633 Kumyks complained to the commander of Terskii Gorod that their purchased and captive Circassians, Nogais, and others had fled there and were not returned.[32]

The first recorded service of Terek Cossacks also was connected with Terskii Gorod, where they worked occasionally as couriers, guards, escorts, and fighters.[33] Russian historians such as Popko often date the beginning of the Terek Cossacks as a service estate to their first service at Terskii Gorod.[34] But this is as misleading as the Soviet claim that the "voluntary unification" of the Kabardians, Chechens, and others dates from the first petition of loyalty of particular mountain clans. Just because some Cossacks periodically worked for a Muscovite frontier outpost, it does not mean that they or their communities were bound to the state. As will be evident below (and as Popko and many other historians have shown), there is ample evidence to suggest that they were still fundamentally independent.

The origins of the officially recognized Terek host are thus somewhat cloudy. Unlike the Greben host (see Chapter 3), there is no official record of a Terek host being officially created, recognized, or submitting to the state, but there were Cossacks working in Terskii Gorod in its early years. By 1623 there were 500 resident Cossacks on the payroll there, but the number of actual servitors fluctuated with irregular provisioning and salary payment from the center.[35] Although they probably participated in the campaigns against the Shamkhal of Tarku, it seems as if the major military service of the Terek Cossacks in this period was in the 1614 Astrakhan campaign against Ivan Zarutskii, the last pretender of the Time of Troubles, and Marina Mniszech.[36] When Peter I transferred the garrison of Terskii Gorod to Sviatoi Krest in 1724, Terek Cossacks were sent there; when Sviatoi Krest was abandoned in 1735, two new Cossack hosts were created out of the remnants of the Cossacks in the region and the Terek host came to an end (see Chapter 3).

At the same time it is clear from the few extant primary sources from the seventeenth century, that in various spots in the northeast Caucasus lived "free Cossacks," whom Terskii Gorod commanders were only casually aware of, and who often only incidentally pop up in the sources. As early as 1581 there were reports of "fugitive Cossacks" living at the mouth of the Terek. As late as 1650, the *voevoda* of Terskii Gorod was evidently not terribly familiar with them. When he dispatched a Tezik, or resident Persian, to search for mulberry trees, he discovered them growing between Cossack villages, a half-day's trip up the Terek River.[37]

Free Cossack or Slavic communities appear repeatedly in sources from this period, but leave as many questions as answers. A Georgian sent to Moscow in 1665 found the remains of a town called "Chechen" that had once apparently been established by Russians at the foot of the mountains on the Chechen River.[38] In 1619, Fedor Kotov, a Moscow merchant traveling to Persia, visited Terskii Gorod and mentioned Cossack fortifications (*ostroshki*) along the mountain ridge and Cossacks laying in wait for belligerent Tatars along the Terek River.[39] A 1640 report to the Posol'skii prikaz (Foreign Office) said that "Cossacks lived along the Terek and along the Sunsha [Sunzha] and in other spots in fortified towns and in fishing camps, on the sea and on the rivers and in the reeds and in the steppe."[40] And, who were the "Kuban Cossacks" whom Muscovite servitors alerted the Astrakhan *voevoda* to in 1692?[41]

The most common reference to Cossacks in the North Caucasus before the eighteenth century relates to free Cossacks, or "criminal fugitive Cossacks" (*vory beglye kazaki*) as the Posol'skii prikaz called them, plundering native villages, attacking travelers, and pirating on the Caspian Sea. Mountain people, and Persian and Ottoman diplomats, frequently petitioned the tsar for protection against these highwaymen and pirates. They took captive Turkish couriers and attacked Turkish armies (1583, 1584); they plundered Kumyk villages close to the Terek, taking captives, horses, and weapons (1589); they attacked a Kabardian prince en route to Terskii Gorod and took his horse and weapons and killed one of his peasants (1645); they attacked caravans of Kumyk servants of Russia and stole 100 of their horses and sold them to Don Cossacks (1650).[42]

When Adam Olearius visited Terskii Gorod in 1636, hundreds of Cossacks in ships tried to attack his vessel, only to be rebuffed by *strel'tsy*. A Don Cossack ataman reported in 1647 that they were plundering in several boats along the Caspian and had attacked Gilian and Baku. In 1650, a Muscovite servitor in Astrakhan said that pirate Cossacks on the Caspian had been so disruptive that they interrupted the madder trade to Persia, causing prices of madder to skyrocket. Petitions of Persian diplomats regularly accused the Terek and Astrakhan *vodevody* of receiving booty.[43]

Çelebi wrote about Cossacks plundering along the Caspian coast, attacking the fortress of Koisu, south of Endirei, Gilian, and Baku:

> In spite of the peaceful relations between the Moscow kingdom and Iran, in several places they fall on the fortresses and towns of Iran along the bank of the Caspian Sea...and destroy them...The people of Iran are very frightened of these Muscovite Cossacks.[44]

It is curious that oral tradition has the Terek Cossacks turning to Ivan IV for protection against the mountain people; the reality was that Kabardians and Kumyks petitioned for protection against the Cossacks.[45]

Free Cossack communities in the North Caucasus in the sixteenth and seventeenth centuries also had contacts with other Cossacks from the Volga, the Don, and Ukraine. Their communities grew as they received fugitive *strel'tsy*,

Cossacks, other servitors, schismatics, and natives escaping social oppression; they shrank as others headed north to resettle, trade, or plunder.[46] Terek Cossacks participated in the major Cossack revolts of the seventeenth century, the Bolotnikov and Razin uprisings. The most famous Terek Cossack rebel in this period was probably the "False Peter" (Petrushka) who sailed north with, according to Solov'ev, 4,000 other Terek Cossacks, to link up with Bolotnikov and plunder up and down the Volga. Stenka Razin began his outlaw career as a pirate of the Caspian (and lower Volga) and used Chechen Island, off the coast where the Terek issues into the Caspian Sea, as one of his bases.[47] Cossacks also forged bonds with native villages of the Caucasus. Already in 1633, Kumyks complained to the commander of Terskii Gorod that their wives were fleeing to Cossack villages and were sheltered there, regardless of whether they converted to Christianity or not.[48]

By the time the Cossacks were formally enrolled in Russian service in 1720, then, they had already lived in the region for two centuries as independent settlers, occasional servitors, pirates, and brigands. They came to the North Caucasus from various places—including southern Russia and the North Caucasus—intermarried with native women, and joined forces with and fought against native communities. We can assume that their villages appeared and disappeared, that their populations ebbed and flowed as inhabitants were killed, taken captive, joined with other settlers, moved in, and moved out. And Chechens, Kumyks, Kabardians, and others also settled in Terskii Gorod, took up service, and became Terek Cossacks themselves. These were the first roots from which North Caucasus Cossack society grew. In the eighteenth century, the Russian state would begin to re-create that society by establishing a solid presence there with new forts, new Cossack villages, and waves of new settlers who became Terek Cossacks. The first step, though, was to get the original Cossacks to cross over and become full-fledged, dependent state servitors.

Notes

1. I. D. Popko, *Terskie kazaki so starodavnikh vremen* (St. Petersburg: Tipografiia Departamenta udelov, 1880), 11-17; I. Kravtsov, *Ocherk o nachale Terskago kazach'iago voiska* (Khar'kov: Tipografiia I. M. Varshavchika, 1882), 66; V. A. Potto, *Dva veka Terskago kazachestva* (Vladikavkaz: Elektropechatnia tipografiia Terskago oblastnogo pravleniia, 1912), 1: 12-14; I. V. Bentkovskii, *Grebentsy* (Moscow: Russkaia topolitografiia, 1889), 3-11; S. A. Kozlov, "Popolnenie vol'nykh kazach'ikh soobshchestv na Severnom Kavkaze v XVI-XVIII vv.," *Sovetskaia etnografiia*, no. 5 (September-October 1990): 47-49. Kozlov's article, based on original archival research, is one of the best and most sophisticated works on the origins of the Terek Cossacks, and he rightly emphasizes their diverse ethnic, regional, and social origins, but still downplays the native component. A modern Soviet uncritical review of historians' claims on the origins of the Terek Cossacks is L. B. Zasedateleva, "K istorii formirovaniia Terskogo kazachestva," *Vestnik Moskovskogo universiteta*, series 9, istoriia, 3 (1969): 53-55.

2. E. N. Kusheva, *Narody Severnogo Kavkaza i ikh sviazi s Rossiei (vtoraia polovina XVI-30-e gody XVII veka)* (Moscow: Izdatel'stvo Akademii nauk SSSR, 1963), 244, 292; Zasedateleva, "K istorii formirovaniia," 54-55.

3. "Istoricheskiia svedeniia o Grebenskom kazach'em polku," *Sbornik Obshchestva liubitelei kazach'ei stariny,* no. 4 (1912): 28-29; G. Maliavkin, "Kak poshlo na Rusi kazachestva (kazach'e predanie)," *Terskiia vedomosti,* 1 January 1892, 2; S. Pisarev, *Trekhsotletie Terskago kazach'iago voiska. 1577-1877* (Vladikavkaz: Tipografiia Terskago oblastnago pravleniia, 1881), 1, 19-21; P. A. Vostrikov, "Stanitsa Naurskaia, Terskoi oblasti," *Sbornik materialov dlia opisaniia mestnostei i plemen Kavkaza,* no. 33 (1904): section 2, 103.

Endirei often appears in Russian sources as Enderi or Endrei; as of 1990 its official name is Endirei. See A. P. Shikhsaidov, T. M. Aitberov, and G. M.-P. Orazaev, *Dagestanskie istoricheskie sochineniia* (Moscow: Nauka. Izdatel'skaia firma "Vostochnaia literatura," 1993), 205.

4. "Vospominaniia o Grebenskikh kazakakh i Kavkazskoi linii," *Kavkaz,* 4 October 1856, 313-14.

5. I. Abozin, "Vozrazhenie," *Voennyi sbornik* 26, no. 8 (1862): 489-90; Bentkovskii, *Grebentsy,* 3-10.

6. I. A. Rodionov, *Tikhii Don* (Tipo-litografiia T-va "Svet," 1914; reprint, St. Petersburg: Petropolis, 1994), 38.

7. V. N. Tatishchev, *Istoriia Rossiiskaia* (Moscow-Leningrad: Izdatel'stvo Akademii nauk SSSR, 1962), 1: 278; P. L. Iudin, "Byla-li Andreevka kolybel'iu Tertsev?" *Zapiski Terskago obshchestva liubitelei kazach'ei stariny,* no. 10 (October 1914): 35-42; Shikhsaidov, Aitberov, and Orazaev, *Dagestanskie istoricheskie sochineniia,* 205-07.

8. "Materiialy dlia statistiki Kizliarskago polka Terskago kazach'iago voiska," *Voennyi sbornik,* no. 12 (December 1869): 207-09. Russians often used "Tatar" to mean a mountain person, and not necessarily an ethnic Tatar or even a Turkic-speaking person.

9. I.-G. Gerber, "Opisanie stran i narodov vdol' zapadnogo berega Kaspiiskogo moria. 1728 g," in *Istoriia, geografiia i etnografiia Dagestana XVIII-XIX vv.,* ed. M. O. Kosven and Kh.-M. Khashaev (Moscow: Izdatel'stvo vostochnoi literatury, 1958), 60-70. Stavropol' was the Russian name for the region immediately south of the Terek along the Caspian sea.

10. "Opisanie Grebenskikh kazakov XVIIIv.," *Istoricheskii arkhiv* 5 (September-October 1958): 181-83; Aleksandr Rigel'man, *Istoriia ili povestvovanie o Donskikh kazakakh* (Moscow: Universitetskaia tipografiia, 1846), 138-39; "Materialy Ekaterinskoi zakonodatel'noi komissii," *Sbornik Imperatorskago russkago istoricheskago obshchestva,* no. 115 (1903): 487, 457; "Istoricheskoe svedenie. (Raport komanduiushchago Kizliarskim polkom podp. Alpatova 31 Iiulia 1854 goda no. 4530)," *Sbornik Obshchestva liubitelei kazach'ei stariny,* no. 2 (1912): 3-4.

11. I. A. Gil'denshtedt [Johann Anton Güldenstädt], *Geograficheskoe i statisticheskoe opisanie Gruzii i Kavkaza* (St. Petersburg: Imperatorskaia akademiia nauk, 1809), 21-23; G. A. Tkachëv, *Stanitsa Chervlennaia. Istoricheskii ocherk* (Vladikavkaz: Elektropechatnia tipografiia Terskago oblastnogo pravleniia, 1912), 29-39.

12. Willard Sunderland, "Russians into Iakuts? 'Going Native' and Problems of Russian National Identity in the Siberian North, 1870s-1914," *Slavic Review* 55, no. 4 (1996): 806-25; Richard W. Slatta, *Gauchos & the Vanishing Frontier* (Lincoln: University of Nebraska

Press, 1983; repr. 1992), 7-9.

13. *Slovo o polku Igoreve*, ed. N. M. Pavlov (Moscow: Universitetskaia tipografiia, 1874), 26; *The Russian Primary Chronicle*, trans. and ed. Samuel H. Cross (Cambridge, Mass.: Mediaeval Academy of America, 1953), 84, 134, 145; S. A. Belokurov, ed., *Snosheniia Rossii s Kavkazom* (Moscow: Universitetskaia tipografiia, 1889), 455; V. A. Kuznetsov, *Ocherki istorii Alan* (Vladikavkaz: Ir, 1992), 209-10.

14. N. K. Dmitriev, "O Tiurkskikh elementakh Russkogo slovaria," *Leksikograficheskii sbornik* 3 (1958): 17, 23, 24, 26, 27, 29, 36; Dzh. N. Kokov, *Kabardinskie geograficheskie nazvanie* (Nal'chik: Kabardino-Balkarskoe knizhnoe izdatel'stvo, 1966), 154-59; Dzh. N. Kokov and L. Dzh. Kokova, *Kabardino-Cherkesskie familii* (Nal'chik: "Elbrus," 1993), 54-61; P. Ia. Chernykh, *Istoriko-etimologicheskii slovar' sovremennogo russkogo iazyka* (Moscow: Russkii iazyk, 1994), 1: 57, 396, 555; W. Barthold, "Kazak," in *E. J. Brill's First Encyclopedia of Islam 1913-1936* (repr. Leiden-New York-Koln: E. J. Brill, 1993), 4: 837; V. I. Abaev, *Istoriko-etimologicheskii slovar' Osetinskogo iazyka* (Moscow and Leningrad: Akademiia nauk SSSR, 1958), 1: 366-67.

15. V. B. Vinogradov and T. S. Magomadova, "O vremeni zaseleniia Grebenskimi kazakami levogo berega Tereka," *Istoriia SSSR* 6 (November-December 1975): 160-61.

16. V. O. Kliuchevskii, *Russkaia istoriia. Polnyi kurs lektskii v 3 kn.* (Moscow: Mysl', 1995), 2: 218.

17. T. Kh. Kumykov and E. N. Kusheva, eds., *Kabardino-russkie otnosheniia v XVI-XVIII vv.: Dokumenty i materialy* (Moscow: Izdatel'stvo Akademii nauk SSSR, 1957), 1: 302-03

18. Evliia Chelebi [Evliya Çelebi], *Kniga puteshestviia* (Moscow: Izdatel'stvo "Nauka," 1979), 2: 116, 124.

19. V. I. Abaev, *Istoriko-etimologicheskii slovar' Osetinskogo iazyka* (Leningrad: Nauka, 1973), 2: 273-74.

20. A. I. Shavkhelishvili, "K voprosu o pereselenii Checheno-Ingushskikh plemen s gor na ravninu," *Izvestiia Checheno-Ingushskogo respublikanskogo kraevedcheskogo muzeia* 10 (1961): 112-16.

21. Potto, *Dva veka*, 12-14. Potto stands out among pre-revolutionary historians of Cossacks for his search for native as well as Russian origins of Terek Cossacks.

22. U. Laudaev, "Chechenskoe plemia," *Sbornik svedenii o kavkazskikh gortsakh* 6 (1872): 6-8; M. Afanas'ev, "Selenie Kostek, Khasav-Iurtovskago okruga, Terskoi oblasti," *Sbornik materialov dlia opisaniia mestnostei i plemen Kavkaza* 16 (1893): 88.

23. George Vernadsky, "Russia, Turkey, and Circassia in the 1640's," *Südost-Forschungen* 19 (1960): 139; V. B. Vinogradov and T. S. Magomadova, "Gde stoiali Sunzhenskie gorodki?," *Voprosy istorii*, no. 7 (1972), 205-08; B. B. Piotrovskii, ed., *Istoriia narodov Severnogo Kavkaza s drevneishikh vremen do kontsa XVIIIv.* (Moscow: Nauka, 1988), 330.

24. Some of the most important travelers in Muscovite history—Fedor Kotov, Adam Olearius, Jan Struys—visited Terskii Gorod on their way south.

25. Vernadsky, "Russia, Turkey, and Circassia," 134-45; Carl Max Kortepeter, *Ottoman Imperialism During the Reformation: Europe and the Caucasus* (New York: New York University Press, 1972), 26-31.

26. Chantal Lemercier-Quelquejay, "Cooptation of Elites of Kabarda and Daghestan in the Sixteenth Century," in *The North Caucasus Barrier: The Russian Advance towards the Muslim World*, ed. Marie Bennigsen Broxup (New York: St. Martin's Press, 1992), 18-44. See also Muriel Atkin, "Russian Expansion in the Caucasus to 1813," in *Russian Colonial Expansion to 1917*, ed. Michael Rywkin (London: Mansell, 1988), 139-47; Firuz Kazemzadeh, "Russian Penetration of the Caucasus," in *Russian Imperialism from Ivan the Great to the Revolution*, ed. Taras Hunczak (New Brunswick: Rutgers University Press, 1974), 239-42.

Some Kabardians who pledged allegiance to Moscow turned out quite well. The daughter of Temriuk, Maria, married Ivan IV. Temriuk's son and nephew became boyars and the later, Boris, was the first of the princely clan of Cherkasskii, one of the most illustrious noble families in Muscovite and Russian history. See Lemercier-Quelquejay, "Cooptation of Elites," 42; N. A. Baskakov, *Russkie familii Tiurkskogo proiskhozhdeniia* (Moscow: Izdatel'stvo "Nauka," 1979), 80-81.

27. Lemercier-Quelquejay, "Cooptation of Elites," 39-40; Atkin, "Russian Expansion," 147-47; V. A. Potto, *Kavkazskaia voina* (St. Petersburg: Tipografiia R. Golike, 1885; reprint, Stavropol': Kavkazskii krai, 1994), 1: 16.

28. N. P. Gritsenko, *Goroda Severo-Vostochnogo Kavkaza i proizvoditel'nye sily kraia* (Rostov-on-Don: Izdatel'stvo Rostovskogo universiteta, 1984), 48.

29. N. B. Golikova, *Ocherki po istorii gorodov Rossii kontsa XVII-nachala XVIII v.* (Moscow: Izdatel'stvo Moskovskogo universiteta, 1982), 41.

30. Gritsenko, *Goroda Severo-Vostochnogo Kavkaza*, 34; N. P. Gritsenko, *Sotsial'no-ekonomicheskoe razvitie Priterechnykh raionov v XVIII-pervoi polovine XIX vv.* (Groznyi: Izdatel'stvo gazety "Groznenskii Rabochii," 1961), 16-20; Golikova, *Ocherki po istorii gorodov*, 32-33; Belokurov, *Snosheniia Rossii s Kavkazom*, 554-57; Kusheva, *Narody Severnogo Kavkaza*, 294-95. Most ethnographers and historians have concluded that Akintsy were Chechens, but a minority say they were Ingush, or closely related. See E. I. Krupnov, *Srednevekovaia Ingushetiia* (Moscow: Nauka, 1971), 37-38.

31. I. Popko, *Terskie kazaki*, viii-xii.

32. E. N. Kusheva and others, eds., *Russko-Dagestanskie otnosheniia XVII- pervoi chetverti XVIII vv. (Dokumenty i materialy)* (Makhachkala: Dagestanskoe knizhnoe izdatel'stvo, 1958), 110.

33. Kusheva, *Narody Severnogo Kavkaza*, 292-93; G. A. Tkachëv, "Bitva 14 Maia 1614 g. pod Astrakhan'iu i eia znachenie v istorii Rossii," *Zapiski Terskago obshchestva liubitelei kazach'ei stariny*, no. 7 (July 1914): 21-30.

34. Popko, *Terskie kazaki*, iii-vi, viii-xii.

35. Kusheva, *Narody Severnogo Kavkaza*, 292; Bentkovskii, *Grebentsy*, 23-28; Popko, *Terskie kazaki*, 190; Zasedateleva, "K istorii formirovaniia," 59; "Rospis sluzhilym liudiam," 456-67.

36. Tkachëv, "Bitva 14 maia," 21-30; F. Ponomarëv, "Materialy dlia istorii Terskago kazach'iago voiska s 1559 po 1880 god," *Voennyi sbornik* 23, no. 10 (October 1880): 353-54; Belokurov, *Snosheniia Rossii s Kavkazom*, 545-53; "Otpiska streletskago golovy Khokhlova k voevodam kniaziu Odoevskomu i Golovinu," *Akty istoricheskie* 3 (1841): 14-15; "Otpiska Terskago voevody Golovina Astrakhanskim voevodam kniaziu Odoevskomu i Golovinu," *Akty istoricheskie* 3 (1841): 17-18.

37. Kozlov, "Popolnenie vol'nykh kazach'ikh soobshchestv," 49; "Otryvok nakaza Astrakhanskim voevodam, boiarinu kniazu Mikhailu Pronskomu, okol'nichemu Timofeiu Buturlinu i Il'e Bezobrazovu," *Akty istoricheskie* 4 (1842): 129-44.

38. M. A. Polievktov, *Ekonomicheskie i politicheskie razvedki Moskovskogo gosudarstva XVII v. na Kavkaze* (Tiflis: Nauchno-issledovatel'skii institut kavkazovedeniia Akademii nauk SSSR, 1932), 21-22.

39. F. A. Kotov, "Khozhdenie na vostok F. A. Kotova v pervoi chetverti XVII veka," *Izvestiia Otdeleniia russkago iazyka i slovesnosti Imperatorskoi akademii nauk* 12, no. 1 (1907): 77-78.

40. Quoted in Kozlov, "Popolnenie vol'nykh kazach'ikh soobshchestv," 49.

41. "Otpiski Ivana Volkova i Denisa Serbina Astrakhanskomu voevode knaiziu Petru Khovanskomu," *Akty istoricheskie* 5 (1842): 368-72. For names of other Cossack villages see Kumykov and Kusheva, *Kabardino-russkie otnosheniia*, 1: 193, 226, 256, 315, 302, 303; 2: 29; Vinogradov and Magomadova, "O vremeni zaseleniia," 160-64.

42. Belokurov, *Snosheniia Rossii s Kavkazom*, 73, 79; Kumykov and Kusheva, *Kabardino-russkie otnosheniia*, 1: 35-36, 38, 256; Kusheva, *Russko-dagestanskie otnosheniia*, 180; S. M. Solov'ev, *Istoriia Rosiii s drevneishikh vremen* (Moscow: Izdatel'stvo sotsial'no-ekonomicheskoi literatury, 1961), 12 (book 6): 560-61.

43. Adam Olearii [Adam Olearius], *Podrobnoe opisanie puteshestviia Golshtinskago posol'stva v Moskoviiu i Persiiu v 1633, 1636 i 1639 godakh* (Moscow: Imperatorskoe obshchestvo istorii i drevnostei rossiiskikh pri Moskovskom universitete, 1870), 478; *Donskie dela* (St. Petersburg: Imperatorskaia arkheograficheskaia komissiia, 1909), Russkaia istoricheskaia biblioteka, 26: 569-70; "Otryvok nakaza Astrakhanskim voevodam," 129-44; Popko, *Terskie kazaki*, 73-74. The root of madder (*Rubia* species) was used to dye silk.

44. Chelebi, *Kniga puteshestviia*, 2: 116, 124, 128.

45. Belokurov, *Snosheniia Rossii s Kavkazom*, 535.

46. Kozlov, "Popolnenie vol'nykh kazach'ikh soobshchestv," 47-56.

47. *Vosstanie I. Bolotnikova: Dokumenty i materialy* (Moscow: Sotsekgiz, 1959), 84, 109-10; S. M. Solov'ev, *Sochineniia* (Moscow: Mysl', 1989) 8: 435; *Krest'ianskaia voina pod predvoditel'stvom Stepana Razina: Sbornik dokumentov* (Moscow: Izdatel'stvo Akademii nauk SSSR, 1954), 1: 120, 140-41; Ia. Ia. Streis [J. J. Struys], *Tri puteshestviia* (Moscow: Ogiz - Sotsekgiz, 1935), 198-99, 211.

48. Kusheva, *Russko-dagestanskie otnosheniia*, 110.

3

Formation and Colonization

I was in Kiev, in Poland, in Egypt, in Jerusalem, and on the Terek River.
—Pugachev to Iaik Cossacks in 1772

If you lose your harvest, go to the plains; if you lose your wits, go to the mountains.
—Ossetian saying

The nature of the Terek Cossacks changed radically in the first few decades of the eighteenth century. They suffered from raids, attacks, epidemics, and demographic catastrophe. Their communities were augmented by the first official state settlement of Cossacks to the North Caucasus. And they were constituted, for the first time, as official regiments, bound to the Russian state, and subordinated to the War College. A considerable population of free Cossacks still existed outside the confines of the Russian estate system, but from then on, most Cossacks' fortunes ebbed and flowed at least partially in relation to the Russian state. Within the next century a massive resettlement of population, both spontaneous and state-directed, flooded the original Cossack communities and created a considerable Cossack force in the North Caucasus that was crucial to the Russian colonization and conquest of the region. Thus, the history of the Terek Cossacks as a number of officially recognized hosts, in contrast to loose communities of independent settlers, begins in the eighteenth century. In that sense, the Russian state created the Terek Cossacks.

The "Crossing Over"

Why did the original Cossacks of the North Caucasus, those known as the Greben Cossacks, resettle to the north in the late seventeenth or early eighteenth century, establish five villages on the left bank of the Terek River, and attach themselves more firmly to Russia?[1] The Cossack myth interprets this move in national terms—as fulfilling a long-held desire to "reunify" with Russia—but the reality was probably more mundane, and less definitive.[2]

Since Cossack villages already existed on the left bank of the Terek, the "crossing over" and resettling to the north side of the river—if indeed this occurred—was less dramatic than is often made out. Except for the khanates along the Caspian Sea, there were few fixed "territorial homelands" for the people of the North Caucasus in the seventeenth and eighteenth centuries, Cossacks included. Mobility was an essential part of life in an area where good land was often scarce and where political fluidity and turbulence were endemic. In fact, Terskii Gorod itself was relocated several times for security reasons and to occupy better, drier land.[3] One of the earliest sources on the Greben Cossacks, an anonymous mid-eighteenth century description, has them settling in three villages north of the Terek already in 1666 or earlier, and then building two more villages as their communities grew with fugitive *strel'tsy* and Cossacks.[4] To what extent, then, did the Cossacks come to the state by relocating, and to what extent did the state come to the Cossacks?

From what can be pieced together from the sources, the early years of the eighteenth century were particularly turbulent in the North Caucasus. The "Kuban Tatars" attacked the Terek region almost every year and in 1708 Terskii Gorod was seized and burned.[5] It also seems there was a general population reshuffle during this period that could have been responsible for some of the destabilization. When the Kalmyks arrived in the lower Volga region in the early seventeenth century, they gradually pushed the Nogai Tatars from the Astrakhan steppe west, some to meadows of the Kabardians in the north central Caucasus. The subsequent Kabardian pressure on the Chechens may have made things more difficult for the Cossacks.[6]

At any rate, the earliest primary sources that mention the resettling of the Greben Cossacks, attribute it to "frequent and powerful attacks on them by the neighboring mountain people, which brought them continual unrest and a loss of people and livestock." In 1728, Gerber specifically pointed to attacks by Tatars, Chechens, and residents of Endirei (mostly Kumyks).[7]

If the Cossacks migrated for security reasons, the Terek River was probably more significant as a defensive cover than any military support that the skimpy garrison of Terskii Gorod could provide. The Terek is 100 to 640 yards wide and because of the great height from which it flows, runs fast all the way to Kizliar. It is especially ferocious—and treacherous to cross—during the period of snow thaw and rain in the mountains from April to September and often overflows its banks and floods the environs.[8]

The Cossacks were also pulled north by the opportunities offered by life on the plain. The move north was in keeping with long-term migration patterns in the North Caucasus, and in most mountain regions: downward for more land and better opportunities. The Terek River was a trade conduit that led to Terskii Gorod, and, across the Caspian, to Astrakhan to the north, Iran to the south, and on to further points. Astrakhan was, at the time, Russia's "window on the

East" with Persian, Indian, and Armenian bazaars; permanent quarters for Indian, Bukharan, Persian, Tatar, and Armenian traders; and a lively trade with the Caucasus, Iran, Turkey, Central Asia, and India.[9]

So there were many reasons why the Cossacks probably found it useful to relocate a bit northward. How did their relationship to the state change as a result? As of 1720, the Greben host was officially subordinated to the governor of Astrakhan and, as of 1721, to the War College. We should not imagine that these acts fully integrated the Cossacks into the empire—even after Russia recognized the Greben Cossacks as an official regiment, subordinated to the military chain of command, their relationship to the state remained somewhat tenuous. Up to 1819, they retained the right to elect their ataman and other top officials.[10] Even more curious is the fact that in 1765, 1768, 1778, and as late as 1799 one village of the Greben host, Chervlennaia, entered into independent treaties with their trans-Terek neighbors to regulate raiding and land use.[11] And not all of the local "Cossacks" were official Cossacks, bound to the state. According to a 1744 report of the Kizliar commander Obolenskii, the Greben host, then numbering 450 men, claimed that if needed (and if paid), they could equip 1,500 to 2,000 for war without difficulty—"they said that there are many in the forests in the mountains and hunters (*gulebshchiki*) in the steppe whom they could get if the need arose."[12]

It was also a much weakened community of Greben Cossacks that submitted to Russian authority in 1720. They suffered much from the folly of Peter the Great: in 1717 the Greben Cossacks took part in one of the most disastrous and ill-conceived expeditions in Russian history, the mission to the khanate of Khiva in Central Asia. Among other things, Peter wanted to reconnoiter little-known Central Asia, to make the khan of Khiva a Russian subject, and most importantly to establish trade links with India. So in 1717 he dispatched Aleksandr Bekovich Cherkasskii with a detachment of over 2,000, including 500 Greben Cossacks, to Khiva. The son of a Kabardian prince who was kidnapped as a child, baptized, and raised by Boris Golitsyn, Cherkasskii was one of many Russified natives who commanded Terek Cossacks in the eighteenth century.[13]

Cherkasskii led his troops on a long trek through the desert and by the time the group reached Khiva, they were short of food and water and had lost many horses. The khan then tricked them into splitting up their forces, and massacred or took into captivity nearly the entire detachment. After this disaster, "to vanish like Bekovich," became a popular expression in the Russian language.[14]

Apparently all 500 Greben Cossacks "vanished" alongside Cherkasskii—killed or taken into slavery—and hundreds of Cossack families became fatherless back home along the Terek. Only two inhabitants of the relocated villages returned, and they only after many years of captivity.[15] It was in the wake of this great population loss that the Greben Cossack communities on the left bank of the Terek formally submitted to Russian authority in 1720.

Early Military Colonization

In the early eighteenth century, Russia also began the long process of building up its military and colonial presence in the North Caucasus by resettling people and constructing forts and villages. The first state-directed settlement of people to form a new Cossack host in the North Caucasus was connected with the ill-fated fort of Sviatoi Krest, another brainchild of Peter the Great.

During his Persian campaign of 1722, Peter visited Terskii Gorod, located in the lowlands of the Terek delta, on a small island between the branches of the Terek. According to the governor of Astrakhan, A. P. Volynskii, in 1721 it was lower than the main branch of the Terek and the lakes of stagnant water in the streets and the courtyards had created an unhealthy living environment. The emperor too found it a wet and generally unsuitable place, and ordered a new fort, Sviatoi Krest, to be built to replace it. The location of the new fort was some 130 miles to the south along the Agrakhan branch of the Sulak River and nearly the entire Terskii Gorod garrison was transferred there. Terskii Gorod was eventually dismantled and according to legend, the very spot where it had been located disappeared under the rising waters of the Caspian Sea. It too vanished like Bekovich.[16]

The fort was named Sviatoi Krest, Holy Cross, because, according to oral tradition, a Christian Greek colony once existed there, named Stavropol', Greek for "the town of the cross." It was founded as part of Peter's push to conquer the northern provinces of Iran along the Caspian Sea, including the Shamkhal of Tarku, Derbent, Baku, and Gilian. This new Christian beachhead on the border of the ancient Muslim region of Dagestan was to have a not-so-blessed existence.[17]

To defend the fort, by ukazes of 1723 and 1724, Peter ordered 1,000 families of Don Cossacks to settle on the Sulak and Agrakhan Rivers and form the Agrakhan Cossack host.[18] All the Terek Cossacks and the Chechen and Ingush Okotskaia quarter were then resettled to Sviatoi Krest.[19] Only the Greben Cossacks remained behind on the Terek.

The area that Peter selected for the new fort and Cossack villages turned out to be even more unsuitable than the lower Terek. More exposed, it was frequently attacked by the Shamkhal of Tarku. The area was also low and often flooded. Because of the scarcity of wood, Cossacks lived in dark, wet, and extremely unhealthy earthen huts. As a result, the "plague" (*morovaia iazva*, most likely malaria) killed large numbers of Cossacks. Many families were completely wiped out. After a decade of misery, Russia abandoned Sviatoi Krest in 1735-1736; by then only 200 of the Agrakhan host could be mustered for service at the new fort of Kizliar. Of the 1,000 Terek Cossacks garrisoned at Sviatoi Krest, at most 172 were still alive in 1729.[20]

Although Peter initiated the region's state-sponsored colonization, his legacy in the North Caucasus was not a positive one. He destroyed the oldest

Russian town in the region, once an important trading and service center. And through ill-conceived and ill-fated imperial adventures, he wreaked havoc on Cossack society there. Sviatoi Krest and the Agrakhan host disappeared into the dust of history, like Terskii Gorod and the Cherkasskii forces before them, and Russia retreated to the lower Terek to rebuild on firmer foundations. The next fort was named much more modestly, most likely after the Turkic-named river there, Kizliar.[21]

The Kizliar Period

Kizliar would be the first Russian fort to last and it eventually became the cornerstone of the Caucasus Military Line. The remnants of the Agrakhan and Terek hosts were transferred back to the lower Terek region and formed into two new hosts—the Terek-Kizliar host and the Terek-Semeinoe host. The Okochan and Novokreshchen servitors were enlisted in the Terek-Kizliar host.[22] With the Greben regiment to the west, ten official Cossack villages now dotted the lower Terek.[23]

Up until the end of the eighteenth century, Kizliar remained the center of Russian activity in the North Caucasus and a powerful economic magnet for natives and Cossacks alike. This period marked the high point of Russian-native cooperation in the region. Before the mass settlement of peasants to the North Caucasus steppe, the Russian forces remained economically dependent upon local economies and before the mass settlement of Cossacks and other colonists, there was a continual attempt to recruit natives for service. The state's involvement in the region was relatively limited until the end of the century. The systematic conquest of the Caucasus was not possible until the Caucasus fortified line was built in 1777-1778 and large numbers of Cossacks and peasants were resettled to the south; it did not begin until large numbers of regular troops entered the fray in the nineteenth century.

Russian settlement in the North Caucasus in our period may be divided into three stages. As has been shown in Chapter 2, from the 1560s up to 1721, free Cossack villages appeared along the eastern Terek and Sulak and in the mountains to the south, and the first Russian forts were built in the river valleys. Only in the second stage (1722-1775) did the Russian government begin resettling a significant number of Cossacks and other service people. Several new forts were built along the Terek, including the first two permanent ones, Kizliar and Mozdok. During the third stage (1776-1860) the military line was completed and pushed further into the mountains. Cossacks were resettled all along the line, the Zaporozhian Cossacks were reconstituted as the Black Sea Cossacks and awarded lands in the Kuban region, and the resettlement and spontaneous migration of large numbers of peasants began. The Russian influx was simultaneous with a great reshuffling of Caucasian populations, including the immigration of Armenians and Georgians; a movement of

Ossetians, Chechens, and Ingush from the mountains to the foothills and plains; a migration of Nogais from the steppe across the Kuban River and to the Ural, Crimean, and Caspian steppes; and finally a massive out-migration of perhaps 700,000 Circassians in the 1850s and 1860s.[24]

Russians, then, faced demographic uncertainty in the North Caucasus up until the nineteenth century—only at the end of the eighteenth century did Russians become a slight majority in the province, which still did not include the unconquered mountain region beyond the Terek and Kuban Rivers. Kizliar and Mozdok remained largely non-Russian even later.[25]

As happened earlier with Terskii Gorod and Sviatoi Krest, as soon as the new fort of Kizliar was erected, a large number of Caucasian peoples settled there, including Chechens, Kabardians, Persian traders, Georgians, and Armenians. By 1773 there were seven native quarters in Kizliar.[26] At about the same time, the population of Kizliar stood at 4,197—not including the non-resident garrison (1,277 men). Ninety-two percent were Georgians, Armenians, Chechen, Ingush, Persians, Kazan Tatars, and Circassians.[27] At the turn of the century, there were only three Orthodox churches and one monastery in Kizliar, in comparison to four mosques and two Armenian churches.[28] As a collegiate councilor wrote in 1810, "Kizliar is a town unique among Russian *uezd* towns, with a diverse population, mostly of Asian peoples" extracting a good profit from viticulture, sericulture, and trade.[29] Kizliar's population grew to 5,464 by 1789 and to 9,106 by 1825. It remained the largest town in the North Caucasus until Stavropol' surpassed it sometime between 1825 and 1856.[30]

Kizliar, and the next Russian fort-town in North Caucasus, Mozdok (founded in 1763), were largely Armenian and Georgian. In the eighteenth and the nineteenth centuries, the Russian government expended much effort luring these Transcaucasians to the North Caucasus. In fact, the first major land grant in the North Caucasus was awarded in 1710 to an Armenian from Karabakh, Safar Vasil'ev, for the cultivation of silkworm-producing mulberry gardens in the Kizliar region. Many Armenians from Turkey and Persia followed and settled in the Terek River basin; other Armenians fled there from mountain, Nogai, or Crimean captivity. By 1789, over half of the population of Mozdok was Armenian and Georgian; by 1796 Armenians outnumbered Russians three to one in Kizliar; and in 1797 nearly 3,500 more Armenians resettled along the Caucasus Military Line from khanates in Dagestan and along the Caspian Sea. Armenians engaged in silk production and viticulture and were the backbone of regional trade in the North Caucasus. Georgians practiced agriculture, horticulture, and viticulture and some later became Cossacks.[31]

The resettlement of the Greben Cossacks to the north of the Terek River and the establishment of a permanent Russian presence seems to have also accelerated the Chechen and Ingush northward migration. Already in the late sixteenth century, Chechens and Ingush had resettled to form the Okotskaia quarter at Terskii Gorod. When the Cossacks moved away, more Chechens relocated north to get better land for their sheep and cattle and to develop their agriculture. It is difficult to establish exactly when Chechens and Ingush founded their villages in the plains, but there is little doubt that there was a major move north in the eighteenth century. By the end of the century, dozens of Chechen and Ingush villages dotted the right banks of the Terek and the Sunzha.[32]

The nineteenth-century Chechen publicist, Umalat Laudaev, wrote that this migration was a major turning point for the Chechens. Up until then, it seems they had mostly lived in the mountains. Now they lived in the plains, developed their agriculture, and came increasingly into contact and conflict with the Russian state and the Cossacks.[33]

One of the best known, and largest, new settlements was Devlet-Girei, located on the right bank of the Terek. Devlet-Girei was a Kabardian in Russian service, a captain at Kizliar, and the son of major general prince El'murza Cherkasskii, the ataman of the Terek-Kizliar host. When the Chechen community of Germenchuk resettled to the lower Sunzha in 1747-1748 and pledged allegiance to Russia, Devlet-Girei was appointed their overlord, and he resettled to the new village. He moved again in 1760 after Chechens attacked his house and chopped off his wife's hand for her gold bracelet. The site he chose for his new settlement was pasture land of the Chechens and the neighboring Kumyk village of Bragun, and for the next several years he fended off Chechen and Kumyk attacks. The Kizliar commander did not want to involve himself openly in the conflict, out of fear of angering the others, but he did lend him material and diplomatic support. By 1766 the land dispute seems to have been settled and Devlet-Girei's new village began to develop. Thanks to its close position to the Cossack villages and Kizliar—and the trading privileges granted to him by the Russians—the village prospered and attracted Chechen, Kumyk, and Kabardian immigrants. By 1784 it had grown to 400 households and in 1799 one of Devlet-Girei's descendants split off to found another village (Novyi Iurt or Bamat-Iurt) six kilometers to the east. By 1859, Devlet-Girei Aul, or as it was now called Staryi-Iurt, was the most populous Chechen village, with a population of 7,100.[34]

As soon as a permanent Russian presence was established along the Terek, groups of native peasants and slaves also settled in the fort-towns and stanitsas (Cossack villages), often causing serious diplomatic complications. One of the first notorious captivity incidents involved Russian protection of native fugitives. In 1774, the botanist Samuel-Gotlieb Gmelin, on a research expedition in the Caspian region, was captured in Dagestan by the sovereign (*utsmi*) of Kaitag, Amir-Hamza. Some 200 of his subject families had fled years earlier to Russian protection and he demanded either their return or a payment of 30,000 rubles in exchange for Gmelin.[35]

Others also complained: Kumyks periodically petitioned the Kizliar commander about the flight of their slaves to Kizliar.[36] Beginning in the 1740s,

Kabardian princes and lords continually protested to the Russian government about the flight of their slaves to Russian settlements. And in 1742, Kabardian lords petitioned the Russian empress Elizabeth Petrovna, complaining that their captives and slaves were fleeing to Cossack villages, where the Cossacks accepted them and pretended that they had converted to Christianity (so Cossacks could keep them without compensation).[37]

Nationalist and Islamist historians of the North Caucasus tend to downplay the very real attraction that Russian forts and Cossack villages held for many peoples of the northeast Caucasus during the eighteenth century. The archives are filled with native petitions asking for trading privileges in Kizliar and Mozdok, for Russian protection against enemies, for Russian mediation in local disputes, for permission to resettle closer to the Terek or in a Russian fort-town. True, declaration of loyalty usually did not extend beyond a clan and certainly was much less than "the voluntary unification" of a non-existent state to Russia. But we should not overlook the fact that as early as the mid-sixteenth century, locals were turning to Russia—even traveling to Moscow—for their own self-interest. As soon as forts and stanitsas were raised in the North Caucasus, they began to have an effect on North Caucasian society and pull some Caucasians into their orbit.

On the other hand, Russian nationalist and Soviet historians tend to exaggerate the significance of the various oaths of allegiance and to downplay the dependence of the Russian forts on natives and the importance of non-Russians in the colonization process. The "Russian" society coming into existence in the North Caucasus in the eighteenth century was multicultural and multiethnic, with the "Russian" component in the decided minority.

In these early years of Russian and Cossack settlement, natives played a vital political role. The first ataman of the Terek-Kizliar host was a Kabardian, El'murza-Bekovich Cherkasskii. He entered Russian service in 1720 and advanced to the rank of general in 1744. To the end of his life, according to Russian sources, he could read and write only in "Tatar." Two of his sons later commanded the same host. One of them, Temir-Bulat, also commanded the Terek-Kizliar host and was one of the first two Terek Cossacks to reach the rank of major. His importance was projected by his two-story wooden house, the only such structure in Kizliar in 1775. The other major was Petr Tatarov, another Kabardian, who entered service in 1718. There were many other native Caucasians in the top ranks of the Terek-Kizliar host.[38]

According to Ioann-Iakub Lerkhe, a doctor who visited the North Caucasus in 1745 en route to Persia, the brother of Aleksandr Bekovich Cherkasskii, Elligursa, was a colonel in Kizliar and was then "still a fervent Muslim."[39] Another native Caucasian, Kazbulat-Murza Taganov, became the commander of Mozdok. He was the son of a Nogai *amanat*—a captive held in collateral as part of a treaty—in Kizliar, who managed to escape. Kazbulat-Murza was subsequently taken to St. Petersburg, taught Russian, converted, and entered into Russian service.⁴⁰ And, Mozdok was founded by a Kabardian in Russian service—Kurgok Konchokin. His son, Nikolai Cherkeskii-Konchokin, reached the rank of lieutenant colonel, knew Russian like a native, but lived mostly in Kabarda.⁴¹

Cossacks Along the Terek

So, amidst this strong native presence, at the edge of the fledgling fort of Kizliar, the first Cossack communities began to establish themselves. The Greben host was the oldest and was considered the most ethnically mixed. It had not been moved to Sviatoi Krest for fear that the Cossacks might flee back to the mountains.⁴² The Greben Cossacks lived in five villages along the lower Terek and up to the formation of the Mozdok regiment in 1765, they were at the western edge of Russian power in the North Caucasus. According to a 1744 report by the Kizliar commander, they had 450 active-duty Cossacks, and claimed that they could put as many as 2,000 into service if they were compensated.⁴³ Although it is impossible to say how many lived in their villages, the number of active-duty Cossacks remained around 500 for the rest of the century.⁴⁴ According to I. P. Falk in 1775, many Armenians lived in their village Novogladkovskaia and Armenian and Tatar traders lived in another, Shchedrinskaia.⁴⁵ Many Georgians fleeing captivity also settled among the Greben Cossacks. For a long time they lived outside the Russian estate system, which meant that they had no service requirements and did not have to pay taxes. Only in 1824 were they officially enrolled as Cossacks.⁴⁶

The weakest hosts during this period were those formed from the Agrakhan host's remnants—the Terek-Semeinoe and the Terek-Kizliar hosts. The Terek-Semeinoe host resettled in three villages between Kizliar and the land of the Greben host. They were named the Terek-Semeinoe host ("Terek-family host") most likely because they were so weak they received salaries not just for active male Cossacks, but also for wives, children, orphans, widows, and church servants.⁴⁷ They were permitted to have a smaller number of active-duty Cossacks, about 450, which it remained until the end of the century.⁴⁸ Originating from the Don Cossacks, they seem to have been predominantly Slavic.

According to the Terek-Semeinoe host's Greben neighbors in 1744, they were a weak unit, unable to defend themselves against attacks, "from carelessness are robbed and killed," and some deserted to either the Don or the Kuban.⁴⁹ The commander of Kizliar, Obolenskii, concurred, saying that because of their poverty, many were deserting: "it is not possible for them to have hopes to improve things in the future, especially since, because of their wretchedness, they have not the means with which to build themselves up."⁵⁰ It is true that they had a hard time keeping their population steady—when they arrived on the Terek they had 452 families; as of 1744, this number had been reduced to 422.[51]

To ease their service burdens, the Terek-Semeinoe host was merged with the Greben host in 1745. The separate halves never got along and quarrelled over who to elect as ataman and how to divvy up service. One of the more remarkable documents from this period is a 1755 letter from local Kumyks requesting that the Greben candidate, Ivan Ivanov, be selected over the Terek-Semeinoe candidate, "because the behavior of Don Cossacks is unknown [to us]" and because Ivan Ivanov, or Kara-Ivan as they called him, "is highly gifted in handling affairs both among Christians and Muslims, his conduct is established, and he is a well-known person to all."[52] He was elected, but the two sides continued to quarrel and were re-divided in 1755 (and Ivanov remained ataman of the Greben host).[53]

The Terek-Kizliar host was formed by uniting the remainder of the Terek Cossacks stationed at Sviatoi Krest with the "newly converted" and Okochan servitors. They totaled only 169 service Cossacks in 1735. Because of their small number and knowledge of local languages, they were freed from direct military service and worked mostly on diplomatic missions in the North Caucasus and Crimea. Local commanders also sent Cossacks and Kalmyks throughout the North Caucasus to find recruits to work in the host as couriers and in other non-military capacities.[54]

The Terek-Kizliar host settled to the east of Kizliar on the lower Terek's worst land. Their numbers remained anemic through the century—in 1750 the War College authorized their number of active service Cossacks at 177, in 1791 at only 178, and in 1804 they had only 142 serving Cossacks.[55] About one-third of them in 1767 were "newly converted" and Okochan, and about one in ten still lived south of the Terek.[56]

As of the mid-eighteenth century, the numbers of Cossacks in all these first official hosts were still relatively small—1,162 active-duty Cossacks. They all served in pretty much the same capacity—as guards, couriers, manual laborers, and border sentries—and by all accounts had little time to devote to their households or domestic economies.[57]

Expansion West

The next stage of Cossack formation in the North Caucasus began after the foundation of the Russian fortress of Mozdok in 1763. Mozdok was the site of a village founded by the Kabardian Kurgok Konchokin, who had resettled from south of the Terek and converted to Christianity in 1759. A small Russian fortification was built there in 1763 and Konchokin became prince Cherkesskii-Konchokin and was awarded the rank of lieutenant colonel. Mozdok was upgraded to a strong fortress in 1770 with an independent garrison as in Kizliar. With this, Russian influence extended all the way up the middle course of the Terek, well into the north-central Caucasus.[58]

Mozdok quickly became a magnet for peasants, slaves, and captives fleeing from the Kabardian lands. A Kabardian delegation was sent to St. Petersburg in 1764 to request that the fortress be destroyed, that they be compensated for Christian fugitives, and that any other fugitive subjects of theirs be returned. These requests were, of course, denied. At the time there were more than 200 converted Kabardians in Mozdok. The ambivalence of Kabardians towards the Russian presence—and the lure of Russian trade—is reflected in the fact that the same delegation asked for reduced commercial tariffs at Kizliar.[59]

With Mozdok beckoning, in 1767 a reportedly 10,000 Kabardian peasants—surely an exaggeration—fled to the adjacent area between the Terek and the Malka Rivers and erected a bridge across the Terek as an escape route. Despite promises of Russian protection by the commander of the Kizliar fortress, the peasants reached an agreement with their lords concerning lower taxes and the right to flee to other proprietors, and many returned. In 1771 after another Kabardian petition, Catherine the Great agreed to return fugitive Kabardian slaves and to pay fifty rubles for each Christian.[60] This decision was made because Russia did not want to aggravate its relations with the Ottoman empire (which considered Kabarda a feudal dependency) and because it was thought that many converted Kabardians had no real interest in Christianity.

Russia turned its attention instead to the Ossetians, supposedly "wayward Christians" who had become the objects of special missionary activities. The resettlement of Ossetians from the mountains to the valleys began with the founding of Mozdok and then Vladikavkaz in 1784. In fact, the original plan for Mozdok called for a fortified settlement—Ossetian Fortress—to which Ossetians, Georgians, Armenians, other "people of Christian nations" and mountain people wanting to convert would be invited to resettle, where they would have freedom to construct churches, and practice their faith and where Muslim residences would be prohibited. Although this plan never materialized, the intention of making Mozdok a magnet for Ossetian resettlement remained. It was in Mozdok that the Ossetian Commission opened its first missionary school for Ossetian children in 1764.[61]

Ossetian resettlement increased in the 1820s when general Ermolov began removing Kabardians from the area of the Georgian Military Highway and replacing them with Ossetians. Ossetians resettled from the mountains in large numbers through the 1830s; by the 1840s there were some 21,000 Ossetians living in the Vladikavkaz plain.[62] Many enrolled in Cossack service.

To settle Mozdok, the Russian government enticed natives willing to convert and move there with gifts of rubles. Thanks to this, the number of migrants from the mountains quickly grew and out of them the 100-strong Mozdok Mountain command was formed in 1765 from converted Kabardians, Ossetians, Kumyks, and other mountain people. They were used mostly for convoy service between Mozdok and Tiflis.[63]

Mozdok was located a good sixty-five miles west from the westernmost village of the Greben Cossacks and the number of mountain migrants was not large enough to create a native force to protect this distance. To cover the area, new Cossack villages were settled along the middle course of the Terek by Don and Volga Cossacks.[64] First, in 1770, 100 families of Don Cossacks formed Lukovskaia stanitsa on the outskirts of Mozdok. They worked mostly as cannoneers in Mozdok and operated the town ferry across the Terek.[65] In the same year, 517 Cossacks from the Volga host and 250 families from the Don were resettled into five villages between Mozdok and the westernmost territory of the Greben host and named the Mozdok regiment.[66] In 1777, 200 households of converted Kalmyks were added to the Mozdok regiment—they were initially settled in Cossack villages, but soon returned to their nomadic lifestyle in the Mozdok steppe. In 1799, a sixth Mozdok regiment village was created when the militia in the Volga town of Saratov was transferred. Three hundred thirty-five families resettled and they all became Cossacks.[67]

Massive Colonization and Expansion South

At this point, the Russian presence in the North Caucasus was still restricted and tentative. The population of the stanitsas and forts numbered in the thousands rather than the tens of thousands.[68] Military operations had been extremely limited. Without large numbers of peasants growing grain, colonization—and conquest—was threatened. Cossacks had their hands full with service requirements and could not grow enough grain to feed themselves, but provisioning from internal Russia was difficult and sometimes the goods and salaries never arrived. Although the Russian presence had not yet provoked large-scale native resistance, the roots of conquest had been planted. Widespread settlement, massive peasant colonization, frenzied fort and town building, and extensive military operations began in the next few decades and culminated in Ermolov's brutal reign as the commander of the Separate Caucasus Corps (1816-1827) and the war with Shamil (1834-1859).

To further protect Russian interests in the North Caucasus, in 1777 the government embarked on the construction of a series of fortresses and Cossack villages, stretching from Mozdok to Azov. In two years, ten new forts were thrown up and many of the old ones were strengthened. As a result, a system of new forts appeared in the North Caucasus steppe, including Georgievsk, Ekaterinograd, and Stavropol'. Families of Cossacks resettled from the Volga and the Khoper to forts and stanitsas all along the line. Retired soldiers also moved there. Then in 1784, four fortresses were built on the right bank of the Terek, the southernmost, Vladikavkaz, on its upper reaches. Finally, at the end of the eighteenth century, under the cover of the Mozdok-Azov Line, large numbers of peasants began to settle on the rich agricultural land of the steppe.[69]

As part of the new push for colonization, the Volga regiment was formed in 1777 from the remaining half of the Volga Cossacks and 700 families were resettled in five villages between Mozdok and Stavropol'. Although there was considerable opposition to the move, by 1778 4,640 were resettled.[70]

The new settlement push provoked the first large-scale North Caucasian resistance to Russian colonization. From 1785 until his capture at Anapa in 1791, the Chechen Mansur (or Ushurma) preached holy war and led raids along the line supported by an army of thousands. He attacked Kizliar in 1785 and also forced the Russians to abandon Vladikavkaz and a number of other fortresses in the upper Terek region.[71]

But Mansur could not stop the wheels of Russian conquest from rolling on. The next stage of Terek Cossack formation occurred in 1824 when general Ermolov shored up the line between the Mozdok and Volga regiments with new Cossack villages. He innovatively created the Mountain regiment by combining already existing Cossack, native, and state peasant settlements and villages into a Cossack regiment. Thus, overnight, a new regiment was created with 5,500 individuals, made up mostly of Russians and Ukrainians, but with a minority of Kabardians, Ossetians, and other mountain people.[72]

At the same time, Ermolov expanded the Volga host by attaching to it existing Cossack and state peasant villages and one native village, Babukovskii Aul. This village was founded in 1790 by Kabardians, Abazians, and Tatars and it became the largest Muslim Cossack center. By 1853 it numbered 1,044 male Muslim Cossacks. When four state peasant villages were transformed into Cossack stanitsas and attached to the host in 1832, it brought the total population to 10,500, including 1,150 active duty Cossacks.[73]

After this expansion of the Volga host, the state pushed the Russian fortified line further south into the Caucasus mountains and into the foothills of the Sunzha region. This expansion met with particularly fierce resistance because it cut off the mountain people from their winter pasture lands and best agricultural lands, and because the construction of new fortifications was often accompanied by the destruction of native villages and the forced resettlement of the residents.[74]

This Russian penetration south of the Terek River was long in coming. The initial motive, however, was not the conquest of the North Caucasus, but to secure a transportation route to the Transcaucasus after the Georgian kingdom of Kartlo-Kakheti became a part of the Russian empire with the Georgievsk Treaty of 1783. The first step had been the construction of the Georgian Military Highway and the foundation of the fortress of Vladikavkaz—"the ruler of the Caucasus"—in 1784, at the point where the steep ascent of the Caucasus mountains begins. With the Mansur uprising in 1787, it was soon abandoned, the Ossetians who had resettled there escaped to the mountains, and Vladikavkaz was not reconstructed until 1795.[75]

To strengthen the defense of the Georgian Military Highway, which opened for travel in 1801, Russia began a new series of population shuffles. First, military commanders moved Ossetians from the Dar'ial gorge at the top of the highway to the Vladikavkaz plain to prevent them from threatening the highway. They also granted land and salaries to other mountain Ossetians to resettle around Vladikavkaz to provide manual labor and additional defense for the fort. Ermolov also used Ossetians and Kabardians to guard the lower part of the Georgian Military Highway and in the 1820s began to settle the plain with mountain villagers. By the beginning of the 1830s, there were over twenty settlements of migrants from the mountains.[76]

With the beginning of the war with Shamil, the situation along the Georgian Military Highway became more precarious and often out of control. From the spring of 1835, parties of mountain people often broke into Russian territory and Shamil tried to attack the highway several times. To deter such attacks, in 1837, two Ukrainian Cossack regiments—formed in 1831 to fight the Polish rebels—were resettled to the Vladikavkaz region. They helped to form eight stanitsas of the Vladikavkaz regiment, along with Cossacks from already existing Caucasus regiments; migrants from Russia and Ukraine; and families of soldiers who had formed two military colonies in 1832. The population was predominantly Russian and Ukrainian.[77]

Finally, Ermolov also began the gradual colonization of the area east of Vladikavkaz along the Sunzha River. He first penetrated the area with the founding of a series of ominously named forts and camps in 1818-1819: Groznaia ("menacing"), Pregradnyi ("barrier"), Zlobnyi ("malicious"), Vnezapnaia ("unexpected," as in a surprise attack), and Burnaia ("violent"). But the permanent settlement of Cossacks in the Sunzha region began only in 1845 when the Sunzha regiment was formed, mostly by resettlers from other Caucasus Cossack regiments and from the Don. Some local Cossacks settled in this more spacious but viciously contested region by their own free will; others were forced to move by their stanitsa. Seven Cossack villages were formed in the middle course of the Sunzha by 1,105 families of Don Cossacks, 1,063 families of Terek Cossacks, and 670 families of Kuban Cossacks. In 1852, eight more stanitsas were created along the lower course of the Sunzha and the regiment was split into First and Second Sunzha regiments.[78]

Peasants, Fugitives, and Drifters

With Cossacks and forts stringing along the Terek and Kuban Rivers, migration to the North Caucasus—both legal and illegal—exploded. Mass legal resettlement to the North Caucasus began under Catherine the Great. Each new fortress acted as a magnet for non-military settlers from all over Russia. Some 68,000 peasants resettled in 1781-1784 and by 1784, fourteen peasant villages had been formed. Some 68,000 more moved there by the beginning of the nineteenth century.[79]

Most of the migrants were state peasants and most came from southern Russian provinces. During this period (up to the nineteenth century) most of the "peasant" settlers were *odnodvortsy*, descendants of southern and eastern frontier settlers of the sixteenth and seventeenth centuries, who by the late eighteenth century were little different in legal status from state peasants. Another major flow of resettlement occurred in 1824-1830. By 1830 some 53,500 state peasants lived in the Caucasus *oblast'*.[80]

The resettlement of state peasants to the North Caucasus was encouraged by granting the settlers a tax-free period, usually from one-half to three years. The majority was allowed to settle where they wanted—most moved to the steppe region in the north-central Caucasus around Stavropol'. State land was plentiful and productive there, unlike in the lower Terek region. Peasants were needed to develop the region's agriculture so that Cossacks would cease to be dependent on state provisions and trade with the mountain people (and so that the state could purchase provisions locally rather than import them from internal Russia). But there was also a chronic need for more Cossacks—to provide military support, defend the borders, and provide manual labor for Cossack villages. This created a trade-off between peasant-economic colonization and Cossack-military colonization, and peasant settlement sometimes created land disputes between peasants and Cossacks. Also, as we have seen, one way the state tried to remedy the shortage of Cossacks was to convert local state peasants into Cossacks, buttressing the military line, but weakening its economic foundation by eliminating farmers.[81]

It would be a mistake to view the Terek Cossacks solely through the narrow prism of the official Russian presence in the North Caucasus. One of the prominent features of "Russian" society in the North Caucasus was its fluidity—at the edges of the officially constituted forts and villages were free-flowing populations and large stateless areas.

The North Caucasus had long been a refuge for people on the run. Fleeing Cossacks, *strel'tsy*, serfs, state peasants, religious schismatics, convicts and criminals, and slaves and servants from the Caucasus mountains all made their way to the North Caucasus, and many ended up enrolled in a Cossack regiment. Others lived as drifters or on the margins of officially registered communities. Sometimes they came alone, like the serf Nikolai Shipov, who fled to the North Caucasus twice in the 1830s and was taken in by local Armenian traders.[82] Sometimes large groups escaped there, such as the 1,500 Don Cossacks who built a small village on the Kuma River in the thick of the forest in the 1680s during the schism; or the 2,000 refugees from the Bulavin uprising who fled to the Kuban and formed the so-called Nekrasov Cossack host.[83] After he was captured, Pugachev testified to the lure of the North Caucasus as a place of refuge. Recounting how he advised his brother-in-law, a Don Cossack in Taganrog, where to escape to, he warned against the former Zaporozhian lands and recommended the North Caucasus: "if you are ready to run then run to the Terek, our families live there, there are many people there, plenty of rivers and forest, you will be able to live there, and the local people are hospitable to strangers." Pugachev himself fled to the North Caucasus in 1772 and enrolled in the Terek-Semeinoe host; en route he joined up with fugitives from Siberian factories who were also running to the Terek.[84] Even after the Terek Cossacks became clients of the Russian state in 1720, free settlement and independent living remained possible—for individuals and for groups—well into the nineteenth century. It is difficult to track down the history of these settlements since their very purpose was to remain invisible to the Russian state. But local history and local lore contain enough references to free settlers to conclude that this frontier freedom was an important and enduring part of the social landscape.

There was considerable peasant flight to the North Caucasus—peasants joined resettlements of state peasants or Cossacks, or they founded settlements of their own, sometimes undetected for decades. According to folk tradition, many of the villages of the North Caucasus, with names such as Privol'noe ("free") and Naidennoe ("found," presumably named for its discovery by a traveler), were initially hideouts for bands of fugitive serfs. Petrovskoe on the Kalaus River was supposedly founded by the fugitive serf Petr Burlak, who settled in its dense forest in the 1750s and joined neighboring "Tatar" villages in banditry. Other fugitive serfs later joined Burlak, many with their families, and a Russian village came into being, deep in the woods. The Burlatskii ravine on the right bank of the Buivola River sheltered fugitive peasants who supposedly settled there to escape military duty and landlords, and to lead a life of robbing and plundering. Nikolinobalkovskoe was supposedly named after the bandit Nikola who also lived near the Kalaus River with his band.[85]

It is unwise to try to extract too much from local foundation myths; we can never be sure if these folk memories correspond to actual origins. On the other hand, there certainly were plenty of opportunities to live "between the cracks" in the North Caucasus, on the Russian side of the Caucasus Military Line and in the mountains. Until the founding of Mozdok in 1763, the official Russian presence was limited to the lower Terek. Even after the construction of the Mozdok-Azov Line in 1777, Russian outposts stretched only along a single, thin line, with great distances between forts. The bulk of the North Caucasus steppe, not to mention the lands beyond the Terek and the Kuban, remained uncontrolled by the Russian state.[86]

This gradually changed during the next half century with the addition of new forts on the existing military line, the building of new fortified lines to the south and to the west, and the completion of the Georgian Military Highway. But even so, there were plenty who carved out a free existence in the forests of the foothills, the mountains beyond the Terek, the swampy lowlands along the Caspian and Black Seas, or the vast and sparsely populated steppe. Iosif Debu, the colonel of the Second Brigade of the Caucasus Line, reported in 1829 that various types of vagrants, fugitives, and deserters, many with families, lived in the swamps in the environs of Kizliar and worked in fishing gangs and in

Kizliar. At the same time, free, armed bands hid along the streams and coves at the edges of Temriuk.[87]

In 1857, the provincial government attempted to disperse a settlement of Russian bandits at Dzhelan' in the Stavropol' steppe: they simply moved to the Sukhaia-Buivola River between Stavropol' and Georgievsk and continued to attack traveling traders. Another well-known refuge for Russian soldiers and Cossacks who deserted from various garrisons and regiments was the village of Bashly, not far from Derbent.[88] Cossacks of the Line and Black Sea Cossacks formed "haidamak" gangs that attacked farmsteads in the late 1840s. The aura of the free life beyond the bounds of the state led some nineteenth-century Cossacks to imagine that Stenka Razin still lived in the forest in the Caucasus mountains.[89]

Many people also lived undiscovered and unencumbered in the major towns and Cossack villages of the North Caucasus. A lieutenant colonel of the gendarmes in Kizliar wrote in 1842 that he often met mountain people who lived in the town for many years with no status (*"bez vsiakikh vidov"*), with no official permission, and often in hiding from some crime.[90] The phenomenon of rootlessness was common enough that the Greben Cossacks sang a folk song about a homeless wanderer, whose ataman was "the light of the moon."[91]

State peasant and serf flight to the North Caucasus received particular attention from the authorities in the 1820s through the 1840s. Nicholas I made a special announcement on 12 May 1826 that rumors of freedom in the Caucasus were lies and that all who tried to flee there would be punished with the full force of the law. On 16 February 1827, he issued regulations by which all fugitive serfs were recognized as Cossacks if they had been included on the Cossack registers of 1816 and had a family, a domestic economy, and had done military duty; the rest were to be returned to their masters.[92] But nothing could stop the flight to the Caucasus—thousands were caught fleeing in the 1830s and 1840s, mostly from the southern provinces, some with false passports, some enticed by returning fugitives and on occasion by armed bands from the south. Most seem to have hoped to receive freedom, land, and status as a Cossack.[93]

To curtail peasant flight from Voronezh province, in 1837 the governor installed new border guards at all bridges and roads leading south to the lands of the Don Cossacks and tried to curb passport forgery by forbidding *uezd* treasuries from selling, without prior approval, stamped paper used for tickets. The Minister of War was so alarmed by the movement south that he proposed the construction of a temporary cordon, stretching from Astrakhan and Saratov to Ekaterinoslav province, to keep peasants and serfs from escaping to the Caucasus![94]

But despite all this, rootlessness and flight were still perpetual concerns for local authorities. The first issue of *Stavropol'skiia gubernskiia vedomosti*, in 1850, reported the disappearance of 108 peasants from Voronezh who were supposed to be enrolled in the Volga host.[95] It is not known if they returned to Voronezh; if they fled to the mountains, the swamps, or the steppe; or if they dispersed to already existing Cossack and state peasant villages. Governors reported annually on the number of fugitives caught in Stavropol' province: in 1845 they nabbed 348, then 202 in 1846, and 191 in 1847.[96] During 1850-1852, the governor of Stavropol' announced in the same newspaper the catch of 342 "vagrants" (*brodiagi*) (114/year average), sometimes as many as thirty a month.[97] Surely many more remained undetected.

Although it is difficult to document the magnitude, a good number of peasants who made it to the Caucasus ended up, sooner or later, as Cossacks. Up to the mid-nineteenth century there was a great labor shortage in the North Caucasus, which meant that Cossacks had difficulty keeping their fighting numbers up and also—because of service requirements—in establishing successful economies. It was all to the advantage of the different hosts and regiments, then, to accept fugitives. It was also to the advantage of local officials to look the other way since they were mainly concerned with keeping up a viable fighting force, which meant maintaining an adequate number of Cossacks both to fight and to work in their villages in order to provide the necessary economic base. The Ministry of Internal Affairs discovered in 1833 that Cossack regimental leaders were enrolling fugitive serfs as workers and that some commanders gave fugitive serfs passports so they could return to their home villages and talk others into fleeing to the Caucasus line.[98] Peasants also became Cossacks in the North Caucasus by administrative decree. Dozens of state peasant villages were simply converted into stanitsas and added to existing hosts. Two mass conversions of state peasant villages occurred—fourteen were "cossackized" in 1784 and thirty-three in 1832—and many more were converted individually or in small groups in the early nineteenth century.[99]

It should be reiterated that not all who found themselves enrolled as Cossacks in the North Caucasus went by their own volition. The North Caucasus was not just a freedom frontier; like Siberia it was also a region of forced resettlement. As we have seen, Don, Volga, Khoper, and Ukrainian Cossacks were resettled by the thousands to the North Caucasus in the course of the eighteenth and nineteenth centuries. Most forced resettlement was relatively peaceful, but Cossacks actively opposed resettlement on two occasions—the worst one involved fifty Don Cossack regiments.[100]

The government also forced thousands of "vagrants" to resettle to the North Caucasus. On 12 February 1829 the State Council approved measures that *brodiagi* in the Caucasus *oblast'*, along with those in Ukrainian and southern provinces, be given to the Cossacks of the line as laborers for a three-year period, after which those of good behavior were to be enrolled as Cossacks. According to one source, in the course of three years 10,000 such people joined the regiments of the line. Cossacks also purchased workers from mountain people who likewise became indentured servants and then joined up as Cossacks.[101]

So the Cossack villages that came into being in the North Caucasus were formed from several distinct frontier movements—the original free migration; forced resettlement of Cossacks and "vagrants"; peasant and Cossack flight from Russia; Chechen, Ingush, Kumyk, Kabardian, Ossetian, Armenian, and Georgian flight, migration, and forced resettlement from the mountains; and free migration of state peasants. By the nineteenth century, a motley string of settlements stretched along the Terek: predominantly old-settler, Old Believer Cossack villages; Georgian and Armenian Cossack villages; Orthodox Ukrainian Cossack villages; Ossetian and Kabardian Cossack villages; ethnically diverse old fort towns such as Kizliar and Mozdok; and the newer fortress town of Vladikavkaz, ringed by Ossetian suburbs. To the north, the Russian civil administrative center of Stavropol' dominated the steppe and was surrounded by mostly Russian state peasant villages. Kalmyks of the Mozdok regiment also lived in the steppe, moving their animals and tents with the seasons. To the south were planted smaller, wilder, more exposed forts and Cossack villages such as Groznyi. And at the margins floated a nebulous population of fugitive serfs, deserters, schismatics, mountain migrants, and wanderers of other sorts.

The Cossack population had reached 86,538 by 1851. The largest units were the Sixth brigade (the former First and Second Volga regiments) (26,127), the Mountain regiment (15,612), and the Mozdok regiment (14,215). The smallest were the Vladikavkaz regiment (4,192), the Kizliar regiment (5,395), and the First Sunzha regiment (10,044).[102]

The heartlands from whence Cossacks came and to which some retained family connections were equally diverse—mostly the Cossack Don and Volga, peasant Ukraine and south Russia, the mountains and steppe of the North Caucasus, and the Transcaucasus. Native peoples of the North Caucasus, Muslims included, served in every capacity in the Cossack regiments and up to the end of the war with Shamil, Muslims occasionally commanded Christians. As of 1853, there were seventy-three native North Caucasian (or "Asian" as they were officially called) staff and chief officers in the Line host, including Chechens, Kabardians, Digorians, Kumyks, and Circassians. In the Mountain, Vladikavkaz, Mozdok, Sunzha, Greben, and Kizliar regiments, at least forty-one out of forty-six were Muslim.[103]

The Terek Cossacks were socially and ethnically diverse, with ties to many "interiors," with heritages of free settlement and forced resettlement, living on a frontier that offered many opportunities to escape. This social landscape of settlement contributed to a sometimes uncertainty of loyalty. Not that Cossack villages were hotbeds of anti-imperial rebellion, but their loyalty often could not be taken for granted. As we shall see, Cossacks were able to work within this context to secure certain freedoms and occasionally work against the policies of the Russian state.

Notes

1. The oft-cited date for the migration in 1711, but I can find no primary source to support a concentrated migration in a particular year. See I. Debu, "O nachal'nom ustanovlenii i rasprostranenii Kavkazskoi linii," *Otechestvennyia zapiski* 18, no. 48 (1824): 282; I. Popko, *Terskie kazaki so starodavnikh vremen* (St. Petersburg: Tipografiia Departmenta udelov, 1880), 94-97; "Istoricheskiia svedeniia o Grebenskom kazach'em polku," *Sbornik Terskago obshchestva liubitelei kazach'ei stariny*, no. 4 (1912): 27.

2. I. Abozin, "Vozrazhenie," *Voennyi sbornik* 26, no. 8 (1862): 489-90; "Vospominaniia o Grebenskikh kazakakh i kavkazskoi linii," *Kavkaz*, 4 October 1856, 313-14.

3. N. B. Golikova, *Ocherki po istorii gorodov Rossii kontsa XVII-nachala XVIII v.* (Moscow: Izdatel'stvo Moskovskogo universiteta, 1982), 32.

4. "Opisanie Grebenskikh kazakov XVIII v.," *Istoricheskii arkhiv*, no. 5 (September-October 1958): 182.

5. "Materialy Ekaterinskoi zakonodatel'noi komissii," *Sbornik Imperatorskago russkago istoricheskago obshchestva* 115 (1903): 457; Golikova, *Ocherki po istorii gorodov*, 4, 31; "Istoricheskiia svedeniia," 28-29; Popko, *Terskie kazaki*, xii; "Materialy dlia statistiki Kizliarskago polka Terskago kazach'iago voiska," *Voennyi sbornik*, no. 12 (December 1869): 207-09.

6. Popko, *Terskie kazaki*, 84-85; N. G. Volkova, *Etnicheskii sostav naseleniia Severnogo Kavkaza v XVIII-nachale XX veka* (Moscow: Izdatel'stvo "Nauka," 1974), 82-84.

7. "Opisanie Grebenskikh kazakov," 182; I.-G. Gerber, "Opisanie stran i narodov vdol' zapadnogo berega Kaspiiskogo moria. 1728 g.," in *Istoriia, geografiia i etnografiia Dagestana XVIII-XIX vv.*, eds. M. O. Kosven and Kh.-M. Khashaev (Moscow: Izdatel'stvo vostochnoi literatury, 1958), 60.

8. F. G. Chernozubov, "Ocherki Terskoi stariny (1832-1837). Nabegi khishchnikov," *Zapiski Terskago obshchestva liubitelei kazach'ei stariny*, no. 7 (1914): 10-13; Popko, *Terskie kazaki*, 365-67; I. A. Gil'denshtedt [Johann Anton Güldenstädt], *Geograficheskoe i statisticheskoe opisanie Gruzii i Kavkaza* (St. Petersburg: Imperatorskaia akademiia nauk, 1809), 2-3; I. P. Falk, "Zapiski puteshestviia akademika Falka," *Polnoe uchenykh puteshestvii po Rossii* (St. Petersburg: Imperatorskaia akademiia nauk, 1824), 6: 57-58; M. N. Gersevanov, *Ocherk gidrografii Kavkazskago kraia* (St. Petersburg: Tipografiia Ministerstva puti soobshcheniia, 1886), 45-46.

9. Golikova, *Ocherki po istorii gorodov Rossii*, 7-19. For Astrakhan's trade with Asia, see A. I. Iukht, *Torgovlia s vostochnymi stranami i vnutrennii rynok Rossii* (Moscow: Rossiiskaia akademiia nauk. Institut Rossiiskoi istorii, 1994) and Stephen Frederic Dale, *Indian Merchants and Eurasian Trade, 1600-1750* (Cambridge: Cambridge University Press, 1994), 78-127.

10. *Polnoe sobranie zakonov Rossiiskoi imperii* [hereafter *PSZ*] (St. Petersburg: Tipografiia II otdeleniia sobstvennoi Ego Imperatorskago Velichestva kantseliarii, 1830), 6: 277, 367; "Istoricheskiia svedeniia o Grebenskom kazach'em polku," 28-29; Popko, *Terskie kazaki*, 197-98. Ermolov abolished the right to elect *voisko* ataman, captain (*esaul*), color bearer (*znamënshchik*), clerk (*d'iak*), and the village atamans.

11. "Istoricheskiia svedeniia," 36-37; Popko, *Terskie kazaki*, 328-29; G. A. Tkachëv,

Stanitsa Chervlennaia. Istoricheskii ocherk (Vladikavkaz: Elektropechatnia tipografii Terskago oblastnago pravleniia, 1912), 53-56. For an accessible copy of one of the treaties, see Iu. A. Galushko, *Kazach'i voiska Rossii* (Moscow: Informatsionno-izdatel'skoe agentstvo "Russkii mir," 1993), 185.

12. I. I. Dmitrenko, "Materialy k istorii Terskago kazach'iago voiska," *Terskii sbornik* 4 (1897): 75.

13. Aleksandr Markov, *Petr Pervyi i Astrakhan'* (Astrakhan': Izdatel'stvo "Forzats," 1994), 28-29; Evgenii V. Anisimov, *The Reforms of Peter the Great*, trans. John T. Alexander (Armonk and London: M.E. Sharpe, 1993), 256-57; S. G. Agadzhanov and A. Il'iasov, eds., Kh. Agaev, M. Annanepesov, comps., *Russko-turkmenskie otnosheniia v XVIII-XIX vv. Sbornik dokumentov* (Ashkhabad: Izdatel'stvo Akademii nauk Turkmenskoi SSR, 1963), 46, 48.

14. Markov, *Petr Pervyi*, 29-30; "Istoricheskoe svedenie. (Raport komanduiushchago Kizliarskim polkom podp. Alpatova 31 Iiulia 1854 goda No. 4530)," *Sbornik Obshchestva liubitelei kazach'ei stariny*, no. 2 (1912): 4-5; Vladimir Dal', *Tolkovyi slovar' zhivogo velikorusskogo iazyka* (St. Petersburg-Moscow: Izdanie T-va M. O. Vol'f, 1907; repr., Moscow: A/O Izdatel'skaia gruppa "Progress," "Univers," 1994), 3: 1310; V. I. Dal', "Poslovitsy Russkago naroda," *Chteniia v Imperatorskom obshchestve istorii i drevnostei Rossiiskikh pri Moskovskom universitete* 4 (October-December 1861): 363.

15. I. D. Popko, *Terskie kazaki so starodavnikh vremen* (St. Petersburg: Tipografiia Departmenta udelov, 1880), 97-101; P. A. Vostrikov, "Stanitsa Naurskaia, Terskoi oblasti," *Sbornik materialov dlia opisaniia mestnostei i plemen Kavkaza* 33 (1904): section 2, 117-20; G. A. Tkachëv, ed., *Grebenskie, Terskie i Kizliarskie kazaki* (Vladikavkaz: Elektropechatnia tipografiia Terskago oblastnago pravleniia, 1911), 167-68; I. V. Bentkovskii, *Grebentsy* (Moscow: Russkaia topolitografiia, 1889), 36-37.

16. Golikova, *Ocherki po istorii gorodov*, 32; P. G. Butkov, *Materialy dlia novoi istorii Kavkaza s 1722 po 1803 god* (St. Petersburg: Tipografiia Imperatorskoi akademii nauk, 1869), 1: 20, 32-33; F. I. Soimonov, *Opisanie Kaspiiskago moria i chinennykh na onom Rossiiskikh zavoevani* (St. Petersburg: Imperatorskaia akademiia nauk, 1763), 72; V. P. Lystsov, *Persidskii pokhod Petra I* (Moscow: Izdatel'stvo Moskovskogo universiteta, 1951), 92-93; D. Vasil'ev, "Zagadka starogo Kizliara (Kizliar do 1735 goda)," in *Voprosy istorii Dagestana (dosovetskii period)*, ed. V. G. Gadzhiev (Makhachkala: Dagestanskii filial Akademii nauk SSSR, 1974), 1: 39; V. G. Gadzhiev, ed., *Russko-dagestanskie otnosheniia v XVIII-nachale XIX v. Sbornik dokumentov* (Moscow: Nauka, 1988), 45; Petr Khitsunov, "Snosheniia Rossii s severnomiu chastiiu Kavkaza," *Kavkaz*, 20 April 1846, 64.

17. Butkov, *Materialy dlia novoi istorii Kavkaza*, 1: 20, 32-33; I. V. Rovinskii, "Khoziaistvennoe opisanie Astrakhanskoi i Kavkazskoi gubernii," *Trudy Stavropol'skoi uchenoi arkhivnoi komissii*, no. 2 (1910): section 4, 50-52; Iu. Shidlovskii, "Zapiske o Kizliare," *Zhurnal Ministerstva vnutrennikh del*, no. 4 (1843): 190. On Peter's policy in the northeast Caucasus see Muriel Atkin, "Russian Expansion in the Caucasus to 1813," in *Russian Colonial Expansion to 1917*, ed. Michael Rywkin (London: Mansell Publishing, 1988), 147-50; Firuz Kazemzadeh, "Russian Penetration of the Caucasus," in *Russian Imperialism from Ivan the Great to the Revolution*, ed. Taras Hunczak (New Brunswick: Rutgers University Press, 1974), 243-45; and Lystsov, *Persidskii pokhod*.

18. *PSZ*, 7: 252; "Pokhodnoi zhurnal Petra Velikago. 1722," *Pokhodnye i putevye*

zhurnaly imp. Petra I-go, 1855: 64; "Ukaz Senata o poselenii Donskikh kazakov na zemliakh, raspolozhennykh po reke Sulak," in *Russko-dagestanskie otnosheniia XVII-pervoi chetverti XVIII vv. (Dokumenty i materialy)*, ed. M. M. Ikhilov and others (Makhachkala: Dagestanskoe knizhnoe izdatel'stvo, 1958), 110; Butkov, *Materialy dlia novoi istorii Kavkaza*, 1: 78; Aleksandr Rigel'man, *Istoriia ili povestvovanie o Donskikh kazakakh* (Moscow: Universitetskaia tipografiia, 1846), 140-41; "Materialy dlia statistiki Kizliarskago polka Terskago kazach'iago voiska," *Voennyi sbornik*, no. 12 (December 1869): 210; "Istoricheskoe svedenie," 8-9.

19. N. P. Gritsenko, *Sotsial'no-ekonomicheskoe razvitie priterechnykh raionov v XVIII-pervoi polovine XIX vv.* (Groznyi: Izdatel'stvo gazeta "Groznenskii Rabochii," 1961), 16-20; Butkov, *Materialy dlia novoi istorii Kavkaza*, 1: 77.

20. Butkov, *Materialy dlia novoi istorii Kavkaza*, 1: 78, 143; "Materialy dlia statistiki Kizliarskago polka," 209; Popko, *Terskie kazaki*, xii-xiii; N. Toporov, *Opyt'' meditsinskoi geografii Kavkaza* (St. Petersburg: Tipografiia Iakova Treia, 1864), 73-74; "Istoricheskoe svedenie," 5-6. For a good, brief summary of the Sviatoi Krest period, see N. P. Gritsenko, *Goroda Severo-vostochnogo Kavkaza i proizvoditel'nye sily kraia* (Rostov-on-Don: Izdatel'stvo Rostovskogo universiteta, 1984), 75-83.

21. A. P. Shikhsaidov, T. M. Aitberov, and G. M.-P. Orazaev, *Dagestanskie istoricheskie soch
eneniia* (Moscow: Nauka. Izdatel'skaia firma "Vostochnaia literatura," 1993), 235-36.

22. Butkov, *Materialy dlia novoi istorii Kavkaza*, 1: 154-55.

23. S. Pisarev, *Trekhsotletie Terskago kazach'iago voiska. 1577-1877* (Vladikavkaz: Tipografiia Terskago oblastnago pravleniia, 1881), 19-20; "Materialy dlia statistiki Kizliarskago polka," 211; Rigel'man, *Istoriia ili povestvovanie o Donskikh kazakakh*, 138-39.

24. Alan W. Fisher, "Emigration of Muslims from the Russian Empire in the Years After the Crimean War," *Jahrbücher fur Geschichte Osteuropas* 35 (1987): 356-71. One of the best general sources on population movements in the North Caucasus is Volkova, *Etnicheskii sostav naseleniia Severnogo Kavkaza*.

25. V. M. Kabuzan, *Narody Rossii v XVIII veke. Chislennost' i etnicheskii sostav* (Moscow: Nauka, 1990), 227; N. I. Voronov, ed., *Sbornik statisticheskikh svedenii o Kavkaze* (Tiflis: Kavkazskii otdel Imperatorskago russkago geograficheskago obshchestva, 1869), section 2, part B, 20-21; Butkov, *Materialy dlia novoi istorii Kavkaza*, 1: 156; Gritsenko, *Goroda Severo-vostochnogo Kavkaza*, 103.

26. Gil'denshtedt, *Geograficheskoe i statisticheskoe opisanie Gruzii*, 21-23; Gritsenko, *Goroda Severo-vostochnogo Kavkaza*, 86-87.

27. F. Ponomarëv, "Materialy dlia istorii Terskago kazach'iago voiska s 1559 po 1880 god," *Voennyi sbornik* 23, 10 (October 1880): 364-65.

28. N. Blagoveshchenskii, ed., *Sbornik svedenii o Terskoi oblasti* (Vladikavkaz: Tipografiia Terskago oblastnago pravleniia, 1878), 93-94; L. M. Maksimovich and A. Shchekatov, *Geograficheskii slovar' Rossiiskogo gosudarstva* (Moscow: Universitetskaia tipografiia, 1804), 3: 454-55.

29. Steven, "Kratkaia vypiska iz puteshestviia g. kollezhskago sovetnika Stevena po Kavkazskomu kraiu v 1810 godu," *Severnaia pochta* 59 (1811): no pagination.

30. Gritsenko, *Sotsial'no-ekonomicheskoe razvitie*, 71-72; L. V. Kupriianova, *Goroda Severnogo Kavkaza vo vtoroi polovine XIX veka* (Moscow: Nauka, 1981), 39. For a good

summary of the history of Kizliar see Gritsenko, 84-113.

31. Ashot Ioannisian, ed. *Armiano-russkie otnosheniia v pervoi treti XVIII veka. Sbornik dokumentov* (Yerevan: Izdatel'stvo Akademii nauk Armianskoi SSR, 1984), 2: 37-41; B. B. Piotrovskii, ed. *Istoriia narodov Severnogo Kavkaza s drevneishikh vremen do kontsa XVIII v.* (Moscow: "Nauka," 1988), 374, 463; Gritsenko, *Sotsial'no-ekonomicheskoe razvitie*, 35-36; N. G. Volkova, "O rasselenii Armian na Severnom Kavkaze do nachala XX veka," *Istoriko-filologicheskii zhurnal* 3 (1966): 260; Volkova, *Etnicheskii sostav naseleniia Severnogo Kavkaza*, 200-201; Iosif Debu, *O Kavkazskoi linii i prisoedinennom k nei Chernomorskom voiske* (St. Petersburg: Tipografiia Karla Kraiia, 1829), 54-59; Platon Zubov, *Kartina Kavkazskago kraia prinadlezhashchego Rossii, i sopredel'nykh onomu zemel'* (St. Petersburg: Tipografiia Konrada Vingebera, 1834), 2: 125-26; Voiskovoe khoziaistvennoe pravlenie, *Statisticheskiia monografii po izsledovanniu stanichnago byta Terskago kazach'iago voiska* (Vladikavkaz: Tipografiia Terskago oblastnago pravleniia, 1881), 320-21.

32. Gritsenko, *Goroda Severo-vostochnogo Kavkaza*, 92; Gritsenko, *Sotsial'no-ekonomicheskoe razvitie*, 21-23; "Opisanie Grebenskikh kazakov," 182; S. B. Bronevskii, *Noveishiia geograficheskiia i istoricheskiia izvestiia o Kavkaze* (Moscow: Tipografiia S. Selivanovskii, 1823), 2: 175-76; E. I. Krupnov, *Srednevekovaia Ingushetiia* (Moscow: Nauka, 1971), 24.

33. A. I. Shavkhelishvili, "K voprosu o pereselenii Checheno-Ingushkikh plemen s gor na ravninu," *Izvestiia Checheno-Ingushskogo respublikanskogo kraevedcheskogo muzeia* 10 (1961): 120-22; B. A. Kaloev, "Iz istorii Russko-Chechenskikh ekonomicheskikh i kul'turnykh sviazei," *Sovetskaia etnografiia*, no. 1 (January-February 1961): 41-43; Gritsenko, *Sotsial'no-ekonomicheskoe razvitie*, 14-16, 21-23; Laudaev, "Chechenskoe plemia," 6-8, 19-23, 50.

34. I. P. Falk, "Zapiski puteshestviia akademika Falka," *Polnoe uchenykh puteshestvii po Rossii* 6 (1824): ii-iii; Butkov, *Materialy dlia novoi istorii Kavkaza*, 1: 259-60; Ia. Z. Akhmadov, "Iz istorii Checheno-russkikh otnoshenii," in *Voprosy istorii Dagestana*, ed. V. G. Gadzhiev (Makhachkala: Dagestanskii filial Akademii nauk SSSR, 1975), 2: 295-300; Tkachёv, *Stanitsa Chervlennaia*, 53-56; A. P. Berzhe, *Chechnia i Chechentsy* (Tiflis: Kavkazskii otdel Imperatorskago Russkago geograficheskago obshchestva, 1859), 77.

35. *Akty sobrannye Kavkazskoi arkheograficheskoi komissieiu* [hereafter *AKAK*] (Tiflis, 1866), 1: 87. Gmelin died in captivity.

36. Gadzhiev, *Russko-dagestanskie otnosheniia*, 125-126, 147, 204.

37. N. A. Smirnov and U. A. Uligov, eds., *Kabardino-russkie otnosheniia v XVI-XVIII vv. Dokumenty i materialy* (Moscow: Izdatel'stvo Akademii nauk SSSR, 1957), 2: 103-04.

38. P. L. Iudin, "Sostav kazach'ikh voisk na Kavkaze v 1767 g.," *Zapiski Terskago obshchestva liubitelei kazach'ei stariny* 4 (April 1914): 5-9; Gritsenko, *Goroda severo-vostochnogo Kavkaza*, 89; Falk, "Zapiski puteshestviia akademika Falka," 65; Butkov, *Materialy dlia novoi istorii Kavkaza*, 1: 258; 3: 117.

39. Ioann-Iakub Lerkhe, "Prodolzhenie izvestiia o vtorom puteshestvii doktora i kollezhskago sovetnika Lerkha, v Persiiu, s 1746 do 1747 goda," *Novyia ezhemesiachnyia sochineniia* 63 (1791): 73-74.

40. Butkov, *Materialy dlia novoi istorii Kavkaza*, 1: 176.

41. Butkov, *Materialy dlia novoi istorii Kavkaza*, 1: 516-517.

42. Butkov, *Materialy dlia novoi istorii Kavkaza*, 1: 79.

43. Dmitrenko, "Materialy k istorii Terskago kazach'iago voiska," 75.

44. "Opisanie Grebenskikh kazakov," 182; Falk, "Zapiski puteshestviia akademika Falka," 60; Rigel'man, *Istoriia ili povestvovanie o Donskikh kazakov*, 138-39.

45. Falk, "Zapiski puteshestviia akademika Falka," 62-63.

46. Popko, *Terskie kazaki*, 262-63; Debu, "O nachal'nom ustanovlenii i rasprostranenii Kavkazskoi linii," 289.

47. "Istoricheskoe svedenie," 10-13; L. B. Zasedateleva, "K istorii formirovaniia Terskago kazachestva," *Vestnik Moskovskogo universiteta*, series 9, history, no. 3 (1969): 60; Popko, *Terskie kazaki*, xiii-xvi.

48. "Materialy dlia statistiki Kizliarskago polka," 211; Falk, "Zapiski puteshestviia akademika Falka," 60.

49. Dmitrenko, "Materialy k istorii Terskago kazach'iago voiska," 76.

50. Dmitrenko, "Materialy k istorii Terskago kazach'iago voiska," 74.

51. Dmitrenko, "Materialy k istorii Terskago kazach'iago voiska," 75.

52. Gadzhiev, *Russko-Dagestanskie otnosheniia*, 88; Dmitrenko, "Materialy k istorii Terskago kazach'iago voiska," 85-88.

53. Dmitrenko, "Materialy k istorii Terskago kazach'iago voiska," 90; Popko, *Terskie kazaki*, 188-89; P. L. Iudin, "Iz-za vlasti," *Zapiski Terskago obshchestva liubitelei kazach'ei stariny* 9 (September 1914): 39-42.

54. Butkov, *Materialy dlia novoi istorii Kavkaza*, 1: 153-55; Gritsenko, *Goroda severovostochnogo Kavkaza*, 88-89.

55. Rovinskii, "Khoziaistvennoe opisanie Astrakhanskoi i Kavkazskoi gubernii," 52-53; "Istoricheskoe svedenie," 5-6; "Materialy dlia istorii Severnogo Kavkaza," *Kavkazskii sbornik* 18 (1897): 392-94; "Vzgliad na Kavkazskuiu liniiu," *Severnyi arkhiv* 2 (January 1822): 174-77.

56. Iudin, "Sostav kazach'ikh voisk na Kavkaze," 9-10.

57. Dmitrenko, "Materialy k istorii Terskago kazach'iago voiska," 56; Iudin, "Sostav kazach'ikh voisk," 10-19; Butkov, *Materialy dlia novoi istorii Kavkaza*, 1: 508.

58. A. G. Kuchiev, ed., *Gorod Mozdok: Istoricheskii ocherk* (Vladikavkaz: RIPP im. Gassieva, 1995), 16-24; Butkov, *Materialy dlia istorii Kavkaza*, 1: 516-17.

59. *AKAK*, 1: 81, 85.

60. B. B. Piotrovskii, *Istoriia narodov Severnogo Kavkaza s drevneishikh vremen do kontsa XVIII v.* (Moscow: Nauka, 1988), 395; Smirnov and Uligov, *Kabardino-russkie otnosheniia*, 2: 269-73; Butkov, *Materialy dlia novoi istorii Kavkaza*, 1: 317-19.

61. B. P. Berozov, *Pereselenie Osetin s gor na ploskost' (XVIII-XX vv.)* (Ordzhonikidze: Ir, 1980), 56-59; Smirnov and Uligov, *Kabardino-russkie otnosheniia*, 2: 219.

62. B. A. Kaloev, *Osetiny*, 2nd ed. (Moscow: Nauka, 1971), 65.

63. Zasedateleva, "K istorii formirovaniia Terskogo kazachestva," 61; I. Debu, "O nachal'nom ustanovlenii i rasprostranenii Kavkazskoi linii," *Otechestvennyia zapiski* 19, no. 51 (1824): 51-52; B. A. Kaloev, *Mozdokskie Osetiny* (Moscow: Akademiia nauk SSSR, 1951), 8-10; *Polnoe sobranie zakonov*, 17: 189. In 1824 they were entered into the newly formed Mountain regiment.

64. P. L. Iudin, "S Khopera na Kavkaze," *Zapiski Terskago obshchestva liubitelei*

kazach'ei stariny 11 (1914): 5-12.

65. *PSZ*, 19: 5-7; Pisarev, *Trekhsotletie Terskago kazach'iago voiska*, 22-24; Debu, *O Kavkazskoi linii*, 64-66.

66. *PSZ*, 19: 5-7; Popko, *Terskie kazaki*, xvii-xix.

67. P. [L.] Iudin, "Mozdokskie Kalmyki," *Zapiski Terskago obshchestva liubitelei kazach'ei stariny* 12 (December 1914): 29-31; Zubov, *Kartina Kavkazskago kraia*, 2: 129-30; Debu, *O Kavkazskoi linii*, 63-64; Pisarev, *Trekhsotletie Terskago kazach'iago voiska*, 22-24; Popko, *Terskie kazaki*, xvii-xix.

68. I. P. Falk estimated it at some 3,500 males in 1773, but this is nothing more than a very rough estimate. Falk, "Zapiski puteshestviia," 60-64.

69. Kupriianova, *Goroda Severnogo Kavkaza*, 24; Piotrovskii, *Istoriia narodov Severnogo Kavkaza*, 450-52; L. B. Zasedateleva, *Terskie kazaki* (Moscow: Izdatel'stvo Moskovskogo universiteta, 1974), 205.

70. Popko, *Terskie kazaki*, xxi-xxv; Debu, "O nachal'nom ustanovlenii i rasprostranenii Kavkazskoi linii," 54-56; A. Sosiev, "Stanitsa Ekaterinogradskaia. Istoriko-statisticheskii ocherk," *Terskii sbornik* 5 (1903): 4-6; I. [A.] Biriukov, "Neskol'ko glav iz istorii Volzhskago kazach'iago voiska," *Sbornik Obshchestva liubitelei kazach'ei stariny* 4 (1912): 4-9; I. A. Biriukov, "Iz istorii Volzhskago kazach'iago voiska," *Zapiski Terskago obshchestva liubitelei kazach'ei stariny* 1 (January 1914): 21-29; Zasedateleva, *Terskie kazaki*, 205.

71. "Ocherk voennoi zhizni Kavkazskikh lineinykh kazakov," *Russkii invalid*, 9 January 1849, 21; Iu. Shidlovskii, "Zapiski o Kizliare," *Zhurnal Ministerstva vnutrennikh del*, no. 4 (1843): 196-206; Paul Henze, "Circassian Resistance to Russia" in *The North Caucasus Barrier*, ed. Marie Bennigsen Broxup (New York: St. Martin's Press, 1992), 75-76; Nart, "The Life of Mansur," *Central Asian Survey* 10, no. 1/2 (1991): 81-92.

72. Pisarev, *Trekhsotletie Terskago kazach'iago voiska*, 30-31; Zasedateleva, *Terskie kazaki*, 207; Popko, *Terskie kazaki*, xxvi-xxvii; Kaloev, *Mozdokskie Osetiny*, 8-10.

73. Popko, *Terskie kazaki*, xxi-xxv; Pisarev, *Trekhsotletie*, 27-30; Rossiiskii Gosudarstvennyi Voenno-Istoricheskii Arkhiv [RGVIA], f. 1058, op. 1, d. 325, ll. 32-33; Khorunzhii Eloev, "Stanitsa Georgievskaia. Istoriko-ekonomicheskii ocherk," *Terskii sbornik* 5 (1903): 82-83.

74. One of the best descriptions of this "military-economic blockade," as they call it, is in M. M. Bliev and V. V. Degoev, *Kavkazskaia voina* (Moscow: "Roset," 1994), 148-81.

75. *Geodezicheskaia s''emka i kratkoe opisanie goroda Vladikavkaza* (Vladikavkaz: Vladikavkazskii gorodskii komkhoz, 1928), 13; Blagoveshchenskii, *Sbornik svedenii o Terskoi oblasti*, 59-61.

76. B. P. Berozov, *Istoricheskie etiudy (iz istorii vozniknoveniia Osetinskikh sel i kazach'ikh stanits)* (Vladikavkaz: Izdatel'stvo Severo-Osetinskogo gosudarstvennogo universiteta im. K. L. Khetagurova, 1992), 7-9, 35-38, 42-48.

77. Popko, *Terskie kazaki*, xxviii-xxix; Pisarev, *Trekhsotletie Terskago kazach'iago voiska*, 33; Berozov, *Istoricheskie etiudy*, 17-19, 22-23; P. Nitsik, "Byvshiia voennyia poseleniia na Voennom-Gruzinskoi doroge," *Terskiia vedomosti*, 25 January 1887, 3-4; F. P. Ponomarëv, "Materialy po istorii Terskago kazach'iago voiska. 2-i Malorossiiskii polk," *Terskii sbornik* 6 (1903), 149.

78. Pisarev, *Trekhsotletie Terskago kazach'iago voiska*, 33; Popko, *Terskie kazaki*,

xxx; Fedor Chernozubov, "Ocherki Terskoi stariny," *Russkii arkhiv* 3 (1912): 459-61; Zasedateleva, *Terskie kazaki*, 208-09; *Polnoe sobranie zakonov Rossiiskoi imperii. Sobranie vtoroe* (St. Petersburg: Tipografiia II otdeleniia sobstvennoi Ego Imperatorskago Velichestva kantselarii, 1853), 27: 759.

79. G. N. Prozritelev, "Pervyia russkiia poseleniia na Severnom Kavkaze i v nyneshnei Stavropol'skoi gubernii," *Trudy Stavropol'skoi uchenoi arkhivnoi komissii* 5 (1913): section 1, 1-7.

80. A. P. Pronshtein, *Don i stepnoe Predkavkaz'e XVIII-pervaia polovina XIX v.* (Rostov-on-Don: Izdatel'stvo Rostovskogo universiteta, 1977), 58-60; Prozritelev, "Pervyia russkiia poseleniia na Severnom Kavkaze," 6-10; I. [V.] Bentkovskii, "Materialy dlia istorii kolonizatsii Severnogo Kavkaza," *Stavropol'skiia gubernskiia vedomosti*, no. 37 (1883): 1-2.

81. Pronshtein, *Don i stepnoe Predkavkaz'e*, 58-60; A. I. Arkhipov, "Neskol'ko svedenii o sovremennom sostoianii sel'skago khoziaistva na Kavkaze," *Moskvitianin*, no. 6 (November 1851): 126; RGVIA, f. 1058, op. 1, d. 297, ll. 116-19.

82. N. Shipov, *Istoriia moei zhizni* (St. Petersburg: Tipografiia V. S. Balasheva, 1881), 426-30.

83. Popko, *Terskie kazaki*, 80-84; N. G. Volkova, "Madzhary (iz istorii gorodov Severnogo Kavkaza)," *Kavkazskii etnograficheskii sbornik* 5 (1972): 65-66.

84. N. Dubrovin, *Pugachev i ego soobshchniki* (St. Petersburg: Tipografiia I. N. Skorokhodov, 1884), 135, 138.

85. A. L. Narochnitskii, ed., *Istoriia narodov Severnogo Kavkaza (konets XVIII v.-1917)* (Moscow: Nauka, 1988), 59; A. Tvalchrelidze, *Stavropol'skaia guberniia v statisticheskom, geograficheskom, istoricheskom i sel'sko-khoziaistvennom otnosheniiakh* (Stavropol': Tipografiia M. N. Koritskogo, 1897), 269, 382, 399.

86. The Mozdok regiment, for example, had five villages covering sixty-six miles (or one village per thirteen miles). See Biriukov, "Iz istorii Volzhskago kazach'iago voiska," 26.

87. Debu, *O Kavkazskoi linii*, 342-43; F. Shcherbina, "Beglye i krepostnye v Chernomorii," *Kievskaia starina* 6 (June 1883): 244-45.

88. Tvalchrelidze, *Stavropol'skaia guberniia*, 452-53; "Iz proshlogo Dagestanskoi oblasti (po mestnym arkhivnym dannym)," *Dagestanskii sbornik* 2 (1904): 199.

89. I. Mikhailov, "Pover'ia i predrazsudki rybakov pribrezhnyi Kaspiiskago moria," *Kavkaz*, 25 April 1853, 126.

90. V. A. Golobutskii [V. O. Holobutskyi], *Chernomorskoe kazachestvo* (Kiev: Izdatel'stvo Akademii nauk Ukrainskoi SSR, 1956), 372-73; Rossiiskii Gosudarstvennyi Istoricheskii Arkhiv [RGIA], f. 1268, op. 1, d. 424, l. 4.

91. Tkachëv, *Grebenskie*, 159-60.

92. Narochnitskii, *Istoriia narodov Severnogo Kavkaza*, 59; A. V. Fadeev, *Ocherki ekonomicheskogo razvitiia stepnogo predkavkaz'ia v doreformennyi period* (Moscow: Izdatel'stvo Akademii nauk SSSR, 1957), 146.

93. For a representative sampling of serf attempts to flee to the North Caucasus see A. V. Predtechenskii, ed., *Krest'ianskoe dvizhenie v Rossii v 1826-1849 gg. Sbornik dokumentov* (Moscow: Sotsekgiz, 1961), 223-25, 579, 659, 748; E. A. Morokhovets, *Krest'ianskaia reforma 1861 g.* (Moscow: Gosudarstvennoe sotsial'no-ekonomicheskoe izdatel'stvo, 1937),

49-50; Shcherbina, "Beglye i krepostnye," 244-45; N. Varadinov, *Istoriia Ministerstva vnutrennykh del* (St. Petersburg: Tipografiia Ministerstva vnutrennykh del, 1861), 3: book 2, 292; 3: book 3, 57, 45.

94. Predtechenskii, *Krest'ianskoe dvizhenie*, 672.

95. "O rozyske krest'iane," *Stavropol'skiia gubernskiia vedomosti*, 1 January 1850, 1.

96. RGIA, f. 1268, op. 3, d. 275, l. 10.

97. *Stavropol'skiia gubernskiia vedomosti*, 25 March 1850, 137; 8 April 1850, 161; 27 May 1850, 249; 22 July 1850, 366; 5 August 1850, 394-95; 16 September 1850, 469-70; 28 October 1850, 556-57; 11 November 1850, 585; 15 November 1850, 600; 18 November 1850, 613; 25 November 1850, 624; 2 December 1850, 640-41; 9 December 1850, 656-57; 16 December 1850, 673; 30 December 1850, 698; 6 January 1851, 4; 5 February 1851, 39-40; 24 February 1851, 73-74; 3 March 1851, 84; 17 March 1851, 107; 21 Apr. 1851, 171-72; 5 May 1851, 192-93; 19 May 1851, 216-17; 9 June 1851, 268-69; 16 June 1851, 286; 14 July 1851, 352; 11 August 1851, 412-13; 18 August 1851, 425; 25 August 1851, 436; 13 October 1851, 522-23; 27 October 1851, 550; 3 November 1851, 562, 577; 17 November 1851, 595; 15 December 1851, 661; 5 January 1852, 2; 16 February 1852, 87-88; 15 March 1852, 147; 22 March 1852, 168; 29 March 1852, 186; 26 April 1852, 244; 17 May 1852, 291; 24 May 1852, 308; 14 June 1852, 354; 19 July 1852, 411; 20 September 1852, 549-550; 4 October 1852, 577; 1 November 1852, 634; 22 November 1852, 673. Most (38 percent) reported that they did not know to which estate they belonged. The rest were mostly serfs (33 percent) and state peasants (13 percent).

98. For cases of Cossacks enrolling fugitives see Predtechenskii, *Krest'ianskoe dvizhenie*, 225; Shcherbina, "Beglye i krepostnye," 240-41; Varadinov, *Istoriia Ministerstva vnutrennykh del*, 3: book 1, 509-10.

99. G. N. Prozritelev, "Pervyia Russkiia poseleniia na Severnom Kavkaze i v nyneshnei Stavropol'skoi gubernii," *Trudy Stavropol'skoi uchenoi arkhivnoi komissii* 5 (1913): section 1, 14; Popko, *Terskie kazaki*, 388, 398; I. Bentkovskii, "Byvshee Kavkazskoe lineinoe kazach'e voisko i ego nakaznye atamany (1832-1860 g.)," *Kubanskii vedomosti*, 26 January 1891, unofficial section, 1-2.

100. Bruce W. Menning, "Cossacks Against Colonization: Mutiny on the Don, 1792-1794," in *East Central European Society and War in the Pre-Revolutionary Eighteenth Century*, Gunther E. Rothenberg, Béla K. Király, and Peter F. Sugar, eds. (Boulder: Social Science Monographs; New York: Distributed by Columbia University Press, 1982), 470-90; P. L. Iudin, "S Khopera na Kavkaze," *Zapiski Terskago obshchestva liubitelei kazach'ei stariny* 11 (November 1914): 12-23.

101. Popko, *Terskie kazaki*, 299-301, 426-28; Fadeev, *Ocherki ekonomicheskogo razvitiia*, 146-47.

102. RGVIA, f. 1058, op. 1, d. 452, ll. 4-8, 31, 68, 123, 178, 204, 224-225.

103. RGVIA, f. 1058, op. 2, d. 382, ll. 65-157, 190.

4

The Ecology of Settlement

Славный, пышный, быстрый Терек прорыл горы и леса.
Прорви етот берег, унеси меня с собой.

The famous, glorious, rapid Terek broke through the mountains and forest.
Break through this bank and carry me with you.

—Terek Cossack song

A fast river never makes it to the sea.

—Ossetian saying

A person is spoiled by another person, but the land is spoiled by water.

—North Caucasus mountaineer saying

В лесочке комарики сильно уродились;
Почто сильно уродились? Девки удивились.

In the wood, the mosquitoes were born in great numbers;
Why so many? The girls were amazed.

—Terek Cossack humorous song

Frontier history is incomplete without an ecological component. Some of the most imaginative and influential histories of American frontiers in the last few decades have been environmental histories; one could go so far as to say that the American frontier is the birthplace of the subdiscipline.[1] This is because of the American contribution to frontier historiography: the environment emerges from the background and plays a leading role in the history of frontiers, where settlers try to construct new communities in unfamiliar ecological contexts. How settlers are transformed by and how they transform their landscapes are integral parts of their struggles and opportunities.

An environmental history of settlement in the North Caucasus is particularly inviting; there are few regions in the world with such extremes and diversity of nature, including the numerous microclimates of the mountains and the foothills, the cycles of flooding and drought in the valleys, and the contrast of the mountains with the steppe—near desert along the Caspian Sea—and the swampy Terek lowlands. Here the camel butts heads with the ox, the buffalo with the mountain goat. This was a very different environment from the Russian and Ukrainian heartlands from which many Terek Cossacks came, and their struggle to adapt was a major part of their story. The colonization of the North Caucasus was not only conditioned by the environment; sometimes the environment played a primary role and determined the success or failure of colonization. And the Cossacks who settled in the North Caucasus altered that environment. At the least, this environmental history gives nuance to the myth of Cossack as pathfinder, forging into uncharted territory and mastering new lands for the tsar. As this chapter will show, at least in the North Caucasus, the lands rather mastered the Cossacks.[2]

The Terek Cossacks settled mostly in the Terek River valley, a relatively narrow strip of more or less wooded land between the steppe and the mountains. An important ecological divide separated Cossacks of the Terek-Kumyk lowlands, to the east of Mozdok (which I will call the lower Terek region), and the Cossacks of the Stavropol' plateau and the heights of Central Ciscaucasia (the upper Terek, upper Kuma region). The Terek-Kizliar and Terek-Semeinoe hosts and the Greben regiment lived in the former; the Mountain, Volga, and Vladikavkaz regiments lived in the latter; the Sunzha and Mozdok regiments straddled the two zones.[3]

The land of the lower Terek was, in general, wetter, saltier, and sandier; swamps flooded the Terek delta and sands blew between the Terek and the Kuma. Along the Caspian to the north of Kizliar, salt deposits dotted the steppe. As an observer described them in the mid-nineteenth century, "deep pits, pasted all over with salt, scattered over the steppe like empty bowls." The land here was less suitable for agriculture, although in some areas in the steppe, with irrigation, a fair grain crop could be grown. But the lower Terek was known more for its horticulture (grapes and other fruits) and rice paddies than for its grain.[4] In general, the further to the west, the less water-logged and the better the land along the Terek was; the swampiest lands belonged to the Terek-Kizliar and the Terek-Semeinoe hosts. The steppe land also improved, from near desert along the Caspian Sea to fertile chernozem to the west of Mozdok.[5]

Besides the varying suitability of the soil for agriculture (see Chapter 5), the three main ecological challenges that Terek Cossacks faced involved deforestation, flooding, and the sickness which these processes helped to create.

Deforestation

Thanks to Tolstoi's story, "The Wood Felling," and to the concentration on the military history of the North Caucasus, the dominant impression is that the Russian army deforested the region to eliminate the woodland cover of hostile tribes and by hacking out ever more military roads. Indeed, the army was incredibly destructive in places, especially in Chechnia (see below). But deforestation was a more complicated process, fueled mostly by the insatiable need for lumber and firewood in the villages sprouting up in, and at the edge of, the steppe. Wherever Cossacks and peasants settled in the North Caucasus, the narrow bands of accessible forest along the river valleys soon receded and in many spots disappeared. The demand for wood was so great that it was shipped in from the interior of Russia at great cost and obtained locally in a high-volume trade with the people of the mountains (see Chapter 6).

There is abundant anecdotal evidence concerning the deforestation—and the attendant environmental affects—caused by colonization. The difficulty is in establishing the timing and the extent of the destruction. Travel accounts and other anecdotal evidence can be misrepresentative, pointing to a clearing here or a forest there as a general landscape. Forest conservation measures provide a different type of evidence, but we do not always know if these were put into effect in anticipation or as a result of deforestation. If the latter, they do not necessarily help determine the timing. Spore and pollen analyses are very useful in reconstructing historic forests, but they only reveal long-term trends and not the sawdust and wood smoke of the human time frame. Toponyms also help to suggest where forests and specific types of trees once grew; they say nothing about when they disappeared. But if all these types of sources are put together, some general trends of deforestation and environmental change can be established.[6]

According to spore and pollen studies, the steppe has been encroaching on the forest (and the desert on the steppe) for many centuries. Pollen and spore analysis from sites in what is now the northeast Caucasus steppe suggests a diffusion of forest-steppe in the middle of the first century B.C.E., with parcels of mezolithic forest including beech, lime, pines, birch, and nut trees, and ferns. Topographers studying the sands have concluded that during the same period, the Kuma was a full-flowing mountain river (by the nineteenth century it petered out in the steppe, fifty miles from the Caspian Sea), which could suggest greater forest cover. Soil from the pre-Mongol middle ages has less tree pollen, but still reveals an abundance of fern spores and pollen from plant species that have long since disappeared, including nut and lime trees, hornbeam, and *Gramineae*. Today all of the pollen from the same region comes from semi-desert plants. As the botanist I. P. Falk described it in 1775, "the entire Kuma steppe has the appearance of a dried-up sea and is treeless, wavy, sandy, and partly covered with clay and salt plains."[7]

Others have concluded that the mysterious steppe town of Madzhary, which still existed in the thirteenth century, could not have survived in a forestless region. Falk went so far as to claim—based on a mistranslation of an Arabic tombstone inscription—that the town faded away when its inhabitants left for the mountains because of a shortage of forest. It was a popular theory through the nineteenth century; at the least it shows that many in the North Caucasus during the eighteenth and nineteenth centuries were conscious of the precariousness of settlement in a treeless region.[8]

Archaeologists, paleobotanists, and topographers concur that the mass distribution of sand and the attendant change in the distribution of plant species occurred in the late middle ages and especially after the Mongol period. They attribute the bulk of the change to human intervention. The North Caucasus steppe had long been a region of pasture for steppe nomads and mountain people; the overpasturing of livestock by Nogais, mountain people, and others destroyed the top vegetation layer and uncovered the sand beneath it. Overgrazing can cause such environmental destruction, and such a thesis is plausible. But pollen and spore study is in its infancy in Russia and previous research has sometimes been ideologically biased, in an effort to prove the "irrational" animal husbandry of pre-Soviet peoples. Without more, and more objective, research, including the study of long-term climatic change, any conclusions as to the cause of deforestation in the middle ages must remain tentative at best.[9]

On the other hand, there is abundant evidence of wood shortages and deforestation during the late eighteenth and nineteenth centuries. Deciduous species grew on both sides of the Terek for a mile or two, but as forts and Cossack villages sprang up, the forest shrank and Cossacks had to obtain wood from further afield. Already in the mid-eighteenth century—when the Cossack population along the Terek was still rather small—there were reports of Terek-Semeinoe Cossacks journeying to the Kumyk plain south of the Terek and to Greben Cossack land in search of wood. The Kizliar commander recommended in 1744 that the Greben ataman closely guard their forest, "so that there will not be a shortage of forest in times of need." The commander of the Caucasus Military Line, general Gudovich, observed around 1770 that there was no forest in the environs of Kizliar and that residents obtained their firewood from higher up the Terek and most of their lumber from towns along the Volga.[10]

Güldenstädt confirmed this picture when he visited the Terek in the early 1770s. He reported that the Terek was nearly devoid of trees up to Kizliar; the forest began only at the Greben Cossack village of Starogladkovskaia and stretched up the river to the west. Mozdok (Circassian for "thick forest") had a forest to the south and the steppe to the north. All of the villages of the Mozdok regiment were "sufficiently wooded."[11] On the other had, the Cossacks of Chervlennaia of the Greben host were so concerned about their forest reserves that in 1765 they signed a treaty with the trans-Terek village of Devlet-Girei whereby the latter was not to cut the forest along the Terek's south side without Chervlennaia's permission. As late as the 1830s, these Cossacks crossed the Terek to cut the forest they considered their own on the right bank.[12]

By the 1820s, after the mass settlement in the North Caucasus had well begun, Cossacks experienced more wood shortages. Lieutenant general Rtishchev was so concerned about the situation that he reported to Alexander I in 1812 that the forest,

> in previous times, about fifteen years ago, was found in complete abundance and perfectly preserved, but having been put under the authority of the forest administration it has been reduced excessively so that in a short time one should expect it to be completely destroyed.

According to colonel Debu, the Terek-Semeinoe and Terek-Kizliar hosts, and parts of the Volga regiment were in need of forest. Now only two of the Mozdok Cossack villages had sufficient forest, "but because it is not protected, we can expect that it will soon be completely destroyed."[13] Writing in 1834, Platon Zubov agreed that the Mozdok Cossack forest was skimpy, but claimed that the Volga Cossacks still had plenty.[14]

The situation became more severe in the 1840s. By 1844, the Greben Cossack ataman was complaining about the destruction of their forest and firewood shortages in Chervlennaia. The commander of the Vladikavkaz regiment, M. S. Il'inskii, reported insufficient forest along the Terek and near the Georgian Military Highway. The Cossacks and military colonists of the upper Terek resorted to illegal cutting of the expansive forest of Kabarda and the latter were selling it all along the Caucasus Military Line.[15] According to an anonymous local writer, the forests in the upper Kuma region were in very poor shape by 1848—"the greater part of the residents of [Stavropol'] province suffer an extreme need of forest for building, artisanal work, and heating." The governor of Stavropol' province confirmed this in his annual report, warning that the state forest in the province was insignificant "and with each year noticeably grows scarcer, such that the price for firewood recently has increased very much, especially in the town of Stavropol'." Although extensive forests grew in the foothills and the mountains of Kabarda, for most settlers it was too far away and too costly to cut and haul; thus Stavropol', Georgievsk, and Piatigorsk imported lumber from the north via Novocherkassk, and Kizliar and Mozdok via Astrakhan. As S. D. Nechaev observed in the spa region of the upper Kuma, "each log, each board of the best structure here have sailed over two thousand versts (1,325 miles)." He suggested that it cost more to build a sizeable house here than in Moscow.[16]

Official estimates of the extent of forest in the Stavropol' province are extremely unreliable, since there was no general land survey during this period, a shortage of officials to inspect and estimate forests, and no distinctions were made between the health, type, or age of the trees. But based on information from the Forest Department of the Chamber of State Properties, in 1844-1845, the amount of state forest had shrunk from 29,988 dessiatines [about 81,000 acres] to 27,261 dessiatines [73,600 acres], that is by 9 percent, in just one year. By 1850, state forest plots decreased 24 percent from 19,561 dessiatines [52,800 acres] to 14,825 dessiatines [40,000 acres].[17]

Indeed, a turning point seems to have occurred in the 1840s—it was then that the first large-scale forest conservation measures were attempted in the North Caucasus. Up until 1845, each stanitsa controlled its own forest, under the general oversight of the regimental commander. This changed in 1845 when a system of host forests was created, controlled by the host government and managed by the new office of host forest warden. With this, two large host forests were established along the Caucasus Military Line and Cossacks could cut stanitsa forests only with permission of the regimental government, and only in the fall and winter. But just how effective were the new rules? The wardens responsible for inspecting the forests did not receive salaries, so the host forester often worked alone and was limited to one inspection a year.[18] Also, the apportioning of stanitsa forests was hardly calculated or equitable. At least in Chervlennaia, according to one resident, Cossacks lined up on a designated day at the end of February and when the ataman gave the signal, leapt on their horses and rushed to the wood with ax in hand, first come, first served.[19]

Further regulations were passed in 1847, following the recommendations of the host ataman who warned that, "the forest is in an impoverished condition, such that there is practically no workable timber." His main concern seems to have been that Cossacks were using too much young forest for firewood. An imperial ukaz adopted all of the ataman's recommendations, which among other things required Cossacks to plant twenty-five trees annually and forbade them to heat their houses and the regimental headquarters with wood. Instead, they were to use reeds, weeds, and manure bricks (*kiziak*) "which accumulates in great quantities in every courtyard, so this use will have the advantage of cleaning up the courtyards."[20]

The scarcity of heating fuel was a perennial concern for North Caucasus settlers. The use of reeds, weeds, scrub, and manure was nothing new— Cossacks had always fed these, and anything else combustible they could get their hands on, into their stoves. Everyone in the North Caucasus—Cossacks, steppe nomads, and mountain people—heated with manure bricks as a favorite fuel, but it had an important disadvantage. The more manure went up in smoke, the less was applied to fields and gardens to increase fertility. Manure was especially needed in the lower Terek region, where soil was the poorest; unfortunately this was also one of the most deforested regions and so Cossacks preferred to shovel the "black gold" into their stoves rather than their fields. Even so, their demand for heating fuel remained insatiable: it seems little usable wood was overlooked. When the fortress of Urukhskoe was abandoned in 1843, all of its buildings were demolished and used as firewood. A story was told about an inn in Mozdok that received so little business that it closed down and the billiard table was chopped up for firewood. The lack of fuel could be so severe that sometimes, regiments hauled firewood with them during expeditions across the Terek, especially in Dagestan.[21]

Another major demand for wood was as lumber for houses, state buildings, and other structures. The first settlers along the Terek often adopted local practices—and adapted better to their environment—by building with adobe bricks, reeds, clay, and wattle. Travelers were often surprised to find so few wooden or stone buildings in Kizliar. Of the 2,084 private houses registered in Kizliar in 1846, only 20 percent were made of wood (and only one of stone).[22]

The Cossacks of the lower Terek combined Russian-style wooden and Caucasian-style clay/wattle architecture. The Greben Cossacks especially were known for their mixed building traditions. Nearly every Cossack had a long and narrow, flat-roofed Caucasian *saklia*, usually constructed out of adobe bricks and a larger, pitched-roof Russian *khata* made from logs. As the host economic administration described it:

> After the other stanitsas, where most of the buildings are of wattle, adobe, or smooth wood, it is as if you are carried away to some Great Russian village of some forested province: wooded, framed *izbas*, often of oak, and with pitched, high roofs, ornamented on the peak of the gable, with window jambs, and decorated with carvings. But to your astonishment, you also see low Chechen *saklias*, standing in the same courtyard and right next to the Russian *izbas*.

The family lived in the warmer *saklia* in the winter, which was less expensive to heat, and moved to the drafty wooden houses in the summer. The latter had chinks in the walls and were raised off of the silty and sometimes flooded ground, so they were very cold and uninhabitable in the winter. Occasionally Cossacks lived in Nogai or Kalmyk felt tents, especially when they went to their fields in the steppe.[23]

The Cossacks who settled later in the North Caucasus, along the upper Terek and the upper Kuma, and the peasants who moved to the steppe, built more in the Russian and Ukrainian style with wood. The houses in Mozdok, Georgievsk, and Stavropol' were almost all constructed of wood.[24] This was often difficult in the tree-hungry steppe and settlers there resorted to raiding (and destroying) forests, including a protected one near the village of Pokoinoe. Armenians and Russians building near Madzhary looted the ruins of the ancient town for bricks, flagstones, and other materials. They built floors, counters, and benches with Arabic- and Tatar-inscribed tombstones.[25]

Cossacks and state engineers also hacked away at the receding forest to obtain wood for fascines and weirs, which were used to try to restrain the Terek from flooding fields and villages. Engineers made 100,000 fascines for just one weir at the Greben Cossack village of Novogladkovskaia. According to the commander of the Kizliar regiment Alpatov, between 1847 and 1853, engineers strengthening the river bank created 25,000 to 200,000 fascines annually. As a result, the regiment's and many Cossack villages' forests were destroyed and Cossacks had to purchase even vineyard stakes. The commander of the Kizliar regiment in 1855, Sukhodol'skii, asked that reeds be used for fascines instead of wood because so little of their forest remained.[26] In the wet lower Terek basin, there was no shortage of reeds.

They were fighting a losing battle—the ax proved no match for the river. Removing the forest cover from the drainageway into the Terek only hastened the flooding. The role of trees in reducing water run off—and erosion—was little known in Russia in the nineteenth century: the humusy forest soil absorbs water, the leaves break the rain's impact on the soil, the roots help hold river banks in place. There is a certain pathos to observe the same commanders report the forest's disappearance and in nearly the same breath express dismay at the nearly annual, very destructive flooding of the Terek.[27]

The military-led war against the forest began in earnest also in the 1840s, when Ermolov created the Sunzha regiment and began his systematic conquest of Chechnia. Every winter, beginning in 1845, army troop detachments pushed further into Chechnia, spending a month and sometimes two felling trees. They chopped out wide clearings for fortifications and roads. Main roads were cut the width of the distance of two cannon shots, lesser roads the width of one or two rifle shots, and in general trees were removed where it was feared that enemy Chechens could hide before an attack.[28]

Chechens vigorously resisted this deforestation. The push up the Sunzha was one of the war's bloodiest episodes and the woodcutters' progress was followed in the newspaper *Kavkaz* as if it was battle news, with the amount of forest destroyed duly noted. Shamil supposedly sent 10,000 men to defend this forest, but to little avail.[29] The same paper reported in 1849 that after the wood-clearing operations of 1846-1847, "Lesser Chechnia has taken on a completely new appearance."[30] The deforestation was compounded by a "multiplier effect" whereby those Chechens not killed during the aggression resettled deeper in the forest and hacked out new clearings for their grain fields and pastures.[31]

Both the military deforestation and the widespread wood trade between Chechens, Kabardians, and others with the Russians must have made a serious impact on the wood stock of Shamil and his forces. Sometime between 1847 and 1853, Shamil promulgated laws restricting woodcutting and prohibiting wood trade with Russians.[32] The maps of Chechnia and Ingushetiia are covered with toponyms derived from tree species that no longer exist there, including yew, chestnut, and plane trees; the great number of names with "oak" (*"nozhai"*) suggests the onetime existence of a large oak forest. This silva had not yet disappeared by the mid-nineteenth century, but the axes were making their progress. By 1855, K. Samoilov depicted the Chechen plain from south of the Sunzha to the Terek, "not long ago one enormous forest" as significantly deforested, either by the military or residents clearing glades for sowing.[33]

Ecology does not respect political boundaries, and Russian troops and Cossacks also suffered from the deforestation south of the Terek. Occasionally the troops cut down Cossack forests during their road building operations. Firewood only became scarcer for troops south of the Terek. For example, when soldiers laid a road in 1859 from Sulak to Vedeno, it took them a week to get to the forest thirteen miles away, cut their firewood, and haul it back. Also, the hydrology of the region only became worse for those who lived along the Terek (see below).[34]

But the sound of the ax continued to echo through the woods. By the late 1850s and early 1860s, reports of wood shortages, expensive firewood, and embattled forests became louder and more frequent. In 1856, agronomist A. I. Deichman wrote that except for the area next to the main ridge of the Caucasus mountains, the Caucasus *oblast'* was without significant forest and lumber was imported, firewood expensive, and nearly everyone heated with manure bricks. In 1859, colonel Murav'ev inspected the Cossack forests and found most of them in sorry shape. Except for the Volga regiments and the First Sunzha regiment, which had no forests of their own but used those of their neighbors, all of the regiments suffered at least some shortages and for the Mountain, Vladikavkaz, Mozdok, Kizliar, and villages of the Greben regiment, the situation was extreme.[35]

A. Viskovatov reported that there were only small groves of trees left in the environs of Stavropol' and along the Kuma by 1860. In the same year an anonymous writer in *Voennyi sbornik* claimed a shortage of forest all along the Caucasus Military Line, despite the fact that many stanitsas had been founded not long before in the middle of forests. The scraggy forest growing along the Terek was "a meager remnant of the previous forests." He said that the Cossacks heated their homes very poorly and in the winter had to wear warm clothes inside. In Avariia, the cost of brushwood shot up from ten to twenty kopeks per load in 1843 to twenty-five silver rubles per cubic sazhen (a little less than a cubic foot) in 1860. Ataman Sokolov confirmed this picture in the same year, reporting to the chief of staff of the Caucasus army:

> It is well-known that the banks of the Kuban, Laba, Urup, Terek, Malka, and others were once covered with thick forests of which now remains only a scrawny forest suitable for brushwood and stakes and in some places for wooden plows and poles; in many places not even a trace of such forest remains.[36]

The next attempt at forest conservation comes from this period. After the head commander of the Caucasus corps, Murav'ev, took a trip through the host lands in 1855 and noticed that the Cossack forests were exhausted, an imperial ukaz was promulgated in 1856, which laid down a detailed set of rules on forest cutting, planting, the wood trade, and the heating of homes and offices. Forest wardens were to be salaried and new inspectors were to patrol markets and trade bazaars for illegal wood trade. A more detailed schedule of fines and punishments was established for Cossacks who traded or illegally cut wood, or failed to plant or haphazardly planted the requisite twenty-five willows or poplars a year. This ukaz included many other precise prohibitions and regulations about which trees could be cut, when, and by what methods. It also reaffirmed that "the heating of houses, more than anything else, exposes the forest to destruction" and decreed again that all Cossacks heat only with reeds, weeds, straw, manure bricks, scrub, and deadwood.[37]

It seems as if such forest conservation measures came much too late. By the 1860s, there was widespread mourning over the forests that had recently been destroyed the North Caucasus. A. Domanskii wrote of the forests that had disappeared from the banks of the rivers and the wide ravines of Kabarda, reminding readers that Mozdok was named for the "dense forest" that bordered it, which had now vanished. Individual species had reached an enormous size:

Existing to this day are individual stumps two arshins [about four and one-half feet] in diameter, a trough for watering livestock made from an entire oak fifteen arshins long [thirty-five feet], and finally, entire houses constructed from ash boards of enormous width; all of this testifies to the size of the forests that once covered the banks of the Terek.

The same author once met a Mozdok resident whose father built his house out of just one oak from the Mozdok forest. But now:

The old dense forest is completely destroyed and in its place have appeared small wood lots of young trees, terribly overgrown with shrubs, and new plantings of pussy willows and aspens that were planted not long ago in spaces between the vineyards. Our foothills are completely bare and only here and there, on the north slope, in deep ravines, can be seen woody spots, oases of a sort, consisting of old, mutilated trunks, the remnants of giants of the past, with withered branches and tall stumps sending out young shoots.[38]

Geographer D. L. Ivanov wrote in 1886 of the great soil erosion of the Stavropol' region, a result of settlement and deforestation. Villages such as Dubovka ("oak") and Berestovok ("birch bark"), named for their silva, were denuded of forests; areas that had been rich in trees, shrubs, and wildlife were transformed into bare slopes, gullies, gorges, and weeds. When founded in 1790, Kruglolesskoe ("forest-encircled") had been surrounded by a thick forest.

By the end of the nineteenth century only a "pitiful remnant" survived on the west side and the village was now known by locals simply as Krugloe ("round"). The story of Chernolesskoe ("black forest"), founded by Russian settlers in 1799, was typical:

> According to old-timers, the village was probably named "Chernolesskoe" because at the time of its founding there grew along the entire stretch of the Tomuzlov River large trees, exclusively of deciduous species. Wild pigs and goats were found in abundance in the forest; there were even deer and bears which had made their way from the forest of the Caucasus mountains. In our time, not even vestiges of this forest remain.[39]

As Ivanov correctly pointed out, one of the results of the great deforestation was a degradation of the land. As the trees were cut in the steppe, streams dried up and land dried out; as trees were cut along the Terek and in its drainageways, flooding and siltation worsened. Doctor Toropov, the head physician at the Kutais military hospital, was probably correct to see a connection between forest clearing, land drainage, and the improvement of health in some foothill and plains regions of the North Caucasus. But his maxim that "a person who settles in a feverous climate makes it healthy" did not hold for the lower Terek. It had always been swampy and relatively unhealthy there (see below). But the residents suffered further from the forest clearing undertaken by their up-river brethren—much of the eroded soil created by deforestation in Chechnia and Kabarda ended up in the lower Terek. As siltation worsened, the delta spread and along with it the habitat for malaria-carrying mosquitoes. The same swamps that provided reeds for construction and heating hatched mosquitoes by the millions.[40]

Flooding

Deforestation causes water problems, which Cossacks suffered in great measure. "Terek, son of the mountains" as they affectionately called it, was a provider and destroyer. Those Cossacks—and anyone else—who settled too far into the steppe risked water shortages and drought (and a lack of wood). They also suffered power shortages since mills could be built only on rapidly flowing rivers such as the Terek. But those who settled too close to the Terek had to endure unhealthy, boggy environs and regular flooding.

The Russian foothold in the lower Terek region had always been a soggy one. Both Terskii Gorod and Sviatoi Krest were built in wet, unhealthy spots. Kizliar was perhaps even worse. It was surrounded by swamps, standing lakes, and shifting branches of the Terek that made it—at different points in its history—an island. During rainy or snowy periods and when the Terek flooded, the streets of Kizliar would turn to muck and the clay houses soaked up so much water that, according to Falk, who was there in 1775, clay dripped from the roofs and the floors became so muddy that one would get stuck if he stood still for too long. As Debu wrote in 1829, "In general the soil there is so water-logged that every three steps you run into a deep pit, filled with water, and so salty that when the pit dries out it's as if it was plastered with salt."[41]

By all accounts, Kizliar was a very unhealthy town. The air was thick with "miasmic" clouds. Fevers were common. Toropov wrote in 1864 that it was hard to find a person there with a healthy facial color, and added, "it would be impossible to choose a place more unsuitable to good hygiene than Kizliar."[42]

The Terek-Semeinoe and the Terek-Kizliar hosts settled in the same swampy lowlands of the lower Terek, where floods were common. What Debu laconically described for the Terek-Semeinoe host held for both: "Swamps and reeds safeguard their borders: during full water the Terek overflows both our bank and the opposite bank, making creeks, which form swamps, which are disadvantageous to the settlements." During the Terek's summer flooding, water sometimes stood over four feet deep in Terek-Semeinoe stanitsas and vineyards. In general, the further up the Terek you went, the drier the land was, but the river flooded almost all Cossack villages at one time or another and swampy environs were by no means limited to the lower Terek. According to a 1843 survey of the Georgian Military Highway, even villages of the Vladikavkaz regiment in the upper Terek were plagued with floods and bogs. The same held for the upper Kuma.[43]

When Güldenstädt visited the lower Terek in the early 1770s, he recommended resettling Kizliar and the Cossack villages to the right bank of the Terek, where the soil and the climate were better and the harvests more plentiful. But Kizliar and the Cossack villages had been intentionally planted on the left bank of the Terek to take advantage of the cover that the river afforded against enemies to the south. Unfortunately, the Terek "covered" entirely too much land to the north and the Cossacks who patrolled the river in the summer watched not just for enemy movements but also rising waters. In fact in summer months when the Terek raged, the water was the greater threat; when the rising level promised danger to a village, an alarm was sounded and all of the residents rushed to strengthen the bank's ramparts with fascines. As Lermontov wrote in *A Hero of Our Time*, "The people and the rivers are as bad as each other—there's no depending on them!"[44]

As was mentioned in Chapter 3, the Terek was a formidable river. It issued from the highest mountains in Europe, and rushed fast all the way to Kizliar, especially from April to September when the snow was thawing or it was raining in the mountains. Güldenstädt noted that in July and August, its level rose eight to ten feet above normal; the river became furious and flooded many spots. He added, "in many places it not only overflows the bank but makes new branches, filling up the old one with sand, to which it adds trees, and not infrequently even rafts, which it has carried from the mountain." In the lowest spots in the delta below Kizliar, it flooded in the spring and occasionally changed its course. According to an 1834 army survey of the region, all of the stanitsas to the east of the Greben village of Shchedrinskaia flooded regularly.[45]

Rivers have histories, just like anything else, and the Terek did not remain static over the centuries, or even over decades. The Cossacks recognized the river's active role in their lives, personalizing it with a name and patronymic, and giving it a dynamic—and often destructive—personality in folk tales and songs.[46] And indeed, it seemed to be a living creature. A. A. Litvinov observed remarkable changes from 1841 when he first surveyed part of the Kizliar *uezd* to 1863 when he returned to the same spot, most of which was caused by a change in hydrology:

> In the place of a swamp could be seen the dry steppe and not infrequently plowed fields; where the river had run before, now signs of its flow were hardly noticeable and in many places not visible at all; where there was a lake now is a swamp, reeds, or a fine meadow; and on the other hand, where there was before meadows and the steppe, now there drifted impassible sandy mounds (*bugry*).

Many of the branches of the Terek delta were flowing in a completely different place and the main branch of the Terek itself had changed direction from above Kizliar. The entire delta was continually on the move—finding a reliably dry spot among these shifting currents was difficult. Also, over time the alluvium from the mountains and the soil erosion upstream built up the Terek, so that in many places in the lower Terek it was level with the roofs of stanitsa buildings. This made flooding all the more likely and all the more dangerous when it happened.[47]

The settlers, though, were not innocent victims of unfriendly forces of nature; they contributed to "the rage of the Terek," and not only through deforestation. Cossacks and others also tried to manipulate the river for their own ends with canals and dams, and in the process often did more harm than good. Canals were cut mostly for two purposes: mills and irrigation. Peter I did order a moat to be built between the Agrakhan and Sulak Rivers so that Sviatoi Krest would be surrounded and protected by water. Perhaps the soggy failure of that fort discouraged others to lay moats. General Potapov repeated the mistake sometime around 1770 when, fearing an attack, he deepened an irrigation canal from the Terek to the Borozda and removed the sluice. The invasion never materialized, but the Terek rushed through the canal and flooded roads; other branches became stagnant, ruining fishing spots and trade conduits.[48]

Most canals were cut for irrigated agriculture—a necessity for most Cossacks living along the Terek. They dug canals for a couple of miles to their fields in the steppe and released the water in the spring, flooding a predetermined area and bringing nutrient-rich silt to the unmanured land. By fall, the flooded area was ready to plow; if some of the water had not drained, they simply plowed the drier spots or cut new canals to lead it away. Every year Cossacks, women mostly, dug new canals or deepened old ones. As Ponomarëv put it, "the work is very hard and exhausting, but necessary because without them the residents would be without grain, vegetables, and vineyards."[49] Without water and fertilizer their fields were barren.

Unfortunately, the canals also became unintentional flood channels. General Gudovich—sent by Catherine the Great to determine how to strengthen the Russian defense in the North Caucasus—reported that in 1765 the Terek broke through an irrigation canal, flooded Kizliar, and changed its course to make Kizliar a wet, unhealthy island. The Borozda River—one of the branches of the Terek delta—was also originally an irrigation canal; another branch—the Prorva ("the break")—sprouted from it in 1813.[50]

Three new canals were constructed in the early 1850s, the most famous being the Eristov canal, which led from the Malka (a Terek feeder) for more than 130 miles to the steppe. It was one of the grand construction projects of the region, the inspiration of ataman Eristov of the Mountain regiment. And some of the Cossacks benefited from it, at least for a period. In the words of the commander of the regiment, colonel Tovbich, in 1855:

> Now this steppe (which before was without water and nearly useless) is furnished with advantages, such that now, as there never was before, there is plowing, the sowing of grain, and pasturing of horse herds and sheep, and it's supposed that in time farmsteads and water mills will be built and forest planted.[51]

Not all, though, reaped a bountiful harvest. At the beginning of its course, the canal was cut too steeply so that a rapid flow of water quickly eroded it into a seventy-foot-deep ravine. Occasionally livestock and even people fell into it and died. As the canal approached Mozdok, the slope rapidly declined, the water became stagnant, and a swamp grew from the deposited eroded soil. Because it was irregularly repaired and cleaned, banks collapsed and sluices decayed; many stanitsas complained that it flooded their pastures and roads and asked that it be destroyed. The Greben Cossacks requested the same for the Shchedrinskii canal, which they contemptuously nicknamed the Shchedrinskii ditch.[52]

Terek-Kizliar Cossacks dug canals from the Terek into the Dolobna, hoping to lead wild carp there; nothing is reported on their fish catch, but the canals flooded all their low-lying lands. The Second Sunzha regiment cut a canal for a water mill. In 1856 the engineer, captain Rypinskii, reported that because the mill was located on such a low spot, the feeder canal had formed a large swamp. "Up to that time," he said, "not only was there not a swamp here, but instead a large forest, the traces of which are noticeable yet today." Others claimed that the swamp ruined the climate and caused sickness. Such mishaps explain why the Kizliar regiment, after allowing Nogais to build a canal through one of their villages, bound them to specific monetary compensation in case of flooding.[53]

Sometimes Cossacks or their commanders tried to dam canals or unruly river branches, but this often created entirely new water problems. In 1850 the commander of the Kizliar regiment dammed a branch of the Elga-Burgun in the Terek delta. When the water flow in the Terek increased as a result, a new branch popped out at Dubovskaia stanitsa and flooded fruit gardens and vineyards on the right side of the Terek. Toropov claimed that in the upper Kuma region, it was swampy and feverous precisely where Cossacks had built weirs and mills. Sometimes, down-river villages suffered from a water shortage when weirs were built up river. When two Terek feeders were dammed in 1855 to divert water for the Vladikavkaz regiment stanitsa of Ardonskaia, Arkhonskaia stanitsa suffered a complete water loss. Afterwards, Arkhonskaia residents had to travel over five miles to get water.[54]

The Prorva proved to be particularly stubborn. After the flood of 1809, it became the Terek branch with the most water and up to 1847 it frequently flooded Cossack fields, gardens, and residences. Cossacks of Borozdinskaia moved their village closer to the steppe because of flooding in 1814. Engineers built weirs to restrain it, first in 1847, and then when they collapsed, again in 1852. As a result, the Prorva shallowed because water rushed into the Talovka branch of the Terek, flooded the environs, and sometimes cut off all roads between Sosoplinskaia stanitsa and Kizliar. The Prorva, meanwhile, silted up, grew even shallower, and fishing at its mouth suffered. It was used to water the best land in the Kizliar regiment and Cossacks feared that it would soon dry up. So in 1854, work commenced on widening the mouth of the Prorva and blocking the Talovka so Cossacks would be able to continue to water their fields. By 1855, not much had changed—the Talovka flooded Kizliarskaia stanitsa; at the same time the commander of the Kizliar regiment reported that there was so little water in the Prorva that he feared great harm. By the next decade, though, the Prorva sloshed to the brim and recommenced massive flooding.[55]

The flood of 1863 was probably the decade's worst. In July the heavy snow thaw in the mountains quickly raised the Terek's level and in a short time it was lapping over the earthen flood walls in the stanitsas above Kizliar. Soon the water began to leak through the wall at Dubovskaia, formed a 200-foot break and "an enormous mass of water streamed through," flooding many of the villages, farmsteads, and roads in the environs and forming a new path to the sea. Water rushed through the Prorva, once again devastating Borozdinskaia, flooding the gardens and fields, carrying away the shocks of harvested grain, and deluging the stanitsa itself, so that residents had to resettle temporarily to another stanitsa and farmstead. The three hardest hit stanitsas (Dubovskaia, Borozdinskaia, and Aleksandrovskaia) reportedly suffered losses to the sum of around 180,000 rubles and more than 100 houses carried away by the water. Not much progress, it seems, had been made since 1809.[56]

Over time, floods took a large toll on Cossack villages, especially in the lower Terek. They frequently forced Cossacks to relocate their villages either further from the river or to a less flood-prone area along the river. In the Greben regiment, Cossacks of Shchedrinskaia moved several of their houses away from the river bank before 1775, lest they be washed away. The entire stanitsa was moved in 1823, as were Novogladkovskaia and Starogladkovskaia in 1814, Kurdiukovskaia in 1812, and Chervlennaia in 1816, the latter after a flood destroyed some 200 gardens. In the Terek-Kizliar host, as we have seen, Borozdinskaia moved in 1814; Dubovskaia moved in 1790 when the stanitsa was severely flooded and all of its vineyards and orchards destroyed.[57]

Further, as with the 1863 flood, property losses could be enormous. The flood of 1767 ruined Greben Cossack harvested and unharvested grain; hay in ricks, haycocks, and in the field; vineyards; meadows; and in Novogladkovskaia and Chervlennaia, sections of the villages were flooded. They applied to the governor of Astrakhan for financial assistance, but were turned down. The same experience was repeated, usually on a smaller scale, over and over again.[58]

Flooding also helped ruin the most important sector of the Cossack economy of the lower Terek—viticulture. Over time, floods destroyed entire vineyards—soil was washed away and roots were exposed or rotted by standing water. Poorly drained soil also brought salinization as salt was drawn to the surface with evaporation. The only way to rid the soil of excess salt was to wash it away with water led from the Terek through canals. But this was time-consuming, laborious work and useless if the vineyard was in a lowland and did not drain properly. At least as early as the 1820s, Cossacks and residents of Kizliar complained about the frequent floods harming their vineyards and decreasing their grape harvest. Beginning in the 1830s, large numbers of vineyards were abandoned and changed into steppe or meadow or swampy lowland. In Kizliar, for example, in 1819 over 13,500 acres of land was in vineyards; by 1838 only 11,000 acres remained. The number of vineyards there decreased from 1,269 to 964 from 1836 to 1828. In the Kizliar regiment, wine production at Starogladkovskaia plummeted from 612,000 liters in 1849 to 130,200 liters in 1856. At Kurdiukovskaia, it dropped from 228,000 to 78,000 liters in the same period.[59]

Cossacks also suffered when their scarce labor force had to abandon field work and other domestic labor to build, maintain, buttress, and repair levees, which by 1850 stretched for over sixty miles along the Terek. For most of their history, Terek Cossacks were responsible for all of this work. From 1846 on, some major dike work was done under the direction of the communications' engineer, with hired workers, paid for by state and host money. But up until then, it was a communal responsibility of the stanitsa and even after 1846, the engineers left many vulnerable spots that had to be shored up by the

Cossacks.[60]

Earth, wattle, and fascines could not tame the Terek. Water sill flooded during the summer months, breaking through the walls and causing great devastation at the low spots along the levees. In the summer of 1846, the Terek flooded over 100 feet west of the embankment at Mozdok and sunk Kizliar beneath six feet of water. Residents paddled in boats along the streets and courtyards trying to save their property. They could not remember such a bad flood in a very long time. Many Cossack gardens, especially in the Kizliar regiment, were destroyed; fields were flooded and covered with silt.[61]

The flood of 1855 drenched fields and gardens in Kizliar for two square miles, flooding the entire left side of the town, raising some houses from their foundations and completely flooding others. Residents abandoned their property, hopped in boats, and paddled to the dry side of town. Again, old-timers claimed it was the worst flood in memory.[62] And every year, engineers cut down more trees, with which to patch up weirs and dikes. The Kizliar regimental government reported in 1859 that strengthening the banks of the Terek, Prorva, and Talovka for the entire distance of the regiment was an extreme necessity, but they did not have the labor or the materials to do it, since the engineer of communications had destroyed almost all of their forest for fascines. It was a wet, vicious circle. And a diseased one.[63]

Disease

The history of colonization and frontier settlement has been bound up with the history of disease. Often, colonists have been the purveyors of disease, bringing new pathogens for which colonial peoples have no resistance. This was the deadly experience in North and South America, Australia, New Zealand, and Oceania; according to Alfred Crosby, the ease of the conquest of the Americas is in no small measure related to the sickness and death that Europeans unleashed on the native peoples. "It was their germs," Crosby writes, "not these imperialists themselves, for all their brutality and callousness, that were chiefly responsible for sweeping aside the indigenes and opening the Neo-Europes to demographic takeover."[64]

But in other parts of the world, empires struck back with pathogens of their own and colonial settlement became, to use Philip Curtin's term, "death by migration." Europeans needed temperate climates to succeed in demographic takeover and establish "neo-Europes." As Crosby reminds us, within those familiar latitudes, colonists spread like an escaped weed species:

> The only nations in the Temperate Zones outside of Asia which do not have enormous majorities of European whites are Chile, with a population of two-thirds mixed Spanish and Indian stock, and South Africa, where black outnumbered whites six to one. How odd that these two, so many thousands of miles from Europe, should be

exceptions in *not* being predominantly pure European.

European colonists were demographically defeated in the tropics by malaria, yellow fever, cholera, and tuberculosis.[65]

The Caucasus is not in the tropics, but cholera and especially malaria killed settlers by the thousands. As in all of Europe at the time, doctors tended to attribute the fevers to the miasmic climate. The author of a geographic survey of the region, Nadezhdin, claimed that the Terek and the Sunzha regions were among the most feverous places in the North Caucasus, but everywhere up to 1,000 feet above sea level, warmth, wetness, and verdure produced a poisonous miasma. Swampy areas were the worst, because plant decomposition was more prevalent there. Toropov depicted a similar "medical geography"—wherever it was green, wet, and warm, unhealthy miasmas wafted. He too pointed to the particular danger of the Kizliar lowlands, along the Terek and Sunzha tributaries, and wherever rivers and canals flooded the lowlands and millponds.[66]

Others drew a connection between fevers and the overconsumption of fruit. This was just as plausible as the miasma theory, because the vineyards and fruit gardens were most numerous in the same areas—including the lower Terek—where there was the worst flooding and the most fevers. And floods raged, fruits were harvested, and fevers spread all at the same time—from late June to September. On the other hand, the steppe tended to be dry and healthy, and if anything was grown it tended to be grain or grass rather than fruit.[67]

The salient factor in creating conditions ripe for malaria was, of course, standing water providing a habitat for the appropriate mosquitos. And as we have seen, flooding occurred because colonists settled in the lowlands and worsened the region's hydrology for human habitation. The stump, the flood, the swamp, the fever—all were part of the same ecology. In the soggy, sickly areas, one was more likely to die from "swamp fevers" than from raiding Chechens or Kabardians.

The sickest fort-towns in the North Caucasus seem to have been Kizliar, Georgievsk, and Mozdok. Up to 1749, there apparently was little complaint about the conditions in Kizliar. But then rice was planted, almost to the walls of the fortress itself, and sickness increased so much that sometimes it was difficult to find enough people to staff the guard posts. According to the staff doctor of the medical chancellery in 1750 there were 1,369 men in the field hospitals of three regiments of the regular army sick with fever and diarrhea. Things were so bad that the army removed the Navaginskii and the Kurinskii regiments from Kizliar and replaced them with the Tenginskii and Samarskii regiments in June 1751. But by 1752, 323 of the Tenginskii regiment and 293 of the Samarskii regiment had died of epidemic diseases. In 1755, another 875 were added to these regiments, but within six months fifty-one had died and the rest were sick and in no condition to work.[68]

The medical chancellery sent a new doctor to Kizliar in 1755 to study and improve the situation. William Gevitt [Hewitt?] served in Kizliar for only one-half year, but in that time he wrote a valuable "medical topography." Gevitt was told that after 1749 when rice was planted near the fortress, the air became heavier. People who worked in the rice fields became sick, turned yellow, got diarrhea, and became feverish. In 1751, the head commander of Kizliar prohibited the cultivation of rice close to Kizliar, but the sickness continued. No doubt what had been observed was the symptom and not the cause of the problem; the same low topography that permitted rice cultivation made for swampy terrain and provided habitat for disease-bearing mosquitoes. The irrigation canals that watered the numerous fruit gardens, vineyards, and rice paddies in and around Kizliar only made things wetter. Commanders sensed a link between horticulture and the sickness and at one time or another banned not only rice cultivation, but also cotton growing, silkworm breeding, and even the sale of fruit, wine, and vegetables. As Chistovich noted, such measures only served to increase contraband; the sickness raged on. In 1798, for example, 652 in the Kizliar garrison died from sickness. A. M. Pavlov visited Kizliar between 1824 and 1835 and reported that in the summer, two to three and sometimes up to five people died per week because of the unhealthy climate.[69]

Travelers who visited Kizliar almost always mentioned the dank atmosphere and ill health. In the early 1770s, Güldenstädt wrote that all around Kizliar it was wet and swampy, with much standing water, and the air was thick and miasmic. Falk observed in 1775 that Kizliar dried out only in the summer and that the dampness was very harmful to health. Gudovich in 1792 reported that Kizliar was now an island, surrounded by swamps, frequently flooding, and permeated with unhealthy air and sickness. Shidlovskii, a correspondent for the Ministry of Internal Affairs, visited Kizliar in 1843 and remarked that "a winy, stuffy atmosphere begins to pour over you when you approach the town." The roads were so wet and muddy in spring and autumn that it was impossible to travel on the streets by vehicle or on foot. Oxcarts would remain stuck for months. Irrigation canals rotted with spent yeast from the distilleries and fumes from the surrounding swamps contributed to the generally unhealthy climate.[70]

Georgievsk, on the upper Kuma, was no better. Locals called it "the cemetery of collegiate assessors" because of the high rate of death there. The site of a Cossack stanitsa of the Volga regiment, Georgievsk had a brief period of glory when it became the capital of the *namestnichestvo* (region ruled by governor-general) in 1802. But as the sickness persisted and more and more state servants died, the capital was switched to the healthy steppe town of Stavropol' in 1824. Locals were divided as to the cause of the great sickness in Georgievsk. One school of thought claimed that the drinking water was overloaded with unhealthy minerals since it came from the mineral-rich mountains. The others more accurately pointed to the accumulation of water in the plain, which formed swamps around the town.[71]

Observers in Mozdok sounded similar refrains. Güldenstädt in the early 1770s said that, even though it was situated at a low, wooded spot, because it abutted the steppe to the north, the air there was clean and healthy. But Falk reported in 1775 that:

> The people and the cattle are very lively, but few of the people live to a very only age. Of the 1,400 of the garrison, from 1 January 1770 to 1 July 1773, 888 died mostly from "swamp fever" [gnilaia goriachka] and diarrhea [probably dysentery].

He claimed that the unhealthiness was caused by the adobe-walled houses, which would change rapidly from cold to warm and soak up moisture during wet weather. In 1815 Mozdok was described as hot and unhealthy in the summer because of its low situation and the swamps that neighbored it on the east and north sides. The flooding Terek made the environs wet and "threatens to carry off the very town in time." Kriukov noted in 1852 that the wide, stagnant irrigation canals harmed the health of the residents. Apparently, the stagnant Eristov canal made things worse in the mid- to late 1850s and fevers increased.[72]

Swamps, mosquitoes, and fevers did not discriminate based on estate. The state peasant village of Pokoinoe, founded in 1766 on the Kuma River by peasants from southern provinces, was so named, according to a resident, because so many died from "swamp fever" (they became pokoiniki, deceased). The Nogai Tatars named the village "bad place." There is also abundant evidence that the same conditions often existed in Cossack villages outside the fort-towns. The usual sickness was probably malaria and the most unhealthy areas were from Kizliar to Chervlennaia, around Mozdok and Georgievsk, and the lower course of the Kuma, from Aleksandrovskaia stanitsa to the Caspian. Again and again records report standing water, reeds, swamps and swamp sickness, "extraordinary and in autumn generally impassable muck," hordes of mosquitoes, and fevers.[73]

Up to 1820, regimental doctors were scarce to nonexistent, and even after that Cossacks seemed to prefer, in Popko's words, "old women and people who pose as physicians." To treat malaria they used amulets containing live spiders, snake skins, or prayers, sprinkles of Candlemas water, and other spells and potions. The materia medica of the military doctors, which included salt, chalk, Spanish fly (dried beetles), hemp, and hemlock, was not much more effective. According to military figures, the proportion of those dying from disease did improve as the century wore on—from one out of nine in 1837 to one out of forty-one in 1862—but this probably had more to do with a reorientation of settlement from the wetter, unhealthier areas to the relatively healthier north central and north west Caucasus steppe.[74]

The military accounts of the conquest of the North Caucasus have done a superb job depicting the eco-warfare that Russian troops waged against their enemies, burning and trampling fields, befouling streams, destroying water reservoirs, chopping down trees, smashing fords, and diverting streams. But Russia also unwittingly practiced eco-warfare against itself and this affected Cossack communities in important ways. The anemia of the lower Terek Cossack economy was caused at least in part by the economic and demographic consequences of the environmental changes described in this chapter. Deforestation, for example, made them more dependent on traders from the mountains—as will be discussed in Chapter 6, every stand of trees that the army chopped down boosted the Cossack demand for a commodity that their trans-Terek neighbors could best supply. Flooding and erosion, caused in part by deforestation, washed away the profits from viticulture, which had been the strongest branch of their economy, and in general worsened agricultural land. Sickness and death removed much-needed labor power from their communities— labor that not only would have boosted their chronically labor-short economy, but presumably also would have gone towards extremely necessary "public works" projects such as dike building and swamp drainage. Braudel has written about the great labor power and capital that were necessary to transform the Mediterranean plains into agricultural land and the connection between the shortage of labor and capital and malaria in the plains. In the North Caucasus, the capital and labor were in short supply and the swamps and sickness remained.[75]

Russian literary figures, travelers, and historians created an image of the perils in the North Caucasus, where Chechens and others swooped down from the mountains to plunder, kill, and kidnap. The main danger, though, was more mundane. Disease probably carried off more people than any enemies from across the Terek, and it should be emphasized that these were diseases of poor settlement and environmental transformation, not diseases of war. Nor should Cossacks and other settlers be viewed as innocent victims. They manipulated their environment in harmful ways—removing forest cover, cutting canals, and altering the course of the Terek and other rivers—all of which had severe consequences downstream. It seems they had enough hands to worsen the region's hydrology, soils, and disease regime, but not enough to fix them.

Notes

1. See, for example, such classics as Carl Ortwin Sauer, *The Early Spanish Main* (Berkeley: University of California Press, 1966), Alfred W. Crosby, *The Columbian Exchange* (Westport: Greenwood, 1972), and William Cronon, *Changes in the Land* (New York: Hill and Wang, 1983). The French and British were studying the historical dimensions of the environment and nature decades earlier, but the oldest environmental history journal as such is *Environmental History*.

2. For a brief, general overview of the environment of the North Caucasus see Yu. P. Badenkov and others, "Caucasia," in *The Earth as Transformed by Human Action*, ed. B. L. Turner, II (Cambridge and New York: Cambridge University Press with Clark University,

1990), 513-31.

3. I. P. Gerasimov, ed., *Kavkaz*. Seriia "Prirodnye usloviia i estestvennye resursy" (Moscow: Izdatel'stvo "Nauka," 1966), 315.

4. I. V. Rovinskii, "Khoziaistvennoe opisanie Astrakhanskoi i Kavkazskoi gubernii po grazhdanskomu i estestvennomu ikh sostoianiiu," *Trudy Stavropol'skoi uchenoi arkhivnoi komissii*, no. 2 (1910): section 4, 41-42, 58; Gerasimov, *Kavkaz*, 324-25.

5. Rossiiskii Gosudarstvennyi Istoricheskii Arkhiv (RGIA), f. 1268, op. 1, d. 839a, ll. 40-41; Iu. Shidlovskii, "Zapiski o Kizliare," *Zhurnal Ministerstva vnutrennikh del*, no. 4 (1843): 162; I. I. Dmitrenko, "Materialy k istorii Terskago kazach'iago voiska," *Terskii sbornik*, no. 4 (1897): 77; I. Debu, "O nachal'nom ustanovlenii i rasprostranenii Kavkazskoi linii," *Otechestvennyia zapiski* 18, no. 48 (1824): 274-79, 290-93; N. Toropov, *Opyt'' meditsinskoi geografii Kavkaza* (St. Petersburg: Tipografiia Iakova Treia, 1864), 70-75, 92-94; S. A. Chekmenev, ed., *Nekotorye voprosy sotsial'no-ekonomicheskogo razvitiia iugo-vostochnoi Rossii* (Stavropol': Ministerstvo prosveshcheniia RSFSR. Stavropol'skii gosudarstvennyi pedagogicheskii institut, 1970), 6-7; Gerasimov, *Kavkaz*, 214-19, 323-24.

6. For an excellent brief discussion of such environmental history methodology, and its pitfalls, see Cronon, *Changes in the Land*, 6-10.

7. R. V. Fedorova, "Primenenie sporovo-pyl'tevogo analiza v arkheologicheskikh issledovaniiakh prikaspiia i predkavkaz'ia," *Sovetskaia arkheologiia*, no. 1 (1959): 286-90; E. I. Krupnov, "Za ekonomicheskoe vozrozhdenie raionov prikaspiiskoi nizmennosti," *Sovetskaia arkheologiia*, no. 3 (1963): 4-8, 10-12; I. P. Falk, "Zapiski puteshestviia akademika Falka," *Polnoe uchenykh puteshestvii po Rossii* (St. Petersburg: Imperatorskaia akademiia nauk, 1824), 6: 91.

8. I. Bentkovskii, *Reka Kuma i neobkhodimost' uluchshit' eia ekonomicheskoe znachenie* (Stavropol': no publisher given, 1882; repr. from *Stavropol'skie gubernskie vedomosti*, nos. 27, 28 [1882]), 10-11; Falk, "Zapiski puteshestviia akademika Falka," 96; L. I. Lavrov, *Epigraficheskie pamiatniki Severnogo Kavkaza* (Moscow: Izdatel'stvo "Nauka," 1966), 2: 127; "Vzgliad na Kavkazskuiu liniiu," *Severnyi arkhiv*, no. 2 (January 1822): 169.

9. Krupnov, "Za ekonomicheskoe vozrozhdenie raionov prikaspiiskoi nizmenosti," 10-12; V. I. Deniskin, "Razvitie zemledeliia u terskikh kazakov i izmenenie prirodnykh uslovii. (K postanovke problemy)" in *Arkheolog-etnograficheskii sbornik*, V. B. Vinogradov, ed. (Groznyi: Checheno-Ingushskii nauchno-issledovatel'skii institut istorii, iazyka i literatury pri Sovete Ministrov Checheno-Ingushskoi ASSR, 1976), 4: 270-72.

10. Ia. Chistovich, "Kizliar i ego meditsynskaia topografiia za 100 let do nastoiashchago vremeni," *Voenno-meditsinskii zhurnal* 78 (1860): 10-19; Dmitrenko, "Materialy k istorii Terskago kazach'iago voiska," 58, 79; F Ponomarëv, "Materialy dlia istorii Terskago kazach'iago voiska s 1559 po 1880 god," *Voennyi sbornik* 23, no. 10 (October 1880): 364-65.

11. I. A. Gil'denshtedt [Johann Anton Güldenstädt], *Geograficheskoe i statisticheskoe opisanie Gruzii i Kavkaza* (St. Petersburg: Imperatorskaia akademiia nauk, 1809), 2-3, 16-18.

12. "Istoricheskiia svedeniia o Grebenskom kazach'em polku," *Sbornik Obshchestva liubitelei kazach'ei stariny* 4 (1912): 35-36, 52-53; G. A. Tkachëv, *Stanitsa Chervlennaia. Istoricheskii ocherk* (Vladikavkaz: Elektropechatnia tipografii Terskago oblastnago pravleniia, 1912), 53.

13. Quoted in I. Popko, *Terskie kazaki so starodavnikh vremen. Istoricheskii ocherk* (St. Petersburg: Tipografiia Departmenta udelov, 1880), 182; Debu, "O nachal'nom ustanovlenii i rasprostranenii Kavkazskoi linii," 276-77, 293; Iosif Debu, *O Kavkazskoi linii i prisoedinennom k nei Chernomorskom voiske* (St. Petersburg: Tipografiia Karla Kraiia, 1829), 47-51, 53-54, 66-68.

14. Platon Zubov, *Kartina Kavkazskago kraia prinadlezhashchago Rossii, i sopredel'nykh onomu zemel'* (St. Petersburg: Tipografiia Konrada Vingebera, 1834), 126-28, 130-32.

15. Popko, *Terskie kazaki*, 212-14, 360-62; F. P. Ponomarëv, "Materialy po istorii Terskago kazach'iago voiska. 2-i Malorossiiskii polk," *Terskii sbornik*, no. 6 (1903): 213-14.

16. A. V...v, "Kratkii ocherk Stavropol'skii gubernii v promyshlennom i torgovom otnosheniiakh," *Kavkaz*, 22 May 1848, 82-84; RGIA, f. 1268, op. 3, d. 275, l. 21; f. 1268, op. 4, d. 308, l. 30; S. D. Nechaev, "Otryvki iz putevykh zapisok o Iugo-Vostochnoi Rossii," *Moskovskii telegraf*, no. 7 (1826): section 1, 31-32.

17. RGIA, f. 1268, op. 1, d. 839a, l. 27; f. 1268, op. 1., d. 839a, l. 148; "Smeta i taksa na otpusk iz kazennykh dach Stavropol'skoi gubernii lesnykh materialov na 1850-1851 gody," *Izvestiia Kavkazskago otdela Imperatorskago russkago geograficheskago obshchestva* 5, no. 4 (1878): supplement, 30-31.

18. Rossiiskii Gosudarstvennyi Voenno-Istoricheskii Arkhiv (RGVIA), f. 1058, op. 1, d. 432, ll. 1-4.

19. Tkachëv, *Stanitsa Chervlennaia*, 127-28.

20. RGVIA, f. 1058, op. 1, d. 428, ll. 29-34, 96-97.

21. Ponomarëv, "Materialy po istorii Terskago kazach'iago voiska," 223; I. Slivitskii, "Ocherki Kavkaza i Zakavkaz'ia. Kazatskii khutor i staroobriadcheskie skity v Ishorakh," *Kavkaz*, 27 November 1848, 190; M. Liuventseev, "Razskaz Mozdokskago Armianina," *Kavkaz*, 23 August 1850, 261; Kh. I. K., "Khoziaistvennyia zametki," *Kavkaz*, 21 January 1850, 23-24; A. I. Deichman, "Neskol'ko slov o Kavkaze v sel'sko-khoziaistvennom otnoshenii," *Zapiski Kavkazskago obshchestva sel'skago khoziaistva* 2 (1856): 94-95; A. O., "Rubka lesa," *Voennyi sbornik* 16 (1860): section 2, 97-100.

22. Chistovich, "Kizliar i ego meditsynskaia topografiia," 10-19; Gil'denshtedt, *Geograficheskoe i statisticheskoe opisanie Gruzii i Kavkaza*, 22-23; Falk, "Zapiski puteshestviia akademika Falka," 64-67; Shidlovskii, "Zapiski o Kizliare," 171-73, 185-87; RGIA, f. 1268, op. 2, d. 887, l. 60.

23. Rovinskii, "Khoziaistvennoe opisanie Astrakhanskoi i Kavkazskoi gubernii," 52-53; A. Rzhevuskii, ed., *Tertsy. Sbornik istoricheskikh, bytovykh i geografichesko-statisticheskikh svedenii* (Vladikavkaz: Tipografiia Oblastnago pravleniia Terskoi oblasti, 1883), 231-35; Voiskovoe khoziaistvennoe pravlenie, *Statisticheskiia monografii po izsledovaniiu stanichnago byta Terskago kazach'iago voiska* (Vladikavkaz: Tipografiia Terskago oblastnago pravleniia, 1881), 234-36; Petr Egorov, "Dorozhnyia zapiski o Kavkaze i Severnom Dagestane, 1851 goda," *Russkii invalid* 177 (1851): 733-35; Gil'denshtedt, *Geograficheskoe i statisticheskoe opisanie Gruzii i Kavkaza*, 24.

24. RGIA, f. 1269, op. 2, d. 887, l. 60; "Goroda Stavropol'skoi gubernii," *Izvestiia Kavkazskago otdela Imperatorskago russkago geograficheskago obshchestva* 5, no. 4 (1878): supplement, 14-17; Z...v, "Puteshestviia. Poezdka iz Mozdoky," *Tiflisskiia vedomosti,*

10 July 1830, n.p.; A. V. Fadeev, *Ocherki ekonomicheskogo razvitiia stepnogo predkavkaz'ia v doreformennyi period* (Moscow: Izdatel'stvo Akademii nauk SSSR, 1957), 232.

25. G. N. Prozritelev, *Stavropol'skaia guberniia v istoricheskom, khoziaistvennom i bytovom otnoshenii* (Stavropol': Tipografiia "Proletarii," 1925), 2: 11-12; G. N. Prozritelev, ed., "Iz proshlogo Severnogo Kavkaza. Materialy dlia istorii g. Stavropolia i Stavropol'skoi gub." *Trudy Stavropol'skoi uchenoi arkhivnoi komisii*, no. 2 (1910): section 4, 25; P. Khitsunov, "O mestonakhozhdenii i razvalinakh goroda Madzhar, Stavropol'skoi gubernii, v Piatigorskom uezde," *Kavkaz*, 2 April 1849, 51-52; A. Tvalchrelidze, *Stavropol'skaia guberniia v statisticheskom, geograficheskom, istoricheskom i sel'sko-khoziaistvennom otnosheniiakh* (Stavropol': Tipografiia M. N. Koritskogo, 1897), 219-20.

26. RGVIA, f. 1058, op. 1, d. 380, ll. 19, 125-26; f. 1058, op. 1, d. 381, l. 88.

27. RGVIA, f. 1058, op. 1, d. 380, ll. 125-26, 130; f. 1058, op. 1, d. 381, ll. 9, 40, 46, 64, 88, 194-97. There is some indication that mountain people of the North Caucasus recognized the role of forests in preventing erosion or at least the utility of forest-conservation measures. Chechens, Kabardians, Ossetians, and others had sacred groves that were protected from cutting and there were prohibitions against felling trees by river heads, lakes, and streams. See T. P. Kaznacheeva, "Cherty obshchnosti zemledel'cheskoi kul'tury i ekologicheskikh predstavlenii narodov Severnogo Kavkaza v dorevoliutsionnyi period," in *Problemy agrarnoi istorii narodov Severnogo Kavkaza v dorevoliutsionnyi period*, V. P. Nevskaia, ed. (Stavropol': Stavropol'skii gosudarstvennyi pedagogicheskii institut, 1981), 84-85; A. M., "Religioznye obriady Osetin, Ingush i ikh soplemennikov, pri raznykh sluchaiakh. II. Prazdniki," *Kavkaz*, 13 July 1846, 110-12.

28. K. Samoilov, "Zametki o Chechne," *Panteon* 23, no. 9 (September 1855): section 3, 67-69; V. A. Potto, *Kavkazskaia voina v otdel'nykh ocherkakh, epizodakh, legendakh i biografiiakh* (St. Petersburg: Tipografiia R. Golike, 1885), 2: part 1, 107-18.

29. See for example, "Pis'mo k redaktoru iz Dagestana," *Kavkaz*, 19 January 1846, 9; "Vnutrenniia izvestiia Kavkaza," *Kavkaz*, 26 January 1846, 14; "Kavkaz," *Kavkaz*, 1 February 1847, 18.

30. "Kavkaz," *Kavkaz*, 26 February 1849, 34.

31. A. P. Berzhe, *Chechnia i chechentsy* (Tiflis: Kavkazskii otdel Imperatorskago russkago geograficheskago obshchestva, 1859), 2-4; Samoilov, "Zametki o Chechne," section 3, 58-60.

32. R. Sh. Sharafutdinova, "Eshchë odin "Nizam" Shamilia," *Pis'mennye pamiatniki vostoka* (1975): 168-71.

33. E. M. Murzaev, *Toponimika i geografiia* (Moscow: Nauka, 1995), 65-66; Deniskin, "Razvitie zemledeliia u terskikh kazakov," 271-73; Samoilov, "Zametki o Chechne," section 3, 58-60. Berzhe, writing in 1859, concurred. See Berzhe, *Chechnia i chechentsy*, 2-4.

34. RGVIA, f. 1058, op. 1, d. 427, ll. 3-4; G. Prozritelev, ed., *Iz proshlago Severnago Kavkaza. Vospominaniia starago kavkaztsa otstavnago vakhtera Mefodiia Stepanovicha Soloduna* (Stavropol': Tipografiia Gubernskago pravleniia, 1914), 15.

35. Deichman, "Neskol'ko slov o Kavkaze," 94-95; RGVIA, f. 1058, op. 1, d. 426, ll. 3-21.

36. A. Viskovatov, "Obshchii kharakter prirodi i cheloveka na Kavkaze," in *Priroda i liudi na kavkaze i za kavkazom* (St. Petersburg, 1869), 1-2; A. O., "Rubka lesa," section 2, 97-102; RGVIA, f. 1058, op. 1, d. 426, ll. 45-46.

37. RGVIA, f. 1058, op. 1, d. 432, ll. 1-4.

38. A. Domanskii, "Sel'skokhoziaistvennyia zametki iz nadterechnago kraia," *Kavkaz*, 30 August-11 September 1864, 382. See also "Materialy dlia statistiki Kizliarskago polka Terskago kazach'iago voiska," *Voennyi sbornik*, no. 12 (December 1869): 234.

39. D. L. Ivanov, "Vliianie russkoi kolonizatsii na prirodu Stavropol'skago kraia," *Izvestiia Imperatorskago russkago geograficheskago obshchestva* 22, no. 3 (1886): 224-54; Tvalchrelidze, *Stavropol'skaia guberniia*, 14, 62, 204.

40. Viskovatov, "Obshchii kharakter prirodi i cheloveka," 1-2; Toropov, *Opyt'' meditsinskoi geografii*, 72-75, 92-94.

41. On Terskii Gorod and Sviatoi Krest see F. A. Kotov, "Khozhdenie na vostok F. A. Kotova v pervoi chetverti XVII veka," *Izvestiia Otdeleniia russkago iazyka i slovestnosti Imperatorskoi akademii nauk* 12, no. 1 (1907): 77-78; D. Vasil'ev, "Zagadki starogo Kizliara (Kizliar do 1735 goda), " in *Voprosy istorii Dagestana (dosovetskii period)*, V. G. Gadzhiev, ed. (Makhachkala: Dagestanskii filial Akademii nauk SSSR. Institut istorii, iazyka i literatury im. G. Tsadasy, 1974), 3: 39. On Kizliar, Debu, *O Kavkazskoi linii*, 23-26, 47-51; Chistovich, "Kizliar i ego meditsynskaia topografiia," 10-19; Gil'denshtedt, *Geograficheskoe i statisticheskoe opisanie Gruzii i Kavkaza*, 19-20.

42. Ponomarëv, "Materialy dlia istorii Terskago kazach'iago voiska," 363-64; Falk, "Zapiski puteshestviia akademika Falka," 65-67; Toropov, *Opyt'' meditsinskoi geografii*, 74.

43. Gil'denshtedt, *Geograficheskoe i statisticheskoe opisanie Gruzii i Kavkaza*, 16-17; Debu, "O nachal'nom ustanovlenii," 274-75, 278-79; Debu, *O Kavkazskoi linii*, 47-51; Ponomarëv, "Materialy po istorii Terskago kazach'iago voiska," 219-22; Toropov, *Opyt'' meditsinskoi geografii*, 72-75, 92-94.

44. N. P. Gritsenko, *Sotsial'no-ekonomicheskoe razvitie priterechnykh raionov v XVIII-pervoi polovine XIX vv.* (Groznyi: Izdatel'stvo gazety "Groznenskii Rabochii," 1961), 30-31; Voiskovoe khoziaistvennoe pravlenie, *Statisticheskiia monografii*, 238-39; M. Iu. Lermontov, *Izbrannye sochineniia* (Moscow: "Khudozhestvennaia literatura," 1983), 667.

45. Gil'denshtedt, *Geograficheskoe i statisticheskoe opisanie Gruzii i Kavkaza*, 2-3, 5-8; Falk, "Zapiski puteshestviia akademika Falka," 57-58; Popko, *Terskie kazaki*, 365-67. See also P. P. Nadezhdin, *Kavkazskii krai: Priroda i liudi*, 3d ed. (Tula: Tipografiia Vladimira Nikolaievicha Sokolova, 1901), 65-67.

46. See, for example, "The Rage of Terek, Son of the Mountain" and an accompanying song in Popko, *Terskie kazaki*, 223-41, 505; F. Butova, "Stanitsa Borozdinskaia, Terskoi oblasti, Kizliarskago okruga," *Sbornik materialov dlia opisaniia mestnostei i plemen Kavkaza*, no. 7 (1889): 119-20.

47. A. A. Litvinov, "Ob izmeneniiakh techeniia r. Tereka i beregov Kaspiiskago moria s 1841 po 1863 god," *Zapiski Kavkazskago otdela Imperatorskago russkago geograficheskago obshchestva* 6 (1861): section 4, 83-86; Popko, *Terskie kazaki*, 365-67. See also M. N. Gersevanov, *Ocherk gidrografii Kavkazskago kraia* (St. Petersburg: Tipografiia Ministerstvo putei soobshcheniia, 1886), 45-46, 57.

48. "Pokhodnoi zhurnal Petra Velikago. 1722," *Pokhodnye i putevye zhurnaly imp. Petra I-go* (1855): 64; Falk, "Zapiski puteshestviia akademika Falka," 58; Gil'denshtedt, *Geograficheskoe i statisticheskoe opisanie Gruzii i Kavkaza*, 3-4.

49. F. Ponomarëv, "O zemledel'cheskikh zaniatiiakh zhitelei Kizliarskago kazach'iago

82

polka," *Zapiski Kavkazskago obshchestva sel'skago khoziaistva* 15, no. 4 (1869): 130-31; "Materialy dlia statistiki Kizliarskago polka," 228-29.

50. Ponomarëv, "Materialy dlia istorii Terskago kazach'iago voiska," 363-64; "Materialy dlia istorii Severnago Kavkaza 1787-1792," *Kavkazskii sbornik* 18 (1897): 446; Shidlovskii, "Zapiski o Kizliare," 163-64.

51. Quoted in S. F. Golovchanskii, "Kniaz' Georgii Romanovich Eristov i kanaly— Eristovskii i Kursko-Mar'inskii," *Zapiski Terskago obshchestva liubitelei kazach'ei stariny*, no. 12 (December 1914): 5-13.

52. Gersevanov, *Ocherk gidrografii*, 66-67; Toropov, *Opyt'' meditsinskoi geografii*, 191; Deniskin, "Razvitie zemledeliia u terskikh kazakov," 271-73.

53. Debu, "O nachal'nom ustanovlenii," 275; RGVIA, f. 1058, op. 1, d. 385, ll. 2-3; d. 502, ll. 30-31.

54. Arkadii Iziumov, "Stanitsa Aleksandriiskaia," *Terskiia vedomosti*, 30 July 1873, 3; Toropov, *Opyt'' meditsinskoi geografii*, 92; RGVIA, f. 1058, op. 1, d. 386, ll. 2-3.

55. RGVIA, f. 1058, op. 1, d. 380, ll. 163-64; f. 1058, op. 1, d. 381, ll. 194-97, 201; I. Shabanov, "Predkhranitel'nyia mery, prinimaemyia protiv razlivov Tereka," *Kavkaz*, 28 March 1863, 155-58; Gersevanov, *Ocherk gidrografii*, 58-61; "Istoricheskoe svedenie. (Raport komanduiushchago Kizliarskim polkom podp. Alpatova 31 Iiulia 1854 goda No 4530)," *Sbornik Obshchestva liubitelei kazach'ei stariny*, no. 2 (1912): 16; Debu, "O nachal'nom ustanovlenii," 278-79.

56. E. Butovaia, "Stanitsa Borozdinskaia, Terskoi oblasti, Kizliarskago okruga," *Sbornik materialov dlia opisaniia mestnostei i plemen Kavkaza* 7 (1889): 3-5; Litvinov, "Ob izmeneniiakh techeniia r. Tereka," 86-90.

57. Falk, "Zapiski puteshestviia akademika Falka," 62; Tkachëv, *Stanitsa Chervlennaia*, 29, 61-63; "Istoricheskoe svedenie," 15-16; "Materialy dlia statistiki Kizliarskago polka," 216.

58. Popko, *Terskie kazaki*, 214-22; RGVIA, f. 1058, op. 1, d. 381, ll. 9, 40, 64, 194-97.

59. Deichman, "Neskol'ko slov o Kavkaze," 45-49; Debu, "O nachal'nom ustanovlenii," 278-79, 290-93; S. P. P. V., "Vinogradnyia zavedeniia v Kizliare," *Kavkaz*, 12 October 1846, 164; I. Shabanov, "Predokhranitel'nyia mery prinimaemyia protiv razlivov Tereka," *Kavkaz*, 24 March 1863, 151-52; Gritsenko, *Sotsial'no-ekonomicheskoe razvitie priterechnykh raionov*, 49-51; RGIA, f. 1268, op. 1, d. 839a, ll. 44-46; RGVIA, f. 1058, op. 1, d. 410, l. 4.

60. RGVIA, f. 1058, op. 1, d. 380, l. 40; Popko, *Terskie kazaki*, 209-11, 214-17; G. A. Vertepov, "Khoziaistvennoe polozhenie nizov'ev reki Tereka," *Terskii sbornik* 6 (1903): 19-20.

61. RGVIA, f. 1058, op. 1, d. 381, l. 9; I. Shabanov, "Predokhranitel'nyia mery, prinimaemyia protiv razlivov Tereka," *Kavkaz*, 17 March 1863, 137-38; Vertepov, "Khoziaistvennoe polozhenie nizov'ev," 19-20; "Vnutreniia izvestiia Kavkaza," *Kavkaz*, 5 August 1846, 121; 31 August 1846, 139; 7 September 1846, 142.

62. Nikolai Krasovich, "Navodenie v Kizliare," *Kavkaz*, 31 August 1855, 291.

63. RGVIA, f. 1058, op. 1, d. 426, ll. 19-21.

64. Alfred W. Crosby, *Ecological Imperialism: The Biological Expansion of Europe, 900-1900* (Cambridge: Cambridge University Press, 1986), 196. See also Alfred W. Crosby, Jr., *The Columbian Exchange* (Westport, Connecticut: Greenwood Press, 1972).

65. Philip D. Curtin, *Death by Migration: Europe's Encounter with the Tropical World*

in the Nineteenth Century (Cambridge: Cambridge University Press, 1989); Alfred W. Crosby, "Ecological Imperialism: The Overseas Migration of Western Europeans as a Biological Phenomenon," in *The Ends of the Earth*, Donald Worster, ed. (Cambridge: Cambridge University Press, 1988), 104.

66. Nadezhdin, *Kavkazskii krai*, 93-94; Toropov, *Opyt'' meditsinskoi geografii*, 3, 74, 92-94, 186. The information on cholera is sketchier, but we do know that there was an epidemic in 1847, which hit Mozdok and Vladikavkaz regiments and killed at least 279. See "Kavkaz," *Kavkaz*, 11 October 1847, 161; Tkachëv, *Stanitsa Chervlennaia*, 147; A. Pliushch, "Stanitsa Urukhskaia. Istoriko-ekonomicheskii ocherk," *Terskii sbornik* 5 (1903): 97; P. Nitsik, "Byvshiia voennyia poseleniia na Voenno-Gruzinskoi doroge," *Terskiia vedomosti*, 5 March 1887, 2.

67. RGIA, f. 1268, op. 1, d. 839a, l. 39; "Materialy dlia statistiki Kizliarskago polka," 223-25.

68. Chistovich, "Kizliar i ego meditsynskaia topografiia," section 3, 3-10.

69. Chistovich, "Kizliar i ego meditsynskaia topografiia," section 3, 27-33; A. [M.] Pavlov, *O aziiatskikh narodakh, obitaiushchikh v iuzhnoi Rossii* (St. Petersburg: Tipografiia Kh. Gintsa, 1841), 5.

70. Gil'denshtedt, *Geograficheskoe i statisticheskoe opisanie Gruzii i Kavkaza*, 19-20; Falk, "Zapiski puteshestviia akademika Falka," 65; "Materialy dlia istorii Severnogo Kavkaza," 446; Shidlovskii, "Zapiski o Kizliare," 165, 173-74.

71. G. N. Prozritelev, "Istochnik Karabin. K istorii goroda Stavropolia," *Sbornik svedenii o Severnom Kavkaze* 11 (1914): 1-11; Nadezhdin, *Kavkazskii krai*, 360-61; "Goroda Stavropol'skoi gubernii," *Izvestiia Kavkazskago otdela Imperatorskago russkago geograficheskago obshchestva* 5, no. 4 (1878): supplement, 14-17; Mikhail Kriukov, "Goroda Stavropol'skoi gubernii," *Stavropol'skiia gubernskiia vedomosti*, 8 April 1850, 168.

72. Gil'denshtedt, *Geograficheskoe i statisticheskoe opisanie Gruzii i Kavkaza*, 16; Falk, "Zapiski puteshestviia akademika Falka," 59-60; Gr. Gord...v, "Puteshestviia. Poezdka iz Pol'shi za Kavkaz," *Tiflisskiia vedomosti*, 20 February 1830, n.p.; Kriukov, "Putevyia zametki," *Izvestiia Kavkazskago otdela Imperatorskago russkago geograficheskago obshchestva* 5, no. 4 (1878): supplement, 62-63; Gersevanov, *Ocherk gidrografii*, 66-67.

73. Tvalchrelidze, *Stavropol'skaia guberniia*, 408; Popko, *Terskie kazaki*, 297-98; Debu, *O Kavkazskoi linii*, 288; "Materialy dlia statistiki Kizliarskago polka," 228-29; Voiskovoe khoziaistvennoe pravlenie, *Statisticheskiia monografii*, 238-39; Tkachëv, *Stanitsa Chervlennaia*, 9; RGVIA, f. 1058, op. 1, d. 385, ll. 2-3.

74. Popko, *Terskie kazaki*, 208, 297-98; Toropov, *Opyt'' meditsinskoi geografii*, 3.

75. Fernand Braudel, *The Mediterranean and the Mediterranean World in the Age of Philip II*, trans. Siân Reynolds (New York: Harper & Row, 1972), 1: 60-85.

Illustration 4 A Cossack watchtower (drawing by A. P. D'iakonov)

Illustration 5 A Greben Cossack in a watchtower scans the horizon
(drawing from an album by P. I. Chelishchev)

Illustration 6 *A Cossack Forager* (Theodore Horschelt)

Illustration 7 *Lieutenant Fediushkin of the Greben Cossack Regiment and His Wife* (watercolor album of Prince Gagarin)

5

Land Without Labor:
The Cossack Economy

He who plows, eats; he who doesn't plow, lives poorly.

—Mountaineer saying

A Cossack without a horse is not a Cossack.

—Cossack saying

A man without a weapon is simply a woman with a long beard.

—Dagestanian saying

The foundation of Cossack life and Cossack service was their home economy. Cossacks were expected not only to fight for the empire, but also to establish successful economies, economies that would provide the material base for their military service and integrate the frontier into the all-Russian economy. As the Vladikavkaz regimental government optimistically ordered in 1840,

> each married Cossack is obliged to find means to provide for himself and his family, and is also obliged to make haste over his own safety and in linking his economic life with his military life; he should not only be an industrious warrior and agriculturist, but also...should engage in animal husbandry, apiculture, and all types of handicrafts and manufacture based on the example of his native neighbors.[1]

In the same breath he commanded that Cossacks become productive and acknowledged their lag behind the natives to the south. This important economic aspect of cossackdom has been slighted in the West, because historians have concentrated on questions of military service and political integration.

The success or failure of Cossack service cannot be understood without digging deep into the history of Cossack economies—their health or sickness was crucial not only to the settlers themselves, but also to the entire Russian imperial enterprise. Since the Cossack system was supposed to be self-sustaining, the issue of sustenance had direct political importance. With ailing economies, Cossacks would not be able to provide for themselves or to equip their regiments. Since reproduction depends on production, weak Cossack economies could make their communities demographically unviable and they would slowly fade away.

Furthermore, Russian dreams about the economic integration of the borderlands—and the drawing in of native peoples to Russian civilization through inexorable economic forces—directly depended on the Russian frontier economy which was anchored in the Cossack communities well into the nineteenth century. As A. P. Thornton wrote about the colonial experience in Madagascar, "'Civilization' does not contact 'barbarism'...What happens is, that men make contact with other men. Or, with other kinds of women." Of course political power helps to determine, as the Russians put it, *kto kogo* or who gets the better of whom, when representatives of different nations come into contact on the frontier. But so does economic power. How could officials in St. Petersburg hope to draw the Caucasus mountain people into Russian civilization if the agents of that civilization whom the later encountered were poor and partially economically dependent on the mountain people themselves? As the Ossetians said, "Even God doesn't like a poor man."[2]

The Terek Cossacks had an extremely difficult time establishing successful economies. Land was abundant, but often of very poor quality. More importantly, since they suffered a chronic labor shortage, Cossacks strained to use the land, regardless of quantity or quality. The lack of able bodies and strong arms structured Cossack life in important ways. This chapter will examine the labor shortage and then sketch out the major branches of the Terek Cossack economy—agriculture, viticulture, and animal husbandry.

One of the most important facets of North Caucasus society was the dearth of labor. The rarest type of settlement was that predominant in the rest of Russia: the serf-based manorial village. In 1857 less than 3 percent of the population of the North Caucasus (Stavropol' province and Terek and Kuban *oblast'*s) was serf; except for sparsely settled Arkhangelsk and Siberia, it was the region of the empire with the lowest percentage of serfs.[3] Other sources of labor were also scarce since harsh service requirements removed male Cossacks from their home economies for a good part of their lives (see Chapter 8). This shortage colored the social world of the Terek Cossacks. They and their commanders tried all means possible, including those outside of the law, to make up for their lack of field hands. Occasionally Cossacks went awol to get back to their homes and farms to work (see Chapter 8). We also saw in Chapter 3 how they sheltered peasant fugitives from the interior of Russia.

Peasants streamed to the North Caucasus from adjacent provinces—sometimes straight from their villages, sometimes after legally working a stint on the Volga or the Caspian. Some hid out in the forests or the swamps and worked in Cossack fishing gangs or hired themselves out for seasonal labor; others were immediately welcomed into the labor-starved Cossack farms and villages. Nicholas I, not known for his flexibility, had to yield to this inexorable pressure for Cossack labor. According to an 1827 statute, all fugitive peasants who had carved out a place for themselves in Cossack villages by 1816— marrying, establishing a domestic economy, and entering military service— were legally recognized as Cossacks and allowed to stay put.[4]

The government also forced thousands of vagrants, criminals, and war prisoners to resettle to the North Caucasus. This practice dated back to the seventeenth century, when Latvian, German, and Polish prisoners of war, along with criminals, disgraced people, and religious schismatics, were sent to work in prisoner brigades or as free laborers. The government also dispatched French prisoners of war in 1815 to build flood walls to protect the Cossack villages.[5]

Later, officials concentrated on "vagrants" (*brodiagi*)—people caught without a passport, including peasant fugitives, escaped prisoners, and others who had fled their place of residence, their service, and their legal estate to wander freely across the vast Russian empire or to move to another region and assume a different identity. On 12 February 1829 the State Council approved measures that *brodiagi* in the Caucasus *oblast'*, along with those in Ukrainian and southern provinces, be given to the Cossacks of the line as laborers for a three-year period, after which those of good behavior were to be enrolled as Cossacks. Some Cossack commanders were not keen about this, fearing, in the words of the commander of the Terek-Semeinoe regiment, "that they would try to pervert the most radical residents to evil deeds, and because the Cossacks are always on service, such workers would remain in their homes, close to the Cossacks' wives and children," easy prey for lawlessness and corruption. He feared that they would commit crimes, teach others to steal, and eventually flee to the mountain people and join in on attacks against the Cossacks. The commander of the Terek-Kizliar host worried about Muslim Cossacks using Christian workers. But the other regimental and host commanders saw the great advantage of an infusion of labor power and simply cautioned against sending those whose records tainted them as being potentially harmful. According to one source, in the course of three years 10,000 such people joined the hosts of the line.[6]

The fears, though, seem to have been well founded. Captain Ponomarëv, a staff officer of the Separate Caucasian Corps, reported in August 1830 that *brodiagi* were poor workers who took every opportunity to desert or steal from Cossacks. Perhaps even more threatening, soldiers began to see the possibility of social mobility through vagrancy—lower ranks from the regular army began to desert with the intention of becoming *brodiagi*, being caught and handed over to Cossacks as workers, and thus avoiding the miserable army service and getting a chance at improving their lot by becoming Cossacks.

Apparently the situation became severe—in 1833 the Senate ruled that in the future all *brodiagi* would be sent instead to the regular army or penal battalions.[7]

Cossacks also used the labor of indentured servants, a practice that harked back to the debt servitude of the fifteenth and sixteenth centuries, or even the indentured peasants of the Kievan era, but one that had long since disappeared in the interior of Russia. Mountain people sold slaves and prisoners—other mountain people, Georgians, and Armenians—to the Kumyks of Endirei, who then resold them at Kizliar where there was a great demand for vineyard workers. The commander of the Kizliar fortress reported in 1804 that the residents of Endirei became "well enriched" from this business. Armenians worked as middlemen in this trade too, until they were prohibited by a law of 1804 from "dragging them [slaves] in chains and selling them in Kizliar and at other places." The chattel were called *iasyry*, a Turkic word of Arabic origin meaning slaves or captives, although here they were indentured servants who worked for a period, usually six to eight years, before granted freedom. According to Popko, they often converted to Christianity and after working off their debt, most became Cossacks. Cossacks and other Russian subjects of the North Caucasus also ransomed prisoners from the mountain people, who then became indentured servants if they could not reimburse the purchase price. Although we do not know how frequently this occurred, it was an easy way for those Cossacks who could afford it to pick up an extra hand and gave them a vested interest in mountain kidnapping.[8]

Indentured servitude remained largely unregulated until 1835 when the State Council published a statute, "On the relationship of Caucasus *iasyry* or slaves [*kholopy*] to their owners." Now, instead of working off the purchase price—a practice which invited abuse since the owner could record a higher price than he actually paid for his servant—*iasyry* worked for a specific number of years, based on their age (five-year-olds for twenty-five years, ten-year-olds for twenty years, and so on). It also set a loose standard for the care of *iasyry*, hoping to alleviate cruel labor practices. If we can infer backwards from the different clauses of this statute, the purchasing of *iasyry* had given rise to a legion of strange and illegal practices: Muslims owning Christian servants; parents selling their children, wives their husbands, and sisters their brothers into servitude; individuals purchasing their relatives and using them as *iasyry*.[9]

Some Cossacks also kept slaves. With permission of the army, some 200 households of Kabardians and Abazians founded Babukovskii village on the Kuma River near Georgievsk in 1790; it was incorporated into the Volga regiment in 1821, and then transferred to the Mountain regiment the following year. As a part of the privileges granted to these Muslim Cossacks, they were allowed to keep their slaves. Vorontsov reaffirmed their special position in 1846, banning only the purchase of new slaves and the sale of slaves abroad. By 1853, Babukovskaia stanitsa had 1,044 male Cossacks, three mosques, four mullahs (one Kumyk and three Cossacks), and 510 slaves. It seems as if Vorontsov's ruling had little effect, since the number of slaves reached 682 by 1859. That year, local military authorities discussed freeing the slaves, but the ataman of the Line host recommended against it, suggesting instead that they encourage the stanitsa to disappear simply by letting them go to Mecca.[10]

To further complicate the picture, Cossacks themselves often became free laborers. Because of the constrained economic possibilities in some areas, and the insatiable demand for labor elsewhere, various people, Cossacks included, went in search of work and helped create a labor market in the North Caucasus, decades before it existed in the heartland of Russia. This was not the traditional peasant outmigration of labor, but instead unencumbered individuals freely hiring themselves out for a wage.

Cossacks occasionally worked in other Cossack villages where there was a rich harvest and a need for farm hands, but they also worked for state peasants and for mountain people. The Commander of the Greben regiment reported in 1839, for example, that "many" Greben Cossacks sent their wives and daughters to work for other regiments and for the Ossetians of Mozdok. When locusts destroyed the winter grain of the Magomet-iurtovskaia stanitsa of the First Sunzha regiment in 1854, residents were allowed to go to other regiments to work for grain. According their commander, Cossacks of the First Sunzha regiment were very poor and regularly worked for grain outside of the regiment. In 1855, Cossacks of the Mountain regiment worked in other regiments and state peasant villages after their harvest failed for the eighth year in a row. Others reported that Cossacks regularly went to state peasant villages for seasonal work to earn their grain. Cossack girls, and occasionally men, also worked in Kizliar vineyards for a part of the year.[11]

According to an article in *Kavkaz* in 1848, Cossacks also went to Kabarda to work for rich Kabardians, building houses, mills, stables, working in gardens, and making furniture and other items. Kaloev reported that Terek Cossacks in the twentieth century told him of their tradition, "from time immemorial," of going to Chechen villages to perform agricultural labor. But we probably should not put too much stock in Soviet anthropological field work since it was so distant from our period. It seems, though, that Cossacks did regularly hire themselves out to mountain people—at least enough so that one of the meanings of "Cossack" in Ossetian (*qazaq* or *qazax*) is "hired worker."[12]

The other solution to the labor shortage was to hire large numbers of Nogais, Kalmyks, and mountain people. Russians also migrated to the south for seasonal labor, but Cossacks relied much more on locals, since they were more plentiful and more skilled in the work at hand. Nogais worked in vineyards and at Cossack farms in the steppe. During the 1850s some 15,000 Nogais worked for landlords and Cossacks in the Kizliar *uezd*; they were considered some of the best vineyard workers and were often extremely important to the success of steppe farms. The ability to draw on such labor often determined which

Cossack farms prospered. One of the most productive farms of Chernoiarskaia stanitsa—according to Sosiev, the "granary of the stanitsa"—depended on the labor of families of Nogais who settled in felt tents in the farm in the early 1850s. During harvest time, when labor demands were even higher, other Nogais came in large artels and performed all of the field work, sometimes for money, sometimes for a part of the harvest. Kalmyks were hired in smaller numbers, but were especially valued as cattle hands and horsemen. When horsemen were needed to run the Sixth brigade nursery and tend the Cossack herd, the War Ministry and the ataman ordered that they find three Kalmyks to lead the operation.[13]

The number of mountain people streaming to the Caucasus Military Line to work was even greater. They worked mostly in vineyards and as unskilled laborers, but also as artisans. In 1839, 7,000 mountain people from Dagestan alone went to Kizliar for seasonal labor. In the 1840s, some 18,000 mountain people came annually. At the same time, some 20-25,000 seasonal workers from the mountains lived in Kizliar from spring to autumn, so many that a special office for the assistance of "peaceful non-residents from the mountains" was created in 1842. The governor of the Stavropol' province reported that tens of thousands of natives came to the province in 1850, to work as unskilled laborers, artisans, and in light industry (*promyshlenniki*).[14]

Mountain people nearly monopolized the artisanal work along the line, skilled as they were as smithies, metalworkers, swordsmiths, gunsmiths, coopers, cobblers, cart-makers, leatherworkers, and saddlemakers. The labor-intensive wine industry never would have survived without this supply of seasonal workers, who were numerous, available at the right time, and often quite knowledgeable about the difficult art of viticulture. When Shidlovskii described the mountain people filling the Kizliar square labor market, his resentment—and fear—of Russian dependency on their erstwhile enemies was as palpable as his "Orientalist" cultural arrogance:

Each tribe positions itself on the square in separate groups, sitting on their feet, with short pipes sticking in their teeth, mostly without shirts, covering their chests with scrappy, shaggy *burka*s [felt cloaks]. It is possible to identify the name and location of the *aul* [native village] which the savages came from by the different cuts of their sheepskin caps. Waiting to be hired, they converse, or in the local expression "mumble slyly," incessantly, baring their teeth that are white like elephant's tusks. Theft and brigandage, wheaten bread, and gunpowder—bread as the highest delicacy and gunpowder as their hope for the future—are the usual subjects of their conversations. Easily read on their faces, however, is the clear expression of the only thoughts that occupy them: "I don't have a slice of bread...I put my last leaf of tobacco in the pipe...My barefoot wife cuts her feet to pieces on the rocks...Look out giaour that you don't run into me tomorrow beyond the Terek!"[15]

He could call them "wild half-humans" all he wanted; the fact was that the

Russian frontier economy relied upon them, both for unskilled and highly skilled labor. In 1811, major general Del'potso, who had been in service in the Caucasus since 1795 and was the former commander of the Vladikavkaz fortress, pleaded for the free passage of Kabardians, Kumyks, Ossetians, and peaceful Chechens to the Russian side, not just to trade but also because of their great importance in farmwork, viticulture, and handicrafts. As he said, "from them come the majority of the skilled craftsmen who live in our borders, towns, and settlements" and "many workers for harvesting, hay cutting, cultivating vineyards, threshing, and other work."[16] Of course, the mountain people were dependent too, on these Russian towns and villages for seasonal employment.[17]

Looking over this variegated social landscape of slaves, indentured servants, soldier-vagrant-Cossacks, Cossack bondsmen, free laborers, and monopolies of native skilled craftsmen, it is hard to believe that we are still in nineteenth century Russia! The social history of imperial Russia embraced far more than the usual categories; microhistories of other borderland regions will doubtless reveal similar complexities. Our understanding of legal estate and social class needs to allow for and further explore this frontier diversity. Why was the social landscape so different in the North Caucasus? Because without nobles moving there and populating the land with serfs and without an abundant supply of peasant laborers and artisans from Russia, Cossacks had to innovate and use means within their grasp to secure labor. Because local commanders and other officials needed the Cossacks to be vigorous and fertile, it was to their advantage to give in to local irregularities. The frontier, as all who spent any time there realized, had a logic of its own.

Because of the varying suitability of land, the Terek Cossacks also had a more diversified economy than that which existed in the interior of Russia. Cossacks of the lower Terek, where the land was wetter, saltier, sandier, and in general less fertile, specialized in viticulture, distilling, sericulture, and fishing. Viticulture was much more important there than agriculture; because of harvest failures lower Terek Cossacks often had to purchase grain. Both steppe and river valley land became more fertile further to the west; Cossacks of the middle and upper Terek had a more successful agriculture and in general a more boisterous economy. They were largely self-sufficient in grain and some regiments raised a surplus of cattle and sheep, which they traded at the livestock markets of Georgievsk and Stavropol'. The richest lands—and by the mid-nineteenth century the largest harvests—were in the Stavropol' chernozem steppe.[18]

The grain culture of the Cossacks concentrated on wheat (Derbent and Kuban varieties), rye, millet, oats, and barley. Armenians grew rice—known locally as "Saracen millet" or "Saracen Yerevan millet"—in the low spots along the Terek and the Sunzha; some Cossacks picked up rice cultivation from the Armenians, but most could not because of the high labor requirements. They also had to forego the excellent grain substitute buckwheat because of the extra work it required to hull the seed into groats. Buckwheat had been an important supplemental crop in Russia since the middle ages. But Terek Cossacks could not say, along with their brethren to the north, that "Buckwheat kasha is our mother," to their great disadvantage since buckwheat can be grown in—and used to improve—poor soil. When a local writer Stepanov visited the villages of the upper Terek, he was surprised to learn that the Ukrainian Cossacks cooked kasha mostly out of millet instead of buckwheat. The Greben Cossacks sometimes resorted to porridge made from wild garlic, steppe sorrel (*Rumex* spp.), or watermelon pulp.[19]

Although it is difficult to generalize, according to the sparse statistics compiled by the governor of Stavropol', grain yields for the Line Cossacks in the 1840s and 1850s varied from barely over one to one, to five to one. With these types of yields, farmers could not build up much of a surplus to defend against future hardship. As a writer for *Kavkaz* confirmed,

> In these stanitsas everything is in such short supply that they hardly have enough for their own needs and if a Cossack goes to sell his grain, livestock, or wheat in town, then it is because he is forced to do so from extreme need and not because of a surplus.

According to P. A. Shatskii, up to the 1870s, the Cossacks of the Terek still could not produce enough grain to feed themselves and had to rely on imports, mostly from the interior of Russia, but also by mid-century from Stavropol' province.[20]

Besides poor land, what kept the grain harvests so low? Cossacks faced the same type of problems that plagued agricultural settlers in other frontier regions—a shortage of labor, an unfamiliar and often destructive climate, and whirlwinds of voracious locusts. The chronic labor shortage discussed above was sometimes compounded by other temporary difficulties. In the spring of 1847, for example, a rich harvest was developing for the Vladikavkaz regiment, but then a cholera epidemic hit that so devastated the work force that Cossacks were not able to plant their winter grain. Sometimes Cossacks had to abandon their planting or postpone their harvest for a few weeks when there was flooding, an attack, or even rumors of a pending attack. As William Cronon reminds us in his environmental history of the making of Chicago, the timing of a wheat harvest is crucial; a few days late and the plant can topple from its own weight or scatter seeds to the ground. In turbulent regions, maize was the superior crop, since it can remain on the stalk for a longer period and is protected from wind, rain, and even the death of the plant, by its husk. Growing upright on its stalk, it is also harder to trample than other grains. It seems the Chechens realized the great advantages of maize, because once it was introduced sometime around the late eighteenth/early nineteenth century, maize became an increasingly important crop to them; Samoilov claimed that by the mid-nineteenth century it was their main crop. Maize, beans, and pumpkins were the subsistence base of Shamil's forces in the mountains. Most Cossacks, on the other hand, did not widely cultivate maize during this period, and their harvests suffered as a result. Maize also would have been an improvement over rye and millet, entire crops of which would be cast into oblivion in one day by the annual summer eastern winds in the lower Terek region.[21]

Locusts occasionally devastated even the richest farmland. Nikolaevskaia stanitsa of the Vladikavkaz regiment grew wheat and millet on their fertile, well-watered land and often reaped excellent harvests. But in other years locusts destroyed their grain. They came for five years in a row in the 1850s, appearing in June and leaving only in mid-September, devouring all of the grain from Stavropol' to Vladikavkaz. S. D. Nechaev described the terror of a North Caucasus locust swarm in 1826 with appropriate military metaphors:

> In July more than once the wind carried in entire clouds of locusts. This gluttonous insect, covered with a hard shell like armor and endowed with extraordinary strength in legs that are as hard as metal, can perhaps only be destroyed with a considerable amount of work and only in small numbers. In these conditions, that is, having reached its full development, a locust is afraid only of noise and in general depends on puffs of wind. Irregular gusts sometimes collect so many locusts in one place that it seems they usurp the sun's rays. Fall into their boisterous deluge and you think you see a winter snowstorm pouring snow in big chunks, the toneless noise of the beating of their wings sounds like a rapid river flowing over your head. Meanwhile, as one group covers the ground—to rest or from satiation—the other group continues on its way and then in turn lands when the first takes off. Thus, there is no army anywhere that can stop them. In a few hours, and sometimes a few days, another horde files in and with a noisy swarm flies by and clears a place for others, who often, as if on purpose, appear for a gorging of the last remains of the camp meal of the predecessors.[22]

There were many years when entire stanitsa grain harvests were destroyed by locusts, sometimes covering fields, if the regimental reports can be believed, for over 100 square miles, and causing hundreds of thousands of rubles of damage. After the locusts arrived, crowds of Cossacks banged on basins and frying pans, they whacked the intruders with brooms, drove them into wide ditches and then buried them with soil, and attacked "with cattle, spades, harrows, by crushing them, by slapping them, with fire," but to little avail. Sometimes entire village populations, including children strong enough to hold tools, marched out to destroy locusts. Nechaev even recommended gun and cannon fire to drive the invaders away, realizing full well that they would simply regroup and assault different fields.[23]

Some of the richest farmland belonged to the Vladikavkaz regiment and it sometimes reaped a bountiful harvest. The most serious obstacle preventing further agricultural development there was the lack of labor power. As a writer in *Kavkaz* commented in 1861, "they'd be happy to hire workers, and at a good price, but none are to be found." Some of the Cossacks were former military colonists who actually had to be instructed in plowing, planting, and other agricultural work by outside Cossacks. Their prospects for developing agriculture were so dismal that the chief of staff of the Separate Caucasian Corps general Kotsebu asked that neighboring Kabardians be allowed to pasture livestock within the bounds of the land of Aleksandrovskaia. "And besides," as Nitsik said about Cossacks of the regiment, "to steer a plow with a gun hung over the shoulder and a sword at the side is very awkward."[24]

Russian agricultural colonization of the North Caucasus was not secure until large numbers of state peasants had put down roots in the steppe; the Cossacks were simply too busy to produce dependable agricultural surpluses and feed themselves. By 1830, some 53,500 state peasants lived in the Caucasus *oblast'* (see Chapter 3); it was the plows of these "grain guys," as some were called, which conquered the steppe and fed the cities, forts, and stanitsas. Of course it took a while for these settlers to establish successful farms—as late as 1833 widespread crop failure and famine beset the Stavropol' province, sending 40,000 peasants temporarily back to the interior provinces of Russia. This agricultural failure was partially caused by the conversion of thirty-three state peasant, Armenian, and Tatar settlements into Cossack villages in the same year; defense took priority over colonization and thousands suffered extreme hunger as a result. By the late 1840s and the 1850s, though, peasants produced regular surpluses of grain, which they sold to Cossack hosts and even exported to Taganrog and Rostov. According to Shatskii, it was not until the 1870s and 1880s that Cossacks quit importing grain from the interior of Russia and that Stavropol' province became the great granary of the North Caucasus.[25]

Luckily for the Cossacks of the lower Terek, their land which was so unsuitable for growing grain was one of the best areas for viticulture in the North Caucasus. Greben Cossacks grew grapes, made wine, and sold it at Terskii Gorod already in the mid-seventeenth century; they probably picked up the art, and the vines, in Dagestan. The Kizliar region became the center of viticulture in the North Caucasus, especially after Armenians and Georgians began settling there—and competing with the Cossacks—in the eighteenth century. Cossacks made a crude red wine called *chikhir* and they also distilled their wine "in the French style" into brandy, known throughout Russia as *kizliarka*. By the 1760s and 1770s, Cossacks and Armenians sent large amounts of wine from Kizliar to Astrakhan.[26]

The Russian state realized the potential for developing viticulture in the North Caucasus as early as 1650, when two Russians trained in viticulture by Germans in Astrakhan were sent to the Terek to make wine. Throughout the eighteenth and nineteenth centuries, the government concocted various schemes to promote viticulture along the Terek, encouraging foreign settlement;

opening a school of viticulture in Kizliar in 1807; importing French, German, and Crimean vines; and bringing in Georgian potters to teach Cossacks how to make wine storage jugs, which the Greben regiment was particularly interested in since their land was too wet for wine cellars.[27]

St. Petersburg also latched on to the developing industry as a revenue source, creating state monopolies and levying tariffs, which sometimes harmed the winemaking and distilling of the Terek Cossacks. In 1757, an injunction from empress Elizabeth prohibited the Greben and Terek-Semeinoe hosts from freely selling wine in Astrakhan and Kizliar, requiring them to sell it at a fixed low price to the Astrakhan horticultural bureau. After four years of declining profits, the War College complained to the Senate that this monopolistic measure had crippled the economy of the Greben host and it successfully petitioned that they be allowed to resume the free trade of their one important commodity. The Cossacks traditionally were allowed to sell their *kizliarka* duty-free, but in 1820, an excise was levied on this brandy, which sent the petitions flying to St. Petersburg. This time, they fell on deaf ears, no doubt because of the great take for the state. A writer for *Severnyi arkhiv* marveled in 1813 at the revenues Kizliar provided from the two-ruble banknote excise per *vedro* (about twelve liters) of spirits: "and thus, a tiny, ugly, dirty *uezd* town at the edge of a nearly uninhabited province, the town of Kizliar, brings to the treasury from one of its articles of trade, about 500,000 rubles of income."[28]

Wine and brandy production peaked in the early decades of the nineteenth century. With the continental blockade and disruptions of the Napoleonic Wars curtailing the import of wines and spirits, alcohol from the North Caucasus made a splash in the Russian market. *Kizliarka,* especially, was sent to the Nizhnii Novgorod trade fair, Moscow, St. Petersburg, Riga, and other Russian cities. In the 1820s, Kizliar vineyards alone produced some 24 million liters (over 6 million gallons) of wine and 2.4 million liters (634,200 gallons) of spirit, almost all of which was exported to Russia. The Greben Cossacks produced some 2.6 million liters (685,000 gallons) of spirit in the late 1820s. Over 23,000 acres of vineyards stretched along the lower Terek.[29]

But gradually increased competition, excises, and soil degradation destroyed the Cossack viticulture and distilling industry. Terek Cossacks complained bitterly about local Armenians and Georgians crowding out their once-profitable industry. Up to a point, they were right. Armenians and Georgians held limited service requirements and could devote more time to their business than the Cossacks. They came to control the distilling industry in the lower Terek and forced the Cossacks into a position of dependence. After European wine imports resumed, the market for North Caucasus wine collapsed and Cossacks sold their wine to distillers for conversion into *kizliarka.* Prices for this also dropped and the industry became more concentrated. In Kizliar, the number of distilleries dropped from forty-six in 1810 to eleven in 1847. Cossack distilleries dropped from thirty-five in 1830 to twenty-two in 1839 to ten after 1845. Greben Cossack distilleries dropped from twenty-eight in 1830 to six in 1853. Most Cossacks had little choice but to sell their wine to be processed and profited by others.[30]

But in the long run, Armenians and Georgians—just like the Cossacks—suffered from collapsing demand and the deterioration of lower Terek vineyards. The volume of spirit produced in Kizliar fell from 2,472,288 liters in 1829 to 238,440 liters in 1846. Prices plunged from sixty ruble banknotes per *anker* (forty liters) in 1817, to thirty rubles in 1829 to about twenty-seven rubles in 1835. Already in 1824, the Mozdok and Terek-Semeinnoe hosts complained of the gradual ruining of their grape harvest by the flooding of the Terek, which salinized—and eroded—vineyard soil. There are reports from the 1830s of vineyards being abandoned and turning into steppe or disappearing behind grass and reeds. By 1856 A. I. Deichman reported for the Caucasian Agricultural Society that most of the wine made along the Terek was used for local consumption; the price had fallen so low that it barely covered transportation costs for export to Nizhnii Novgorod. By 1868 *Terskiia vedomosti* reported that the Greben Cossacks brought in no significant income from their viticulture, selling their wine mostly on the spot, mostly in exchange for goods, at fifty kopecks a *vedro*.[31]

As viticulture faded in importance to the Terek Cossacks, animal husbandry expanded and helped shift west the economic center of gravity in the region. All of the Terek Cossack regiments raised cattle, sheep, and horses for their own use; the Greben Cossacks also raised buffalo, used occasionally as draft animals but mostly for their milk. Only the Mozdok regiment, though, had a dependable surplus of cattle and sheep, which they sold at local trade fairs or drove north to Russia. The Volga regiment also raised a surplus of sheep. The Cossacks relied on Kalmyk and Tatar breeds of cattle, horses, and sheep, in addition to Kabardian and Circassian horses.[32]

Besides labor power, the greatest constraint on animal husbandry was the availability of pasture and meadowland. The Mozdok regiment succeeded so well because of its proximity to the rich Mozdok steppe, and because they had about 2,000 Kalmyks enrolled in the regiment (as of 1840). The later, with their limited service requirements, were left to tend their animals in the steppe; in the mid-nineteenth century, they drove up to 8,000 head of livestock a year to the local trade fairs.[33]

In the other regiments, Cossack husbandry suffered from a shortage of pasture and hay. Historians and contemporaries have criticized Cossacks for letting their animals fend for themselves in the steppe and not cutting hay to feed them in the winter or during drought. Given the extreme labor shortage, the free-range method made the most sense. But it did have its drawbacks. In the northeast Caucasus, where the steppe was arid, and where there was competition with Nogai and Kalmyk animals, livestock had a poor feed base. The grass was so scarce that Kizliar residents sometimes had to mix hay with reeds and pasture sheep on the grass roofs of their houses; the Greben Cossacks were known to feed their livestock the roofs of their outbuildings. Occasionally a severe winter caused the mass death of free-ranging livestock.[34]

Specializing in livestock might have made sense given the frequent fighting in the Cossack lands. As John McNeill has pointed out in his environmental history of the Mediterranean mountains:

> Chronic warfare and brigandage improved the logic of producing goods that were easily transported and easily hidden, and of crops that need not be harvested at any particular time. Thus the rise of popular wars helped spread reliance on livestock and potatoes and discouraged wheat, tree crops, and most cash crops. Seminomadic transhumance, for instance, had two signal advantages in conditions of insecurity. It encouraged people to store their wealth in highly mobile forms, and gave them two places to call home.

That, in fact, is exactly how the Chechens ran their economies: they specialized in maize and sheep. The latter, besides being easily movable, were less particular about food than cattle and could be hidden in ravines or mountains.[35]

The Terek Cossacks did not grow much corn or potatoes, and faced rustlers to the north and the south. If Cossacks pastured their animals too close to their enemies south of the Terek, they risked raids of the mountain people; those stanitsas of the upper Terek that were furthest away from the steppe suffered mostly from these mountain raids. If Cossacks left their animals untended in the steppe, they risked raiding by Nogai rustlers; the Greben regiment suffered the most from the attacks of Nogais. Even more insurmountable for the would-be cattle baron, or simply the ordinary Cossack rancher looking for pasture, was the competition of the Nogais, who had hundreds of thousands of heads of livestock in the steppe, and held limited service obligations, mostly the upkeep of post stations.[36]

For all of these reasons, Terek Cossacks never developed steppe ranching to the degree that Nogais, Kalmyks, or the Black Sea Cossacks (later renamed the Kuban Cossacks) did. In 1849, the Cossacks of the Line had only 271 steppe farmsteads, compared to the 2,548 of the Black Sea regiment. Most of those 117 farmsteads of the Terek Cossacks in 1851 belonged to the Mozdok regiment (sixty-seven).[37]

Although not all Cossacks lived in poverty, we must conclude that their part in the economic colonization of the North Caucasus was a complete failure. In fact, Terek Cossacks depended on others: on state peasants for grain and on mountain people for plants, animals, skilled and unskilled labor, and as we will see in Chapter 6, weapons, clothing, and food. Their rice came from Persia, their wheat from Derbent and the Kuban, their grapevines from Dagestan, their horses from Kabarda, their sheep and cattle from the Nogais and Kalmyks, who worked as their herders and breeders. In that other great frontier of the Russian empire, Siberia, Cossacks could make good by extracting furs from their native neighbors. In the North Caucasus Cossacks did not extract, they gratefully received: trade goods, plant and animal culture, skilled and unskilled labor power, and the products of local manufacture.

As we have seen, the economic difficulties of the Cossacks stemmed from their poor land, labor shortage, and state policy that encouraged Armenian and Nogai competition and siphoned off viticulture profits with excises. And many Cossack were poor, especially Cossacks of the lower Terek as their traditional bases of livelihood withered in the nineteenth century. According to the commander of the Greben regiment in 1839, his Cossacks were so poor that most of them did not own work animals and one plow was shared per ten households. A Cossack N.C.O. from the Kizliar regiment said that they also used "a common plow." The ataman of the Caucasus Military Line host reported in 1838 that even his officers often had such a poor domestic economy that they could not afford to hire workers; the families usually carried out all of the field and house work themselves. Cossack villages of the better-off regiments could be rendered destitute overnight: after a fire destroyed one-third of Zheleznovodsk of the Volga regiment, it became one of the poorest spots in the North Caucasus, "a haunt for sufferers," as *Kavkaz* described it in 1856. A Moscow merchant who was taking the mineral waters there was so moved by the poverty that he began a charity drive among his colleagues to rebuild their church and help out the poor Cossacks.[38]

Most troubling for the imperial mission, though, were the persistent reports that Terek Cossacks could not equip themselves. The commander of the Greben regiment noticed in 1839 that some of his Cossacks did not own horses. In 1844, the ataman of the Line host reported to the commander of the Line host Gurko that the situation was even worse: Cossacks of the Greben, Mountain, Mozdok, and Semeino-Kizliar regiments were so poor that they could not provide their own arms or horses, or feed their families.[39]

Finally, after an inspection of the host in 1855 revealed that many Cossacks lacked horses and arms, the host commander ordered a full review of fighting readiness. The results were surprising. More than 50 percent of the active-duty Cossacks in all of the regiments had no horse (except for the Sixth brigade, where 48 percent were horseless). The First Sunzha and Greben regiments were the worst—74 percent were without horses in the former, 79 percent in the later. The commander of the First Sunzha regiment appended a note to his report explaining that his Cossacks were so poor that they simply did not have the means to purchase horses. Their harvest failed regularly, and their sickly domestic economy was based on their one "trade"—hauling state provisions. This was an alarming deficiency that undermined the foundation of cossackdom; as Cossacks were wont to say, "A Cossack without a horse is like a soldier without a gun."[40]

Unfortunately, these "soldiers" also lacked guns—in most of the regiments the number of active-duty Cossacks who were poorly armed or without arms ranged from 36 to 56 percent. The solution that the host chief of staff recommended was to direct Cossacks to purchase more horses and weapons from mountain traders! That, as we shall presently see, was what Terek Cossacks had always done.[41]

There is no more powerful symbol of the gaps in the Cossack economy—and in the Russian empire—than these horseless, weaponless Cossacks forced to turn to their mountain "enemies" for their most important equipment. The Cossack system was reasonably good at populating the military border; the privileges of the estate pulled many people into Cossack service. At the same time, the Cossack system had a weak foundation on a frontier such as the North Caucasus, where fighting was endemic and economic opportunity often scarce. In the economic balance of power, they were outgunned by their mountain neighbors.

Notes

1. B. P. Berozov, *Istoricheskie etiudy (iz istorii vozniknoveniia Osetinskikh sel i kazach'ikh stanits)* (Vladikavkaz: Izdatel'stvo Severo-Osetinskogo gosudarstvennogo universiteta im. K. L. Khetagurova, 1992), 19-22.

2. A. P. Thornton, "Jekyll and Hyde in the Colonies," *International Journal* 20 (1965): 226-27; G. A. Dzagurov, *Osetinskie (Digorskie) narodnye izrecheniia* (Moscow: Glavnaia redaktsiia vostochnoi literatury, 1980), 67.

3. V. M. Kabuzan, *Izmeneniia v razmeshchenii naseleniia Rossii v XVIII-pervoi polovine XIX v.* (Moscow: Nauka, 1971), 167-70.

4. Iosif Debu, *O Kavkazskoi linii i prisoedinennom k nei Chernomorskom voiske* (St. Petersburg: Tipografiia Karla Kraiia, 1829), 342-43; N. P. Gritsenko, *Sotsial'no-ekonomicheskoe razvitie priterechnykh raionov v XVIII-pervoi polovine XIX vv.* (Groznyi: Izdatel'stvo gazety "Groznenskii rabochii," 1961), 32-33, 85-87; A. V. Fadeev, *Ocherki ekonomicheskogo razvitiia stepnogo predkavkaz'ia v doreformennyi period* (Moscow: Izdatel'stvo Akademii nauk SSSR, 1957), 146.

5. I. D. Popko, *Terskie kazaki so starodavnikh vremen* (St. Petersburg: Tipografiia Departamenta udelov, 1880), 70-73; Rossiiskii Gosudarstvennyi Voenno-Istoricheskii Arkhiv [RGVIA], f. 1058, op. 1, d. 380, ll. 234-35.

6. Popko, *Terskie kazaki*, 299-301, 426-28, 449-55; Fadeev, *Ocherki ekonomicheskogo razvitiia*, 146-47.

7. Popko, *Terskie kazaki*, 449-55.

8. Iu. Shidlovskii, "Zapiski o Kizliare," *Zhurnal Ministerstva vnutrennykh del*, no. 4 (1843): 179-81; A. I. Akhverdov, "Opisanie Dagestana. 1804 g.," in M. O. Kosven and Kh-M. Khashaev, eds., *Istoriia, geografiia i etnografiia Dagestana XVIII-XIX vv.* (Moscow: Izdatel'stvo vostochnoi literatury, 1958), 213; *Polnoe sobranie zakonov Rossiiskoi imperii s 1649 goda* [hereafter *PSZ*] (St. Petersburg: Tipografiia II otdeleniia sobstvennoi Ego Imperatorskago Velichestva kantseliariii, 1839-1843), 28: 245; V. S. Shamrai, "Istoricheskaia spravka k voprosu o iasyriakh na Severnom Kavkaze i v Kubanskoi oblasti i dokumenty otnosiashchietsia k etomu voprosu," *Kubanskii sbornik* 12 (1907): 169-73; Popko, *Terskie*

kazaki, 32-33, 229-301, 321, 426-28; *Akty sobrannye Kavkazskoi arkheograficheskoi komissieiu [AKAK]* (Tiflis: Tipografiia Kantseliarii glavnonachal'stvuiushchego grazhdanskoi chast'iu na Kavkaze, 1875), 6: part 2, 445-46.

I have also come across evidence of free Cossacks falling into indentured servitude. In the late 1840s, a Cossack of the Mozdok regiment bound himself to the noble P. I. Shalikova for three years in exchange for her promise to free a serf he wanted to marry. In 1813, Cossack elders of Chervlennaia took 900 ruble banknotes from Cossack Fillip Fediushkin for stanitsa needs and awarded him a retired Cossack to work until the loan was repaid. Since both of these incidents came to light only because of conflicts, we must assume that there were other such cases where everything worked out smoothly. See N. Samarin, "Dorozhnyia zametki," *Severnaia pchela,* no. 134 (1862): 555; G. A. Tkachёv, *Stanitsa Chervlennaia. Istoricheskii ocherk* (Vladikavkaz: Elektropechatnia tipografii Terskago oblastnago pravleniia, 1912), 17-18.

9. *PSZ,* 10: 421-24.

10. I. L. Omel'chenko, *Terskoe kazachestvo* (Vladikavkaz: Ir, 1991), 94-95; RGVIA, f. 1058, op. 1, d. 325, ll. 32-33; f. 1058, op. 1, d. 539, ll. 2, 9-10, 29-35, 37-39.

11. "Istoricheskiia svedeniia o Grebenskom kazach'em polku," *Sbornik Obshchestva liubitelei kazach'ei stariny,* no. 4 (1912): 27; Fadeev, *Ocherki ekonomicheskogo razvitiia,* 156; RGVIA, f. 1058, op. 1, d. 360, ll. 105, 168, 196-97; f. 1058, op. 2, d. 512, l. 49; f. 1058, op. 2, d. 512a, ll. 54-55; f. 1058, op. 2, d. 1139a, ll. 1-4; "Materialy dlia statistiki Kizliarskago polka Terskago kazach'iago voiska," *Voennyi sbornik,* no. 12 (1869): 229-30; F. Ponomarёv, "O zemledel'cheskikh zaniatiiakh zhitelei Kizliarskago kazach'iago polka," *Zapiski Kavkazskago obshchestva sel'skago khoziaistva* 15, no. 4 (1869): 130-34; P. Dziubenko, "Vinodelie na Kavkaze," *Russkaia mysl'* 7, no. 8 (1886): section 2, 115-16.

12. A. V...v, "Kratkii ocherk Stavropol'skii gubernii v promyshlennom i torgovom otnosheniiakh," *Kavkaz,* 22 May 1848, 82-84; B. A. Kaloev, "Iz istorii Russko-Chechenskikh ekonomicheskikh i kul'turnykh sviazei," *Sovetskaia etnografiia,* no. 1 (1961): 44; V. I. Abaev, *Istoriko-etimologicheskii slovar' Osetinskogo iazyka* (Leningrad: Nauka, 1973), 2: 273-74. In Finland also in the early nineteenth century, *kasakka* meant, according to Keith Bosley, "an itinerant worker, popularly supposed to be of Cossack origin." See *The Kanteletar,* trans. Keith Bosley (Oxford: Oxford University Press, 1992), 182.

13. Gritsenko, *Sotsial'no-ekonomicheskoe razvitie,* 80-83; Dziubenko, "Vinodelie na Kavkaze," 115-16; Steven, "Kratkaia vypiska iz puteshestviia g. kollezhskago sovetnika Stevena po Kavkazskomu kraiu v 1810 godu," *Severnaia pchela,* no. 59 (1811): n.p.; Z. Sosiev, "Stanitsa Chernoiarskaia," *Terskii sbornik,* no. 5 (1903): 64-66; I. Slivitskii, "Ocherk Kavkaza i Zakavkaz'ia. Bugry," *Kavkaz,* 18 September 1848, 145-47; RGVIA, f. 1058, op. 1, d. 407, ll. 47, 183-84, 264-65.

14. Fadeev, *Ocherki ekonomicheskogo razvitiia,* 168-69, 188-91; A. L. Narochnitskii, ed., *Istoriia narodov Severnogo Kavkaza (konets XVIII v.-1917 g.)* (Moscow: Nauka, 1988), 76; Gritsenko, *Sotsial'no-ekonomicheskoe razvitie,* 80-83; Rossiiskii Gosudarstvennyi Istoricheskii Arkhiv [RGIA], f. 1268, op. 5, d. 356, l. 21.

15. Shidlovskii, "Zapiski o Kizliare," 174-75.

16. *AKAK* (Tiflis: Tipografiia Kantseliarii glavnonachal'stvuiushchego grazhdanskoi chast'iu na Kavkaze, 1870), 4: 334-35.

17. For more on these seasonal workers from the mountains, see RGIA, f. 1268, op. 1,

d. 424, ll. 24, 67; Steven, "Kratkaia vypiska," n.p.; A. [M.] Pavlov, *O aziiatskikh narodakh, obitaiushchikh v iuzhnoi Rossii* (St. Petersburg: Tipografiia Kh. Gintsa, 1841), 27; M, "Tatarskoe plemia na Kavkaze," *Kavkaz*, 19 November 1859, 509-10.

18. "Statisticheskie svedeniia o Kavkazskoi oblasti i Zemle voiska Chernomorskago," *Zhurnal Ministerstva vnutrennykh del* 2, no. 3 (1830): 183-206; 3, no. 4 (1830): 123-30; Gritsenko, *Sotsial'no-ekonomicheskoe razvitie*, 42-44; A. P. Pronshtein, ed., *Don i stepnoe Predkavkaz'e XVIII-pervaia polovina XIX v.* (Rostov-on-Don: Izdatel'stvo Rostovskogo universiteta, 1977), 114-15; Voiskovoe khoziaistvennoe pravlenie, *Statisticheskiia monografii po izsledovaniiu stanichnago byta Terskago kazach'iago voiska* (Vladikavkaz: Tipografiia Terskago oblastnago pravleniia, 1881), 232-34; Debu, *O Kavkazskoi linii*, 23-26; I. V. Rovinskii, "Khoziaistvennoe opisanie Astrakhanskoi i Kavkazskoi gubernii," *Trudy Stavropol'skoi uchenoi arkhivnoi komissii*, no. 2 (1910): section 4, 41-42, 58

19. Gritsenko, *Sotsial'no-ekonomicheskoe razvitie*, 42-44; V...v, "Kratkii ocherk Stavropol'skii gubernii," 15 May 1848, 79-80; 5 June 1848, 90-92; P. Stepanov, "Beglye ocherki Kabardy," *Kavkaz*, 19 October 1861, 442-44; P. Gulebiakin, "Grebentsy" in A. Rzhevuskii, ed., *Tertsy. Sbornik istoricheskikh, bytovykh i geografichesko-statisticheskikh svedenii* (Vladikavkaz: Tipografiia Oblastnago pravleniia Terskoi oblasti, 1888), 238-39; "Vzgliad na Kavkazskuiu liniiu," *Severnyi arkhiv*, no. 2 (1822): 181; Vladimir Dal', *Tolkovyi slovar' zhivogo velikorusskogo iazyka* (Moscow: Izdatel'skaia gruppa "Progress," "Univers," 1994), 1: 973.

20. RGIA, f. 1268, op. 2, d. 887, l. 66; op. 3, d. 275, l. 54; op. 4, d. 308, l. 76; V...v, "Kratkii ocherk Stavropol'skii gubernii," 22 May 1848, 82-84; P. A. Shatskii, "Izmeneniia struktury posevnykh ploshchadei predkavkaz'ia na protiazhenii XIX veka," *Istoriia gorskikh i kochevnykh narodov Severnogo Kavkaza*, no. 3: (1978): 87; Fadeev, *Ocherki ekonomicheskogo razvitiia*, 160.

21. P. Nitsik, "Byvshiia voennyia poseleniia na voenno-gruzinskoi doroge," in Rzhevuskii, *Tertsy*, 62-63; Kulebiakin, "Grebentsy," 238-39; I. Shabanov, "Predokhranitel'nyia mery, prinimaemyia protiv razlivov Tereka," *Kavkaz*, 28 March 1863, 155-58; William Cronon, *Nature's Metropolis: Chicago and the Great West* (New York and London: W. W. Norton, 1991), 100; V...v, "Kratkii ocherk Stavropol'skii gubernii," 82-84; Gritsenko, *Sotsial'no-ekonomicheskoe razvitie*, 37-40; I. Debu, "O nachal'nom ustanovlenii i rasprostranenii Kavkazskoi linii," *Otechestvennyia zapiski* 18, no. 48 (1824): 286-88; K. Samoilov, "Zametki o Chechne," *Panteon* 23, no. 10 (1855): section 3, 45-46; B. A. Kaloev, "Zemledelie u gorskikh narodov Severnogo Kavkaza," *Sovetskaia etnografiia*, no. 3 (1973): 50-51; Voiskovoe khoziaistvennoe pravlenie, *Statisticheskiia monografii*, 237-40; Stepanov, "Beglye ocherki Kabardy," 442-44; Iu. Zagorskii, "Vosem' mesiatsev v plenu u gortsev," *Kavkazskii sbornik* 19 (1898): 231; RGVIA, f. 1058, op. 2, d. 1150, l. 86.
The agronomist Geevskii tried to promote the use of maize in Russia in 1864, pointing to its great success in the Caucasus. Maize did not become a major crop in Russia until the twentieth century. V. Geevskii, *Vozdelyvanie i upotreblenie kukuruzy* (Tiflis: Tipografiia Glavnago upravleniia namestnika Kavkazskago, 1864), 2-4.

22. Stepanov, "Beglye ocherki Kabardy," 442-44; S. D. Nechaev, "Otryvki iz putevykh zapisok o Iugo-vostochnoi Rossii," *Moskovskii telegraf*, no. 7 (1826): section 1, 40-41; "Statisticheskiia svedeniia o Kavkazskoi oblasti," 3, no. 4 (1830): 126.

23. Popko, *Terskie kazaki*, 212-14, 360-62; "Materialy dlia statistiki Kizliarskago polka," 228-32; RGVIA, f. 1058, op. 1, d. 346, l. 67; op. 1, d. 360, ll. 1-2; op. 1, d. 359, ll.

21, 32, 36, 54, 57, 59, 79-81, 104, 122, 133-34, 148, 192, 199; Nechaev, "Otryvki iz putevykh zapisok," 40-41.

24. Stepanov, "Beglye ocherki Kabardy," 442-44; Berozov, *Istoricheskie etiudy*, 19; F. P. Ponomarëv, "Materialy po istorii Terskago kazach'iago voiska. 2-i Malorossiiskii polk," *Terskii sbornik*, no. 6 (1904): 149-52, 168-89, 218-19; Nitsik, "Byvshiia voennyia poseleniia," 52, 60-61. On the agriculture of this regiment, see also Voiskovoe khoziaistvennoe pravlenie, *Statisticheskiia monografii*, 138-58, 417-24; Sosiev, "Stanitsa Chernoiarskaia," 64-69.

25. G. N. Prozritelev, "Pervyia Russkiia poseleniia na Severnom Kavkaze i v nyneshnei Stavropol'skoi gubernii," *Trudy Stavropol'skoi arkhivnoi komissii*, no. 5 (1913): section 1, 13; V...v, "Kratkii ocherk Stavropol'skii gubernii," 15 May 1848, 79-80; I. Bentkovskii, "Byvshee Kavkazskoe lineinoe kazach'e voisko i ego nakaznye atamany (1832-1860 g.)," *Kubanskiia vedomosti*, 26 January 1891, unofficial section, 1-2; RGIA, f. 1268, op. 4, d. 308, ll. 27, 32; op. 5, d. 356, l. 23; I. S. Efimovyi, "O sovremennom sostoianii torgovli v gorode Stavropole," *Kavkaz*, 16 August 1852, 196-97; RGVIA, f. 1058, op. 1, d. 277, l. 1; Shatskii, "Izmeneniia struktury," 87.

26. *Akty istoricheskie, sobrannye i izdannye Arkheograficheskoiu komissieiu* 4 (1842): 177-79; Popko, *Terskie kazaki*, 65-66, 116-17; N. P. Gritsenko, *Goroda severo-vostochnogo Kavkaza i proizvoditel'nye sily kraia V-seredina XIX veka* (Rostov-on-Don: Izdatel'stvo Rostovskogo universiteta, 1984), 96-98; "O vinodelii v Rossii," *Zhurnal Ministerstva vnutrennykh del* 3, no. 4 (1839): 107-22.

27. *Akty istoricheskie*, 177-79; "Zametki k istorii vinodeliia i vinogradarstva v Kizliare," *Trudy Kavkazskago obshchestva sel'skago khoziaistva* 30, no. 4 (1885): 329-36; 30, no. 5 (1885): 349-58; Pronshtein, *Don i stepnoe Predkavkaz'e*, 119; Gritsenko, *Goroda severovostochnogo Kavkaza*, 96-98; A. I. Deichman, "Neskol'ko slov o Kavkaze v sel'skokhoziaistvennom otnoshenii," *Zapiski Kavkazskago obshchestva sel'skago khoziaistva* 2 (1856): 45-49; "O vinodelii," 107-22; Kh. I. K, "Khoziaistvennyia zametki," *Kavkaz*, 18 January 1850, 18-20.

28. "Zametki k istorii vinodeliia," no. 4 (1885): 329-36; P. G. Butkov, *Materialy dlia novoi istorii Kavkaza s 1722 po 1803 god* (St. Petersburg: Tipografiia Imperatorskoi akademii nauk, 1869), 1: 97-101; Popko, *Terskie kazaki*, 175-77, 443-48; "Vzgliad na Kavkazskuiu liniiu," *Severnyi arkhiv*, no. 2 (1822): 181-82; "Istoricheskiia svedeniia o Grebenskom kazach'em polku," 51-54; Gritsenko, *Sotsial'no-ekonomicheskoe razvitie*, 49-53.

29. Gritsenko, *Goroda severo-vostochnogo Kavkaza*, 96-98; Popko, *Terskie kazaki*, 175-77; Rovinskii, "Khoziaistvennoe opisanie," 60-61.

30. Samarin, "Dorozhnyia zametki," 638; Popko, *Terskie kazaki*, 309-11, 443-46; Debu, *O Kavkazskoi linii*, 54-59; Platon Zubov, *Kartina Kavkazskago kraia prinadlezhashchago Rossii* (St. Petersburg: Tipografiia Konrada Vingebera, 1834), 122-25; Dziubenko, "Vinodelie," 115-21; "Statisticheskiia izvestiia o Kavkazskoi oblasti i Zemle voiska Chernomorskago," *Zhurnal Ministerstva vnutrennykh del* 3, no. 5 (1830): 111-17; Gritsenko, *Sotsial'no-ekonomicheskoe razvitie*, 51-53; RGIA, f. 1268, op. 1, d. 839 a, ll. 44-46; "Istoricheskiia svedeniia o Grebenskom kazach'em polku," 33-34; RGVIA, f. 1058, op. 1, d. 350 ll. 2-4; d. 457, l. 228.

31. Gritsenko, *Sotsial'no-ekonomicheskoe razvitie*, 49-53; "Zametki k istorii vinodeliia," 30, no. 5 (1885): 349-54; Debu, "O nachal'nom ustanovlenii," 278-79, 290-93; Gritsenko, *Goroda severo-vostochnogo Kavkaza*, 96-98; Deichman, "Neskol'ko slov o Kavkaze," 45-

49; "Neskol'ko slov o nastoiashchem polozhenii Grebenskikh kazakov," *Terskiia vedomosti*, 10 June 1868, 94; S. P. P. V., "Vinogradnyia zavedeniia v Kizliare," *Kavkaz*, 12 October 1846, 164.

32. "Statisticheskiia svedeniia o Kavkazskoi oblasti," 3, no. 4 (1830): 131-48; "Statisticheskiia svedeniia o Kavkazskoi oblasti i zemle voiska Chernomorskago," *Zhurnal Ministerstva vnutrennykh del* 2, no. 3 (1830): 193; 3, no. 4 (1830): 133, 141; RGIA, f. 1268, op. 1, d. 839a, ll. 43-44.

33. "Statisticheskiia svedeniia o Kavkazskoi oblasti," 3, no. 4 (1830): 131-48; P. Iudin, "Mozdokskie Kalmyki," *Zapiski Terskago obshchestva liubitelei kazach'ei stariny*, no. 12 (1914): 29-31.

34. Samarin, "Dorozhnyia zametki," 555; Popko, *Terskie kazaki*, 173; RGIA, f. 1268, op. 4, d. 308, ll. 16-17; Gritsenko, *Sotsial'no-ekonomicheskoe razvitie*, 44-47; Shidlovskii, "Zapiski o Kizliare," 171-73; "Neskol'ko slov o nastoiashchem polozhenii," 94; F. Ponomarëv, "Materialy dlia istorii Terskago kazach'iago voiska s 1559 po 1880 god," *Voennyi sbornik* 23, no. 10 (1880): 364-65. The 1844-1845 winter was especially severe. See Pronshtein, *Don i stepnoe Predkavkaz'e*, 125; A. F. Rebrov, "Zima 1844-1845 goda na stepiakh pri-Kumskikh na Kavkaze," *Zhurnal sel'skago khoziaistva i ovtsevodstva*, no. 3 (1845): 287-92.

35. John P. McNeill, *The Mountains of the Mediterranean World* (Cambridge: Cambridge University Press, 1992), 270; Gritsenko, *Sotsial'no-ekonomicheskoe razvitie*, 45.

36. A. Sosiev, "Stanitsa Ekaterinogradskaia. Istoriko-statisticheskii ocherk," *Terskii sbornik*, no. 5 (1903): 16-24; Debu, *O Kavkazskoi linii*, 54-63, 66-68; Popko, *Terskie kazaki*, 173; Debu, "O nachal'nom ustanovlenii," 286-88; "Istoricheskiia svedeniia o Grebenskom kazach'em polku," 33-34; Andrei [M.] Pavlov, *O Nogaitsakh kochuiushchikh po Kizliarskoi stepi* (St. Petersburg: Tipografiia vneshnei torgovli, 1842), 14-17, 25-26; Deichman, "Neskol'ko slov o Kavkaze," 93-95.

Old Believer Cossacks of the Kizliar regiment did not grow potatoes because their leaves resembled tobacco. Their botanical instinct was correct; both are members of the *Solanaceae* family. Others had to forego potatoes because their land was too wet or too dry. "Materialy dlia statistiki Kizliarskago polka," 230-32.

37. Fadeev, *Ocherki ekonomicheskogo razvitiia*, 151; S. A. Chekmenev, ed., *Nekotorye voprosy sotsial'no-ekonomicheskogo razvitiia iugo-vostochnoi Rossii* (Stavropol': Stavropol'skii gosudarstvennyi pedagogicheskii institut, 1970), 8-9; RGVIA f. 1048, op. 1, d. 452, ll. 19, 35, 72, 127, 183, 211, 231.

38. Popko, *Terskie kazaki*, 199-200, 256-57; "Istoricheskiia svedeniia o Grebenskom kazach'em polku," 51-54; Kulebiakin, "Grebentsy," 235-36; "Materialy dlia statistiki Kizliarskago polka," 228-30; *Kavkaz*, 16 August 1856, 256. On Cossack poverty, see also V...v, "Kratkii ocherk Stavropol'skii gubernii," 82-84; Petr Egorov, "Dorozhnyia zapiski o Kavkaze i Severnom Dagestane, 1851 goda," *Russkii invalid*, no. 177 (1851): 733-35; "Vospominaniia o Grebenskikh kazakov i Kavkazskoi linii," *Kavkaz*, 7 October 1856, 316-17; "Neskol'ko slov o nastoiashchem polozhenii," 94.

39. "Istoricheskiia svedeniia o Grebenskom kazach'em polku," 34-35; Popko, *Terskie kazaki*, 212-14, 360-62.

40. RGVIA, f. 1058, op. 2, d. 512, ll. 13-36; Vladimir Dal', *Tolkovyi slovar' zhivogo velikorusskogo iazyka* (St. Petersburg, Moscow: T-va M. O. Volf, 1905; repr., Moscow:

Izdatel'skaia gruppa "Progress" "Univers," 1994), 2: 176.
    41. RGVIA, f. 1058, op. 2, d. 512, ll. 13-36.

6

Crossing Boundaries: The Trading Frontiers

And really, the Caucasian mountain man, wild and ignorant, shut up in his godforsaken hole, has come to his intelligence only by necessity, so that the skills that he learns in his godforsaken, out-of-the-way house are all that he needs. And no one taught him these, no one gave him examples to follow: from the most thankless areas and from the crudest raw materials he is able to extract for himself that which we obtain only after long investigations entailing great expenditure and after working long hours in factories costing tens of thousands of rubles.

—Iu. Zagorskii, *Kavkazskii sbornik,* 1898

At the trade fair, all are equal and free: an Abazian with a torn cherkeska *shoves an official; a Cossack steps on your foot and swears his heart out for all to hear.*

—*Kavkaz,* 15 May 1848

In the mid-nineteenth century, the Greben Cossacks of the North Caucasus told a story about the origin of Cossack-Chechen enmity two centuries earlier. According to this account, in the early days after the Grebentsy had resettled from the mountains south of the Terek River to the Russian side on the left bank, a specialization of economic functions developed between the Chechens of the mountains and the Cossacks, recently of the valley. The Chechens continued to live off of plunder, attacking villages and travelers as they always had, but now they exchanged their booty with a rich Cossack, Batyrev, who then sold it at Astrakhan for a nice profit. In one plunder exchange Batyrev received an expensive gun, which he decided to keep for himself. When the original owner, a Chechen, spotted the gun and tried to buy it back, Batyrev refused to part with his keepsake; some time later he and his brothers were attacked by the same Chechen and his comrades, the gun was stolen, and all the Batyrevs were killed. Thus began, the story goes, the centuries of hatred, raiding, and killing between Chechen and Cossack across the Terek River and from then on, the Cossacks obtained their booty by attacking their erstwhile colleagues.[1]

It was a popular type of story in the North Caucasus—a successful bandit enterprise falling out over stolen goods, violence, and vendetta. Like most folk memories, there was a fair element of truth and also considerable distortion in this summation of Cossack-Chechen relations. The Cossacks of the North Caucasus did take part in the economy of plunder, but this by no means came to an end in the eighteenth century. The resettling of the Greben Cossacks to the Russian side was an important turning point, but as much because of their new difficulties with the Russian state as any developing animosity towards their old neighbors to the south. And the trade relations between the Cossacks of the Terek and the peoples of the Caucasus mountains did not diminish, but were vital to the Cossack economy into the nineteenth century, even during the period of the most intense warfare of Russian against Chechen. Trade was as important a frontier encounter as was war, and at times war was indirectly dependent upon trade.

The focus in this chapter is on what Daniel H. Usner, Jr. has called "frontier exchange": "networks of cross-cultural interaction through which native and colonial groups circulated goods and services," including "small-scale production, face-to-face marketing, and prosaic features of livelihood."[2] Such processes may appear insignificant from the vantage point of the center; for those at the frontier, they were the foundation of regional economy and shared culture. Frontier exchange is, of course, vital for the livelihood of settlers (and conquerors) on all frontiers and helps to structure native-colonist relationship and dependencies. Russian history and the history of the North Caucasus have focused on what frontier exchange evolved into, in Soviet terms "the drawing of the North Caucasus into the all-Russian market," and not what it meant for regional society, economy, and culture.[3]

The Russian settlement and building of new communities in the North Caucasus created powerful economic demands and opportunities. Cossacks lived at the extremity of the Russian economy, making it difficult and expensive to transport food and other necessities to the Terek River. And besides, Cossacks were supposed to live locally, so to speak, and provide for themselves with the goods at hand. So this growing Cossack community turned to the south with voracious demands and created new markets where mountain people could sell their handicrafts and ply their trades. An examination of local trade reveals not just that Cossacks helped to transform the local economy with many peddlers and merchants continually crisscrossing the military border, but that the goods flowing north from the mountains were essential to the Cossack communities and structured their material culture in many ways. And no matter how many barriers of customs control were erected, and how many disruptions of war, this trade persisted.

To understand Terek Cossack trade in the eighteenth and nineteenth centuries, we must first sketch out an earlier backdrop. The Russian forts and Cossack stanitsas that popped up along the Terek River in the sixteenth and seventeenth centuries were part of the frontier economy of the North Caucasus, an economy that existed in the interstices between three great states (Russia, Persia, and Turkey) and drew nourishment from each, in trade and in plunder. As we have seen, the history of the Terek Cossacks before the eighteenth century is sketchy, but it is clear that they, like most of the peoples of the North Caucasus, supplemented their existence in a less-than-bountiful mountain terrain through thieving and trading. The richest targets for the Cossacks were the Persian merchants sailing to and from Astrakhan, the traders traveling the Caspian coastal road, and the towns along the same. The Cossack pirates of the Caspian were the scourge of Persian merchants; they became so aggressive that Persian traders quit sailing the Caspian for a few years sometime before 1650 and again after 1668 when Stenka Razin and his gang—some of whom were Terek Cossacks—began their Caspian raids.[4] As late as 1737 the Persian consul in St. Petersburg complained of the Russian pirates on the Caspian, operating with some seventy boats from an island base near Baku.[5]

Booty is of limited value without a market—Cossacks or Chechens could only use so much Persian silk or rugs. They had to sell it or trade it for something else and thus the Russian fort town of Terskii Gorod and Astrakhan became important outlets for plundered goods. Petitions from Persian diplomats in the seventeenth century accused the *voevody* of Terskii Gorod and Astrakhan of regularly receiving illicit goods. The Dutch traveler Jan Struys traveled to Terskii Gorod in 1670 where he heard of a prince on the other side of the Terek who habitually gathered an army of 15,000 that went on plundering sprees and then sold the goods at the twice-weekly Terskii Gorod bazaar. The plunder-market nexus was so well established that Astrakhan merchants could put in orders for stolen foreign goods with Terek Cossacks via Russian servitors at Terskii Gorod; they then resold them at relatively low prices at Astrakhan, undercutting the trade of Indian, Bukharan, and Persian merchants there.[6]

It would be wrong, though, to see seventeenth- and early eighteenth-century trade along the Terek as simply a by-product of banditry. The Terek Cossacks made wine and sold it at Terskii Gorod. Even more important, they collected roots of wild madder and sold it to Persian merchants who used it to dye silk and other textiles. According to an Astrakhan tradesman in 1650, Persian ships came by the hundreds to buy madder from Terek Cossacks and that "without this grass there would be no dyeing at all in Persia." In the same year, Aleksei Silin of Kazan reported to tsar Aleksei Mikhailovich that people along the Terek "receive large profits" from madder: they sent many boats filled with large bales of the root to Persia and traders from Persia, Gilian, and Bukhara came to the Terek and exchanged their wares for madder. Cossack traders also traveled to Astrakhan to purchase goods such as sackcloth and lead for resale at Terskii Gorod and across the Terek.[7] Pirates, highwaymen, and marauders, but also traders, wine merchants, and wild plant hunters, the Terek Cossacks of the seventeenth century carved out their niche on a violent but potentially lucrative frontier, far from the center of Russian power.

Whereas their remoteness from the center permitted the Cossacks and Terskii Gorod servitors ample opportunity to enjoy the profit of plunder, it also meant they often had a difficult time receiving food and supplies from the homeland. Grain provisions were sent down the Volga, through Astrakhan, and across the Caspian, but this supply line was long and tenuous and if the food did arrive, it was far from sufficient to feed the local population. There was also little progress in establishing a peasant agricultural base until the early nineteenth century (see Chapter 5).

So the settlers often had to trade for grain with the local population, especially if something disrupted the grain shipment from Russia. The *vodevody* of Terskii Gorod referred to the "Circassian" lands as their granary and if there were harvest failures to the south, the Terek settlers often suffered.[8] During the Time of Troubles in the early seventeenth century, provisions from Russia were cut off and residents of Terskii Gorod bought grain from Kabardians, Kumyks, and the towns of Derbent and Gilian; when there was a bad harvest in the Kumyk and "Circassian" lands a few years later in 1614, the Russian settlers had a difficult time of it until the convoy from the north resumed. In 1672 the supply of Kabardian and Kumyk grain to Terskii Gorod was curtailed because of a campaign by the Crimean khan in those lands and only a few were able to go to the Terek to sell their millet, barley, and vegetables. According to the report of a Terek musketeer, prices for barley and millet skyrocketed and "now Russian people on the Terek suffer great hunger," expending everything on food, including their guns. Many left for what they hoped would be greener pastures.[9]

As long as there was a Russian fort on the Terek, some degree of customs regulation and tariff collection was maintained, but trade was loosely controlled and—outside the palisade walls—totally free. With the founding of Kizliar in 1735 and the Kizliar customshouse in 1755 and the enticement of the Cossacks into Russian service, the state moved a little closer and the customs policies of the center began to have an effect on the frontier trade of the North Caucasus. The rhythms of trade and customs control along the Terek were fairly regular for the next century: the government would impose tariffs or try to channel trade through state trading posts, hoping to garner more income for the treasury. Then the Russian settlements—dependent as they were on a free flow of goods from the south—would suffer, as would the native traders, and customs policy would be relaxed for a decade or two until the next round of control began. The local commanders, realizing the dire straits the forts and settlements could be put in with a cessation of trade, sided with the native traders and the Russian subjects, all of whom petitioned for a free flow of necessary goods. Even the Kabardian delegation that went to St. Petersburg in 1764 to request the destruction of the new Russian fort of Mozdok, asked at the same time for reduced trade tariffs at Kizliar.[10]

The food needs of hungry settlers immediately challenged the new tariff regime. The commander of Kizliar A. A. Stupishin reported to the College of Foreign Affairs in 1761 how the residents of Kizliar were always complaining to him about the trade tariffs "because of a lack of crops in Kizliar" and that the duties on the Kumyks' flour, millet, rice, honey, and walnuts "are bringing them to extreme ruin and grief." Central officials feared that reduced tariffs would lead to an outflow of Russian grain to the mountain dwellers whom they assumed to be destitute and hungry. In order to persuade them otherwise, the next commander of Kizliar, N. A. Potapov, in his 1764 project for mountaineer trade privileges, stated emphatically that grain and fruit should be freely traded "because more will be brought here than taken away." In 1765 the government gave in and allowed duty-free trade by Kumyks and Kabardians of food and other necessities, but only in Kizliar. This was an important decision—one official reported that up to the establishment of the quarantine in Kizliar in the early nineteenth century, the bulk of its grain came from the Kumyks. In 1791, the peoples of Dagestan were also freed from customs in Kizliar.[11]

The appearance of the plague in the North Caucasus at the beginning of the nineteenth century made the Russian government much more concerned about regulating the flow of goods and people across the Caucasus Military Line. After it first appeared in a village near Georgievsk in April 1804, the plague spread back and forth across the Terek to Russian forts and Kabardian villages; by the time it had made its way to the Tatar suburbs of Astrakhan in December 1806, the disease had killed at least 802 people in the Caucasus province and many times more in the uncontrolled areas across the Terek. In 1807-1809 quarantine posts and cordons were created along all of the borders of the Caucasus province and fishing along the Terek was prohibited.[12] The subsequent "Statutes on Trade with the Mountain People" issued by the Committee of Ministers in 1810 inaugurated a new level of trade regulation in the North Caucasus.

By the new rules, six trading posts and four salt magazines were established along the military line, through which mountain goods were supposed to pass, after a "cleansing" period that could last a few or up to forty days. At the trading posts, mountain goods were free of tariffs and they could be exchanged there at fixed prices for state salt and, theoretically, grain. There were bona fide health reasons for quarantining imported goods, but an equally powerful motive behind the new trade cordon was to make the people of the mountains dependent upon Russia for salt, which was almost the only Russian good that stocked the bins of trading posts until they were reorganized and their numbers increased in 1846.[13] This was no small matter, since salt—essential for livestock and preserving food—was scarce in the mountains and the Ingush, Ossetians, and Kabardians especially had few other places to turn to.[14]

Of course, Russian trade policy with the mountain people was directly connected to attempts to conquer the region through winning over, subduing, killing, or exiling the native inhabitants. Creating a salt dependency was one such tool. Forts or the central government also issued periodic bans on selling weapons or materials used for making weapons such as iron and steel. By the nineteenth century, there was also a fair amount of scheming about how to draw the mountain people into the Russian orbit peacefully, through an expansion of trade. This resembled Catherine the Great's project for enlightened rule of the empire's natives, which included plans for whetting the appetite of her steppe people for Russian goods, thereby increasing trade and inculcating among the natives "new modes of behavior" appropriate for imperial subjects.[15]

Plans for the Caucasian tribes ranged from the narrow and practical to the visionary. Colonel M. Chaikovskii proposed to get the belligerents to trade in their weapons and metal for grain and salt; the statesman Platon Zubov held out the visionary hope that trade would create new mountaineer demands for European goods and that gradually "their needs could be increased and luxury goods made a necessity" and they would lay down their arms and become good, civilized Europeans. "Luxury," wrote Zubov, "is the first step towards the education of the wild tribes." Most were more restrained in their dreaming, and argued as did the Viceroy of the Caucasus M. S. Vorontsov, "that trade is one of the most important and effective means towards our *sblizhenie* (drawing together) with the mountain people" and sought to use trade to win trust, change tastes, and make the "wild tribes" dependent upon Russia.[16] But ties of dependency are never clear-cut on distant frontiers, situated as they are at the edge of national economy and state power. The *sblizhenie* that policy makers dreamed of never came to be; instead the opposite happened and trade drew the Cossacks into the world of the mountain people, nativized their material culture, and occasionally led them to subvert state policy.

The Cossacks needed frontier trade as much as the mountain people did and were threatened by every attempt to curtail or cut off trans-Terek exchange. Cossacks traded salt, melons, pumpkins, garden vegetables, sackcloth, cast-iron pots, fish, and fish products mostly to Kumyks, Chechens, and Kabardians, for a wide variety of essential goods—livestock, grain, firewood, lumber, and domestically produced wares such as clothes, carts, and weapons. With the tightening of customs control beginning in the eighteenth century, the Cossacks did what they could to continue their free trade across the Terek. As residents of all of the fort towns of the North Caucasus they suffered just like everyone else from the price increases and periodic shortages caused by tariff policies. The situation in the stanitsas along the Terek was somewhat different because of their proximity to the mountain people and distance from Kizliar officials. At first it seems they simply ignored the rules—the Kizliar customshouse reported in 1765 that Cossacks did not collect tariffs in their stanitsas and that an unregulated free trade continued there, with the collusion of their commanding officers.[17] They also tried to get the tariff policy overturned—one of the instructions of the Greben Cossacks for Catherine the Great's Legislative

Commission of 1767-68 requested that the host be allowed its previous tariff-free trade of salted fish to the mountain people for oxcart wheels, clothes, and other domestic wares, and of Kalmyk horses and cattle for Kabardian and other mountain horses.[18]

As open resistance became less possible, Cossacks diverted more of their trade through well-established underground channels. The history of smuggling is difficult to snoop out since the practice was—by definition—largely invisible. And since Cossacks along the line were the ones responsible for interdiction, a conflict of interest was created and many sentries undoubtedly looked the other way as their village-mates tried to keep the goods flowing.

Smuggling was known to be common—S. M. Bronevskii, who served many years in the Caucasus, called it a normal practice and estimated that the value of contraband trade was over twice that of the official trade with the mountain people. Horses were one oft-smuggled good. Before the establishment of the Kizliar customshouse, Cossacks usually bought Kalmyk horses for a low price and then traded them for the much sought-after Kabardian horses, which were more suitable for the mountain terrain. In the face of the new customs, instead of paying the tariffs Cossacks occasionally raided Nogais in the steppe, stole their horses, and then drove them to the other side of the Terek where they bartered for Kabardian breeds. Cossacks slipped their dug-out canoes across the Terek to trade (and steal) during health quarantines. They also built ferries, which they, mountain people, and Armenians used to subvert the customs regulations. According to the assessor of the Kizliar *okrug* court in 1828, trans-Terek people used such ferries nearly every day to bring food, wood, tools, and more to Shchedrinskaia.[19]

According to Shamil's brother-in-law, Shamil's men even managed to smuggle lead, iron, and steel out of Groznyi and other border forts. Archival sources confirm that there were trade relations between Cossacks and their direct enemies. A Cossack deserter who lived with Shamil near Dargo later testified that Dargo was brimming with textiles purchased at Groznyi and Vozdvizhenskaia forts. Someone was also smuggling gunpowder and gun cartridges to people across the military line, but we cannot pin this directly on Cossacks.[20]

Since the government salt monopoly went to the heart of Cossack frontier exchange, it was natural that salt would be a favorite smuggled commodity. Mountain people would cross the line, buy or trade freely for salt, and then sneak back to the mountains avoiding the customs posts, or Cossacks took their own salt provisions across the river themselves. The inspector of one trading post reported that the sale of salt had nearly stopped at seven posts after new Cossack-manned forts had been established further in the interior of Kabarda in the 1820s—Cossacks would simply bring salt from other towns and trade or sell it to mountain people at these non-quarantine settlements. Another inspector recommended in 1839 the cessation of all "impermissible relations" between Cossacks and mountain people, and particularly the trade in salt. Again in 1851, a trading post inspector, reporting on the fall of the state salt trade, wrote that the Cossacks of the Mountain and Volga regiments "supply the Kabardians with it [salt] in quantities of no small importance through sale and trade, and they, being provided abundant supplies of this necessity by the Cossacks, have no great need for state salt." He went on, "I have no power to cut off this abuse." Finally in 1855, the state finally gave in a bit—in that year the Bureau of Salt Farming allowed Cossacks to sell their salt provisions to the Salt Farming storehouse, "but only with the provision that after this measure the Cossack bootlegging (*korchemstvo*) will be absolutely stopped."[21]

The Cossacks also continued to receive mountain goods through the services of Armenian middlemen. These traders had begun settling in the North Caucasus in the eighteenth century, encouraged by the Russian authorities to move from Persia and the Islamic khanates on the Caspian Sea. The Armenians traveled to the mountain villages, bought or traded for the full range of goods, and then carted their stock back across the line to sell to Cossacks and other settlers. The Armenians of the North Caucasus—living in Kizliar, Mozdok, Cossack stanitsas, and their own villages—were especially well suited for this role and came to dominate the region's trade. They were exempted from service and had special tax-free status until 1836, they spoke mountain languages, and often shared a common culture with the mountain communities from which some had only recently emigrated.[22] Armenian traders sold or traded their imports at a dearer price than the going rate across the military line, and this caused resentment with local officials who upbraided them for their "self-interested motives" and periodically cooked up proposals to ban Armenians from mountain trading. But their enterprising spirit was unrivaled and their profits legendary as they hauled north everything from Circassian honey to Chechen oxcarts.[23]

The most important Cossack sources for mountain goods in the nineteenth century were the trade fairs and bazaars in the fort towns and stanitsas, where Armenians traded their stock, and mountaineers frequented to offer their livestock, grain, and homemade wares. The growing market trade along the Caucasus Military Line was the major reason for the failure of the trading posts—despite the distance, quarantines, and the tariffs and entry fees, the mountain people preferred to engage in the free-flowing commerce of market square, where the prices were unregulated and the goods and customers more plentiful. Travelers to the North Caucasus were often surprised to see the throngs of mountain people in the towns and villages, swamping the local population during market days. Iu. Shidlovskii captured the diversity and vitality of the Kizliar bazaar in 1843:

> You see Ossetians selling cheese and *burkas*, Circassians with green honeycombs of wild bees, Lezghins with copper vessels, Kists and Chechens with muskets and

sabres, Karanogais with sheep and goats, Kalmyk sheepskin coats, coltskin coats, and lambskins, Terek Cossacks with weapons and fish. The Kumyks of Kostek bring firewood and stakes for grape vines, those from Aksai spread out leather and sheep's wool, Armenians and Georgians offer you apples, vegetables, and fruits. And there, closer to the Terek, ruddy Cossacks from Dubovskaia, Chervlennaia, Naurskaia, and other stanitsas of the Terek sit on oxcarts loaded with watermelons, melons, cucumbers, beets, cabbage, etc...Camels, rocking Turkmen on their two-humped, well-loaded backs, tower above the crowds.[24]

Mountain people sold and traded their goods at four types of market venues on the Russian side of the Terek: trade fairs held for several days or up to two weeks once or twice a year, baz_ars (usually open two or three times a week), permanent shops, and informal markets that developed at new forts. By 1849 there were forty-nine trade fairs in the Stavropol' (previously, the Caucasus) province and along the Caucasus Military Line, at Cossack stanitsas, fort towns, and state peasant villages. The most popular trade fair, in the town of Georgievsk, drew around 25,000 people at its peak in the 1850s; the most popular Cossack trade fair, in the stanitsa of Naur, drew up to 11,000. All of the towns and many of the stanitsas and peasant villages also had bazaars and shops. There were 302 permanent shops in the 113 stanitsas along the military line in 1849.[25]

Despite the potential for violence at these multiethnic gatherings where there were plenty of weapons and people who were used to killing each other, markets and bazaars were remarkably peaceful, a tribute more to the importance that they held for all sides than to the ability of the Russian guards to keep control. Self-restraint was the order of the day—at the trade fair of Naur stanitsa, it was said that not a single Chechen had ever been observed to rob or swindle; if they committed some other offense, they were not whacked with the whip or the birch rod as were the Russians and Armenians, but simply sat it out in a pit for a day or two. Of the 78,000 mountain people who came to Kizliar between 1848 and 1852 to work or trade, only fourteen were arrested, jailed, or officially deported.[26]

Life across the line was not so peaceful. As we have seen, the Russian campaign begun in the 1820s for conquest of the mountain tribes included the construction of forts south of the Caucasus Military Line. The spread of these forts caused a massive upheaval in Chechen and Kumyk villages: advancing troops destroyed villages, clear-cut forests, burned fields and gardens, killed resisters, and pushed many people further south and further into the mountains. In areas of the northeast Caucasus, local trade was destroyed or disrupted. When general Ermolov built Groznyi in 1817 and the other first forts of the Sunzha Military Line along the Sunzha and Argun Rivers, he wrecked the local grain trade as Kumyks and Chechens fled to the mountains to escape punitive expeditions. But every historical force creates counter-forces, and the thrust of the army produced eddies of trade in its wake. Once a new fort was constructed, Cossacks settled, and troops billeted, spontaneous barter took place which often evolved into informal bazaars called "*satovki*" (from the Turkish word *satma* meaning "sale").

The fort Vozdvizhenskaia was built in 1844 as part of the Sunzha Line on the spot of the former Chechen village of Chakhkeri. At first the small remaining neighboring population was none too eager to have relations with the fort. After a few years, though, the fort population of up to 6,000 (depending on troop movements), demanding food and supplies, was an irresistible lure and Chechens and Kumyks filed through the gates in large numbers bringing food, cattle, clothes, and weapons; dozens of families began to resettle there. The same occurred near other Sunzha Line forts, most of which had small garrisons and modest bazaars, except for when a detachment of troops moved through, and then, wrote S. Ivanov, "crowds of people buying and selling swarm about as in Moscow's *Gostinyi Dvor*." According to one general, from 1834 to 1840 some 40,000 mountain people came to the Sunzha Line annually to trade and sell.[27]

The centuries of trade between mountaineer and Cossack shaped Cossack material culture and domestic economy. Although the Cossacks always blamed the time-consuming service requirements for their agricultural and artisanal failures, there were also economic, ecological, and practical reasons why mountain goods were so popular. Mountain people traded a wide variety of produce, grain, animals and animal products, handicrafts, and raw materials such as furs and wood; we are concerned here with only a few commodities that help illustrate the importance of this trade to the frontier life of the Terek Cossacks.

As has already been indicated, before the mass settlement of state peasants and the development of a broad agricultural base in the North Caucasus in the mid-nineteenth century, Cossacks frequently traded with mountain people for grain. The ecology of the lower Terek made the Cossacks residing there especially dependent upon purchased grain—they could produce a fair grain harvest in some spots, but only after they cut irrigation canals from the Terek, an extremely labor-consuming task. By the mid-eighteenth century, state grain deliveries were dependable, but still insufficient to meet their needs. And the task of conveying their grain salary from the Caspian Sea to their stanitsas was an arduous undertaking for the Cossacks; they often had to hire Nogais to help, paying them half of the load, which in turn fueled the need to purchase more grain. So they turned to Chechens, Kumyks, Kabardians, and other Cossacks for supplemental wheat, millet, and rice. Before they were pushed away, the lowland Chechens supplied wheat, millet, rice, and maize to both Cossacks and the mountain Chechens. The Cossacks of the central Terek (Mozdok, Mountain, and Volga regiments) were, on the other hand, largely grain self-sufficient.[28]

All of the Cossacks raised sheep and cattle in sufficient quantities for their own use. Horse breeding—much more demanding than cattle or sheep husbandry—was a different matter. Some regiments did not raise horses at all or only in small quantities, and had to trade for or purchase mostly Kabardian horses; others had herds large enough for their own use. But for all of the Tertsy, Kabardian horses (renowned for their gentle temperament, lightness, agility, strength, endurance, quick gallop, strong hoofs, and simple diet) were the most desired. So, as P. Kishenskii observed in 1856, "a good Cossack buys his horse in Kabarda."[29]

The Terek Cossacks also traded for and wore the clothes of the mountain people, especially the *papakha* (tall sheepskin hat), *burka* (felt cloak), and *cherkeska* (long, narrow, collarless coat). In fact, they looked so much like the mountain people that local peasants and travelers in the Caucasus often mistook approaching Cossacks for hostile Chechens or Circassians. In 1828 the head of the Caucasus *oblast'* A. A. Vel'iaminov took the drastic step of ordering Cossacks not to come closer than one-half verst (about one-half kilometer) to peasants working in fields since "the Cossacks of the Line wear identical clothes as the mountain people [and] peasants are not able to distinguish enemies from the Cossacks."[30]

Clothes production was one of the oldest and best-established branches of the mountain domestic economy, so there was always an ample supply of these garments, which were well-suited for local conditions. The *burka* protected riders from rain, snow, cold, heat, and wind, and could serve as a ground cover when resting or sleeping, or be propped up as a small tent. With a *burka* on his shoulders, a rider hid his weapons from sight and protected them from the elements, especially important for flintlocks which were useless when wet. *Cherkeska*s protected the legs of riders without hindering movement and mounted sixteen to twenty cartridges on the chest, a handy spot for quick loading. When the Kizliar commander recommended a tariff-free trade of *burka*s and similar handicrafts in 1765, he made sure to mention their military utility.[31]

Wood was another mountain commodity of great importance to the Cossacks. The Terek River region of settlement, at the edge of the steppe and the foot of the mountains, had only a thin belt of accessible forest (see Chapter 4). Although settlers rarely built wooden houses in the early days of Kizliar and Mozdok, wooden construction became more popular and in places the norm by the late eighteenth century. With the growth in the number of forts, stanitsas, and peasant villages, settlers quickly consumed the forests and there came to be an insatiable demand for not just lumber, but also firewood, vineyard stakes, and various wooden tools and other products. This developed into probably the largest-volume trade with the mountain people; each year Kumyks, Chechens, and Kabardians floated hundreds of rafts down the Terek and led thousands of oxcarts full of wood and wood products to Cossack stanitsas and fort towns. When Shamil attempted to ban trade relations among his peoples with Russia, he made sure to single out the trade in wood; his commanders sometimes attacked mountain wood traders.[32]

Deforestation was one reason why Cossacks also quickly adopted the native oxcart (*arba*). It was light and durable, and with only two large wheels, widely spaced apart, could negotiate a variety of terrains. Cossacks hitched up *arba*s not only for domestic work, but also for state service, since they were responsible for much of the carting work in the North Caucasus. Cossack dependency on the mountain people for *arba*s became a matter of state concern when the imposition of tariffs on cross-Terek trade created such a shortage of *arba*s and *arba* wheels in 1771 that Cossacks were no longer able to cart supplies for the army between Kizliar and Mozdok. They explained that their source had been cut off when the tariff walls went up, and that they did not have the time or the forest to produce *arba*s themselves. The affair went to the Senate, which ordered local commanders to force the Cossacks to trade for *arba*s and pay the required tariffs. *Arba* trade continued to be big business for mountain people through the mid-nineteenth century and they also cornered the market on spare parts, such as wheels.[33]

One of the greatest curiosities of the Russian conquest of the North Caucasus is that Cossacks were armed by mountain silversmiths and metalworkers. The Cossack weaponry—*shashka* (sword), *kinzhal* (dagger), and until the mid-nineteenth century the mountain rifle—was manufactured mostly in native villages and obtained through trade. Weapons production was an ancient craft in the North Caucasus, where the secrets of master craftsmen were highly guarded and passed down from father to son; by the nineteenth century some villages had advanced to the point of dividing up the production process with gun "assembly lines." The Russian esteem for North Caucasian weaponry had an equally long lineage: already in the seventeenth century Russian forts were trading for "Circassian" weapons, coats of mail, and head-pieces and the central government was trying to attract North Caucasus armorers to Astrakhan and Moscow to train apprentices. Tatishchev also raved about the guns and other handicrafts of the Dagestanian village of Kubachi in the first volume of his *Russian History*.[34] Through the nineteenth century the majority of the silversmiths, smithies, and metalworkers in the fort towns of the North Caucasus were mountain people; Kabardian masters were even in Cherkassk making guns and swords for the Don Cossacks. This skewed the development of handicraft production north of the military line—Russians and Cossacks did not engage in metal handicrafts, preferring to obtain weapons from mountain people and other metal goods from the north. Cossacks even went to native villages to get their weapons repaired![35]

Cossacks also obtained a host of military and agricultural accessories from the mountain people—saddles and other horse gear, powder horns, holsters, hoes, sickles, scissors, and other tools. It is striking that the Greben Cossack words for ax and spade are Turco-Tatarisms, perhaps because they had long obtained them from mountain traders. They even used a Turco-Tatarism for the verb "to sell" (*satavat'*).[36]

The mountain economy that was able to flood Cossack markets with so many highly valued goods, in the context of often minimal natural resources and the repeated disruptions of war and conquest, was one of great productivity and sophistication. All families produced handicrafts, and the women—the main producers of textiles and clothes—seemed to be continually working. More than one observer noticed how mountain women were always seen with work in their hands, sewing *cherkeskas* or working a spindle even when walking between villages or trading at Cossack fairs. Mountain people engaged in wool, leather, metal, wood, and silk handicrafts; according to a late-nineteenth-century survey they were involved in a total of thirty-two different domestic industries (compared to the North Caucasus Russians' seventeen). Marggraf compared the industriousness of a Dagestanian village to "some suburb of a large industrial center":

> When you wake up in any Dagestanian village, already at dawn you are startled by the continual noise produced by the knock of looms, by the blows of innumerable hammers hitting metal, and by the squeaks of files. Walk out on the roof of the house that substitutes for a balcony here and you see hundreds, even thousands of hearths smoking below, similar to a small factory.[37]

People living in the alpine region (7,200 to 10,800 feet above sea level) were limited mostly to working with wool, and they lived so far from the major markets that they could not afford to cart their wares there. But their products made it to the Russian side also, with the help of Armenian traders and a system of mountain exchange whereby grain, salt, and other necessities moved up from the plains and wool handicrafts worked their way down from the mountains, sometimes through several exchanges. Some peoples or villages specialized in one or two types of products for trade—for example, several Dagestan and Chechen villages specialized in *kinzhals*, *shashkas*, or guns and the mountain Jews were known for their dressed goat skins and the skins of young lambs (used to make *papakhas*). But mountain people also responded to the Russian market and broadened their product mix. In the first quarter of the nineteenth century some forty different mountain items were registered in trading post lists; by the 1840s the list had more than doubled. By 1848, mountain people sold 149 different products at the Amir-Adzhiiurtovskii trading post, which was founded only the year before.[38]

The plunder-market nexus that was so strong in the seventeenth century continued to exist, although it is difficult to calculate how important it was to the local economy. The large herds of cattle and sheep—sometimes thousands of animals—that Terek Cossacks periodically rustled during punitive raids across the Terek must have, in part, made their way to market.[39] On the other side, the Cossacks were convinced that a good amount of the money that

Chechens received for ransoming captives was spent at Russian trade fairs. When N. Samarin visited the stanitsa of Naur, Cossacks told him that Shamil's men, after releasing the captive Georgian princesses Chavchavadze and Orbeliani in 1854, spent all of the 40,000 rubles ransom money at the Nikolaevskaia stanitsa fair, and that 20,000 rubles was pocketed by one Armenian alone. While this story smacks of frontier boasting, it is true that the ransom money that mountain people collected had to find an outlet and that the markets along the Russian line were the most likely destination. According to Alexandre Dumas, who visited the Caucasus in 1858, sometimes the captors skipped a step and simply made a desired commodity, such as tea, part of the ransom.[40]

Mountain captives were also a venerable commodity of exchange along the North Caucasus frontier. As we have seen, mountain people sold slaves and prisoners to Russian subjects at the chattel market of the Kumyk village of Endirei and at Kizliar itself, until this practice was outlawed in the early nineteenth century. As we will see in Chapter 8, Cossacks also trafficked in Chechen bodies; some even went bounty hunting for "Circassians," hunting them "like game," killing them and trading the bodies to their relatives for money or for Russian captives.[41]

Besides bodies and salt, what did Cossacks have to trade? The Cossack wine trade—their most important trade in the eighteenth century—was in the nineteenth century still a source of profit for Cossacks of the lower Terek, but in decline as a result of state alcohol farming, low prices, and Armenian competition. It was unfortunate that they fixed on a commodity of limited use to their Muslim trading partners. Cossacks still collected madder roots, but after 1757 had to sell them to Russian merchants or their middlemen. Other Cossacks sold some honey, beeswax, or animal skins and the Greben and Volga Cossacks also made a good business as truck farmers.[42]

Trade with the mountain people did not remain static. With the destructive push of Russian forces into the Kumyk and Chechen plains in the 1840s and the establishment of a vibrant agrarian economy in the Kuban region and the North Caucasus steppe, the center of economic gravity in the North Caucasus moved north and west, and the lights of Stavropol', Ekaterinodar, and Vladikavkaz brightened, while those of Kizliar and the lower Terek stanitsas grew dimmer.[43]

Most contemporaries also agreed that by the mid-nineteenth century, Cossack artisanal activity barely existed. A statistical survey of the Caucasus *oblast'* prepared by the Ministry of Internal Affairs in 1830 said:

> the Cossacks settled here, continually on service, do not have time to devote themselves exclusively to any type of handicraft, and the Cossacks that are retired because of old age or infirmity are incapable of it; therefore the women of the regiments engage in handicrafts only as much as is needed to satisfy their domestic demands.

The commander of the Semeinoe-Kizliar regiment reported in 1839 that his Cossacks "do not engage in handicrafts" and wear "Asian" clothes, "which the majority of them buy." Again, in 1856, P. Kishenskii was surprised to observe that industry (*promyshlennost'*) did not exist among the Cossacks and that they purchased all of their needs—*burka*s, guns, Kabardian horses, cloth for *cherkeska*s, leather for boots. It would be good, he advised, for Cossacks to develop some industries such as leatherworks, textiles, viticulture, or agriculture, because then the Stavropol' commissary could buy from them, as could the mountain people, who would in time become dependent on Cossack wares. It was an old dream. In 1859, the regimental government ordered a survey of all factories, handicraft workshops, and the like in the Caucasus Line host. The best they could come up with were thirty-six flour mills in the Mountain regiment. "That is, up to the present time," the report concluded, "no trades have been developed."[44]

Local commanders and observant visitors long realized the importance of local trade to the Cossack economy. Already in 1770, Güldenstädt recommended in a report to the Academy of Sciences that Cossacks be moved to the right bank of the Terek, in part because it would be easier for them to receive cheap grain and livestock from the Chechen village of Bragun. The reorganization of the trading post system in 1846 was encouraged by local commanders for the same reason. Even Prince Vorontsov, the viceroy and commander-in-chief of the Caucasus, devoted time to petty details concerning the day and location for a new bazaar in the Mozdok regiment, where they would trade with Chechens, Kumyks, Sunzha Cossacks, and other "peaceful" mountain people.[45]

Trade along the North Caucasus frontier, perhaps more than anything else, blurred the great divide between the Cossack servants of Russia and the enemy mountaineers. There was a continual flow of goods between the two sides, through legal market relations and underground channels. Even the mountain banditry and kidnapping that so many Petersburg writers represented as a mortal threat to settlers and an affront to Russian morals, stimulated local trade and provided occasional riches for the Cossack markets.

The economy of the mountains was not as backward as many writers and policy makers had imagined; we must conclude that one reason why mountain people never became dependent on Russian manufactured goods was because their economy was more advanced than that of their trans-Terek neighbors, or at least more capable of producing commodities for local trade. And the Cossack hunger for mountain products was not just a result of their remoteness from the center or of service requirements that gave them little time to devote to manufacture and trade. It was also a product of the limitations of their landscape of settlement (hence the grain trade) and the transformation of that landscape by settlers and the army. Every new village that popped up in the tree-hungry steppe and foothills and every stand of trees that was chopped down to create a military road, boosted the demand for an item that the mountain people could best provide. It is also ironic how mountain-Cossack trade was facilitated by the religiously charged policy of encouraging Armenian migration to the Russian, Christian side from Persia and the Islamic khanates along the Caspian Sea. Instead of producing religious division, the resettlement created a social force in the North Caucasus that greatly expanded trade with the Islamic people of the mountains, making it nearly impossible to control by the Russian state. Frontier exchange had a dynamic of its own that often worked against the policies of the center.

Frontier exchange here, as in Usner's Lower Mississippi Valley, brought diverse people together and helped created a syncretic material culture. In both areas, it was a function of the weak commercialization of the economy. In such regions, peripheral as they were to national and world economic systems, imports and exports remained relatively unimportant, and local peoples created local markets that influenced local society in a positive way. The Cossack poverty, which pushed them into a frontier exchange economy, also pulled them into a rich social milieu, where cooperation often took precedence over conflict.[46]

Notes

1. T. M., "Korespondentsiia 'Illiustrirovannoi gazety' s Kavkaza," *Illiustrirovannaia gazeta*, 5 January 1867, 11.

2. Daniel H. Usner, Jr., *Indians, Settlers, and Slaves in a Frontier Exchange Economy* (Chapel Hill: University of North Carolina Press for the Institute of Early American History and Culture, 1992), 6.

3. See, for example, T. Kh. Kumykov, *Vovlechenie Severnogo Kavkaza vo vserossiiskii rynok v XIX v.* (Nal'chik: Kabardino-Balkarskoe knizhnoe izdatel'stvo, 1962).

4. "Otryvok nakaza Astrakhanskim voevodam, boiarinu kniazu Mikhailu Pronskomu, okol'nichemu Timofeiu Buturlinu i Il'e Bezobrazovu," *Akty istoricheskie* 4 (1842): 129-44; I. Popko, *Terskie kazaki so starodavnikh vremen. Istoricheskii ocherk* (St. Petersburg: Tipografiia Departamenta udelov, 1880), 73-74; *Krest'ianskaia voina pod predvoditel'stvom Stepana Razina: Sbornik dokumentov* (Moscow: Izdatel'stvo Akademii nauk SSSR, 1954), 1: 120, 140-41.

5. P. G. Butkov, *Materialy dlia novoi istorii Kavkaza s 1722 po 1803 god* (St. Petersburg: Tipografiia Imperatorskoi akademii nauk, 1869), 1: 168.

6. Popko, *Terskie kazaki*, 73-74; Ia. Ia. Streis [J. J. Struys], *Tri puteshestviia* (Moscow: Ogiz-Sotsekgiz, 1935), 212-14; V. A. Potto, *Dva veka Terskago kazachestva (1577-1801)* (Vladikavkaz: Elektropechatnia tipografiia Terskago oblastnogo pravleniia, 1912), 2: 65.

7. "Tsarskaia gramota Astrakhanskim voevodam kniaz'iam Pronskomu i Volkonskomu, i otpiska ikh Terskim voevodam Volynskomu i Shapilovu, o vydelke vina, dlia opyta, iz rastushchago po Tereku vinograda," *Akty istoricheskie* 4 (1842): 177-79; "Otryvok nakaza," 129-44; N. B. Golikova, *Ocherki po istorii gorodov rossii kontsa XVII-nachala XVIII v.* (Moscow: Izdatel'stvo Moskovskogo universiteta, 1982), 71.

8. "Circassian" (*Cherkes*) was often used to mean mountain person in general and not

specifically the peoples of the northwest Caucasus.

9. B. B. Piotrovskii, ed., *Istoriia narodov Severnogo Kavkaza s drevneishikh vremen do kontsa XVIII v.* (Moscow: "Nauka," 1988), 356; E. N. Kusheva, *Narody Severnogo Kavkaza i ikh sviazi s Rossiei (vtoraia polovina XVI-30-e gody XVII veka)* (Moscow: Izdatel'stvo Akademii nauk SSSR, 1963), 107-08, 299; T. Kh. Kumykov and E. N. Kusheva, eds., *Kabardino-russkie otnosheniia v XVI-XVIII vv.: Dokumenty i materialy* (Moscow: Izdatel'stvo Akademii nauk SSSR, 1957), 1: 333.

10. *Akty sobrannye Kavkazskoi arkheograficheskoi komissii* (Tiflis, 1866), 1: 81 [hereafter *AKAK*].

11. N. P. Gritsenko, *Goroda Severo-vostochnogo Kavkaza i proizvoditel'nye sily kraia V-seredina XIX veka* (Rostov-on-Don: Izdatel'stvo Rostovskogo universiteta, 1984), 109; Kumykov and Kusheva, *Kabardino-russkie otnosheniia*, 2: 215-18, 229-30, 244-50; A. V. Fadeev, *Rossiia i Kavkaz pervoi treti XIX v.* (Moscow: Izdatel'stvo Akademii nauk SSSR, 1960), 63-65; *AKAK* (Tiflis, 1870), 4: 37; V. G. Gadzhiev, "Arkhiv Kizliarskogo komendanta," *Izvestiia Severo-Kavkazskogo nauchnogo tsentra vysshei shkoly. Obshchestvennyi nauk,* no. 2 (1978): 10.

12. V. S. Shamrai, "Kratkii ocherk menovykh (torgovykh) snoshenii po Chernomorskoi kordonnoi i beregovoi linii s zakubanskimi gorskimi narodami," *Kubanskii sbornik* 8 (1902): 363, 383; N. Varadinov, *Istoriia Ministerstva vnutrennykh del* (St. Petersburg: Tipografiia Ministerstva vnutrennykh del, 1858), 1: 133-34, 171; "Iz proshlago Dagestanskoi oblasti (po metstnym arkhivnym dannym)," *Dagestanskii sbornik* 2 (1904): 200-02.

13. Kumykov, *Vovlechenie Severnogo Kavkaza,* 25-28; A. L. Narochnitskii, ed., *Istoriia narodov Severnogo Kavkaza (konets XVIII v.-1917 g.),* (Moscow: "Nauka," 1988), 79-80.

14. Chechens, Kumyks, and the peoples of Dagestan were able to get salt from the Shamkhal of Tarku and the salt lakes along the Caspian Sea south of the Terek. Mountain people could also obtain salt from Circassians who smuggled it in from the Turks. The Russian salt originated at the Mozharskii salt lakes near the Kuma River in the eastern Mozdok steppe. See S. Sh. Gadzhieva, *Kumyki: Istoriko-etnograficheskoe issledovanie* (Moscow: Izdatel'stvo Akademii nauk SSSR, 1961), 73; P. P. Nadezhdin, *Kavkazskii krai: Priroda i liudi,* 3d ed. (Tula: Tipografiia Vladimira Nikolaievicha Sokolova, 1901), 56, 59; Kumykov, *Vovlechenie Severnogo Kavkaza,* 111; A. V...v, "Kratkii ocherk Stavropol'skii gubernii v promyshlennom i torgovom otnosheniiakh," *Kavkaz,* 5 June 1848, 90-92.

15. See Dov Yaroshevski, "Imperial Strategy in the Kirghiz Steppe in the Eighteenth Century," *Jahrbücher für Geschichte Osteuropas* 39 (1991): 221-24.

16. K. V. Sivkov, "O proektakh okonchaniia Kavkazskoi voiny v seredine XIX v.," *Istoriia SSSR* 3 (May-June 1958): 192-96; Platon Zubov, *Kartina Kavkazskago kraia, prinadlezhashchego Rossii, i sopredel'nykh onomu zemel'* (St. Petersburg: Tipografiia Konrada Vingebera, 1834), 1: 71-82; *AKAK,* 4: 835-36; *AKAK* (Tiflis, 1885), 10: 570-72; N. S. Mordvinov, "Mnenie admirala Mordvinova o sposobakh, koimi Rossii udobnee mozhno priviazat' k sebe postepenno Kavkazskikh zhitelei," *Chteniia v Imperatorskom obshchestve istorii i drevnosti Rossiiskikh pri moskovskom universitete* 4 (Oct.-Dec. 1858): section 5, 109-12.

17. Kumykov and Kusheva, *Kabardino-russkie otnosheniia,* 2: 229-30, 237, 239-44; Gritsenko, *Goroda Severo-vostochnogo Kavkaza,* 109-11; Popko, *Terskie kazaki,* 183-84.

18. "Materialy Ekaterinskoi Zakonodatel'noi Komissii," *Sbornik Imperatorskago*

russkago istoricheskago obshchestva, 114 (1903): 490, 492.

19. S. M. Bronevskii, *Noveishie geograficheskie i istoricheskie izvestiia o Kavkaze* (Moscow: Tipografiia S. Selivanovskogo, 1823), section 2, 142-45; Potto, *Dva veka*, vol. 2, 72-73; Popko, *Terskie kazaki*, 177-80.

20. Rossiiskii Gosudarstvennyi Voenno-Istoricheskii Arkhiv [RGVIA], f. 1058, op. 2, d. 547, ll. 3, 12; d. 847, l. 2; d. 1150, ll. 86-89; Georgii Paradov, "Raskaz ochevidtsa o Shamile i ego sovremennikakh," *Sbornik materialov dlia opisaniia mestnostei i plemen Kavkaza* 32 (1903): section 1, 17; N. P. Gritsenko, *Sotsial'no-ekonomicheskoe razvitie priterechnykh raionov v XVIII-pervoi polovine XIX vv.* (Groznyi: Izdatel'stvo "Groznenskii rabochii," 1961), 65-67.

21. Kumykov, *Vovlechenie Severnogo Kavkaza*, 29-35, 110-11; A. V. Fadeev, ed., *Ocherki istorii Balkarskogo naroda (s drevneishikh vremen do 1917 goda)* (Nal'chik: Kabardino-Balkarskoe knizhnoe izdatel'stvo, 1961), 56. RGVIA, f. 1058, op. 1, d. 365, ll. 1-5. Cossacks also illegally sold or traded salt to other non-Cossack Russian subjects. An investigation of 1854 revealed that they usually exchanged salt for grain. See RGVIA, f. 1058, op. 1, d. 362, ll. 1-18.

22. Iu. Shidlovskii, "Zapiski o Kizliare," *Zhurnal Ministerstva vnutrennikh del* 4 (1843): 194-95; N. G. Volkova, "O rasselenii Armian na Severnom Kavkaze do nachala XX veka," *Istoriko-filologicheskii zhurnal* 3 (1966): 259-61; A. [M.] Pavlov, *O aziiatskikh narodakh, obitaiushchikh v iuzhnoi Rossii* (St. Petersburg: Tipografiia Kh. Gintsa, 1841), 34, 47, 52.

23. Shamrai, "Kratkii ocherk," 363, 383, 389; Iosif Debu, *O Kavkazskoi linii i prisoedinennom k nei Chernomorskom voiske* (St. Petersburg: Tipografiia Karla Kraiia, 1829), 80-81; *AKAK*, 4: 334-35; *AKAK*, 10: 570-71; Kumykov, *Vovlechenie Severnogo Kavkaza*, 37-39, 55-56.

24. Shidlovskii, "Zapiski o Kizliare," 174-75. For a similar description of the diversity of the Georgievsk trade fair, or as the author put it, "the most picturesque and endless disorder," see V...v A...i, "Tri pis'ma o Piatigorske. Pis'mo pervoe," *Kavkaz*, 13 September 1847, 145-47.

25. Narochnitskii, *Istoriia narodov Severnogo Kavkaza*, 83; *Izvestiia Kavkazskago otdela Imperatorskago russkago geograficheskago obshchestva* 5, 4 (1878): supplement, 60-61, 346-47; "Iarmarki na Kavkaze," *Kavkaz*, 16 Feb. 1852, 50; A. V. Fadeev, *Ocherki ekonomicheskogo razvitiia stepnogo Predkavkaz'ia v doreformennyi period* (Moscow: Izdatel'stvo Akademii nauk SSSR, 1957), 197, 205-10; "Svedenie o iarmarke, byvshei v Georgievske v den' Sv. Nikolaia, 9 Maia 1850 g.," *Kavkaz*, 20 December 1850, 399; "Svedenie o iarmarke, byvshei v gorode Georgievske v den' Pokrova Presviatyia Bogoroditsy, t.e. 1 Oktiabria 1850 goda," *Kavkaz*, 23 December 1850, 404; RGVIA, f. 1058, op. 1, d. 249, l. 156.

One of the Russianisms to enter the Ossetian language from this period is "*armul'ka*" from the Russian word for trade fair, "*iarmarka*," which in turn comes from the German "*Jahrmarkt*." See V. I. Abaev, *Istoriko-etimologicheskii slovar' Osetinskogo iazyka* (Moscow-Leningrad: Izdatel'stvo Akademii nauk SSSR, 1958), 1: 69 and T. A. Guriev, *Vliianie Russkogo iazyka na razvitie Osetinskoi leksiki* (Ordzhonikidze: Severo-Osetinskoe knizhnoe izdatel'stvo, 1962), 31.

26. N. Samarin, "Dorozhnyia zametki," *Severnaia pchela*, 20 May 1862, 534; M, "Tatarskoe plemia na Kavkaze," *Kavkaz*, 19 Nov. 1859, 509-10.

27. V. A. Potto, *Kavkazskaia voina v otdel'nykh ocherkakh, epizodakh, legendakh i biografiiakh* (St. Petersburg: Tipografiia R. Golike, 1885), 2: 90-91, 97-98; K. Samoilov, "Zametki o Chechne," *Panteon* 23, 10 (Oct. 1855): section 3, 45-46; Fadeev, *Ocherki ekonomicheskogo razvitiia*, 211, 215, 220-21; S. Ivanov, "O sblizhenii gortsev s Russkimi na Kavkaze," *Voennyi sbornik* 7 (1859): 541-47.

28. Potto, *Dva veka*, 64-66; I. V. Rovinskii, "Khoziaistvennoe opisanie Astrakhanskoi i Kavkazskoi gubernii po grazhdanskomu i estestvennomu ikh sostoianiiu," *Trudy Stavropol'skoi uchenoi arkhivnoi komissii*, no. 2 (1910): section 4, 54-55; B. A. Kaloev, "Iz istorii Russko-chechenskikh ekonomicheskikh i kul'turnykh sviazei," *Sovetskaia etnografiia* 1 (Jan.-Feb. 1961): 44; "Statisticheskiia svedeniia o Kavkazskoi oblasti i Zemle voiska Chernomorskago," *Zhurnal Ministerstva vnutrennikh del* 3, no. 4 (1830): 123-30; Fadeev, *Ocherki ekonomicheskogo razvitiia*, 156, 160; Gadzhieva, *Kumyki*, 101-03; Gritsenko, *Goroda Severo-vostochnogo Kavkaza*, 94; Kumykov and Kusheva, *Kabardino-russkie otnosheniia*, 2: 215-16; *Polnoe Sobranie zakonov Rossiiskoi imperii s 1649 goda [PSZ]* (St. Petersburg: Tipografiia II otdeleniia sobstvennoi Ego Imperatorskago Velichestva kantseliarii, 1839-1843), 19: 517-18; Gritsenko, *Sotsial'no-ekonomicheskoe razvitie*, 37-40.

29. Rovinskii, "Khoziaistvennoe opisanie," 52-56; "Statisticheskiia svedeniia," 131-40; A. V-v, "Kratkii ocherk Stavropol'skii gubernii v promyshlennom i torgovom otnosheniiakh," *Kavkaz*, 22 May 1848, 84; P. K. [P. Kishenskii], "Vospominaniia o Grebenskikh kazakakh i Kavkazskoi linii," *Moskovskiia vedomosti*, 13 Sept. 1856, 463-65.

30. N. N., *Zapiski vo vremia poezdka iz Astrakhanoi na Kavkaze i v Gruziiu v 1827 godu* (Moscow: Tipografiia S. Selivanovskago, 1829), 68; G. N. Prozritelev, comp., "Iz proshlogo Severnogo Kavkaza. Materialy dlia istorii g. Stavropolia i Stavropol'skoi gub.," *Trudy Stavropol'skoi uchenoi arkhivnoi komissii* 2 (1910): section 4, 19-23.

31. E. N. Studenetskaia, *Odezhda narodov Severnogo Kavkaza XVIII-XX vv.* (Moscow: "Nauka," 1989), 82-87; Kumykov and Kusheva, *Kabardino-russkie otnosheniia*, 2: 245-48. For a few of the many statistics on this trade, see Kumykov, *Vovlechenie Severnogo Kavkaza*, 62-64, 85-88. *Burkas* also became fashionable with Russian officers serving in the Caucasus— there are well-known portraits of Ermolov, Lermontov, and Bestuzhev-Marlinskii with a *burka* cunningly draped across one shoulder.

32. Fadeev, *Ocherki ekonomicheskogo razvitiia*, 232; Rovinskii, "Khoziaistvennoe opisanie," 52-53; A. P. Berzhe, *Chechnia i Chechentsy* (Tiflis: Kavkazskii otdel Imperatorskago russkago geograficheskogo obshchestva, 1859), 87-89; A. I. Akhverdov, "Opisanie Dagestana. 1804 g.," in *Istoriia, geografiia i etnografiia Dagestana XVIII-XIX vv. Arkhivnye materialy*, eds., M. O. Kosven and Kh-M. Khashaev (Moscow: Izdatel'stvo vostochnoi literatury, 1958), 213-15; A. M. Pavlov, *Kratkoe obozrenie Kavkazskoi gubernii uezdnago goroda Kizliara* (Moscow: Tipografiia Avgusta Semena, 1822), 7; M. Kriukov, "Putevyia zametki," *Kavkaz*, 8 Oct. 1852, 248-50; Narochnitskii, *Istoriia narodov Severnogo Kavkaza*, 82. A total of over 41,000 oxcarts of lumber passed through four central Terek quarantine posts in 1846, 1847, 1849, and 1852. See Kumykov, *Vovlechenie Severnogo Kavkaza*, 65-66, 93-96; R. Sh. Sharafutdinova, "Eshchë odin 'Nizam' Shamilia," *Pis'mennye pamiatniki vostoka* (1975): 168-71; *Kavkaz*, 10 September 1849, 146.

33. *PSZ*, 19: 267-68; Kumykov, *Vovlechenie Severnogo Kavkaza*, 86.

34. Piotrovskii, *Istoriia narodov Severnogo Kavkaza*, 356; Kumykov and Kusheva, *Kabardino-russkie otnosheniia*, 1: 322-27; G. N. Prozritelev, "Kavkazskoe oruzhie," *Trudy*

Stavropol'skoi uchenoi arkhivnoi komissii 7 (1915): section 10, 1-5; Samarin, "Dorozhnyia zametki," 533-34; V. N. Tatishchev, *Istoriia Rossiiskaia* (Moscow-Leningrad: Izdatel'stvo Akademii nauk SSSR, 1962), 1: 241.

35. O. V. Marggraf, *Ocherk kustarnykh promyslov Severnogo Kavkaza s opisaniem tekhniki proizvodstva* (Moscow: Tipografiia S. V. Gur'ianova, 1882), xiv-xl; *AKAK*, 4: 334-35; "Statisticheskiia izvestiia o Kavkazskoi oblasti i Zemle voiska Chernomorskago," *Zhurnal Ministerstva vnutrennikh del* 3, no. 5 (1830): 124-27; F. G. Chernozubov, "Ocherki Terskoi stariny. (1850) S okaziei," *Zapiski Terskago obshchestva liubitelei kazach'ei stariny*, no. 8 (1914): 63-66.

The grooved mountain rifle was praised for its lightness, durability, easy use, and straight shot; see RGVIA, f. 1058, op. 2, d. 988, ll. 9-12.

36. Chernozubov, "Ocherki Terskoi stariny," 63-66; Gritsenko, *Sotsial'no-ekonomicheskoe razvitie*, 61-63; Rossiiskii Gosudarstvennyi Istoricheskii Arkhiv [RGIA], f. 1268, op. 1, d. 424, l. 8. N. A. Karaulov, "Govor grebenskikh kazakov," *Sbornik materialov dlia opisaniia mestnostei i plemen Kavkaza*, no. 37 (1907): section 3, 103-106.

37. Fadeev, *Ocherki istorii Balkarskogo naroda*, 54; Samarin, "Dorozhnyia zametki," 533-34; Marggraf, *Ocherk kustarnykh promyslov*, xiv-xxxv. This quote is actually from an uncited source in Marggraf.

38. Berzhe, *Chechnia i Chechentsy*, 87-89; Piotrovskii, *Istoriia narodov Severnogo Kavkaza*, 280-82; Samarin, "Dorozhnyia zametki," 533; Narochnitskii, *Istoriia narodov Severnogo Kavkaza*, 80; Gritsenko, *Sotsial'no-ekonomicheskoe razvitie*, 67-70.

39. For three particularly lucrative raids, see V. P. Lystsov, *Persidskii pokhod Petra I* (Moscow: Izdatel'stvo Moskovskogo universiteta, 1951), 98; "Materialy dlia statistiki Kizliarskago polka Terskago kazach'iago voiska," *Voennyi sbornik* 12 (Dec. 1869): 213; and F. I. Soimonov, *Opisanie Kaspiiskago moria* (St. Petersburg: Imperatorskaia akademiia nauk, 1763), 102.

40. Samarin, "Dorozhnyia zametki," 534; Alexandre Dumas, *Adventures in Caucasia*, trans. A. E. Murch (Westport, Conn.: Greenwood Press, 1962), 67. Admittedly, Dumas was not the most reliable witness, and must be used with caution.

41. Shidlovskii, "Zapiski o Kizliare," 179-81; Akhverdov, "Opisanie Dagestana," 213-29; *PSZ*, 28: 245; V. S. Shamrai, "Istoricheskaia spravka k voprosu o iasyriakh na Severnom Kavkaze i v Kubanskoi oblasti i dokumenty otnosiashchietsia k etomu voprosu," *Kubanskii sbornik* 12 (1907): 169-73; Popko, *Terskie kazaki*, 299-302, 426-28; Z...v, "Puteshestviia. Poezdka iz Moskvy za-Kavkaz," *Tiflisskiia vedomosti*, 10 July 1830, 3-4.

42. "Statisticheskiia izvestiia," 111-17; Popko, *Terskie kazaki*, 175-77, 309-11, 443-45; *PSZ*, 14: 793-94; Gritsenko, *Goroda Severo-vostochnogo Kavkaza*, 96; Zubov, *Kartina Kavkazskago kraia*, 126-28, 130-32.

43. I. S. Efimovyi, "O sovremennom sostoianii torgovli v gorode Stavropole," *Kavkaz*, 16 Aug. 1852, 196-97.

44. "Statisticheskiia izvestiia," 124-27; F. Ponomarëv, "Materialy dlia istorii Terskago kazach'iago voiska s 1559 po 1880 god," *Voennyi sbornik* 12 (1880): 348-49; P. K., "Vospominaniia o Grebenskikh kazakakh," 463-65; RGVIA, f. 1058, op. 1, d. 349, ll. 3-20.

45. RGIA, f. 1268, op. 1, d. 782a, ll. 7-9, 34; op. 2, d. 614, l. 3.

46. Usner, *Indians, Settlers, & Slaves*, esp. 145-275.

7

Seven Brides for Seventy Brothers: Gender Relations Along the Frontier

It does not suit a Cossack to live alone.

—Terek Cossack saying

On the high mountain stand two crosses,
Under the mountain two friends lay.
A young maiden approached and asked:
Isn't one of you my sweetheart?
And the grave answered: No, he's not here.
The other repeated: Forget about him.

—Greben Cossack song

Split a green oak
Into four parts!
The one who loves another man's wife,
His soul is in paradise.
The one who falls in love with a girl,
Saves his soul.
The one who falls in love with a widow,
Is forgiven his sins.
The one who snatches an old lady,
Has the fever shakes.

—Greben Cossack song

Strange women populate the legends of the North Caucasus. It is curious that both Amazons and sexual captives make their homeland there, that the *Amazonka* and Lermontov's Bela come from the same neighborhood. Amazons are the ultimate misogynist nightmare—women warriors and sexual freaks who have purged all men from their community. The Amazons from antiquity supposedly lived in the nearby Pontic steppe north of the Black Sea and in the

North Caucasus; these sexual monsters were reconfigured in an 1858 fantasy illustration in the journal *Kavkaztsy* of the Amazon company—a mounted force of women warriors, all looking exactly alike, faintly resembling a young Catherine the Great.[1] Sexual captives such as Bela from *A Hero of Our Time* are the ultimate misogynist fantasy—helpless, imprisoned maidens who become submissive, but manage to retain their wildness.

And there were, of course, plenty of "Amazons" and "Belas" on both sides of the frontier in the North Caucasus; plenty of female mountain warriors who hurled rocks and then themselves at the invading Russian troops; plenty of Cossack women who poured boiling water and tar on the mountain people besieging their stanitsa; plenty of captive wives and daughters and sisters in the mountains—Russians and Cossacks and Armenians and Georgians; and plenty of captive mountain women in the Cossack villages.

But there is one spot where the Amazon and the sexual captive myths intersect—in the toponym of Kizliar, the oldest permanent fort-town of the North Caucasus. According to folk tradition, we can trace the founding of Kizliar back to an Amazon or to sexual captives. In one version, a tsar tries to conduct a marriage alliance with a beautiful *Amazonka* who rules a regiment of Amazon warriors. His two sons compete to win her by trying to catch her on horseback. When the youngest is about to snare his prey, the oldest, in a fit of jealousy, lets his arrow fly and kills the Amazon. Thus Kizliar, derives from "beautiful maiden" in Tatar, the *Amazonka* who died and on whose land the tsar founded a fortress in her honor. The "maidens" in the other version are Russian girls who were taken captive by a Kumyk khan. Rather than submit to a forced marriage, they escaped, fled to the Terek, and drowned when trying to cross it.[2]

Kizliar was the most important town in the land of the Terek Cossacks. So the center of gravity of these realms of male fear and fantasy is located in Terek Cossack country. Admittedly, the evidence is slender concerning the creation of these tales and their relevance to the history of the North Caucasus. But when two such potent and opposing symbols of sexual insecurity issue from the same motherland, we should wonder if perhaps something significant was going on between men and women there.

On the surface, Cossack history might seem to be an inherently and exceedingly macho subject. The image that often comes to mind is the Repin canvas of the *Zaporozhian Cossacks Writing a Reply to the Turkish Sultan*—a brotherhood of warriors, armed to the hilt, muscles bulging, threatening the Sultan, apparently with a fair amount of obscenity and barracks humor. And not a woman is to be seen.

As far as the Terek Cossacks are concerned, this picture is wrong. Or rather, it is only half of the story, and often not even that much. Military service, fighting ability, aggression, weapons, and esprit de corps were important parts of Cossack life. But it is impossible to understand the world of the Terek

Cossacks by focusing solely on the military camp. And in many aspects, by the nineteenth century, fighting was the least important part of cossackdom. The primary factors determining which Cossack families prospered were not military prowess or state service, but marriage, reproduction, and women's labor back home. In other words, gender needs to become a category of Cossack history.

The history of Cossack women complicates general notions of patriarchy in Russian society and embroiders on recent work of Barbara Alpern Engel and Christine Worobec, which is sensitive to the possibility of distinct and significant power among Russian peasant women. As we will see, a social history of the frontier reveals that not all women's lives were ruled by "exclusion; dependence and subordination; and imbalance...between their contribution to survival and their rewards," as were Rose Glickman's peasants.[3] Terek Cossack women had great power, founded on economic independence, which their husbands had no choice but to accept.

Although it is impossible to document, the first Cossack settlers in the North Caucasus in the sixteenth and seventeenth centuries were probably mostly, if not exclusively, men. They married with the native women or with women from the north, but gender imbalance was probably an endemic problem until the nineteenth century. For example, the 1781-1784 organized migration of settlers of various classes from Russia to the North Caucasus included some 51,900 men and only 15,700 women, over three men for every woman. Over time, as Cossacks found more sources for brides, with the government's intervention, and the reality that the fighting men died earlier than women, the gender imbalance gradually improved. By the mid-nineteenth century, the balance between men and women among Terek Cossacks was about even.[4]

State officials were very concerned about rooting Cossacks. A married Cossack with a family was better able to provide for himself and equip himself for military service. He was also less likely to desert or to emigrate back to internal Russia or the mountains. So the state worked hard to promote marriage. Women convicts were sent to the North Caucasus from the interior of Russia. Women captives from the mountains were often taken to Cossack villages. Friedrich Wagner reported the unusual incident of a slave ship bound for Turkey filled with Circassian women being overtaken by a Russian steamer, the women captured, and distributed among officers and Cossacks of the Caucasus Military Line.[5]

This type of coerced distribution of women can be seen as a type of state bride theft; the same type of raiding for women occurred in gender-skewed Siberia—it was an understandable solution to an otherwise insoluble problem. What is most remarkable about the Terek Cossacks is not that they received prisoner-brides from the state or that they occasionally raided the mountains for booty and brides, but that they also went galloping north, into Russian provinces for the same purpose, apparently with the tacit approval of the local officials. According to a Cossack colonel, the ritual of the "first campaign" was long practiced by the Greben Cossacks. Once the young Grebentsy came of age, they mounted their horses and were led by old Cossacks—"who knew the way to the Rus'"—to Penza, Samara, and Voronezh provinces where they raided and brought back women and girls to marry, "straight from the saddle to the altar."[6]

The local authorities engaged in a number of other less spectacular but equally effective measures to encourage marriage. In fact, one of the early Cossack regiments, founded in the early eighteenth century, was actually named the Terek Family (Terskoe-Semeinoe) regiment, because they received provisions for the entire family. When the first villages of the Vladikavkaz regiment were established in the late 1830s, married Cossacks were given all sorts of privileges over bachelors—most importantly, they were freed from service and given a monetary bonus once they had set up their homestead. All Terek Cossacks were granted forty-five silver rubles for marrying captives who had converted to Christianity. The government also allowed marriage outside of estate; an imperial decree in 1849 allowed widows of Don Cossacks who had settled to the Sunzha Line in Chechnia to marry lower ranks from the regular army and to enter their new husbands into the Cossack estate. Military colonists were also allowed to marry Cossack women.[7]

So the state did what it could to get women to the Cossacks, to have them marry and put down family roots. Similar interventions occurred on all of the sparsely populated frontiers. The government shipped convict women to Siberian Cossacks in the eighteenth century, including patricides and husband murderers. Troops were quartered along the border of the Black Sea host to make sure women did not marry outside of the host.[8] It is interesting to note that Shamil followed a similar policy with Cossack and soldier deserters. He worked hard at marrying deserters to local girls; he himself sometimes married deserters who had converted to Islam to runaway mountain girls. He passed a regulation abolishing punishment of girls convicted of premarital adultery if they married a converted Russian deserter. And he interceded to get Russian women who had fled to the mountains to marry Russian soldiers and Cossacks there. Sometimes he allowed the Cossack women to choose their husband. In other cases he forced the women to marry certain men. Marriage was a political issue on both sides of the North Caucasus frontier; both sides understood the importance of marriage in creating stable communities and well-equipped fighters.[9]

Marriage was also a political issue from the perspective of the Terek Cossacks, because many of them were Old Believers. This means that two very important challenges stood in their way to marriage. First, many Old Believer Tertsy would not marry into Orthodox families, so their pool of prospective mates was sharply limited. Second, the Terek Cossacks often found themselves without priests, or with illegal priests, to marry them.

Most of the Terek Old Believers were of the priestly sect, but they often had no priests. Sometimes they would simply get married in an Orthodox church and conceal their true faith. More frequently, it seems, marriages were delayed until a fugitive or itinerant priest visited their village who would be pressed into continual and often mass marriage services. Often these priests came from the Irgiz Old Believer monasteries in Saratov *krai*.[10]

One such wanderer was Grigorii Livanov, a defrocked Orthodox priest who appeared at Kalinovskaia in 1856 wearing a yellow Cossack *cherkeska*. Livanov was taken in by the Old Believers there who hid him in various places—in houses in the village, in a hut in a skete half a mile from the village, in a horse trough in a barn, once in an Orthodox household. One time he had to be smuggled out of the village by Kalmyks in an oxcart and taken to a farm twelve miles from the village. And all the while, he performed baptisms and weddings, in secret, mostly at night. Often he performed five marriages at a time in the cramped quarters of a skete hut, reportedly rushing through the service without the proper prayers or readings.[11]

But despite the great limitations Old Believers faced in marriage, they achieved the best gender balance of all of the Russian servitors in their lands. How did they overcome these limitations? They married young and worked out a variety of cohabitation arrangements.[12]

The Terek Cossacks frequently married their daughters to younger boys. We have good information for the villages of the Greben Cossack regiment (predominantly Old Believer) in 1838 and 1839. The rarest type of conjugal union there was one in which men were older than women, only 9 percent of the marriages! Spouses were the same age in 34 percent of the unions; women were older than men "by years" in 31 percent of the unions. At Starogladkovskaia, it was not unusual to find marriages between sixteen-year-old boys and twenty-year-old young women. Approximately 26 percent of the families were headed by widows.[13]

Anecdotal evidence confirms this. Local observers of the Terek Cossacks frequently remarked on their unusual marriage traditions by which Old Believers married adult daughters to sons who had not matured yet, frequently to fifteen- and fourteen-year-old boys. I. Slivitskii, who served with the Tertsy in 1846 and 1847, told the story of an Old Believer who lived in a skete who married his niece to a thirteen-year-old boy who just happened to be visiting. The old holy man said that he had given a vow that none of his children would marry into Orthodoxy. Slivitskii also told of one Cossack woman who said her husband flew kites and played knucklebones. These kinds of marriages were illegal and unrecorded or falsely recorded. They also forced the local authorities to issue regulations in 1820, specifically for the Greben regiment, declaring that husbands and brides must be "of a mature age" at marriage, defined as no younger than eighteen for husbands and fourteen for brides.[14]

Such unusual marriages also occurred in Siberian Cossack communities, and for good reason. When there was great competition for women, there was pressure to marry early so a young Cossack could build a domestic economy before he had to leave for service. To put it crudely, whoever got the girl first, had the best chance. So Cossack families married their boys off as early as possible to the limited stock of girls.[15]

There was also, according to many observers, a loose sexual ethic among the Terek Cossacks. The evidence is rather sketchy, as it would be, but according to an officer who lived among the Grebentsy, married Cossack women and men kept "lovers" in the open. They were called "side" (*pobochnyi*) wives or husbands; it was not considered a vice or a crime to have one and supposedly did not raise any jealousy among the real husbands and wives. When Prince Goriunov inquired at Chervlennaia who certain Cossack women were married to, his landlady habitually told him the last names of both their husbands and their *pobochnyi* husbands. In Chernoiarskaia, the husband had the right to marry again while his wife was still living, if he wanted to leave his inheritance to another. Cohabitation between young widows and unmarried men was also common there. When the village was first settled, there were more of these "unlawful" marriages than lawful ones. According to the church records of Novoosetinskaia church, in Chernoiarskaia and Novoosetinskaia from 1833 to 1839 there were 149 legitimate children and 545 illegitimate children born, an astronomically high rate. (Rural illegitimacy was estimated to be very low in European Russia as a whole, under 2% of live births at the end of the century, because of strict communal customs intended to minimize out-of-wedlock sexual contact.)[16]

Barbara Alpern Engel observed a similar degree of unfaithfulness and illegal cohabitation among peasants in Kostroma province, where there was a high rate of male out-migration. Certainly, as she indicates, there would have been greater possibility and need for such arrangements when the husband was frequently away.[17]

Perhaps another reason why Cossacks tolerated diverse cohabitation arrangements in these villages was because of the complicated legal and semi-legal marital relations that also existed. At the least, the realm of "illegal" marriage shaded into an often confused and diverse realm of "legal" marriages. This was caused by the great mobility of the population through migration, captivity, conversion, and desertion. Husband and wives were often missing a spouse who had been killed, fled, taken captive in the mountains, or simply disappeared. The Orthodox church would not dissolve these marriages for at least ten years. Because of the burden on their economy, there was sometimes great pressure to cohabit and bring a man or woman into the household. Perhaps the diverse cohabitation arrangements that many observed among the Cossacks were solutions to these marriages in limbo.[18]

But there were further complications in marital relations. There are cases of people returning from mountain captivity to find their spouse remarried.

Sometimes former husbands and wives returned from the mountains separately and met up many years later. One woman married a Chechen in captivity, was ransomed to freedom, and had the Chechen's son when she returned to Naur. The Chechen later moved from the mountains to the Russian side and became a Russian subject, but he would not convert and remarry his mountain wife. In another case, a state peasant in captivity married a Chechen and had two sons. He later fled back to the Russian side without his family. Fifteen years later he met up with his wife and children at Novogladkovskaia; they had been purchased from the Chechen by a Greben Cossack who had converted them and was using them as domestic workers. He had to pay to get them back. Further, it was easy to get out of an old marriage and into a new one by converting, either between Islam and Christianity or from Old Belief to Orthodoxy. All of this meant that there were a fair number of former spouses in the vicinity.[19]

Cossack women in the North Caucasus also had the right to flee their spouses. There are many cases of wives simply leaving their husbands. A local writer called it "nearly the custom." Another knew of 100 marriages that had ended with the wife fleeing to her parents, to Groznyi, or to some other fort or village. Sometimes the husband managed to catch his wife and drag her back, but it seems as if a good number got away. The archives are full of cases of wives fleeing to the mountains, to other Cossack villages, and to unknown points. For example, Agafiia Zakharova, the wife of a Cossack of Vladikavkazskaia stanitsa, fled in 1856, taking several dresses and 100 silver rubles. Ul'iana Litvinova left her husband, a Cossack of the First Sunzha regiment, intending to start a new life in Vladikavkaz.[20]

Aside from the obvious human needs, why were brides so important to Cossacks? How was marriage tied to Cossack rooting? Because women Cossacks did nearly all of the work in the Terek Cossack economy. As we saw in Chapter 5 there was a great labor shortage among the Cossack communities in the North Caucasus. Some workers were hired, but the bulk of the work was done by women. Women were the economic heads of the households. They were the ones who made commodities for the market. And the little bit of wage labor that Cossacks engaged in was done by women.[21] As a local observer wrote of the Greben Cossacks:

> A wife is the main wealth of a Cossack, from whence he receives his uniform, weapons, and horse...A wife in the economy and house is an Archimedes lever for him and he feels and sees her power everywhere. And woe to the Cossack who doesn't have such a wife! Then both in the house and in the field—everywhere it is bad for him.[22]

Of course Cossack women did all of the household and kitchen-garden work that was the purview of frontier and peasant women everywhere. In the

North Caucasus, they were also the masters in the wheat fields and the vineyards where Cossack livelihood was made or broken. They planted, tended, harvested, and processed. The crude Cossack wine that the Tertsy were locally famous for was sometimes made by women.[23]

Farming and viticulture are extremely labor-intensive occupations; they were more so in the North Caucasus because of difficulties with water. Irrigation canals were cut to provide water and silt for the plowlands. As we have seen in Chapter 4, the Terek also had to be restrained—flooding was an endemic problem so dams, walls, fascines, and weirs had to be erected. This too was largely women's work.[24] The sources are not clear about the extent of women's work on the Cossack farmsteads (*khutory*) in the steppe where they raised livestock. It seems likely that men controlled this work, since women were needed back home close to the fields and vineyards. But there were widows living on steppe farmsteads, managing their ranches.[25]

Women performed most of the handicraft work in Cossack households and were the ones who entered into the money economy. They spun flax, hemp, wool, they weaved cloth and linen, and they fulled and died cloth. They got a "not insignificant" income from selling vegetables at Kizliar. Non-Russian Cossack women seem to have engaged in handicraft work even more. In Lukovskaia, Ossetian and Circassian women spun, knitted, and wove cloth and they made thick felt *burka*s, and sewed shoes for their own use and for sale. This fits the pattern for non-Cossack native women of the mountains. Still in the late nineteenth century, most of the domestic industry in the North Caucasus was based on women (thirty-nine out of seventy crafts), and more so with mountain people (nineteen out of thirty-four) than with Russians (seven out of nineteen).[26]

Cossack women also performed most of the wage labor that existed in the Cossack economy. At Shelkozavodskaia, nearly all of the women worked at a local silk factory in the 1830s and 1840s until it burned down. The wives and daughters of the Greben Cossacks went to the Mozdok and Terskii regiments and to the Ossetians of Mozdok to work during harvest time to earn grain. Even the women who lived cut off from the world in the sketes on the fringes of the Cossack villages participated in the money economy. Some of the women of the Novogladkovskaia skete hired themselves out during the grape harvest and sold fishing nets and shawls.[27]

Widows also had a special position in Terek Cossack society. Even if there were mature and married sons in the house, when widowed, a Cossack woman became the head of the household. At Starogladkovskaia in 1838-39, one 120-year-old widow was recorded as still the head of her household, despite the fact that she had fifty-one- and thirty-one-year-old married sons living with her. Akulina Nedugova, sixty-seven years old, ruled over her Kurdiukovskaia household and her five sons, aged forty-seven to twenty-five, four of whom were married. She seems to have done very well—the household owned 104 sheep, twenty-six head of cattle, eight work oxen, and four vineyards. The prosperous widow was a fixture of Terek Cossack communities. When her husband died, Zinadia Osipovna, moved back to her native village Chervlennaia, set up a homestead, and farmed, cut hay, made wine, sold, traded, and created a successful enterprise that allowed her to raise her sons for service. Sometimes widows resettled to the farmsteads in the steppe, where the plowland and the pasture was richer. And there were a lot of widows—as cited above, one-fourth of the households of the Greben Cossacks in 1838-1839 were headed by widows.[28]

Often men reserved a certain type of work for themselves, clinging to a narrowly defined task, perhaps to help them symbolically stake out a realm of economic dominance. Greben Cossack women, for example, rarely cut hay. They raked it, stacked it, and carted it, but cutting hay was a man's job. A similar division was practiced at Lukovskaia stanitsa, where women

> turn the cut hay for drying, then they...rake it together with rakes in rows, and from the rows they make hay cocks, drag the cocks with ropes to the place where they have decided to place the haystacks, and then with pitchforks they give them to the men who stand on the haystacks and direct them.[29]

Also, all Terek Cossacks women did not work equally. One can nearly identify the ethnicity or religion of the Cossack community by the type and amount of labor that the women performed. In the predominantly Old Believer communities of the lower Terek, the women preformed the most diverse labor and the men worked the least. In the communities of mostly Orthodox Ukrainian Cossacks, who settled in the North Caucasus later and mostly in the middle Terek region, the men "retained many tints of the farmer" and worked alongside the women in the fields as much as possible.[30]

Non-Russian Cossacks seem to have worked their women the least and to have had a more strict division of labor, with men participating more in the family economy. By Ossetian customary law, labor was strictly divided by gender. Men were not to do women's work under any condition, and vice-versa—they looked down on the Russian habit of making women do all the heavy work of men.[31]

Georgian Cossacks apparently did not allow their women to work outside the house at all. One observer called them "a type of harem women" and claimed that they did not work, even in the house, but simply sat all day. Clearly this is an exaggeration. But Georgian Cossacks were poorer than the other Terek Cossacks and this was directly tied to the cultural limitations on female labor. At Shelkozavodskaia, a predominantly Armenian Cossack village, men did the harvest and garden work.[32]

The main reason why mountain people so often captured women and girls and took them to be married, traded, or ransomed was because they were the easy targets; they were the ones out in the fields and at the vineyards, outside the stanitsa walls, with little or no armed cover. The dominance of women's labor also helps to explain why male Cossacks were so desperate when their women fled or were taken captive in the mountains. As the saying went at Chcrvlennaia, "When the husband leaves, there's a little more to do; when the wife leaves, the entire house goes with her." Men were often put in a difficult position when their women left and they were not allowed to marry again for ten years. In such cases, Cossacks and regiment officials petitioned the church to get their marriages annulled, citing the ruin of their domestic economy. But they had to wait it out ten, and with the slow workings of the bureaucratic machinery, sometimes twelve or thirteen years, long enough to devastate their household if they did not take other measures to get a mate.[33]

The economic predominance of the Terek Cossack women in their home economy also translated to other powers in the house. Women took part in family meetings and in many places were equal to men, although the husband was still considered the head of the family. In many Greben Cossack households, women made all of the economic decisions. According to a local writer, with the Grebentsy, "a husband wouldn't dare even to sell a chicken without his wife." This dominance of elder women in the home economy and equality in the household seems to have improved female-male relations in general there. Parents supposedly accorded daughters-in-law more respect there than in Russian households where the oppression of the daughter-in-law was legendary: "Here daughters-in-law do not hang themselves and do not run away from the oppression of the husband's father and mother and thank God. There has never been such a case with the Greben Cossacks."[34] This contrasted with the often-miserable position of daughters-in-law in Great Russian families, where she was the sexual prey of her father-in-law under the practice of *snokhachestvo*.

There did exist a degree of land discrimination against widows. Widows were generally allotted less plowland than male-headed households; but the most important land—vineyard land, gardens, and the steppe farmstead land—was not reallotted and remained in the family. And if a relatively well-off widow wanted to acquire more plowland, she could lease it from Cossacks who did not have the labor power to use their allotments.[35]

Greben Cossack women were famed for the power they held in their houses. Regionally known as *mamuki*, they ran the household economies with full independence:

> Located continually on service and not receiving either uniform or other necessities of life from the state and at the same time not providing any material use to the family, the husband could not have the predominant influence on the wife, either with labor or with wise instruction, but to the contrary, appeared to his family always as some sort of parasite.

In the Greben Cossack communities, wives even interceded for husbands with their officers.[36]

There was a structural similarity between these Cossack villages and the communities of high male out-migration in Kostroma province documented by Engel. There, men left to engage in skilled trades, but usually not before marrying and establishing a family economy. With men gone, these villages turned into "women's kingdoms," where women did the heavy agricultural work, controlled the domestic economies, had greater independence, cohabited with their lovers, and even participated in the village assembly, sometimes serving as representatives and elders. When the men returned, they were often treated "like guests," and were in general more respectful of their wives, and less likely to tame them with the whip.[37]

One wonders if the Old Believer Terek Cossacks were also influenced to accept handing over such economic and political power to women by the model of the self-governing Irgiz convents of Saratov province. There women had full independence from the men's monasteries in spiritual and economic matters. At Irgiz, the women controlled their own lives and secured their own incomes, from donations, but also by trading vegetables, selling handicrafts, fishing, performing agricultural outwork, and hiring themselves out as readers in the houses of well-to-do Old Believers. At the least, because of the close contact between the Old Believers of Irgiz and the North Caucasus (see Chapter 9), the Terek Cossacks were aware of this center of female power, which made their own communities seem, perhaps, normal.[38]

So where did the men come in? Men left for service, and although they did bring in a little income from this, as far as the women were concerned their main purpose was to distinguish themselves in battle, to accrue military honor. It was kind of an out-migration of charisma. And those who were most devoted to military service, those who were most distinguished for their bravery and military exploits, had the least time for their household economy and were the most dependent on their wives at home.

Greben Cossack wives were even in control of the one item that perhaps was the most important to their husbands' military prowess and charisma— their horses. The Greben Cossack wife tended her husband's horse when he was home—she fed and watered it, cleaned it, and when an alarm sounded, she saddled the horse up and held it by the bridle at the threshold of their house, waiting for her husband. A close observer of the Tertsy wrote, "leading him, she reminded him of his duty and of the reputation of the family which was as dear to her as it was to the *bogatyr'* Cossack." He continued, "she is always ready to contribute hard work if only to see her *dzhigit* husband on a valiant horse, covered with weapons, bound in silver with niello."[39]

Prince Goriunov, who lived in Chervlennaia in 1846, wondered if perhaps a dead Cossack was not worth more to his wife than a live one. He spoke of a "cult of the body" and the lengthy and frequent mourning ceremonies that the women engaged in for their men who had fallen in battle. "Such a death," he wrote, "wasn't considered a loss, but was met with solemn pride by the family." They were often buried in vineyards, where wives, sisters, and granddaughters lamented over their man during work breaks, recounting his military exploits and boasting of his merits (see Chapter 8).[40]

We have come a long way from Repin's swaggering Cossacks. I do not mean to imply that the same gender relations held for other Cossack groups. Within the Terek Cossack communities even, there was a wide variation in the role and position of women. But wherever Cossacks lived, there tended to be a shortage of labor that was compensated by women taking more prominent roles in the domestic economy. For example, Don Cossack women, as Shane O'Rourke has shown, had similar economic power based on the absence of men from the economy. Where the shortage was acute, as in the lower Terek region, women basically controlled the economy.[41]

All Cossacks had to solve the problem of combining lives devoted to fighting and military service with the need to build agricultural economies and families. An extreme solution was practiced by the Zaporozhian Cossacks who totally separated their military world from their domestic world, forming a camp of warriors—the famed *sech*—where women and families were not allowed, or endangered. Reproduction and domestic production (including essential activities such as growing grain) took place back in the villages. Most other Cossacks seem to have practiced a variation on the Terek solution by keeping their community intact, but handing over significant economic control to their women.[42]

Cossack women of the lower Terek also seem to have benefited from the general paucity of good plowland and pasture. The Black Sea (later Kuban) Cossacks along the Kuban and in the Stavropol' steppe had richer agricultural land and larger, more patriarchal families; they were better able to replicate black earth Russian and Ukrainian gender patterns.[43] Poorer agricultural land created smaller families, a greater reliance on military service, and a more diversified economy, where women were in control. The repartitional commune throughout Russia was a patriarchy-perpetuating institution since the allocation of land strips was tied to men, not women; women were apportioned land only as a function of their relationship to men, as wives or widows. Labor power and gender power reinforced themselves. Perhaps Rose Glickman put it best: "Land was a male attribute. Although the land was not the private property of any individual male, the right to land devolved from father to son, or, in the absence of sons, to other male relatives."[44]

But where those strips had less value to the economy, as in the lower Terek, the power associated with them faded. The loosening of patriarchal control in the Russian countryside was, then, not just a function of the spread of capitalist wage relations and industrial employment, described so well by Engel. As the experience of the Terek Cossacks shows, it could also occur in areas where agricultural land, and its gendered power, was poor and where the men left, not because of a capitalist economic pull, but because they served the state.

Further, wherever Cossacks lived, marriage tended to be a political issue. When Cossacks were Old Believers, this was even more the case, and they resorted to a variety of illegal measures and cultural adaptations to overcome their restrictions concerning marriage (and ultimately reproduction), perhaps the most basic and potentially threatening challenge to their communities.

There are also larger ecological and social contexts. On other frontiers, the lack of clergy and paucity of women created a flexible sexual ethic. As Richard W. Slatta has shown for the remote, gender-skewed, and clergy-poor nineteenth-century Argentinean pampas "common-law marriages and concubinage represented normal relationships" and illegitimacy flourished. Maroon communities in Central and South America often practiced various forms of woman sharing; the Leeward Maroons of Jamaica even codified rules regulating the sharing of one woman by more than one man.[45]

The feminization of agriculture occurs in many mountain societies, because the fragile ecology forces a diversification of the economy, and the men are often away from home, tending livestock, selling handicrafts, or working as wage laborers. In many frontier societies the shortage of labor and the difficulties of the work conditions force women into larger economic roles. Here women enjoyed, in the none-too-flattering words of one historian of the American West, "prestige through scarcity."[46] In the North Caucasus these tendencies became accentuated, because the men were removed from the economy. They were displaced to a realm apart, where their main purpose, and sometimes their only purpose, besides making babies, was to win or retain honor for the family, if necessary by dying.

The Terek Cossack communities gave special powers to their women, but they were not Amazons. Many Cossack brides came to the stanitsa by force, but they certainly were not sexual captives. We can understand, though, why a Russian nobleman from St. Petersburg, a Lermontov or a Tolstoi, would have been attracted to and fearful of these women, who, according to the later, were "in most cases stronger, more intelligent, more developed and handsomer than the men."[47]

Notes

1. "Vstrecha Imperatritsy Ekateriny Velikoi Amazonskoiu rotiu," *Kavkaztsy*, 1858. This probably was inspired by the "Amazon" regiment created by Potemkin to greet Catherine the Great on her 1787 trip to the Crimea. See John T. Alexander, *Catherine the Great: Life and Legend* (Oxford: Oxford University Press, 1989), 260.

2. "Legenda o Kizliare," *Terskiia vedomosti*, 3 January 1891, 4; Iu. Shidlovskii, "Zapiski o Kizliare," *Zhurnal Ministerstva vnutrennikh del*, no. 4 (1843): 188-89. In another version they are captured by Circassians. See, "Goroda Stavropol'skoi gubernii," *Izvestiia*

Kavkazskago otdela Imperatorskago russkago geograficheskago obshchestva 5, no. 4 (1878): supplement, 14-17; N. P. Gritsenko, *Goroda Severo-Vostochnogo Kavkaza i proizvoditel'nye sily kraia V-seredina XIX veka* (Rostov-on-Don: Izdatel'stvo Rostovskogo universiteta, 1984), 85-86; N. Semenov, "Drugoe predanie o Kizliare," *Terskiia vedomosti*, 10 January 1891, 4.

3. Rose L. Glickman, "Women and the Peasant Commune," in *Land Commune and Peasant Community in Russia*, Roger Bartlett, ed. (New York: St. Martin's, 1990), 321; Barbara Alpern Engel, "The Woman's Side: Male Out-Migration and the Family Economy in Kostroma Province," *Slavic Review* 45, no. 2 (1986): 257-71; Barbara Alpern Engel, *Between the Fields and the City: Women, Work, and Family in Russia, 1861-1914* (Cambridge: Cambridge University Press, 1994); Christine D. Worobec, "Victims or Actors? Russian Peasant Women and Patriarchy," in *Peasant Economy, Culture, and Politics of European Russia, 1800-1921*, Esther Kingston-Mann and Timothy Mixter, ed. (Princeton: Princeton University Press, 1991), 179-200.

4. Aleksandr Rigel'man, *Istoriia ili povestvovanie o Donskikh kazakakh* (Moscow: Universitetskaia tipografiia, 1846), 138-39. This was originally written in 1778. G. N. Prozritelev, "Pervyia Russkiia poseleniia na Severnom Kavkaze i v nyneshnei Stavropol'skoi gubernii," *Trudy Stavropol'skoi uchenoi arkhivnoi komissii*, no. 5 (1913): section 1, 1-7; Rossiiskii Gosudarstvennyi Voenno-Istoricheskii Arkhiv [RGVIA], f. 1058, op. 1, d. 370, ll. 243-46, 258-59, 279-80, 284-85, 290-91, 296, 370. The 1781-1784 migration was not of Cossacks, but most would become Cossacks.

5. A. Tvalchrelidze, *Stavropol'skaia guberniia v statisticheskom, geograficheskom, istoricheskom i sel'sko-khoziaistvennom otnosheniiakh* (Stavropol': Tipografiia M. N. Koritskogo, 1897), 171. For 1847 rules regulating the distribution of women to Cossack villages, see RGVIA, f. 1058, op. 1, d. 541, ll. 39-40. Friedrich Wagner, *Schamyl and Circassia*, trans. Kenneth R.H. Mackenzie (London: G. Routledge and Co., 1854), 45-46.

6. G. A. Tkachëv, *Stanitsa Chervlennaia. Istoricheskii ocherk* (Vladikavkaz: Elektropechatnia tipografiia Terskago oblastnago pravleniia, 1912), 181-83. For bride stealing in Siberia, see James Forsyth, *A History of the Peoples of Siberia* (Cambridge: Cambridge University Press, 1992), 67-68.

7. B. P. Berozov, *Istoricheskie etiudy (iz istorii vozniknoveniia Osetinskikh sel i kazach'ikh stanits)* (Vladikavkaz: Izdatel'stvo Severo-Osetinskogo gosudarstvennogo universiteta im. K. L. Khetagurova, 1992), 11-14; RGVIA, f. 1058, op. 1, d. 541, ll. 39-40; f. 1058, op. 2, d. 1278, l. 1; F. P. Ponomarëv, "Materialy po istorii Terskago kazach'iago voiska. 2-i Malorossiiskii polk," *Terskii sbornik*, no. 6 (1904): 177-89.

8. N. G. Putintsev, *Khronologicheskii perechen' sobytii iz istorii Sibirskago kazach'iago voiska* (Omsk: Tipografiia Okr. shtaba, 1891), 38-39; F. A. Shcherbina, *Istoriia Kubanskago kazach'iago voiska* (Ekaterinodar: Tipografiia Kubanskago oblastnogo pravleniia, 1910), 830-31.

9. Moshe Gammer, *Muslim Resistance to the Tsar: Shamil and the Conquest of Chechnia and Daghestan* (London: Frank Cass, 1994), 253; Georgii Paradov, "Raskaz ochevidtsa o Shamile i ego sovremennikakh," *Sbornik materialov dlia opisaniia mestnostei i plemen Kavkaza* 32 (1903): section 1, 18; Trifon Vasilikhin, "Ocherk staroobriadchestva v stanitse Kalinovskoi Terskoi oblasti, s 1840 do 1880 g.," *Kavkazskiia eparkhial'nyia vedomosti*, no. 1 (1 January 1881): unofficial section, 30-34.

10. RGVIA, f. 1058, op. 1, d. 320, l. 7; d. 323, l. 4; Episkop Nestrov, "Upravlenie Platona (Liubarskago), Arkhiepiskopa Astrakhanskago i Kavkazskago, Kavkazskoiu pastoriu s 1800 po 1805 g," *Kavkazskiia eparkhial'nyia vedomosti*, no. 3 (1 February 1879): 123; Vasilikhin, "Ocherk staroobriadchestva," 26-29.

11. Vasilikhin, "Ocherk staroobriadchestva," 26-29; no. 2 (16 January 1881): unofficial section, 44-47. For other secret marriages, see RGVIA, f. 14877, op. 1, d. 2935, l. 3. Because of the precariousness of their legal position, other Old Believers were known to conduct mass marriages when the opportunity struck. The first step of the Old Believers in the Astrakhan uprising of 1705-06 was to perform 100 marriages in one day, including underage marriages. They had heard that the state was going to prohibit marriage for seven years and that after that they would have to give their daughters to Germans. See S. M. Solov'ev, "Rasskazy iz Russkoi istorii XVIII veka. Sto svadeb v Astrakhani," in *Chteniia i rasskazy po istorii Rossii* (Moscow: Izdatel'stvo "Pravda," 1989), 584-87.

12. RGVIA, f. 1058, op. 1, d. 334, ll. 10-17, 21-26, 29-36, 40-47, 80-87, 130-35, 141-44, 152-56; d. 370, ll. 243-46, 258-29, 279-80, 284-85, 290-91, 296.

13. "Posemeinye spiski i vedomosti, predstavlennye v komitet po sostavleniiu proekta polozh. o Kavk. Lin. voiske" in I. Popko, *Terskie kazaki s starodavnikh vremen. Istoricheskii ocherk* (St. Petersburg: Tipografiia Departamenta udelov, 1880), 463-487. The village of Shelkozavodskaia was not included because it was made up mostly of Armenian Cossacks. There were nearly no marriages there where the wife was older than the husband.

14. Vasilikhin, "Ocherk staroobriadchestva," no. 3 (1 February 1881): unofficial section, 132-33; I. Slivitskii, "Ocherki Kavkaza i Zakavkaz'ia. Kazatskii khutor i staroobriadcheskie skity v Ishorakh," *Kavkaz*, 4 December 1848, 195-96; Popko, *Terskie kazaki*, 426.

15. N. N. Smirnov, *Slovo o zabaikal'skikh kazakakh* (Volgograd: Komitet po pechati, 1994), 36. A seventeenth-century description of Ukrainian Cossack girls courting the boys and asking their parents for consent is intriguing, but I have no evidence that Terek Cossack young women initiated these marriages. See Guillaume Le Vasseur and Sieur de Beuplan, *A Description of Ukraine*, trans. Andrew B. Pernal and Dennis F. Essar (Cambridge, Mass.: Harvard Ukrainian Research Institute, 1993), 70-71.

16. Tkachëv, *Stanitsa Chervlennaia*, 144-45; A. Sosiev, "Stanitsa Chernoiarskaia," *Terskii sbornik*, no. 5 (1903): 48-52; Engel, *Between the Fields and the City*, 9; Ansley J. Coale, Barbara A. Anderson, and Erna Härm, *Human Fertility in Russia Since the Nineteenth Century* (Princeton: Princeton University Press, 1979), 251-53.

Most of the Cossacks of Chernoiarskaia and Novoosetinskaia were Ossetians and Sosiev attributed their strange sexual unions as part of a hybrid culture of Christian, Islamic, and pagan traditions.

17. Engel, "The Woman's Side," 268.

18. RGVIA, f. 14877, op. 1, d. 354, l. 19.

19. RGVIA, f. 14877, op. 1, d. 683, l. 56; d. 904, ll. 2-4, 8-9; d. 967, l. 2; N. Samarin, "Dorozhnyia zametki," *Severnaia pchela*, no, 134 (1862): 550-55; Popko, *Terskie kazaki*, 299-301, 426-28; RGVIA, f. 14877, op. 1, d. 325, ll. 27-28; d. 487, l. 1-3, 14.

20. Mikhail Zobov, "Iz stanitsy," *Terskiia vedomosti*, 8 January 1875, 2; Vasilikhin, "Ocherk staroobriadchestva," no. 3 (1 February 1881): unofficial section, 132-33; RGVIA, f. 14877, op. 1, d. 3047, ll. 1-2; f. 1058, op. 2, d. 1304, l. 8. For other cases see, for example, f. 14877, op. 1, d. 96, l. 128; d. 504, ll. 1-2; d. 5227, op. 1, ll. 1-2.

21. Popko, *Terskie kazaki*, 212-14, 360-62; V. A. Potto, *Dva veka Terskago kazachestva (1577-1801)* (Vladikavkaz: Elektropechatnia tipografiia Terskago oblastnago pravleniia, 1912), 2: 66-67. Women were also occasionally dragged into service—mostly to perform carting work, but occasionally courier service. And they helped to defend their village from enemy attack, sometimes riding out dressed in *cherkeskas* and *papakhas* with rifles slung across their shoulders. Tkachëv, *Stanitsa Chervlennaia*, 117-18.

22. A. Rzhevuskii, comp., *Tertsy. Sbornik istoricheskikh, bytovykh i geografichesko-statisticheskikh svedenii* (Vladikavkaz: Tipografiia Oblastnago pravleniia Terskoi oblasti, 1888), 250.

23. F. Ponomarëv, "O zemledel'cheskikh zaniatiiakh zhitelei Kizliarskago kazach'iago polka," *Zapiski Kavkazskago obshchestva sel'skago khoziaistva* 15, no. 4 (1869): 134-36; Popko, *Terskie kazaki*, 445-46; "Istoricheskiia svedeniia o Grebenskom kazach'em polku," *Sbornik Obshchestva liubitelei kazach'ei stariny*, no. 4 (1912): 49-51. For general descriptions of women's work, see I. Debu, "O nachal'nom ustanovlenii i rasprostranenii kavkazskoi linii," *Otechestvennyia zapiski* 18, no. 48 (1824): 279-81; I. Debu, *O Kavkazskoi linii i prisoedinennom k nei Chernomorskom voiske* (St. Petersburg: Tipografiia Karla Kraiia, 1829), 51-54; Voiskovoe khoziaistvennoe pravlenie, *Statisticheskiia monografii po izsledovaniiu stanichnago byta Terskago kazach'iago voisko* (Vladikavkaz: Tipografiia Terskago oblastnago pravleniia, 1881), 373-75, 404-09; Rzhevuskii, *Tertsy*, 248-49.

24. Popko, *Terskie kazaki*, 214-17; Potto, *Dva veka Terskago kazachestva*, 68-69.

25. Tkachëv, *Stanitsa Chervlennaia*, 116-18.

26. "Statisticheskiia izvestiia o kavkazskoi oblasti i zemle voiska Chernomorskago," *Zhurnal Ministerstva vnutrennykh del* 3, no. 5 (1830): 124-27; "Vzgliad na Kavkazskuiu liniiu," *Severnyi arkhiv* 2 (1822): 177-78; Debu, "O nachal'nom ustanovlenii," 279-81; Voiskovoe khoziaistvennoe pravlenie, *Statisticheskii monografii*, 404-09; O. V. Marggraf, *Ocherk kustarnykh promyslov Severnogo Kavkaza s opisaniem tekhniki proizvodstva* (Moscow: Tipografiia S. V. Gur'ianova, 1882), xiv-xl.

27. "Opisanie Kavkazskago shelkovodstva," *Sbornik materialov dlia opisaniia mestnostei i plemen kavkaza* 11 (1891): section 2, 16-17; "Istoricheskiia svedeniia o Grebenskom kazach'em polku," *Sbornik Obshchestva liubitelei kazach'ei stariny*, no. 4 (1912): 49-51; Voiskovoe khoziaistvennoe pravlenie, *Statisticheskiia monografii*, 252-58, 318.

28. Potto, *Terskie kazaki*, 484-87; Tkachëv, *Stanitsa Chervlennaia*, 192-93; I. Slivitskii, "Ocherki Kavkaza i Zakavkaz'ia." *Kavkaz*, 27 November 1848, 190-92.

Shane O'Rourke has observed a similar economic power among Don Cossack women in the nineteenth century. They too had a larger role in their families' economies than Russian peasants did, which translated to more control over property. See Shane O'Rourke, "Women in a Warrior Society: Don Cossack Women, 1860-1914," in Rosalind Marsh, ed., *Women in Russia and Ukraine* (Cambridge: Cambridge University Press, 1996), 45-54.

29. Rzhevuskii, *Tertsy*, 248-49; Voiskovoe khoziaistvennoe pravlenie, *Statisticheskiia monografii*, 404-09.

30. Voiskovoe khoziaistvennoe pravlenie, *Statisticheskiia monografii*, 373-75.

31. Ibid, 404-09.

32. Ibid, 376-79; "Neskol'ko slov o nastoiashchem polozhenii Grebenskikh kazakov," *Terskiia vedomosti*, 10 June 1868, 94.

33. G. Maliavkin, "Stanitsa Chervlenaia," *Etnograficheskoe obozrenie*, no. 2 (1891): 32; RGVIA, f. 14877, op. 1, d. 96, l. 128; d. 388, l. 9-18, 45; d. 504, l. 1-2, 32, 38.

F. A. Shcherbina claimed that Black Sea Cossack women were rarely in captivity, because when they were kidnapped by Circassians, their families and military authorities expended all of their energy to conclude an exchange or a ransom quickly. Otherwise, economies suffered. See Shcherbina, *Istoriia Kubanskago kazach'iago voiska*, 830.

34. Sosiev "Stanitsa Ekaterinogradskaia," 16-24; Rzhevuskii, *Tertsy*, 242.

35. L. B. Zasedateleva, "Evoliutsiia obshchiny u Terskikh kazakov v XVI-XIX vv.," *Sovetskaia etnografiia*, no. 1 (1969): 27-29. Sometimes the plowland was divided based on which families did the work digging canals. Since it was mostly women who dug the canals, there the land was divided based on the labor of women. F. Ponomarëv, "O zemledel'cheskikh zaniatiiakh zhitelei Kizliarskago kazach'iago polka," *Zapiski Kavkazskago obshchestva sel'skago khoziaistva* 15, no. 4 (1869): 130-34.

36. Rzhevuskii, *Tertsy*, 250-57, 264-65.

37. Engel, "The Woman's Side," 257-71.

38. Crummey, *The Old Believers*, 130; N. S. Sokolov, *Raskol v Saratovskom krae* (Saratov: Tipografiia N. V. Shtertser i Ko., 1888), 273-73.

39. Rzhevuskii, *Tertsy*, 251-57, 264-65; Tkachëv, *Stanitsa Chervlennaia*, 119-25.

40. Tkachëv, *Stanitsa Chervlennaia*, 165-67; Rzhevuskii, *Tertsy*, 243.

41. O'Rourke, "Women in a Warrior Society," 45-54.

42. D. I. Iavornitskii, *Istoriia zaporoz'kikh kazakiv* (Moscow: Pervaia zhenskaia tipografiia E. K. Gerbek, 1900; reprint, Kyiv: Naukova dumka, 1990), 1: 241-42, 250-51.

One is also reminded of the woodland Indians of eastern North America, where—to the shock of colonists—women performed the agricultural work, so the men could go away to hunt and fight. See William Cronon, *Changes in the Land: Indians, Colonists, and the Ecology of New England* (New York: Hill and Wang, 1983), 44-48.

43. Shcherbina, *Istoriia Kubanskago kazach'iago voiska*, 831; K. V. Chistov, ed., *Kubanskie stanitsy* (Moscow: Izdatel'stvo "Nauka," 1967), 188-200.

The connection between farming and patriarchy apparently stretches back to antiquity in the North Caucasus/Black Sea region. Timothy Taylor writes that the considerable position of Scythian women—Amazon prototypes—probably worsened after the Scythians transformed a good part of their pastoral-based nomad economy into a wheat-export economy, thanks to their contacts with Greek colonists on the north shore of the Black Sea. See Timothy Taylor and T. Sulimirski, "The Scythians," in *Cambridge Ancient History*.

44. Rose L. Glickman, *Russian Factory Women* (Berkeley: University of California Press, 1984), 27.

45. Richard W. Slatta, *Gauchos & the Vanishing Frontier* (Lincoln: University of Nebraska Press, 1983; repr., 1992), 57-60; Richard Price, ed., *Maroon Societies*, 3d ed. (Baltimore: Johns Hopkins University Press, 1996), 18-19.

46. William Forrest Sprague, *Women and the West* (Boston: Christopher Publishing House, 1940; repr., New York: Arno Press, 1972).

47. Leo Tolstoy, *The Cossacks*, trans. Rosemary Edmonds (Harmondsworth: Penguin, 1960), 180.

8

Military Service and Warrior Culture

Слава казачья, а жизнь собачья.
It's a Cossack's glory, but a dog's life.

—Terek Cossack saying

The horrible custom of blood revenge gives rise to an unstoppable series of murder and plunder which in the end would reduce the people to the level of African tigers and lay low the population of this region like the plague if the related customs of hospitality and the peculiar spirit of the bonds of friendship that is famous in the Caucasus under the name of kunachestvo did not place several limits to this torrent of destruction.

—S. D. Nechaev, *Moskovskii telegraf*

Hey you sweeties, don't do this,
Don't do this, don't love those,
Armenians, merchants, or scoundrel-officers.
Love, dearies, Greben Cossacks;
The entire host of Greben Cossacks are great guys,
They're all great guys,
and they're all kunaks with the Chechens.

—Greben Cossack song

Cossacks comprised a military estate—as far as the state was concerned, the entire purpose of cossackdom in the North Caucasus was to defend and help expand the borders of the Russian empire, through military service and permanent settlement. Cossacks saw themselves as warriors and as settlers, saddled with onerous military obligations, struggling to build successful communities in a harsh terrain among sometimes hostile neighbors. In the chronically labor short Cossack villages, the demands of military service often came into conflict with the domestic needs of the stanitsas. Military service and permanent settlement did not always harmonize.

The Cossack system in the North Caucasus created fighters who knew the local terrain and understood the habits of their North Caucasian enemies, counteracting some of the long-term weaknesses of the alien and rather oblivious Russian regular army in the Caucasus. But this was achieved at the expense of a degree of "nativization" of the Cossack forces, with all of the ambivalence towards Russian power that that implied. Terek Cossacks adopted native uniforms, weapons, fighting techniques, and even further, native customs for regulating warfare. The flow of influence was definitely from the south, to the extent that Cossacks were dependent upon their erstwhile enemies for their weapons and often for their horses. Some found the frontier culture so permeable, they had no difficulty crossing over to the other side. As we will see in Chapter 9, Old Believer Cossacks had fundamental differences with the Russian state and occasionally cut their ties completely and fled to the mountains. Others deserted to sow some wild oats with the Chechens or to pursue careers as bandits, holding up travelers and plundering Cossack and peasant villages.

Most Terek Cossacks fought for the tsar, but they also fought for themselves, sometimes on their own terms. What Catherine Wendy Bracewell has described for the Uskoks of Senj—another frontier warrior community along the Christian-Muslim divide of the Habsburg Military Frontier in Croatia—applies equally to the Terek Cossacks, and to their trans-Terek neighbors: "Military operations for the purpose of destroying the enemy and conquering territory were far less a part of border warfare than were plundering raids, usually involving a minimum of confrontation and battle."[1]

Terek Cossacks were not so much conscious empire builders as they were residents on the North Caucasus frontier, which had a fighting code all of its own, and where friends and neighbors were often more important to one's livelihood and security than a barely existent state. That is not to deny that Cossacks spent plenty of time fighting Chechens, Ingush, Kabardians, and others. But they also, at different times, avoided fighting them, fought according to their Caucasian rules, and fought alongside them.

Terek Cossack men were warriors; military training and service structured their lives and their communities. But they were warriors in the Caucasian tradition, who looked like and fought like their enemies. And often for the same purpose—more to acquire honor for their family than territory for the state. The older Cossack communities of the lower Terek were considered the best, and the most nativized, fighters, but all of the Cossacks of the line adopted the weapons, techniques, and the warrior culture of the mountain people, at least partially.

Cossack military training began at an early age and their ritual calendar included many celebrations designed to build fighting skills. At Chervlennaia, boys engaged in the annual "launching of the ships" on Whit Monday. They constructed tiny ships, fully equipped with masts and rigging, and adorned by girls with flags, sails, and tiny dolls. The most beautiful girls launched the ships in the Terek and as they began to disappear from view the boys, dressed in full weaponry, shot at them, competing for accolades. During Shrovetide, mounted Cossack boys did trick riding (*dzhigitovka*) and tried to attack girls armed with sticks. Those who managed to withstand the blows and snatch the booty were rewarded with a kiss.[2]

Shrovetide was a favorite period for military games. As V. Verstennikov, a writer in *Kavkaz*, observed:

> the manner of life is similar to the half-wild mountain tribes who engage in battles with Russians all of their life; the Cossacks are accustomed to imitating them in their entertainments. The mountain people engage in horse races, shooting contests, and dancing during weddings and their holiday Bairam; the Cossacks do this during Shrovetide.

They marched, staged horse races, and took over their villages with daily mock battles, shooting rifles and pistols, brandishing swords, and trying to "kill" or capture their opponents. The highlight was usually the *dzhigitovka*, an ancient type of trick riding which may have originated in the Caucasus. Riding Kabardian horses at full speed, Cossacks shot at targets and performed all sorts of daring stunts. Verstennikov could not contain his excitement when he observed one such display in 1849:

> One galloped at full speed, instantly snatching out a gun from the case six steps in front of the sheaf [target], cocked it, leaned over below the saddle and with a well-aimed shot set fire to the sheaf. Another dashed off after him, standing on the horse and firing from pistols. A third lay down on the saddle, raising his legs up. Another, at full gallop, without stopping, jumped from the horse with one leg, and sat back up again. Another jumped down all the way to the ground, ran with the horse for several yards, and in an instant was up and back on the horse. Over there you see two, standing on their saddles, joining hands and rushing along at full speed. A different one throws himself back, barely holding on to the stirrup with one leg, lying, nearly touching his head to the ground. Another comes off on the front, drags his hand on the ground, and nearly falls. Any hat that falls to the ground is instantly shot to pieces. And if the spectator puts money on the ground, it is carried away in the pockets of dare-devils.[3]

The uniform and weaponry of the Terek Cossacks was also adopted wholesale from the mountain people—perhaps nothing better represents their cultural proximity (see Chapter 6). Travelers continually mistook Cossacks for enemy mountain people because they looked so much alike. Moritz Wagner's first encounter with Line Cossacks in 1843 was typically upsetting: "Their dress and arms are the same as the Circassians, with whom, I at first, confounded them, much to my consternation." John Baddeley—a frequent visitor to the Caucasus at the end of the century—agreed:

No one but a native of the Caucasus, or one who has spent many years there, could possibly distinguish the brigand from the horse-patrol sent to catch him; or, for the matter of that, from the peaceful peasant or, as Scott wrote of England in the eighteenth century, even the country gentleman—a native prince, say—out for pleasure, or for business.[4]

These Cossack warriors in the Caucasian style were a part of the military chain of command in the Russian empire and from the perspective of the center they were an important force in the integration of the North Caucasus into the Russian empire. From the perspective of the frontier, though, Terek Cossacks fought to acquire military glory and the resulting honor in their communities. Although the army, beginning in 1819, appointed the atamans and top regimental officers, it seems as if their own definitions of honor structured the social order of their communities, at least in the lower Terek. In other words, since they were a largely self-governing military community, it was military glory more than economic position, heredity, or education that determined social position. Officers were simple Cossacks who had distinguished themselves in battle; they were usually illiterate and often not much richer than anyone else. If they were Old Believers, as many were in the lower Terek, they were not even legally noble. According to an officer who lived with the Greben Cossacks in 1846 and 1847, when Cossacks sent detachments out to repulse raids on the line, they did not organize themselves in squadrons or other hierarchical formal groupings, but simply rushed out, often led by a "rank and file" old Cossack with the most experience. And officers followed his orders without hesitation. Honor, then—and not estate, class, or rank—was the social signifier that ran like a red thread through Cossack lives, and the lives of their families and communities.[5]

The honor of the family was projected and maintained through fancy weaponry, elaborate uniforms, valuable horses, and mourning rituals. Since the men spent most of their lives fighting, women were also key in the maintenance of family charisma (see Chapter 7). They worked so their husbands could acquire Kabardian horses, Dagestanian *kinzhals*, and all the rest that they needed to project the image of the warrior. The Greben Cossack women made lace from gold and silver silk thread to decorate their husbands' full-dress uniforms. More than one observer noted how stunning the Greben Cossacks could look; Tkachëv described them as richly adorned dandies:

> decked out with gold or silver *kinzhals*, with horn or bone handles on which were also silver buttons; silver-handled *shashki* with silver screws and sheath tips; silver and black or gilded cartridge cases; a silver or gilded setting on a narrow waist belt; silver or gilded setting on the sword belt, bridle, saddle harness, buttons, triggers, *zhirnichka* [box with materials for cleaning weapons], and so on; sometimes even on the heads and screws on the pistols in their belts...such were the old Greben Cossacks, in thin, glittering *cherkeskas*, in satiny embroidered quilted coats, with lambskin

papakhas dashingly cocked at an angle.[6]

As we saw in Chapter 7, military honor was maintained even after death, when Greben Cossack communities engaged in prolonged and elaborate mourning to mark the glory of slain Cossacks. The first step was to save the body. Cossacks tried not to leave any slain comrades behind on the field of battle, and even occasionally pulled corpses out of mass graves so they could return them to their villages. Relatives needed to be given an opportunity to cry over the deceased and publicly read out his deeds and service.

The family often buried the bodies in vineyards, where, during work breaks, wives, sisters, and other women relatives lamented over their warriors, promoting their merits, recounting even the smallest affairs.

> And the more it was possible to list his merits, the more tragic the death of the deceased, the more often and more prolonged was the crying over his grave, the more pride there was in the tone of the words of the mourners, and the more envy was aroused in those who watched.

Funeral feasts were important occasions to continue the mourning. According to Kulebiakin, "Each Cossack troubles more about funeral feasts than about wedding feasts." Feasts were held to honor the dead right after the funeral, the third day after death, then on the fourth day, the twentieth day, the fortieth day, on the one-half year anniversary, the year anniversary, on the birthday of the deceased, and then every year on the anniversary of his death and his birthday. Forty or more relatives would come to each feast. It all totaled up to a great expense for these far-from-rich Cossacks, but was vital in creating the warrior-charisma that was so important to the community.[7]

What type of service did Cossacks hold in the North Caucasus? The popular image is of mounted Cossack warriors banding together in large hosts and after the requisite hooting and hollering and trick riding, engaging in vigorous and mass combat with their enemy. This was not typical. Most Cossack service did not involve military action. And when they were on active duty, they were more likely to be sleepily sitting atop a watch tower or patrolling a deserted river bank with a couple of comrades than actually fighting anyone. When they did fight, it tended to be limited and defensive or retributive.

In theory, Terek Cossacks served from age eighteen to forty-five, in different capacities in four different stages. From eighteen to twenty-one they were in preparatory service, learning to fight, observing battles, and providing support services during campaigns, such as guarding horses. At age twenty-one they entered active service and went on campaigns, either in the Caucasus or elsewhere, guarded the borders, and attended an annual military camp. From thirty-three through thirty-eight they were in the reserves, which in the North Caucasus was practically no different from active service except that they did not have to attend the annual camp. From the age of thirty-nine on, they fulfilled only stanitsa obligations such as guard duty. After they turned forty-five, they were freed from all service. In reality, local observers reported that service began at age fifteen or as young as thirteen and lasted until fifty, sixty, or later. Service records show even seventy- and eighty-year-old Cossacks on duty. The need for able bodies was so great that military officials were forced to press whomever they could into service. As their commander Stenbok said, "in the Greben regiment they define retired Cossacks as those who do not receive provisions for twenty-five years of service and non-serving as those who [simply] have not the estate of serving Cossacks." All physically able men were obliged to serve and those who were unfit still worked as stanitsa or cordon guards when the others were away at battle. Only those Cossacks mobilized for active service received any salary; those who defended their stanitsas, fields, and their part of the military line were considered not mobilized, and served, as the Cossacks said, "for water and grass." Mobilized Cossacks received salary in money, bread, and provisions.[8]

Then there were a host of other obligations for which all Cossacks were responsible. They had to provide quarter and build and maintain roads, bridges, and ferries. They staffed the post stations and provided convoys for mail deliverers, couriers, and travelers. The regular escort across the Georgian Military Highway was tedious and plodding, with Cossacks guarding a long line of carts and carriages. The express courier service (or the "flying post" as it was called) especially exhausted Cossacks and the post horses—up until 1821 when Ermolov decreased its availability, it was often sent three and sometimes four times in a twenty-four-hour period.[9]

One of the other most burdensome obligations was the carting service— Cossacks unloaded material and supplies arriving by ship from Astrakhan and carted it to fortresses-in-construction along the military line. They had to haul their grain salary from the same Caspian piers and when they did not have the carts, the labor, or the oxen available, they got Nogais to help. If the Nogais could not get enough oxcarts, then the Cossacks turned boat-haulers (*burlaki*) and dragged their goods up the Terek on wooden barges. At such times, according to an eyewitness, "it was offensive to see how these born warriors turned into simple *burlaki*."[10] As we have seen in Chapter 4, Cossacks were also largely responsible for building and maintaining the fascines and dikes along the Terek.

As a privileged estate, Cossacks were largely freed from taxes and duties, but the Terek Cossacks did pay dues for the maintenance of the postal service, land dues (*zemskii sbor*), and minor dues for the maintenance of the guard at the lower court (*nizhnyi zemskii sud*). They also had to assign a significant amount of their pasture and hay fields—sometimes up to 1,000 stacks of hay a year—to non-resident regiments.[11]

So the service obligations of the Terek Cossacks were broad and cut deep into their lives. But like most legal relations in the Russian empire, they were also riddled with inconsistency and poorly enforced. The Cossack estate in the North Caucasus did not provide for much coherence. The emperor never promulgated any all-Cossack charter and only in 1845 did the Terek Cossacks receive a systematic legal statute—a modification of the original Don Cossack statute of 1835.[12] Except for a ten-year period from 1776 to 1786 when they were a part of the Astrakhan host, Terek Cossacks, in fact, were not even unified into one host until 1832, when the Caucasus Line host was created. Up until then the Cossacks who lived along the Terek were an inconsistent jumble of hosts and regiments; the hosts (Greben, Terek-Semeinoe, and Terek-Kizliar), traditionally the largest Cossack formation, were often smaller than the regiments, which usually comprised the host.[13]

In practice, their service obligations—that which they did to make them "Cossack"—varied. The Volga regiment, because of its accessible position along the highway leading from the Don Cossack lands to the Caucasus foothills, was recruited for various escorts and commands more often than other regiments. The Greben Cossacks also felt that they were unfairly burdened, complaining to the War College in 1742 that their service burdens were greater than the others,

> because when there is a post to be sent or messengers or dispatches to Astrakhan and couriers to Derbent and travelers dispatched from the Persian side and to other places in the mountains, then only Greben Cossacks are used, since they know the local language and they are always used more in service.[14]

On the other hand, exemptions from service were sometimes granted if the regiment was thought to be particularly poor and weak in numbers. At different times, the Terek-Kizliar, Greben, and Vladikavkaz regiments were partially or totally freed from service because of the vulnerability of their communities. The same applied to military colonies that were later converted to Cossack stanitsas of the Volga and Sunzha regiments, where agriculture and trade were anemic and the residents too ill-equipped and low in numbers to provide any effective border defense. The Ukrainians who settled among the Greben Cossacks beginning in the late 1840s were often excluded from active duty, partly no doubt because of their initial tenuous economic circumstances, but also one suspects because of the condescending attitude the Grebentsy held towards them.[15]

The other exemptions were more systematic. The Kalmyks who joined the Mozdok regiment in 1777 had very limited service requirements, mostly convoy and guard duty. In the Greben regiment, Cossacks could obtain a service exemption for their sons by paying money to the stanitsa administration. Up to the mid-eighteenth century, Greben Cossacks also carried little cordon service because they contracted with the Chechens and others who lived on the right bank of the Terek and the Kabardians who rented land there to patrol the bank (see below).[16]

Still, there was a relentless demand for service and a major theme running through Terek Cossack history is the incessant complaining and petitioning about heavy service requirements crippling Cossack home economies and pointing to the tensions between the twin goals of military service and permanent settlement. As we saw in Chapter 5, the economies of especially the lower Terek Cossacks were always in a precarious position, and this was due in no small part to the labor shortage caused by military service. There were numerous indications that many Cossack communities had to strain to keep up with their obligations. In the early eighteenth century, Cossack women and girls were frequently forced into non-military service such as carting work. In the mid-eighteenth century, under-age boys were enlisted to keep up the active fighting numbers.[17]

Iosif Debu, who served sixteen years on the Caucasus Military Line commanding both the right and left flanks, worried in the 1820s about the overburdening of the Terek Cossacks and their inability to tend to their economies. He made a number of recommendations for limiting and equalizing their service, such as reducing the number of stanitsa guards and stationing active duty Cossacks closer to home so they could tend to their economies when things were slow. But there is no indication that if they were indeed implemented that these limited measures had any effect on actual Cossack service.[18]

In 1839 commander Stenbok warned that all Greben Cossacks served, even the supposedly retired and underaged, well over their legal obligations. They were, he said, on continual service at watchtowers, in secret observation posts, at fords, on convoys, strengthening the river banks, carting, and performing other duties, so that they had less than two days a week free. Anything that they managed to put aside was wiped out during the years of harvest failure. Their poverty was so great, he said, that most of them did not even own work animals and one plow was shared per ten households. The petition of an eighty-some-year-old Cossack of the Mountain regiment to Nicholas I from 1837 reveals a similar situation. He began service in 1781 and fought in campaigns against Kabardians, in Persia, Baku, in the siege of Anapa, and elsewhere. The army released him from service in 1801 because of poor health and rheumatic pain in the legs. But now, in his advanced age, he was being put into service, not just in the stanitsa but also along the cordon and even carting. When he resisted, the commanders threatened him with corporal punishment. "It is deplorable," he pleaded, "that having served in the war, to endure such a reprimand in my old age, but I do not have the strength to carry out the obligations demanded by the commanders."[19]

P. Nitsik claimed that in the 1840s the position of the Vladikavkaz regiment was "extraordinarily difficult" and that they had no time to devote to their domestic economies. Ataman Nikolai made a similar statement to the commander of the Line host Gurko in 1844. He reported that the poorly populated Mountain, Mozdok, Greben, and Semeino-Kizliar regiments suffered from their great burdens. He mentioned in particular billeting and the carting work, which women, children, and old men had to perform since the men were away on service. The fields remained unplowed because of the carting demands and the exhaustion of the work animals. The Cossacks of these regiments, he claimed, could not equip themselves with horses or arms and could not feed their own families. Indeed, about one-half of active-duty Cossacks in 1855 were poorly armed and without horse (see Chapter 5).[20]

Sometimes Cossacks resisted the harsh service requirements that drained their economies of vitality. When the Head Chancellery of Artillery and Fortifications issued an ukaz in 1745 ordering ten people from each stanitsa to take up artillery work, the Greben Cossacks refused. The Kizliar commander pressured them, but the affair went to the Senate which took their side. In 1771, Terek-Semeinoe, Greben, and Mozdok Cossacks refused carting work because of a shortage of oxcarts and oxcart wheels. This time the Senate required them to trade with the mountain people for the equipment and continue their work.[21]

Because of the burdens of service requirements on the Cossack domestic economy, there was also great incentive to shirk or go awol. Occasionally, when convoys were robbed, it was subsequently discovered they had fewer Cossack escorts than required. The Vladikavkaz convoy was attacked and robbed in 1843; the investigation revealed that instead of the five Cossacks who were supposed to comprise the escort, there were only four and two of them were underage. In a separate incident, only one Cossack was on convoy. Ivan Efimovich Frolov, an elderly respected Cossack with a long and distinguished service record, admitted that Greben Cossacks frequently escaped home at night from their field camps in Chechnia—he himself did it and as squadron leader he punished many others for what he called this "inadmissable deviation from the rules of service."[22]

Prince Goriunov served with the Greben Cossacks in the mid-1840s and he too observed them frequently dodging their duty. Cossacks on the cordon paid the commander to be released from duty so they could return home or to their farmsteads to work; Goriunov said that if twenty-five Cossacks were supposed to be on guard, in reality only twelve or thirteen of them were there. And indeed it was difficult to verify the number of Cossacks actually on guard, because it could always be claimed that some were out patrolling for Chechens. For example, at Chervlennaia they told the story of Semen Iankhotov, a cornet who was on guard at a convoy post. It was mowing season, so he let the entire command off to cut hay, leaving only himself and a sentry. When a general came demanding fifteen Cossacks for a convoy, the sentry hid Iankhotov in a manger, covered him with hay, and claimed that everyone was out investigating an alarm. The general continued on without his convoy and as Iankhotov crawled out from the hay, he yelled, "Hey uncle Pashka! It's good you thought of that uncle Pashka." From then on, "hey uncle Pashka" became a humorous catchphrase (*pribautka*) with the Cossacks.[23]

Cossack regiments or hosts rarely went on campaigns or to a battle en masse; they were usually scattered about at various defense lines and theaters of war. At most, they fought in a company (officially 100 men). Cossacks participated in campaigns alongside the regular army, usually in the North Caucasus, but during other wars they were pulled away for foreign campaigns. For example, Greben Cossacks campaigned far away across the Kuban against Circassians in the late eighteenth century and they also participated in the storming of Anapa in 1791, in Persian and Turkish wars in 1826-29, in the Polish campaign in 1831, and in 1802 they helped secure Russian power in Georgia after the East Georgian kingdom of Kartlo-Kakheti was incorporated into the empire. Between 1804 and 1859, the Ekaterinograd Cossacks of the Volga regiment fought against Kabardians, Chechens, and in Dagestan on nearly an annual basis, but were sent to fight against the Ottoman empire in 1829 and during the Crimean War. Between 1829 and 1840, Chernoiarskaia stanitsa of the Mountain regiment was sent to Turkey, then Yerevan, then Chechnia, then Dagestan, and back to Chechnia. At any one time, a regiment was stretched thin. In 1818, the Greben host, for example, had sixty-one Cossacks in Georgia, 143 at Endirei in the Kumyk plain, 135 at Groznyi fortress and the nearby Pregradnyi camp, 446 at cordon posts, 72 in reserve at stanitsas, and 66 on convoy detachments.[24]

When fighting organized campaigns against the mountain people, Cossacks fought with élan and brutality. They had no problem obeying orders to eliminate native villages. For example, after empress Elizabeth gave the order in 1758 because of perceived Chechen disloyalty, Greben and Terek-Semeinoe Cossacks attacked Chechen villages south of the Terek, trampled the unharvested grain and set fire to their houses. Ermolov's push into the Kumyk plain in 1817-21 was the occasion for some of the worst brutality and most ferocious fighting. Cossacks razed Chechen villages to the ground, chopped down forests, trampled gardens, confiscated cattle and other property, and torched grain fields and buildings. Many historians consider this the fatal turning point in the wars of the Caucasus, responsible for the increasing hostility of Chechens and others south of the Terek (see below).[25]

Even after Ermolov, there was always suspicion of native villages close to the cordon line and commanders frequently ordered Cossacks to eliminate these supposed "haunts of brigands" and force the residents to flee to the mountains. In 1847, for example, two and one-half battalions of Cossacks cleared out eleven Chechen villages south of the Sunzha and destroyed their stock of hay and grain in order to push them further away. The following year, fearing that it was a hideout for "plunderers" and other raiders, Cossacks attacked the Kumyk village of Akmet-Tal, drove off their livestock, and burned their grain and hay. The same happened repeatedly during the long decades of the Russian conquest of the Caucasus.[26]

The typical service, though, and that which more than anything else structured the life of the Terek Cossacks, was along the military cordon, the string of stanitsas, watch towers, and secret observation posts that stretched along, and with the Sunzha Line, south of, the Terek. Cossacks there watched for enemy movements, waiting in reserve at their stanitsas, perched atop observation posts, patrolling along the river, or hiding on the bank. The watch towers between the stanitsas and the secret listening posts along the river bank were key to this system of defense.

At night, Cossacks hid along the Terek opposite fords and openings where mountain people were likely to cross. If they caught groups fording the river, from their camouflaged position they could usually turn the exposed enemy away. During daytime, Cossacks sat atop the crude wooden towers next to beacons made of straw or tow smeared with tar or resin. If they spied a group on the attack, then they lit the signal and as soon as the guard of the neighboring stanitsa saw the smoke he fired an alarm shot, locked the gates, and Cossacks grabbed their weapons and assembled, ready to defend or attack. Fire signals passed quickly along the line, and stanitsas dispatched detachments to cut off the raid. Others remained to defend their villages. At least that was the way it was supposed to work.[27]

Although it was often depicted in belles lettres as unexpected and therefore particularly terrifying, there were many regularities to North Caucasus frontier raiding. Attackers usually crossed the river when it was easiest to do so: from October to April when the water was lowest and the nights dark and long. The most dangerous time was when the Terek froze. All was quiet when the Terek flooded from the snow thaw and during the rainy period in the mountains, which was fortuitous since Cossacks had their hands full battling the river.[28]

Shamil's resistance notwithstanding, mountain people usually raided across the border for kidnapping and plunder. Occasionally they attacked in the thousands. One of the most famous massed raids on a major fort-town was Kazi-Mula's [Ghazi Muhammad's] November 1831 invasion of Kizliar, killing 126, capturing 168, and robbing 500,000 rubles worth of money and goods from houses and churches. Residents estimated his forces to be somewhere between 800 and 2,000. Service records of officers of Chervlennaia tell of forces of 3,000, 4,000, and 8,000 attacking between 1840 and 1845. But these were often repulsed without much loss. For example, in 1841, a party of some 3,000 Chechens crossed the lower Terek and began driving off thousands of sheep and cattle. A comparable number of Cossacks from Shchedrinskaia and Chervlennaia and five platoons of chasseurs pursued them and managed to retrieve all of the livestock; only four men were killed on the Russian side and two disappeared. In addition to the ten Chechen bodies left behind, an unspecified number Chechens drowned when the ice broke upon recrossing the Terek.[29]

The typical—and more successful—raid involved much smaller numbers. If the intention was to grab only a few prisoners or several head of cattle from the Cossack line, then a handful of men crossed on foot. If they were heading further into Russian territory, such as to poorly guarded steppe farms, then they crossed in mounted parties of a few dozen. The most important stage of the raid was the crossing. First, the raiders learned of troop strength, weaknesses along the line, and other opportunities from spies, Russian deserters, native villagers who lived close to the Terek, native traders, and others familiar with the Russian side. Their information was sometimes remarkably good. Occasionally small groups were able to sneak into a stanitsa, steal a couple of cows or horses from a Cossack barn and then slip out through a hole in the wattle wall of the stanitsa. In 1846, raids along the lower Terek, where the Old Believer Cossacks observed a strict Lenten fast, became more frequent as Lent progressed and the Cossack bodies weakened; eleven attacks were mounted the week before Easter.[30]

Foot parties usually focused their attack on travelers, women and children working in Cossack gardens, small groups of Cossacks returning to their stanitsa at twilight after a hard day's work, and stanitsa cattle and horses. Mounted groups attacked field workers and drove off large herds of cattle and horses and flocks of sheep. Occasionally raiders appeared to engage in a bit of Islamic aggression, as when a large party of Chechens attacked the state peasant village of Aleksandrovskoe in 1840; besides bundling off captives and driving off the usual livestock, they chopped up fifty pigs. When Chechens attacked Chervlennaia in 1811, they made sure to burn the Cossack stills and twenty casks of Cossack brandy. According to a petition of a retired Cossack lieutenant, they often attacked their alcohol in that manner.[31]

Cossacks usually pursued the raiders no farther than the right bank of the Sunzha. If they were not able to retrieve their stolen livestock, sometimes Cossacks indiscriminately grabbed Chechen herds on the way back to the Terek, occasionally provoking a retaliation by an entirely different group. It was a limited back-and-forth game, with mountain people plundering Cossacks, and Cossacks plundering in return.[32]

Indeed, many of the Cossack attacks seem little different from the plundering raids of the mountain people; they occasionally attacked simply with the purpose of rustling livestock, stealing weapons, and taking bodies to ransom. The battle news in the local paper *Kavkaz* frequently boasted of the "loot" (*dobycha*) that Cossacks hauled back. In 1847, for example, *Kavkaz* reported on two Cossack raids on pasturing animals; in one, "our regiment [Mozdok] returned with valuable loot to the Groznyi fort": 65 head of cattle, 9 horses, and 500 sheep that were pastured on the right bank of the Argun River by Chechens. The service records of Chervlennaia show Cossacks pursuing Chechen invaders, but also making rustling raids of their own on Chechen cattle. Often it was difficult to tell who was pursuing whom: in June 1849 Cossacks drove off 300 head of cattle south of the Sunzha and Argun Rivers; on the way back they were attacked by one of Shamil's forces, which managed to retrieve a part of the herd; then the Cossacks turned around and galloped after them, eventually retrieving all of their hard-earned booty.[33]

The point of all of this raiding and counter-raiding was not to conquer land or to push the enemy away. It was an attempt to transfer property and money. The mountain people targeted livestock and tried to take captives whom they could hold for ransom or sell or exchange in the mountains. As Braudel has shown for the Mediterranean region, winter pastures were often the subject of dispute between mountain people and people of the plains. For example, in the Spanish Navarre:

> This transhumance was a frantic rush down from the mountain in winter—cattle and men hurried to escape the cold of the mountains and flooded into lower Navarre like an invading army. All doors were padlocked against these unwelcome visitors, and every year saw a renewal of the eternal war between shepherd and peasant, first on the way down...and then on the way back.[34]

As Russia gradually cut off Chechens and others from their winter pastures, this "natural" hostility grew sharper. Kidnapping and ransoming prisoners was an ancient vocation in the Caucasus that predated the Russian appearance in the region. It was practiced not only by Muslims, but also by the Christian Ossetians who were supposedly the great allies of Russia in the North Caucasus. Ossetians, just like the others, used captives as a barter good; in fact the Ossetian word for "prisoner" (*wacajrag*) literally means "an article of trade." When Cossacks pursued the raiders, they reckoned their success not only in the comparative body count or in the stolen goods retrieved, but also in the amount of native goods acquired, especially much-needed horses, weapons, and saddles. That is not to say that frontier warfare was only about property—both Cossacks and mountain people used their booty and heroic deeds to accrue honor and all of the social and political benefits that came with it. But the details of raiding and counter-raiding show that this fighting is best understood in the context of frontier culture and local social history rather than as imperial conquest and national resistance.[35]

Indeed, raiding and ransoming were often part of a formal system of local conflict resolution. Mountain people regulated disputes through customary rules—which Russians often lumped under the general term of *baranta* or *baramta*—that determined payment, usually in livestock, for crimes against persons or property. That is, if cattle were stolen or relatives killed or taken captive, the aggrieved party had the right to drive off cattle, sheep, oxen, or horses in retribution. Throughout the eighteenth century the Greben Cossacks regulated disputes with their trans-Terek neighbors through the rules of *baranta*, occasionally formalized by treaty. The 1765 treaty between Chervlennaia and the Kabardian Devlet-Girei and his subjects, for example, held both sides responsible for protecting each other against raiders and for paying fines in the case of theft. This is remarkable not only because the Cossacks regulated relations based on native traditions, but also because one Cossack village had taken upon itself the right to conclude such treaties. A more one-sided agreement was concluded in 1799 with Devlet-Girei's son, which held him and his subjects responsible for Chechen attacks mounted from their territory. At least one officer, the Greben regimental commander Stenbok, felt that this system worked: in 1839 he claimed that when Devlet-Girei and his descendants had responsibility for the land across from the Greben Cossacks, there was significantly less raiding.[36]

Through similar arrangements, Cossacks and their commanders tried to get Kumyk, Chechen, Ossetian, and Kabardian villages on the south side of the Terek to take responsibility for preventing raids on Cossack territory. Many were allowed to settle there with the agreement that they would have to pay for raids through their territory. In the eighteenth and nineteenth centuries, a first line of native defense was attempted, with Chechens settling between the Sunzha and the Terek, Ossetians around Vladikavkaz, and Kabardians and other Circassians along the left bank of the Kuban.[37]

The practice of ransoming captives was also embedded in local tradition. It was not haphazard, but rather a regulated system with formalized rules. First, mediators—Cossacks or natives—traveled to the mountains to investigate the status of the captive. Unless they were bundled off to be married or sold, it was usually not too difficult to find out the condition, and sometimes the location, of the captive. Highly valued prisoners were sometimes inspected by a mediator to assure those putting up the ransom money that the "goods" were indeed in order. Once the price was fixed, Cossacks usually took up a collection to pay for their comrade or relative.[38]

The most lucrative targets were not Cossacks, but high officers in the regular army and their wives and children; the most lucrative Cossack targets were from high Cossack ranks. As far as the mountain people were concerned, the point was to set the ransom price as high as realistically possible—if Cossacks could not raise the money for overpriced captives then the economic purpose of captivity was defeated. Nevertheless, sometimes the captors were willing to wait it out for years until the money was raised and occasionally they simply sold their captive to a labor-hungry neighbor if the ransom was not forthcoming. One grandson of the regimental commander of the Greben Cossacks was held for fifteen years before the silver was raised. On the other hand, if the captive was not so exalted, with the right mediation, captors sometimes lowered the price. The lowest standard price was usually 300 to 400 silver rubles, but cornets, for example, could be ransomed for half that with enough pleading.[39]

Prisoner ransoming was sometimes connected to *baranta* traditions. In 1811, Mozdok Cossacks petitioned general Rtishchev, asking that they be allowed to resume their customary right of conducting *baranta* raids on trans-Terek livestock, "not for our own interests, only for ransoming prisoners." With the prohibition of such an enterprise, they complained, some Cossacks had become completely destitute because of ransom demands that drained their savings or bound them in indentured servitude to those who had provided the money.[40]

Cossacks themselves did not hold their war prisoners for ransom. They usually turned them over to military officials who tried to use them to trade for Russians in captivity. The Cossacks did, on the other hand, deal in bodies. Chechens, like Cossacks, insisted on retrieving the bodies of slain comrades and relatives. Cossacks carried the dead back to their village gates and gathered them along the fence until a mediator arrived with relatives to identify and ransom the bodies. Like the mountain people, Cossacks knew who was who and set a high price for those from rich and notable families. And here too, mediators sometimes got the Cossacks to lower prices for the poor; if they were particularly moved, they sometimes released the body for free.[41]

The success of this ransoming system was linked to the mediators, who were often those known locally as *kunaki*. "*Kunak*" is a Turkic word, which in the Caucasus means a host/friend/protector of a person who comes from outside of the village. The *kunak* is obliged to lodge the visitor; to treat him hospitably; and to defend him, even to the point of death if necessary. Traditions of hospitality—extended even to strangers—were extremely useful in a mountainous region where travel was difficult and often dangerous, currency scarce, and public lodging unavailable. *Kunak*s, though, were more than just the famously generous hosts of the North Caucasus, but rather something akin to blood brothers.[42]

For Cossacks, *kunak*s came to be also escorts and mediators. *Kunak*s literally and figuratively transversed the mountains and the Cossack river valleys; they were conduits linking the different worlds of the Cossacks and the mountain people. Terek Cossacks had Kumyk, Chechen, and Circassian *kunak*s who protected them, ferried information back and forth between Cossack deserters in the mountains and their relatives back home along the Terek, negotiated *baranta* disputes, investigated the location and condition of captives, and brokered ransom deals.[43]

There were also such frontier intermediary types on the Cossack side. The Eroshka character in Tolstoi's *The Cossacks*—who seemed to feel more comfortable with the Chechens than the Russians—was based on one Epishka, an old Greben Cossack. He worked as a translator, a bounty hunter, an escort for honorable mountain people to the Russian side, a horse thief, a mountain trader, and a ransomer. A. L. Chernov, a Mozdok Cossack, ended his career as a warden (*pristav*) of the "peaceful" Chechens living along the Terek. But before that he stole horses, rescued Cossacks from captivity, smuggled contraband goods across the Terek, and according to legend led Russians to attack peaceful Chechens and peaceful Chechens to attack Russians.[44]

Many in the military command were uncomfortable with the Cossack-native interactions and the general strategy of trying to coopt so-called "peaceful" natives to defend against raids. These "peaceful" natives—although nominally pledging loyalty to Russia—were still independent and had neither the means nor the desire to stop raids. Traditional rules of *baranta* are not designed to put an end to mountain raiding, but simply try to provide some rules of the game with which to regulate it. Cossacks of the lower Terek, at least, understood and accepted this arrangement; the military command, on the other hand, insisted on inviolable borders and military obedience. They continually suspected these "peaceful" villages of plotting against the Russian side. As general Potto put it, "Peaceful villages served as a haunt for brigands of all the tribes of the Caucasus; bands are sheltered here before they make a raid on the line; all criminals find a hearty welcome here, and nowhere are there so many Russian deserters." Moritz Wagner described the situation of the Circassians on the left bank of the Kuban with more sympathy, recognizing the difficult situation these people faced: "Hemmed in between the Russians and their opponents, they do their utmost to remain neutral, pledge friendship to both parties, fight one day for the Russians and the next for their compatriots, and act as scouts and spies for both."[45]

Sometimes these villages were attacked by mountain raiders, sometimes they joined in on attacks on the Russian line, sometimes they fought with the Russians to beat back the aggressors. Or they hid behind the village gates and let others do the fighting.[46] Probably the greatest frustration for Russian commanders, though, was the uncertainty, not just of loyalty but of identity. With Kumyks, Chechens, Kabardians, and others in such close proximity, visiting Cossack villages, and buying and selling goods all along the military line, it was often difficult to distinguish "friends" from "enemies." The governor of the Caucasus province noted in 1846 that many mountain people came to Mozdok from Kabarda during bazaar days, all calling themselves "peaceful Kabardians." "But," he went on, "who they really are, except for a small number of well-known people, nobody knows." A traveler made a similar observation in 1833:

> This difficulty in distinguishing our Circassians from the hostile ones inevitably leads to obstacles in restraining the mountain people, who boldly ride along the roads in parties of two or three. To the question, "Where are you from?" he says audaciously in pure Russian that he is from the neighboring *aul*. And how can you detect his lie? How to establish his guilt?[47]

The interactions with these peaceful villages also hampered attempts to use so-called *abrek* or *plastun* commands of dismounted Cossacks beginning in 1846. These were individual or small groups of sharpshooters who hid in bushes or reeds and attacked raiders as they crept by. The idea was not just to mount a secret front line of defense, but to create the fear that there were Cossacks hiding everywhere, "at the river crossing, by the road, in the steppe, in the forest, in the reeds." The main problem was their inability to distinguish the "good guys" from the "bad guys." As Nitsik put it, "such a measure could not be permitted permanently since the bullets of reckless hunters could hit peaceful natives who had...land cutting across here and roads used by all."[48]

One way to clarify this murky situation and establish "guilt" was to try to limit interaction with natives. Throughout the eighteenth century during periods of turbulence, forts occasionally prohibited interaction with mountain people. This was a desperate measure, periodically revived in one form or another, but destined to fail as the economic and political interactions became more complex. For example, the Caucasus *oblast'* head A. A. Vel'iaminov in 1828 despaired of attacks on state peasants:

> since many of the adherents of different faiths (*inovertsy*) who live in the *oblast'*, and also all of the Cossacks of the Line, dress identically as the mountain people, peasants are not able to distinguish the enemies from the Cossacks and the obedient adherents of different faiths and they are exposed to robbery and murder.

To resolve the uncertainty, Vel'iaminov decreed a number of regulations limiting interaction with peasants, including prohibiting armed Muslims, Kumyks, Cossacks, and other "foreigners" from getting closer than 1,750 feet to peasants working in a field.[49]

Ermolov used more aggressive techniques to resolve the uncertainty. During his reign, Ermolov did his utmost to disentangle the Cossack line from native dependencies and traditional culture. He attacked not only mountain villages, but also mountain ways, refusing to play by their rules of the game. Ermolov's first big test was a captivity incident. Pavel Shvetsov, a major in the Georgian grenadier regiment, was on leave from Georgia in 1816, traveling to Kizliar when fifty Chechens jumped out of the thick reeds and started shooting. After a gun battle in which eleven out of Shvetsov's nineteen fellow-travelers were killed, Shvetsov was dragged away by the Chechens and taken to a mountain village where he was held for a ransom of ten oxcarts of silver money, later changed to 250,000 silver rubles.[50]

At about the same time that Shvetsov was taken captive, Ermolov was appointed governor and chief administrator of the Caucasus and commander-in-chief of the separate Caucasus Army Corps—in effect the military and civil ruler of the Caucasus. He would be known for an uncompromising and brutal reign and massacres of entire and often innocent villages in retribution for attacks against the Russian side. Ermolov began his rule in form, ordering all of the Kumyk princes and sovereigns whose land Shvetsov had passed through to be arrested and held under guard; if the prisoner was not freed within ten days, all eighteen were to be hanged from the Kizliar fortress bastions. With this act, the captors lowered their ransom demand to 10,000 silver rubles. Ermolov did not want to pay even this in the name of Russia, so he convinced the Avar khan Sultan Ahmad to pay under the pretext that one of the Kumyk princes was a relative—as Ermolov said, "not giving the appearance that he is doing it by instruction of the Russian government." Ermolov later covertly reimbursed the generous khan. According to the contemporary report in *Russkii invalid*, he exacted the money from peaceful Chechens.[51]

Ermolov probably had been encouraged to act so aggressively by major general Del'potso. In his report on the Shvetsov captivity, Del'potso counseled that it was high time "to make an expedition to punish this barbaric people." Del'potso fumed, as only an Orientalist could, about the Chechens' "wild freedom" and how "their brutality has no limits, while our magnanimity has been exhausted, to no avail." His proposed solution, though, took into account the local balance of power in a way Ermolov never would. True, he recommended a number of measures that Ermolov embraced, such as increasing the military presence along the Caucasus Military Line; pushing the line south to the Sunzha; destroying grain fields of peaceful villagers which supposedly belonged to Chechens; and destroying Chechen villages.

But Del'potso also turned to the Kumyks of Endirei, Aksai, and Kostek, telling *them* to rescue Shvetsov by force of arms and to prevent Chechens from raiding and plundering in the future. Del'potso's demands were unrealistic—he wanted the Kumyks to cut off all contact with Chechens and to kill or take captive every Chechen they encountered from then on. And they were couched in paternalistic threats—if the Kumyks failed to obey, he would come to them "neither as a concerned father nor as an affectionate friend, but as a stern superior, whom you force to use the power of the army against you; then you will know that you yourselves brought on your destruction."[52] Still, it was the last serious attempt to create a front line of native defense against the Chechens. The Orientalist language pointed to the future; the techniques of power pointed to the past.

Ermolov opted only for the negative half of this formula: he repeated the pattern of wanton retribution against "natives" regardless of complicity throughout his reign, flying in the face of local custom and creating an ever-widening circle of enemies. *Baranta* and ransoming traditions limited complicity and retribution to the parties involved. In a region where blood revenge could continue for generations, it was an important way of channeling disputes and appeasing the offended. Ermolov not only ignored this, but insisted that the only way he could bring the natives to heel was to make them collectively responsible for any attack on Russians. He randomly destroyed villages, torched gardens, stole cattle, and clear-cut forests, and indeed eliminated the uncertainty of loyalty of many native villages. But to Russia's loss—the Ermolov system was responsible for the increasing viciousness of the war in the North Caucasus and for Shamil's success is forging an alliance of disparate mountain peoples to fend off the Russians. It was precisely during this period that the warfare in the North Caucasus took on a more political and religious dimension, although still with a good dose of traditional "social-economic" frontier raiding.[53]

Ermolov also tried to clarify the nebulous situation of the peaceful villages along the right bank of the Terek by forcing them to fight against raiders or to move away. "These settlements," he wrote, "no less than the others, were full of brigands, who took part in all of the raids of the Chechens on the line." As he put it, "it would be better to have an empty steppe between the Terek and the Sunzha than to suffer brigandage in the rear of our fortifications." So Ermolov built a new line of Cossack villages and forts south of the Terek along the Sunzha River, attacked suspicious villages, and forced many Chechens and Kumyks to move south, higher up the mountains. Curiously, he hoped to establish a new fringe of peaceful villages around his fortress Groznyi, on the Sunzha, to provide provisions for the regular army and the Cossacks there. But in building the Sunzha Line and indiscriminately attacking villages between the Terek and the Sunzha, he wrecked the local grain trade, which up to then had been an important source of food for Cossacks (see Chapter 6). Then, after altercations with Chechens around Groznyi, the majority of the "peaceful" villages there relocated to the mountains and as Potto wistfully remarked, "from that time on the flowering bank of the Sunzha was deserted." It would be a bloody and extremely difficult three decades before the fury of the Chechens burned itself out and Ermolov's goal of pacification was achieved.[54]

We cannot, and should not try to, ignore the role of the Terek Cossacks in the conquest of the North Caucasus. On the other hand, the master narrative of imperial aggression is not sufficient for understanding the role of fighting and military service in Cossack life. Cossacks were not just soldier-servants of the state, but also frontier settlers—an ambivalence that goes to the heart of cossackdom. Histories of Cossacks or of native resistance in the heroic tradition often overlook this for the glory of battles won and lost.

As Caucasians, Terek Cossacks had a particular understanding of warfare that related more to the creation of honor than the creation of empire. As servants in a chronically labor-short region, their duties were often more mundane, more persistent and plodding, more resented, and considerably less glorious than large-scale warfare. As frontier settlers, they sometimes needed to escape this service to help maintain the economies of their labor-short villages.

When they did engage the enemy, Cossacks could be aggressive and brutal and terribly effective as empire builders. On the other hand, most of the fighting was limited, regulated, and more a function of the way of life in the North

Caucasus than of conquest and resistance. As frontier settlers, Terek Cossacks were drawn into the local fighting traditions and the particular weaponry, uniform, and attempts at conflict mediation of the North Caucasus. Military commanders used Cossacks as agents for imperial policy issuing from St. Petersburg. But the Terek Cossacks often played a more local game that was so beautifully symbolized not just by the fact that they were visually indistinguishable from their enemies, but that they were dependent upon them for their weapons, horses, and uniforms. Military planners in the capital may have hoped for Russian "soldiers" marching in lockstep and the expansion of Russian culture. But in the North Caucasus, the sheep-skin *papakha* and the *kinzhal* from Dagestan come into focus and reveal the local web of relationships that entangled the Terek Cossacks in a frontier culture, a culture that limited their willingness or ability to spread the glory of Russian civilization. As we shall see in the next chapter, nativization could be such a powerful force, that it lured some Cossacks to do something that was even more inconceivable to their rulers—flee to the mountains to desert.

Notes

1. Catherine Wendy Bracewell, *The Uskoks of Senj: Piracy, Banditry, and Holy War in the Sixteenth-Century Adriatic* (Ithaca and London: Cornell University Press, 1992), 45.

2. G. A. Tkachëv, *Stanitsa Chervlennaia. Istoricheskii ocherk* (Vladikavkaz: Elektropechatnia tipografiia Terskago oblastnago pravleniia, 1912), 129-30; G. Maliavkin, "Stanitsa Chervlennaia," *Etnograficheskoe obozrenie*, no. 1 (1891): 115-16.

3. V. Verstennikov, "Maslianitsa v Ekaterinograde," *Kavkaz*, 16 April 1849, 61-62; F. Ponomarëv, "O maslianitse v Kizliarskom kazach'em polku," *Terskiia vedomosti*, 7 May 1870, 2-3.

4. Moritz Wagner, *Travels in Persia, Georgia and Koordistan; With Sketches of the Cossacks and the Caucasus* (London: Hurst and Blackett, 1856), 1: 171; John F. Baddeley, *The Rugged Flanks of the Caucasus* (London: Oxford University Press, 1940), 20; N. N., *Zapiski vo vremia poezdki iz Astrakhania na Kavkaze i v Gruziiu v 1827 godu* (Moscow: Tipografiia S. Selivanovskago, 1829), 68.

5. Tkachëv, *Stanitsa Chervlennaia*, 119-25; P. Kulebiakin, "Grebentsy" in A. Rzhevuskii, ed., *Tertsy. Sbornik istoricheskikh, bytovykh i geografichesko-statisticheskikh svedenii* (Vladikavkaz: Tipografiia oblastnago pravleniia Terskoi oblasti, 1888), 251-52.

6. "Opisanie kavkazskago shelkovodstva," *Sbornik materialov dlia opisaniia mestnostei i plemen Kavkaza* 11 (1891): section 2, 21-22; Kulebiakin, "Grebentsy," 251-52; Tkachëv, *Stanitsa Chervlennaia*, 22-23.

7. Tkachëv, *Stanitsa Chervlennaia*, 165-67; Kulebiakin, "Grebentsy," 243.

8. L. B. Zasedateleva, "Evoliutsiia obshchiny u terskikh kazakov v XVI-XIX vv.," *Sovetskaia etnografiia*, no. 1 (January-February 1969): 33-34; P. Stepanov, "Beglye ocherki Kabardy," *Kavkaz*, 19 October 1861, 442-44; I. Popko, *Terskie kazaki s starodavnikh vremen. Istoricheskii ocherk* (St. Petersburg: Tipografiia Departamenta udelov, 1880), 189-91, 266-71; I. L. Omel'chenko, *Terskoe kazachestvo* (Vladikavkaz: "Ir," 1991), 122; "Istoricheskiia svedeniia o Grebenskom kazach'em polku," *Sbornik Obshchestva liubitelei*

kazach'ei stariny 4 (1912): 51-52.

9. Popko, *Terskie kazaki*, 209-12, 271-72; F. G. Chernozubov, "Ocherki Terskoi stariny," *Zapiski Terskago obshchestva liubitelei kazach'ei stariny* 8 (August 1914): 61-63.

10. V. A. Potto, *Dva veka Terskago kazachestva* (Vladikavkaz: Elektropechatnia tipografiia Terskago oblastnago pravleniia, 1912), 2: 66.

11. Popko, *Terskie kazaki*, 211-12; Zasedateleva, "Evoliutsiia obshchiny," 34-36.

12. Robert H. McNeal, *Tsar and Cossack, 1855-1914* (New York: St. Martin's Press, 1987), 5-11.

13. V. K. Shenk, ed., *Kazach'i voiska* (St. Petersburg: Spravochnaia knizhka Imperatorskoi glavnoi kvartiry; repr. n.p.: Aktsionernoe obshchestvo "Dobral'," 1992), 173-79.

14. Iosif Debu, *O Kavkazskoi linii i prisoedinennom k nei Chernomorskom voiske* (St. Petersburg: Tipografiia Karla Kraiia, 1829), 66-68; quote in I. I. Dmitrenko, "Materialy k istorii Terskago kazach'iago voiska," *Terskii sbornik* 4 (1897): 83-84.

15. Rossiiskii Gosudarstvennyi Istoricheskii Arkhiv [RGIA], f. 1268, op. 4, d. 386, ll. 2-6; f. 1268, op. 5, d. 378, l. 2; ; N. P. Gritsenko, *Goroda severo-vostochnogo Kavkaza i proizvoditel'nye sily kraia V-seredina XIX veka* (Rostov-on-Don: Izdatel'stvo Rostovskogo universiteta, 1984), 88-89; P. Nitsik, "Byvshiia voennyia poseleniia na Voenno-Gruzinskoi doroge," *Terskiia vedomosti*, 25 January 1887, 3-4; Voiskovoe khoziaistvennoe pravlenie, *Statisticheskiia monografii po izsledovaniiu stanichnago byta Terskago kazach'iago voiska* (Vladikavkaz: Tipografiia Terskago oblastnago pravleniia, 1881), 373-74.

16. P. Iudin, "Mozdokskie kalmyki," *Zapiski Terskago obshchestva liubitelei kazach'ei stariny* 12 (December 1914): 29-31; Tkachëv, *Stanitsa Chervlennaia*, 17-18; Potto, *Dva veka Terskago kazachestva*, 2: 65; "Istoricheskiia svedeniia o Grebenskom kazach'em polku," 50, 53.

17. Potto, *Dva veka Terskago kazachestva*, 2: 66-67; F. Ponomarëv, "Materialy dlia istorii Terskago kazach'iago voiska s 1559 po 1880 god," *Voennyi sbornik* 23, no. 10 (1880): 361-62.

18. Debu, *O Kavkazskoi linii*, 282-85.

19. "Istoricheskiia svedeniia o Grebenskom kazach'em polku," 51-52; Popko, *Terskie kazaki*, 362-64.

20. P. Nitsik, "Byvshiia voennyia poseleniia na Voenno-Gruzinskoi doroge," *Terskiia vedomosti*, 5 March 1887, 2; Popko, *Terskie kazaki*, 212-14, 360-62; A. Biriul'kin, "Kazaki," *Terskiia vedomosti*, 19 February 1874, 3.

21. P. L. Iudin, "Iz-za vlasti. (Ocherk iz proshlago soedinennago Grebenskago kazachestva)," *Zapiski Terskago obshchestva liubitelei kazach'ei stariny*, no. 9 (September 1914): 37-39; *Polnoe sobranie zakonov Rossiiskoi imperii s 1649 goda* (Moscow: Tipografiia II otdeleniia Sobstvennoi Ego Imperatorskago Velichestva kantseliarii, 1830), 19: 267-68.

22. F. P. Ponomarëv, "Materialy po istorii Terskago kazach'iago voiska. 2-i Malorossiiskii polk," *Terskii sbornik* 6 (1903): 212, 217; G. A. Tkachëv, ed., *Grebenskie, Terskie i Kizliarskie kazaki* (Vladikavkaz: Elektropechatnia tipografiia Terskago oblastnago pravlenii, 1911), 129-30.

23. Tkachëv, *Stanitsa Chervlennaia*, 116-19.

24. Tkachëv, *Stanitsa Chervlennaia*, 104-05; Popko, *Terskie kazaki*, 274-76, 281-82, 418; A. Sosiev, "Stanitsa Ekaterinogradskaia. Istoriko-etnograficheskii ocherk," *Terskii*

sbornik, no. 5 (1903): 8-9; A. Sosiev, "Stanitsa Chernoiarskaia," *Terskii sbornik*, no. 5 (1903): 40-41.

25. "Materialy dlia statistiki Kizliarskago polka Terskago kazach'iago voiska," *Voennyi sbornik*, no. 12 (December 1869): 213; A. V. Fadeev, *Rossiia i Kavkaz pervoi treti XIX v.* (Moscow: Izdatel'stvo akademii nauk SSSR, 1961), 317; V. A. Potto, *Kavkazskaia voina v otdel'nykh ocherkakh, epizodakh, legendakh i biografiiakh* (St. Petersburg: Tipografiia R. Golike, 1885), 2: part 1, 107-18.

26. "Kavkaz," *Kavkaz*, 1 February 1847, 185; "Kavkaz," *Kavkaz*, 10 July 1848, 110.

27. For general descriptions of the defense system, see Iu. Shidlovskii, "Zapiski o Kizliare," *Zhurnal Ministerstva vnutrennikh del*, no. 4 (1843): 161-62; "Ocherk voennoi zhizni Kavkazskikh lineinykh kazakov," *Russkii invalid*, 9 January 1849, 21; and Popko, *Terskie kazaki*, 255-56, 373.

28. F. G. Chernozubov, "Ocherki Terskoi stariny. (1832-1837) Nabegi khishchnikov," *Zapiski Terskago liubitelei kazach'ei stariny*, no. 7 (1914): 10-13; "O khishchnicheskikh deistviiakh Cherkes i Chechentsev v nashikh predelakh," *Kavkaz*, 31 March 1857, 119-20; I. Slivitskii, "Ocherk Kavkaza i Zakavkaz'ia. Bugry," *Kavkaz*, 18 September 1848, 145-46; "Vnutrenniia izvestiia Kavkaza," *Kavkaz*, 7 September 1846, 142.

29. "Goroda Stavropol'skoi gubernii," *Izvestiia Kavkazskago otdela Imperatorskago russkago geograficheskago obshchestva* 5, no. 4 (1878): supplement, 14-17; Shidlovskii, "Zapiski o Kizliare," 196-206; Tkachëv, *Stanitsa Chervlennaia*, 150-52; Tkachëv, *Grebenskie, Terskie i Kizliarskie kazaki*, 93-96.

30. Chernozubov, "Ocherki Terskoi stariny," 5-10, 13-15; Tkachëv, *Stanitsa Chervlennaia*, 130-31.

31. Chernozubov, "Ocherki Terskoi stariny," 13-15; Ponomarëv, "Materialy po istorii Terskago kazach'iago voiska," 196; Tkachëv, *Stanitsa Chervlennaia*, 47-48.

32. Chernozubov, "Ocherki Terskoi stariny," 15-18; Popko, *Terskie kazaki*, 253-54.

33. "Kavkaz," *Kavkaz*, 19 April 1847, 62; "Kavkaz," *Kavkaz*, 15 March 1847, 42; Tkachëv, *Stanitsa Chervlennaia*, 150-52; "Kavkaz," *Kavkaz*, 16 July 1849, 114.

34. Fernand Braudel, *The Mediterranean and the Mediterranean World in the Age of Philip II*, trans. Siân Reynolds (New York: Harper & Row, 1972), 1: 86.

35. Tkachëv, *Stanitsa Chervlennaia*, 153-57; V. I. Abaev, *Istoriko-etimologicheskii slovar' Osetinskogo iazyka* (Leningrad: "Nauka," 1989), 4: 28-29.

36. Debu, *O Kavkazskoi linii*, 54-63; I. Debu, "O nachal'nom ustanovlenii i rasprostranenii Kavkazskoi linii," *Otechestvennyia zapiski* 18, no. 48 (1824): 283-85; Mary L. Henze, "Thirty Cows for an Eye: The Traditional Economy of the Central Caucasus—An Analysis from Nineteenth Century Travellers' Accounts," *Central Asian Survey* 4, no. 3 (1985): 115-29; T. M., "Korespondentsiia 'Illiustrirovannoi Gazety' s Kavkaza," *Illiustrirovannaia gazeta*, 12 January 1867, 26-27; "Istoricheskiia svedeniia o Grebenskom kazach'em polku," 35-37, 46-48, 51-54; Tkachëv, *Stanitsa Chervlennaia*, 53-56. For a handy copy of the treaty with Devlet-Girei, see Iu. Galushko, *Kazach'i voiska Rossii* (Moscow: "Russkii mir," 1993), 185.

On *baranta* in general, see F. I. Leontovich, *Adaty kavkazskikh gortsev* (Odessa: Tipografiia P. A. Zelenago, 1882), esp. 250-57, 284, 366. According to one customary law of Balkarians and Karachevites collected in 1844, the family of a murder victim had the right to raid the house and winter pasture of the killer and take whatever they could carry away, but only before the body was buried.

What *baranta* actually meant to the mountain people is, of course, a different subject that remains to be investigated. For a perceptive analysis of the evolution of similar customary law among Kazakhs, see Virginia Martin, "Barïmta: Nomadic Custom, Imperial Crime," in *Russia's Orient: Imperial Borderlands and Peoples, 1700-1917*, ed. Daniel R. Brower and Edward J. Lazzerini (Bloomington: Indiana University Press, 1997), 249-70.

37. T. M., "Korespondentsiia 'Illiustrirovannoi Gazety' s Kavkaza," *Illiustrirovannaia gazeta*, 5 January 1867, 11; B. P. Berozov, *Istoricheskie etiudy (iz istorii vozniknoveniia Osetinskikh sel i kazach'ikh stanits)* (Vladikavkaz: Izdatel'stvo Severo-Osetinskogo gosudarstvennogo universiteta im. K. L. Khetagurova, 1992), 35-38; "Poezdka v Gruziiu," *Moskovskii telegraf*, no. 15 (August 1833): 333-34; Potto, *Kavkazskaia voina*, 2: part 1, 86-87; Popko, *Terskie kazaki*, 173-75.

38. Tkachëv, *Stanitsa Chervlennaia*, 165-67.

39. Tkachëv, *Stanitsa Chervlennaia*, 65-67; Tkachëv, *Grebenskie, Terskie i Kizliarskie kazaki*, 119-21; RGVIA, f. 14877, op. 1, d. 756, l. 1, 41; RGVIA, f. 1058, op. 2, d. 637, ll. 1-3.

40. *Akty sobrannye Kavkazskoi arkheograficheskoi komissieiu [AKAK]* (Tiflis: Tipografiia Kantseliarii glavnonachal'stvuiushchego grazhdanskoi chast'iu na Kavkaze, 1873), 5: 843-45.

41. RGVIA, f. 1058, op. 1, d. 541, ll. 39-40; Tkachëv, *Stanitsa Chervlennaia*, 167-68.

42. N. K. Dmitriev, "O tiurkskikh elementakh Russkogo slovaria," *Leksikograficheskii sbornik*, no. 3 (1958): 27-28; A. P. Berzhe, *Chechnia i chechentsy* (Tiflis: Kavkazskii otdel Imperatorskago russkago geograficheskago obshchestva, 1859), 86-87; Shora Nogmov, *Istoriia adykheiskago naroda*, 3d ed. (Piatigorsk: Tipografiia I. P. Afanas'eva, 1891), 32; M. O. Kosven, *Etnografiia i istoriia Kavkaza* (Moscow: Izdatel'stvo vostochnoi literatury, 1961), 126-29. For a description of traditions of hospitality and the responsibilities of *kunaks* in the North Caucasus, see V. K. Gardanov, *Obshchestvennyi stroi Adygskikh narodov (XVIII-pervaia polovina XIX v.)* (Moscow: "Nauka," 1967), 289-326.

43. S. M. Bronevskii, *Noveishie geograficheskie i istoricheskie izvestiia o Kavkaze* (Moscow: Tipografiia S. Selivanovskogo, 1823), section 2, 127-29, 142-45; Fedor Chernozubov, "Ocherki Terskoi stariny. Pobegy v gory," *Russkii arkhiv*, no. 18 (1911): 253-56; N. I. Tolmachev, "Vesti s stoianki," *Kavkaz*, 31 January 1857, 46-47; Debu, "O nachal'nom ustanovlenii," 283-85.

44. N. N. T. [N. N. Tolstoi], "Okhota na Kavkaze," *Sovremennik* 61, no. 1 (1857): 177; Potto, *Kavkazskaia voina*, 2: 135-44.

45. Potto, *Kavkazskaia voina*, 2: part 1, 86-87; Wagner, *Travels in Persia*, 1: 129.

46. See, for example, "Izvestie s Kavkaza," *Kavkaz*, 3 December 1856, 383; "Kavkaz," *Kavkaz*, 10 September 1849, 146; RGVIA, f. 1058, op. 2, d. 1074, l. 1; Sosiev, "Stanitsa Chernoiarskaia," 39-40; Popko, *Terskie kazaki*, 253-54.

47. RGVIA, f. 38, op. 7, d. 128, ll. 5-12; "Poezdka v Gruziiu," 333-34.

48. Petr Egorov, "Dorozhnyia zapiski o Kavkaze i Severnom Dagestane, 1851 goda," *Russkii invalid*, no. 177 (1851): 733-35; Ponomarëv, "Materialy po istorii Terskago kazach'iago voiska," 230; P. Nitsik, "Byvshiia voennyia poseleniia na voenno-gruzinskoi doroge," in Rzhevuskii, *Tertsy*, 62.

49. G. N. Prozritelev, comp., "Iz proshlogo Severnogo Kavkaza. Materialy dlia istoriia g. Stavropolia i Stavropol'skoi gub.," *Trudy Stavropol'skoi uchenoi arkhivnoi komissii*, no. 2 (1910): section 4, 19-23.

50. V. Shvetsov, *Ocherk o kavkazskikh gorskikh plemenakh* (Moscow: Universitetskaia tipografiia, 1856), 60-67; Potto, *Kavkazskaia voina*, 2: part 1, 57-64.

51. Shvetsov, *Ocherk o kavkazskikh gorskikh plemenakh*, 60-67; Potto, *Kavkazskaia voina*, 2: part 1, 57-64; *AKAK* (Tiflis: Tipografiia Kantseliarii glavnonachal'stvuiushchego grazhdanskoi chast'iu na Kavkaze, 1875): 6: part 2, 21, 497; "Ob"iavlenie," *Russkii invalid*, 19 October 1817, 977-78.

Since Ahmad Khan and some 6,000 of his men attacked the Russian troops building the fortress of Vnezapnaia in 1820, he apparently was not the dutiful friend of Russia that Ermolov had hoped. See Moshe Gammer, *Muslim Resistance to the Tsar: Shamil and the Conquest of Chechnia and Daghestan* (London: Frank Cass, 1994), 33.

52. *AKAK*, (Tiflis: Tipografiia Glavnago upravleniia namestnika Kavkazskago, 1873), 5: 874-76.

53. M. M. Bliev and V. V. Degoev, *Kavkazskaia voina* (Moscow: "Roset," 1994), 148-81; Gammer, *Muslim Resistance to the Tsar*, 29-38.

54. A. P. Ermolov, *Zapiski A. P. Ermolova. 1798-1826 gg.*, ed. V. A. Fedorov (Moscow: "Vysshaia shkola," 1991), 304; Tkachëv, *Stanitsa Chervlennaia*, 71-72; Popko, *Terskie kazaki*, 173-75; Potto, *Kavkazskaia voina*, 2: part 1, 86-91, 97-99. Ermolov's memoirs include some rather frank descriptions of the complete destruction of Chechen villages. See, for example, pp. 338-39.

9

Frontier Identities

In my hostile impulsiveness
I craved for freedom to seek
Blinded by that hope
I fled to Chechnia to live.

—"The Confession of Cossack Frolov"

On the famous river,
on the Kushumovka
once lived other Cossacks
from the Don, Nekrasovtsy.
They served, these other Cossacks
faithfully and truthfully;
And for this the Orthodox tsar
loved to reward them,
he gave them much gold.
But now the Orthodox tsar
has become furious with them.
He wants to shave, these other Cossacks,
their mustaches and their beards,
and he wants, the Orthodox tsar
to execute them, to hang them.

—Terek Cossack song

Shchedrinskaia girls are good
Because they have long braids
Because they are stately and tidy.
Nikolaevskaia girls are no good,
Because they have bug eyes
And aren't stately or tidy.

—Greben Cossack song

The Terek Cossacks, like most frontier settlers, occupied a "middle ground" in the Russian empire, where influences from the center mixed with regional culture to produce a rich and unique society. The Cossack myth claims that they were essentially Russian, Orthodox, and patriotic, performing glorious and heroic tasks for the motherland.[1] And of course Cossacks were agents of Russian expansion, clients of a powerful state bent on controlling the region. But as we have seen many times in the course of this study, they were not agents of Russian civilization—the North Caucasus, in a sense, also conquered the Terek Cossacks, and their loyalties and affiliation were pulled in different and often competing directions.

The Russian-controlled region of the North Caucasus had many boundaries—military, political, cultural, religious, social, economic, ethnic—but not all of them were impermeable and many were often quite fluid. Cossacks fought for the state, but they did not always identify with the state. Terek Cossack culture, society, and economy absorbed many native influences; some found the frontier culture so fluid, they had no difficulty crossing over to the other side. Many Cossacks were neither Russian, nor Orthodox; some as we have seen were not even Christian. Old Believer Cossacks had some of the most persistent and irreconcilable differences with the Russian state—some cut their ties completely and fled to the mountains; many more simply battled it out in everyday life with their unwelcome Orthodox neighbors. Other Cossacks deserted to return to their ancestral communities, to spend a few years with the Chechens or to pursue careers as bandits, holding up travelers and plundering Cossack and peasant villages.

This chapter will sketch out the diverse frontier identities of the Terek Cossacks. These identities were formed against the backdrop of the Russian conquest of the region and that experience was an important source of self-identity. But it was not the only source; in the struggles between Christianity and Islam, between Russians and natives, between Russia and "the East," the Terek Cossacks did not fit snugly into either camp.

The Russian state did what it could to try to instill the Terek Cossacks with loyalty and patriotism for the imperial cause. Battles and warriors were commemorated, churches were constructed, imperial images abounded, but the propaganda never completely triumphed. Naming is the first stage of possession and there were many attempts to Russify, Christianize, and symbolically conquer the contested terrain. Forts and villages were planted with loaded names such as Stavropol' ("the town of the cross"), Vladikavkaz ("master of the Caucasus"), Ekaterinograd ("Catherine's town"), and Petrovsk after Peter the Great. But the oldest, and most important "Russian" fort-towns along the Terek were Kizliar, most likely named after the Turkic-named river, and Mozdok, from Circassian words meaning "dense forest." K. F. Gan, an expert on the toponymy of the region, held that the names of two Cossack villages derived from Tatar: Kargalinskaia from "raven" and Kurdiukovskaia from "a fatty sheep tail."[2]

The most usual way of creating imperial bonds was to award Cossacks for faithful service. Beginning in the eighteenth century, a flood of standards, banners, maces, and other awards was sent to the Cossacks for loyalty and excellence in battle. In 1832, the commander of the Greben host located 109 standards and banners, for this, the oldest host.[3] But banners—just like everything else—could have contested meanings in the North Caucasus. For example, the tsar awarded a banner to the Greben regiment in 1832 for its heroism in the Russo-Turkish War of 1828-1829. They wanted to bless it with Old Believer rites, but Nicholas I insisted on Orthodox rites and so it was carried out, under the close observance by the commander of their regiment for resistance. The presiding priest reported an enthusiastic and reverent reception of the imperial grace, but the incident also communicated the domineering position of the Orthodox church, which must have rankled more than a few. Imperial rescripts did not necessarily create imperial sentiment.[4]

Presumably, one of the best ways of instilling imperial allegiance was to draft Terek Cossacks into the Caucasus Line Cossack half-squadron of the imperial convoy, which was created in 1832. Besides having the honor of guarding the emperor, Cossacks in the convoy received a raise, and even better, when they returned to their home regiment they were supposed to be released from active service. The only convoy member whom I have been able to trace, however, was a less-than-well-adjusted Greben Cossack Old Believer. Before his initial presentation, Nicholas I's officials wanted him to shave his beard, which he refused to do for religious reasons. He was awarded a Cross of St. George for bravery in battle and was allowed to keep his beard and apparently served well in the convoy. But after returning to his stanitsa in the North Caucasus, a commander ordered him into service at a night observation post. After refusing and insulting a Cossack noncommissioned officer, he was arrested, tried, found guilty, and his Cross of St. George was taken away. This recalcitrant convoy guard was probably not typical, but the incident does point to the unrelenting service demands of the Terek Cossacks which sometimes forced even the best Cossacks to choose between the demands of service and the domestic needs of their communities.[5]

On the other hand, there were occasions when official attempts to create patriotic attitudes met with great success. The key factor was local relevance. Probably the most popular Cossack commander in the North Caucasus was N. P. Sleptsov. He led the newly created Sunzha regiment from 1845 to his death in 1851, when he fell in battle against the Chechens. This regiment had the difficult task of holding and colonizing the upper Sunzha River, well into Chechen territory, and Sleptsov was apparently much admired by his Cossacks for bold leadership in pushing the Chechens back.

His death made him even more popular, because of the convergence of popular patriotism with official patriotism. After masses of Cossacks crowded into the church where his body lay, state officials quickly realized the utility of creating a cult of Sleptsov. A month after his death the emperor ordered a monument erected in his honor and then the Sunzha stanitsa was renamed the Sleptsov stanitsa. Every year on the anniversary of his death, the village held a memorial celebration. In 1860, this ceremony included a mass and a religious procession to his grave that concluded with six Sunzha Cossack squadrons in parade uniform carrying a banner awarded to them in 1850 for their good work in pacifying the Chechens. After a requiem was sung at the gravesite, holy water sprinkled, and salutes fired, all of the officers, and friends and colleagues of Sleptsov, gathered for a dinner where they sang songs about the heroic commander. Lithograph depictions of the death of Sleptsov, sent by his brother a Saratov merchant, were distributed to the assembled who accepted them, according to a witness, "like a talisman." "These pictures," an eye-witness wrote, "were distributed to every Cossack, who took them with deep reverence, as one after the other tried to grab first the precious gift; those who didn't get a picture were very mournful, some even cried." In 1861 Sunzha Cossacks still told fond stories about the heroic feats of Sleptsov.[6]

Similarly, Cossacks commemorated and long remembered heroic battles. But curiously, the ones that were celebrated were always sieges against Cossack villages—that is, not glorious expansion, but feats of defensive heroism when Cossacks held out against superior numbers long enough for reinforcements—or according to oral tradition, divine intervention—to arrive. No doubt, such attacks were elevated to mythical status because of the focus they provided—Cossacks fought together and for an understandable purpose—and because colonists everywhere prefer to enshrine victims rather than triumphal aggressors. Remember, after all, the Alamo. And Custer.[7]

Terek Cossack songs and tales also reveal their mixed heritage and ambivalence towards Russian power. They sang songs and told stories about Ivan the Terrible, Peter the Great, Yermak the "conqueror" of Siberia, Vladimir of Kiev (who baptized the Rus'), and about famous battles in Russian history. But they also sung of Cossack rebels such as Stenka Razin; about the Nekrasov Cossacks who were persecuted for their Old Belief and fled "across the Danube...with holy justification"; about the Cossack Ivan Frolov, who "craved for freedom...[and] fled to Chechnia to live"; and about Iakov Alpatov, a Terek Cossack who fled twice to the Chechens. Razin was the most popular all-Cossack folk hero—they sang numerous songs and told various legends about him. Some in the mid-nineteenth century imagined that he still lived in the forest of the Caucasus mountains. Once two travelers came upon a naked man living in a cave who claimed to be Razin; from the description he probably was a religious schismatic.[8]

The most famous Cossack deserter of the North Caucasus, and probably the most beloved Terek Cossack folk hero, was Iakov Alpatov, a Cossack from Naur stanitsa of the Mozdok regiment. Alpatov fled twice to the mountains, adopted Islam, married a Chechen, and formed thieving bands of Chechens and other deserters who raided the Caucasus Line and well into the steppe, stealing horses and cattle, taking captives, and killing, from 1842 until he was caught and executed in 1856. Perhaps the most interesting part of the Alpatov story is how he became a Cossack folk hero, despite (or because of?) his famous raids along the line and his conversion to Islam. Many deserters converted to Islam for political reasons and perhaps had little genuine attachment to the religion. Alpatov was different in that he was given the chance to reconvert to Orthodoxy before his execution, but refused and requested a mullah to accompany him in his final hours on earth. Then, right before he was executed he asked a Chechen delegation, in Chechen, to bury his body in their village. Apparently none of this was considered reason to renounce the memory of Alpatov: stories were told about him, a *kurgan* (barrow) was named after him, and at least one song written about the "orphan, bold, [who] decided to escape to the mountains." As a hostile P. A. Vostrikov put it, "Alpatov, because of his cruel and rapacious adventures...was the type of personality that took possession of people's imagination and they made him a subject of tales and legends."[9] The image of Alpatov shone as an example of "true Cossack freedom" and was remembered well into the twentieth century.

It is also important to notice the ease with which Alpatov moved back and forth between the life of an outlaw and the life of a Cossack. He fled, twice, for relatively minor incidents (the first time because he was caught stealing; the second time because he was slapped by the stanitsa chief for refusing to remove his hat). Perhaps most significantly, after he returned from his first desertion, he had little trouble resuming his position in Naur. He lived for two years with the Chechens, converted to Islam, and attacked stanitsas and farmsteads, yet when he gave himself up, he suffered only a short arrest and some strokes with the birch rod and then moved in again with his first wife and returned to regimental service.[10]

There were many Cossacks like Alpatov, who either deserted and fought alongside Shamil, or who simply spent a couple of years in the mountains, raiding the Russian cordon line for booty. We can never be sure how many deserted. One pair of historians who looked into it, Alferov and Chekmenev, wrote that in 1833-1834 alone 1,500 deserted to the mountains. A soldier in the Caucasus army claimed that 30,000 Cossacks and other renegades fought with Shamil. He offers no proof, and this clearly was an exaggeration. But it was common enough so that nearly everyone who returned from captivity in the mountains mentioned seeing deserters. And the archives are full of reports of Cossacks fleeing to the mountains.[11]

Desertion was a perpetual state concern, especially during the period of the most intense military activity in the North Caucasus after 1817. Periodic demands were made for different villages to return Russian deserters and in 1842 Nicholas I ordered local commanders to proffer salt as a bribe. For a period in the 1830s, deserters were shot, but then in 1845 the viceroy of the Caucasus Voronstov issued a proclamation to renegades promising a full pardon for those who returned: "The Commander-in-chief hopes that deserters will hurry to take advantage of the monarchial pardon and mercy, and will not want to remain longer in destitution among the heterodox."[12]

In August 1859, when the war was winding down in the northeast Caucasus, a discussion ensued between the War Ministry and the main command of the Caucasus army about what to do with deserters and captives. As the chief of staff put it:

> In the course of the half-century war which we have waged in the Caucasus, a rather large number of captive and fugitive lower ranks have gradually accumulated in the mountains with the unpacified tribes, who have been with the mountain people for a long time, assimilated their way of life and customs, some marrying, and raising a family, and even converting to Islam,

adding rather hopefully "although most only in outward appearance and not in spiritual conviction." How should they treat such people, "now appearing in significant numbers from their mountain hideaways"? The chief of staff suggested a full amnesty, and rather curiously, proposed to use such nativized Russians to plant "the first seeds of Christianity in the mountains" and to help with the drawing in (*sblizhenie*) of the mountain natives to Russia. As it turned out, the War Ministry granted an amnesty only for those who had not committed any other crimes besides desertion and made their claims within two months. By 30 July 1860, when the two months had elapsed, 642 lower ranks who had fled or were taken captive and converted to Islam had been pardoned.[13]

Why did Cossacks desert? Many, as we will see below, because they were Old Believers and hoped to find religious freedom and/or salvation in the mountains. Others, like Alpatov, because they suffered some indignity such as corporal punishment or because they feared that they would. Filat Aleshchkin of the Greben regiment fled in 1842 because he faced the birch rod for being accused of being drunk on duty. In 1848, Gavril Duriev deserted because he feared corporal punishment after a petty quarrel with another Cossack. Fedor Zamogilin of the Kizliar regiment headed for the mountains in 1850 after losing four sheep he was tending for a prince.[14]

Like Alpatov, most deserters who voluntarily returned to their villages were welcomed back, suffering only minimal punishment. The litmus test was usually whether they had attacked Cossacks or others on the Russian side when they were gone. Commanders implicitly recognized the normalcy of young Cossacks fleeing to live in the mountains with their erstwhile enemies, treating it no more seriously than other acts of youthful exuberance.[15]

Most, but not all, deserters were young men. Extremely unsettling to the Russian authorities was the fact that people of all ages, all faiths, men and women, Slavs and non-Slavs, Cossacks from leading families, Cossacks with long, distinguished service records, chose to desert Russia and run to the mountains. It was one thing for a headstrong twenty year old to get his dander up over some offense and temporarily bolt from authority. It was something altogether different, and much more threatening, when someone like forty-year-old Bairame Erezhepov from the Kizliar regiment, the son of Cossacks, in service for twenty-two years, loaded up an oxcart in August 1842 and slipped away with his family and another. Or when an officer such as lieutenant Atarshchik, brother of two Cossack officers, himself in service for over a decade in St. Petersburg, Poland, and the Caucasus, deserts twice to the mountains, adopts Islam, and takes part in raids on the Russian line. Or when the same Frolov family of Chervlennaia produces a line of distinguished officers, but also Ivan, known by the Kabardian name of Misost, who fled beyond the Kuban to start a new family with the Abadzekhs and fight against the Russians. Or when Greben Cossack women Tat'iana Bagaevskaia and Stepanada Tsyganovka, "reprimanded for debauched behavior," packed their bags and left in 1851.[16]

Such desertions were rejections of Russia, powerful manifestations of the failure to create loyalty and that hoped-for "civilization," which would suck all, Cossack and mountaineer alike, into the Russian orbit. Local commanders, more attuned to the cultural balance of power on the frontier, had few such dashed hopes; their concerns were more down to earth—that deserters would move beyond rejection to aggression. Their fears were well grounded.

Mountain people, including Shamil and his forces, encouraged deserters and welcomed them with open arms. One of the most open calls for desertion was a March 1843 letter from the above-mentioned lieutenant Atarshchik, written on behalf of his new comrades, the Abadzekhs, promising all deserters safe passage in the mountains. As he wrote, "I invite carpenters, smithies, soldiers with guns and gunpowder, drummers...no one will be turned away...whether Pole, German, or Russian." He signed with his Muslim name, Khadzheret Muhammad, adding "I am waiting for you."[17]

Shamil gave those deserters deemed trustworthy a prominent place. He allowed those who converted to Islam to marry Muslim women and to become fully integrated into his community. Shamil singled out such converts for special care, taking strict measures to protect them from the petty oppression of their new neighbors. Captain A. I. Runovskii reported that there were many Russian deserters who converted to Islam, married mountain women and created a happy family life. A Cossack taken into captivity later testified that there were some 300 Russian deserters at Shamil's village of Vedeno, who were looking after artillery, marrying Chechens, dressing in "Circassian coats," and living "sufficiently well." Shamil's son-in-law said that Shamil personally tested their ability, and assigned them work as smithies, artillerymen, mechanics, saddlers, and gunpowdermen. According to the testimony of Cossack deserters and captives, there were 150-500 fugitives with Shamil between 1843 and 1852 at Dargo, who received a salary from Shamil and worked repairing artillery, making iron and gunpowder, and growing maize and cutting hay for Shamil.[18]

Other Russian deserters, like Alpatov, carved out a career in banditry. In the 1840s and 1850s, several Cossack deserters became famous brigands, forming bands with Chechens and others. Some Cossacks believed that all of the Chechen attacks on their farmsteads during these years occurred with the participation of fugitive village-mates who were able to guide the gangs safely through the various Cossack defenses. Such claims sound like inverse boasting, designed to downplay the ability of the Chechens to outwit Cossacks on their own. On the other hand, plenty of Cossacks did participate in such raids. For example, Edyk Batyrev, a fugitive from Babukovskaia, led a band of ten in an 1855 attack on the camp of a lieutenant colonel a few miles from Piatigorsk, taking four people captive. Nestor Daspeev fled from Chervlennaia in 1858 and along with Chechens attacked Cossacks three times in one month, stealing oxen and taking captive one woman and a girl. Six Mozdok Cossacks were exiled to Siberia in 1847 for being suspected of brigandage and having secret contacts with mountain people.[19]

All of these desertions and attacks were extremely disconcerting to Russian authorities and fed a swirl of suspicion concerning Russian cooperation with Shamil. Rumors circulated that he lived in a European-style house built by Russian deserters, that he had a corps of 4,000 "of all nations" built upon an original corps of Russian and Polish deserters, and that Shamil's predecessor, Hamza Bek, was constantly accompanied by Russian bodyguards. There were even stories that the writer Alexander Bestuzhev-Marlinskii, whose body was never recovered after he died in battle in 1837, was alive and fighting alongside Shamil, or was in fact Shamil himself. What is important is not so much the veracity of such rumors, but their currency. That they could exist at all testifies to the uncertainty on this frontier. Because of intermarriage, interactions, conversions, acculturations, and desertions it was often difficult to tell just who was who in the Caucasus. As Pushkin remarked after meeting a Persian court poet between Kazbek and Tiflis, who turned out not to be a "bombastic Oriental" after all but a European-style gentleman, it was best not to judge a person in the Caucasus by his sheepskin cap and painted nails alone. In other words, savages could be gentlemen, enemies could turn out to be friends, but friends could also turn out to be enemies.[20]

Local officials instinctively distrusted native Cossack units, such as the Ossetian village of Chernoiarskaia and the Kabardian village of Babukovskaia. When bandits killed major Surzhikov and took the treasury money he was carrying from Mozdok to Ekaterinograd in 1828, rumors immediately spread about the Chernoiarskaia Ossetians. Within a year, and without solid evidence, the village had been denounced, surrounded by other Cossacks, and eight Ossetians arrested and executed as the robbers. It turned out, though, that

Surzhikov had probably been murdered by three Digorian bandits and a former resident of Chernoiarskaia, one Gulaev, who had earlier fled to the mountains. Gulaev apparently started the rumor about his former villagers.[21]

Military officials accused the Kabardians of Babukovskaia of providing shelter to brigands from beyond the Kuban who preyed on travelers between Piatigorsk and Georgievsk. In 1844, the host ataman agreed that this village was "very harmful to the tranquility of the region" and recommended resettling it. The same rumors continued through the next decade until 1861 when one-half of the village was freed from the Cossack estate and allowed to resettle in Kabarda.[22]

The governor of the Caucasus projected similar fear of and hostility towards various "native" Cossacks, whom he accused of theft and brigandage, without solid evidence, in 1846. His main allegation was that they had continual contacts with Chechens, Kabardians, and other mountain people, often serving as guides for raiders crossing the line, and sometimes joining up with them. His lineup comprised "Circassian," Ossetian, and Armenian Cossacks. The Circassian Zalym Parkhichev, for example, had a Kabardian wife and relatives across the line to whom he passed on stolen horses—"because of his connections with Kabardians and Chechens, he is an extremely harmful person." Nikolai Serebriakov and Matvei Argyshev, Circassians in the Mozdok regiment, "are well-known thieves and continually are in contact with residents and scoundrels from beyond the Terek." Gavrilo Tomov, another Circassian in the Mozdok regiment, had engaged in thievery since 1842, "and although it is well known to all, it is difficult to expose him." Such allegations and fears were founded more in the general cultural fluidity of the North Caucasus than in actual proof of treasonous activity.[23]

Equally terrifying was the fear that Cossacks could be pulled towards nativization by accident and by coercion. In the story of the desertion of Atarshchik, the original sin seems to have been when the father, a translator in Russian service, gave the son to be raised in a Kumyk village so he could learn native languages and follow in the elder's footsteps as a translator. Atarshchik learned Kumyk, Chechen, and Arabic, but he also, as he put it, "involuntarily became accustomed to the everyday life, morals, and customs of the mountain people." According to his testimony, he turned to the mountains after years of service only because his wife and children were murdered and "I imagined the habitual life among the mountain people as the only true and remote refuge." Since Atarshchik fled a second time to the mountains after he returned in 1841 and tried to lure other to desert, his motivation must have been more than just grief.[24]

Similarly, mountain captivity was harmful not just because able bodies and ransom money were lost, but also because of its power to de-Russify. The Cossack deserter Andrei Katov was the son of a Cossack who was taken captive by trans-Kuban mountain people. The elder Katov returned to Russia with a Muslim wife and children, but the latter were baptized and raised in the Armenian church. Apparently it did not take, because Andrei fled beyond the Kuban in 1844. Chechens took seven-year-old Afan'ka Frolov captive in a raid on Chervlennaia. His host family raised him as a Chechen; after only a year he came to identify with them so much that when they resettled pending a Russian attack, he remembered with astonishment that, "it was also frightening to me. We ran from the Russians, from my own, but it was frightening to me, along with the Chechens. I was used to their ways." He also quickly lost his native tongue—"For a year I babbled in Chechen; when I was brought home [after a prisoner trade] I didn't know a single Russian word." Seven-year-old Katiashka of Shchedrinskaia was held in captivity by the Tavlinians for fifteen years; she married twice and had children there. When she was released and returned to her village she refused to give up her trousers for a Russian dress, hitting, biting, and kicking anyone who tried to convert her. Finally, her brothers-in-law from the mountains came and ordered her to wear a dress and to cease thinking about returning home.[25]

Religion did not always stabilize identity either. The North Caucasus was a part of the fault line between Christianity and Islam that stretches from the Balkans through Central Asia. The Russian state tried to push that line further south by Christianizing the region, not so much through missionary activity, but by settling Christians there and getting rid of Muslims. Shamil and many others fought back in the name of Islam. But if this was a religious conflict, it was a confused one indeed. As we have seen, many Muslims were Cossacks, and some Cossacks became Muslims.

Further, conversion to Christianity seems to have been relatively easy, but perceived by outsiders as largely meaningless. Ossetians supposedly retained the taint of paganism and Islam. According to a writer in *Voennyi sbornik*, they "don't seem to have much religious conviction at all." Stepanov, a journalist for *Kavkaz*, wrote that the Ossetians from Kapkai near Vladikavkaz were Christians, but "very bad ones" who made use of a mullah and celebrated Islamic holidays. Another local writer claimed that the Ossetians in Chernoiarskaia mixed up Christianity, Islam, and paganism and practiced polygamy.[26] Lamaist Kalmyks converted to Orthodoxy previous to joining the Mozdok regiment in 1777 when G. A. Potëmkin settled them along the line "to make them acquainted with the essence of law and forget their nomadic life." They quickly abandoned Christianity, retaining only their Christian names and threw off the settled life to return to the steppe. In 1830 there were 1,839 officially Orthodox Kalmyks in the regiment, "who," according to the Ministry of Internal Affairs, "however, are more like pagans because of the nomadic nature of their life and lack of priests." In other words, both settlement and Christianity were required to be civilized. Abozin fixed on the religious deficiencies and called them idol worshippers; Debu concentrated on their wild (i.e., wandering) mode of life, writing that "in their present state they are more like vagrants (*brodiagi*) than people who have entered the ranks of a military command." In 1860, their warden (*popechitel'*) Kostenkov, found Kalmyks along the Kuman River who could not even remember that their parents had been baptized.[27]

From the perspective of the frontier, that which "civilizers" saw as apostasy or religious ignorance was instead the outline of a syncretic religious milieu. In other words, Christianity, Islam, and paganism were not necessarily mutually exclusive. Kizliar Muslim Persians (Teziks) supposedly took offerings to an Armenian church on Sundays. A reporter for *Terskiia vedomosti* claimed that there was a common cult of St. George in Kizliar. "I don't know," he wrote, "if there exists another Christian temple in the world were under the canopy of one vault gather supplicants of such varied faiths as that which occurs in the Church of St. George in Kizliar." Muslims brought offerings of sheep during church holidays. Old Believers in the North Caucasus worshipped the relics of three Muslim Circassians, who, the story went, fled from their village beyond the Terek because they did not want to kill giaours. Sometime after the 1840s, Old Believers sent the bodies to Moscow for canonization. In the late nineteenth century, John Baddeley met an Orthodox priest who allowed pagan customs and "drank reverently to Afsati, the patron saint or god of wild beasts and of hunters." Ossetians, Balkarians, Karachevites, Svans, and Abkhazians all worshiped Afsati, and apparently a few Christians did too.[28]

The "civilizing" power of religion, then, worked poorly for the Russian state; religious affiliation was frequently seen as a weak signifier for allegiance and, since it was often difficult even to fix the boundaries between faiths, a poor determinant of identity. Science did not fare much better. Mountain people were widely respected for their medical arts. Samoilov praised the Chechens' ability to treat wounds with special ointments and mineral baths. Samarin similarly enthused over mountain doctors who could prevent gangrene and pointed to visible evidence of their superiority over Russian physicians: "In the Caucasus one can meet many Russian soldiers, Cossacks, and officers with amputated legs or arms, but I have never seen a single armless or legless mountaineer." Moritz Wagner told of an Ossetian physician at Vladikavkaz, who "was not only celebrated as a medicine man amongst his countryman in the mountains, but had also a considerable practice amongst the Russians, and the regimental doctors were not a little jealous of their barbarous colleague."[29]

Cossacks, then, preferred to turn to "Asian" healers, and also to their own charmers, instead of those purveyors of Enlightenment, Russian doctors. "Everywhere," according to a Cossack N.C.O., "the people have a distrust of doctors and the science of medicine." Tolstoi voiced this in *The Cossacks*, based on his experience living with the Terek Cossacks, when his old Greben Cossack Eroshka grumbles,

I'd long ago have hanged your Russian ones [doctors] if I was the tsar. All they can do is cut at you...If yours ever cured anyone, Cossacks and Chechens would come to be healed, but instead your doctors and colonels send for doctors from the mountains.

Kozlovskii claimed that the only time Cossacks of the Line entrusted themselves to Russian doctors was "in order to avoid publicity about a quickly ensuing death."[30]

The preference for mountain healing over Russian science was but one example of the failure of Russian civilization to sort out loyalties and identities in the North Caucasus. As we have seen many times in this study, it was often nearly impossible determine who was "native" and who was "Russian," who was friend and who was enemy, where "the Caucasus" stopped and "Russia" began. In the local mentality, Cossacks who fled to the mountains were not necessarily disloyal, but necessarily suspected. Natives in Russian service pledged loyalty to the tsar, but did not necessarily mean it. "Peaceful" Chechens were often not peaceful. North Caucasian Armenians, neither of the mountains nor of Russia, were essential to the local economy, but fundamentally untrustworthy, since they lived with the "Russians" and traded in the mountains. Because of the labor shortage, local officials had to rely on just about anybody they could get their hands on to help shore up the military line, but they could fully trust hardly anyone. Orthodox were not necessarily real Christians. Christians who converted to Islam were probably (hopefully) not real Muslims. Enlightened Russian science was denounced as barbaric, but "savage" healers of the mountains were relied on for their knowledge. The local "Russian" that was spoken was equally "non-Russian." Such split identities were most prominently illustrated by the Greben Cossacks who lived in a Caucasian *saklia* in the winter and a Russian *izba* in the summer.[31]

And Christians were not necessarily trustworthy Orthodox. The most important religious fault line in the lives of the Terek Cossack was not between Christianity and Islam, but between Orthodoxy and Old Belief. Cossacks did not cross that divide; it structured their everyday lives, politicized their marriages, split their communities, and fueled a longstanding antagonism with the state that was periodically resolved through desertion.

Cossacks played an important role in the history of Old Belief in the Russian empire, and one that has been neglected by historians apart from the study of the major seventeenth- and eighteenth-century uprisings. Old Believers were not just rebels or monks and merchants who negotiated ways to exist in the realm of the antichrist; they were also state servants who found it possible to serve the antichrist. As such, Old Belief was more than, as Robert O. Crummey put it, "a photographic negative of official society." With the Terek Cossacks— and the Ural Cossacks also—Old Belief was a part of "official society," never entirely well adjusted, always creating tension and suspicion, but, after a century of struggle, an accepted part nonetheless.[32]

Fight over Old Belief began in 1738 when a Kizliar priest Fedor Ivanov tried to force the Cossacks of the Greben host to follow all of the rituals of the Orthodox church, levying a special tax on the host and on their priests and complaining to the bishop of Astrakhan. The bishop admonished them to change their ways, threatening to take the matter to the Holy Synod and to defrock their priests and send them into penal servitude. The Cossacks refused to yield, even after many orders and threats and the incarceration of all of their priests for a period in Kizliar. The struggle continued until 1745, when the host ataman sent three elders to the chairman of the Kizliar Ecclesiastical Board (*dukhovnoe pravlenie*) once again to plead their case, sending with them a petition, which included the threat that "our affairs are frontier affairs (*delo nashe ukrainoe*)" and that the Cossacks would "disperse" (*razbredutsia*) if the tax was not lifted. After this, the spiritual and civil authorities stopped threatening the Cossacks and let them practice their own religion in their own way. But their hunt for proselytizers and wandering priests continued.[33]

During the same period, local authorities began to seek out and apprehend suspicious holy people living in Cossack villages or in the woods nearby. The then-thick forest of the North Caucasus offered many places for Old Believers to hide, and from the early eighteenth century, religious fugitives began to found small monasteries known as sketes. The Kizliar commander periodically sent dragoon detachments through the forests to try to round them up, but the faithful posted sentries in tall trees who would warn when troops were approaching and all would flee across the Terek to safety. They did catch a few, such as the Cossack Alpat who lived in Novogladkovskaia stanitsa and went about in monastic dress, barefoot, carrying an iron staff, and the hermit Andrei Vasil'ev who lived in the woods near Starogladkovskaia.[34]

Beginning in 1751, nearly every year Old Believer preachers were discovered agitating near Kizliar and the villages of the Greben host and receiving protection and material support from the Cossacks and the stanitsa chiefs. In 1751, four were caught—two Don Cossacks, a peasant, and an Abazian with Old Believer books—in the forest near the Greben stanitsas. In 1756, Fedor Stepanov—a Nogai Tatar who led a skete near Shchedrinskaia—was handed over to the Astrakhan consistory. In 1759, three more were caught in the forest along the Terek River. After a dragoon intercepted an oxcart heaped full of Old Believer manuscripts, old books, monks' cloaks, and iron chains (*verigi*) in 1760, the Astrakhan consistory tried to get the Kizliar commander to double his efforts to catch schismatics hiding in and near Greben villages, and also sent an ukaz to the host ataman Ivan Ivanov ordering him not to let them into the stanitsas and to turn in any he might discover. Ivanov refused to comply, and the chancellery of the Kizliar commander warned that the Cossacks could easily flee across the Terek if pressured.[35] The church then gave up hunting down the Old Believers and sketes began to be founded in the open, right next to the stanitsas. The local change corresponded to Peter III's and Catherine the Great's general tolerance towards Old Believers beginning in 1762, but issued from immediate—and more relevant—concerns.[36]

In the eighteenth century, local commanders especially feared that Old Believer Cossacks would collude with or desert to join the so-called Nekrasov Cossacks, Don Cossack Old Believer refugees from the Bulavin uprising who lived in the lower Kuban region, mounting raids on the Russian settlements with the Kabardians and siding with Turkey in the Russo-Turkish war of 1768-1774. Local sources reported that Nekrasovites periodically sent delegates to the Greben Cossacks to entice them to leave for greener pastures. General De Medem was so concerned about collusion in 1774 that he prohibited all residents of Kizliar and Mozdok from interacting with people beyond the Terek and he ordered that the Greben Cossacks be called into service only with great caution. His fears seem to have been warranted. Nekrasov Cossacks joined up with 10,000 Kabardians in the 11 June 1774 attack on Naur. Days before the attack, they had been in the area appealing once again to the Greben Cossacks to abandon their allegiance to Russia. That was apparently the last stand of the Nekrasovites in the North Caucasus; in 1778 they moved to Anatolia and began their existence as Cossacks of the Ottoman empire.[37]

Even after the Nekrasovites disappeared and Old Belief was decriminalized, tensions continued to exist between Orthodox and Old Believers. Old Believers were continually watched for proselytism or anti-state activity. Orthodox priests investigated suspicious priests and services and compiled lists of parishioners not receiving confession. Then, in the first half of the nineteenth century, official persecution of Old Believers revived—they were not allowed to hold services or fix up their prayer houses, and their priests, usually fugitives, were turned away. Oppression could come from the highest order—when Nicholas I visited the North Caucasus in 1838, according to the commander-in-chief Baron Rozen, during the inspection of the Greben regiment he noticed several officers with Old Believer beards and ordered that they shave.[38]

According to official numbers in 1830 there were 19,555 schismatics, mostly Old Believers, in the Caucasus *oblast'* and the Black Sea host, compared to 166,734 Orthodox and 81,366 Muslims. In the Line host in 1846 there were 21,487 schismatics (20,246 Old Believers) compared to 67,511 Orthodox. The actual number was probably higher, since Old Believers sometimes claimed they were Orthodox or avoided being counted. Also the Ministry of Internal Affairs encouraged local officials to swell the ranks of the Orthodox by declaring in 1850 that illegitimate children of Old Believers and sectarians who were subsequently married in the Orthodox church and pledged to raise their children in the true faith would be counted as legitimate. (As we saw in Chapter 7, some Old Believers married in the Orthodox church, and illegitimate children were not rare.) Most of the Old Believers were in the Greben regiment (6,540 in 1846), but they could be found, in varying numbers, almost everywhere. As Slivitskii observed in 1846-47, "in each stanitsa there are several Old Believer families who live in their own circle, avoiding association with the Orthodox." The village-by-village proportion of Old Believers to Orthodox varied widely. In the Greben regiment, Old Believers tended to live in predominantly Old Believer villages, the most in Chervlennaia where in 1848 there were 3,193 and only eleven people of different faiths. In the Mozdok regiment, where there was the next largest representation of Old Believers (3,636 in 1846), it varied from mixed denominational villages to villages where Old Believers were in the great minority.[39]

Cossack religious animosity took many forms. Most reports on mixed-religion Cossack villages claimed that Orthodox and Old Believers were distrustful and sometimes contemptuous of each other. Occasionally Old Believers jeered Orthodox during religious processions, covered their ears so as not to hear the singing, and did not remove their hats. Religious hatred could also transcend rank—when the newly appointed ataman went to Chervlennaia to introduce himself in 1846, the lady of one house yelled at him for crossing her threshold "with dirty paws," calling him both a "damned non-Christian" and an "accursed Muscovite." Often tensions were heightened by the typical resentment by old immigrants (Old Believers) of new immigrants (Orthodox). At Novogladkovskaia, when Ukrainian Orthodox began moving there in 1848, the Old Believers grudgingly apportioned them swampy lands to settle on. As the Greben Cossacks were reported to say to their new comrades-in-arms, "We are native Cossacks and were born here; you are peasants, peasants through and through." The Old Believer Greben Cossacks of Shchedrinskaia chopped up the plows and oxcarts of neighboring Orthodox Cossacks in 1860, claiming they were encroaching on their land. Animosity was compounded by cultural and ethnic differences. In general, Old Believers were more ethnically Russian and North Caucasian, they practiced agriculture less, had been Cossacks longer, and were considered the best fighters. The Orthodox tended to be more Ukrainian, only recently Cossacks, and more attracted to farming. And they often spoke different languages: at Umakhan-Iurtovskaia—half Orthodox and half Old Believer—the former spoke Ukrainian and the latter spoke Russian, Chechen, and Kumyk.[40]

The most visible manifestations of the separation of Old Believers from the world of the Orthodox were their sketes on the edge of their villages. There Old Believers lived contemplative lives apart from their village-mates, praying and living in poverty. As the host government described them, "Passing through [the stanitsa] in some secluded corner you may see something like a sacred grove, enclosed by a high fence, behind which are visible the roofs of miniature Russian huts. These are Old Believer sketes." It seems that mostly elderly women lived in these sketes. But when an investigator for the regiment visited the Novogladkovskaia skete he also found two "lively old maids" under forty and he could not figure how they ended up there. Apparently, others besides

Cossacks went to sketes to escape the world. The same investigator spoke with one eighty-year-old woman from Moscow, who had lived there for fifteen years and had a wide reputation as a particularly holy and knowledgeable Old Believer. There were also rumors—sometimes no doubt true—of fugitive peasants, soldiers, and priests hiding out in sketes.[41]

Occasionally, Old Believers were driven from reclusion to mass protest. Once, for example, when an Old Believer priest was about to be arrested in Chervlennaia, Cossack women surrounded his house armed with oven prongs, sticks, pokers, and rifles and surrendered him only after soldiers fired cannon shots over their heads. Such rebellions, though, were rare; mostly Old Believers kept to themselves, sheltered their priests, and avoided major confrontations with the Orthodox church or the state. The more typical protest was flight and desertion, either to a small, secluded monastery in the woods or to the mountains.[42]

A small but significant trickle of Old Believer Cossacks to the mountains began on 27 November 1849 when five Cossacks from Chervlennaia fled to the mountains, taking with them icons, holy books, bronze crosses, rosaries, incense, and wax and leaving behind the message "we have gone on the path of Christ." They had heard tales of Old Believer monks and Nekrasov Cossacks living in the mountains and decided to seek them out and live a life of religious purity. This religious dream was a local variation of the popular nineteenth-century legend of "the town of Ignat," where Ignat Nekrasov still lived, somewhere beyond the Arabian desert. Enchanted by such stories, the original pilgrims were later joined by three more (two from Chervlennaia and one from Shchedrinskaia) who were searching for "forty stanitsas of freemen and an Old Believer monastery." The stream of desertions from the same and other villages continued—eight more from Chervlennaia, one from the Kizliar regiment, then fourteen from Kalinovskaia, then a doctor's assistant from the Kizliar regiment, four from Mekentsaia, two more from Kalinovskaia, and four from Alkhan-Iurt. Dozens deserted in the next few years; they were all given a place to settle and lived under the protection of Shamil.[43]

Nicholas I no doubt fueled this exodus, and a general atmosphere of distrust, by his assaults on other Old Believer communities in the Russian empire. By 1841, the Irgiz monasteries had been attacked by troops, monks and nuns exiled, and others forced into *edinoverie*, an officially sanctioned version of Old Belief, under the hierarchy of the Orthodox church. The attacks on the Vyg community were more muted, but more persistent, and by the late 1840s had significantly undermined the foundations of this important center of Old Belief.[44]

It is certainly no coincidence that the intolerant reign of Nicholas I corresponded to a renewed militancy among Old Believers. In the 1830s and 1840s, Ural Cossacks deserted to search in Siberia, the Altai mountains, and China, for the Kingdom of the White Waters (*Belovode*), a mythical Old Believer commune said to exist "across the waters." In the 1850s, Ural Cossacks apostatized in mass from Orthodoxy and *edinoverie* back to Old Belief. In the 1840s and 1850s, Terek Cossacks fled to Shamil.[45]

To calm things down, in 1850, the commander of the Line warned that it was an insult to call Greben Cossacks "schismatics" (*raskolniki*), and that to prevent further umbrage all should be called Old Believers (*Starovertsy*), reserving the former term for "harmful" sects such as the Dukhobors and Shore-dwellers (*Pomortsy*). In 1850, the commander of the Greben regiment created a special commission to investigate the reasons for these desertions. It was discovered that a regular flow of communications existed between the religious colony far in the mountains and the stanitsas of the Line, with the help of Chechen intermediaries. Authorities intercepted several letters between the deserters and their village-mates in 1851 and 1852, some of which spoke of the reign of the antichrist in Moscow. The sentiment may have been widespread among this group—when four Cossacks fled from the Sunzha regiment in 1852, one left behind a "testament" that denounced "the precursor of the antichrist, that is Nicholas I." After Cossacks captured one of the original pilgrim/deserters Timofei Iankhotov in June 1852 when he returned to his stanitsa to entice more Cossacks to the mountains, he was sentenced to be executed. The local commander and the ataman of the Line Cossacks intervened and got the sentence reduced to running the gauntlet twice and enrollment in a criminal brigade—they feared his execution would increase "fanaticism" and lead to more desertion. All of the other deserters who returned were treated even more gently, facing only a short-term detention or corporal punishment; some were not punished at all. Then in December the host government warned the secretary (*dezhurstvo*) that all correspondence concerning the conversion of "schismatics" to Orthodoxy should be as secret as possible.[46]

Apparently, the gentler approach did not entirely work. In 1855, three Old Believer Cossacks from the Mozdok and Greben regiments ran off to the mountains; one had been seen earlier with the book "How to Save Yourself in the Wilderness." After one of the deserters, Ivannenkov, returned, he reported seeing a deserted monastery in the mountains.[47]

Most Cossacks, of course, did not desert. The Terek Cossacks on the whole accepted their relationship with the Russian state, and were happy to receive land, salaries, and provisions as a part of the bargain. Most were not Old Believers. Most Old Believers apparently did not think that the antichrist ruled over the Kremlin, since they were content to stay put in Russia. And the local military officials were comfortable enough with Old Believers in their units that they had no problem accepting state peasant Old Believers into the host in 1852. But it is also true that Old Belief provided a conduit for anti-state activity and local turbulence ever since the schism occurred in the seventeenth century. And time and time again, the state was forced to back down and allow Old Believers their way, including the freedom to desert, the most powerful rejection of Russian, and imperial, identity.[48]

There is nothing novel in the imperial government's restrained approach towards Cossack dissent. After all, as Isabel de Madariaga reminds us, most of the 10,000 Cossack and other prisoners taken in the liberation of Kazan at the end of the Pugachev uprising were let completely off of the hook. After taking a new oath of loyalty, Catherine the Great released them without punishment and even granted the rebels travel stipends to speed their journeys home.[49] That was the price Russia had to pay for relying on the Cossack system at the extremity of empire, where the power of the apparatuses of government, army, and Orthodox church faded. What is surprising is the fact that Russia had to allow such rebellious behavior as late as the mid-nineteenth century, amidst the most protracted and costly imperial expansion, and one that was unrivaled in the creation of modern Russian national identity.[50]

There is no evidence that the Terek Cossacks had a particularly strong dynastic allegiance as did, for example, the Grenzer of the Croatian Military Border who looked to the Habsburg emperor as the defender of their privileged status from the Croatian nobility. On the other hand, the Terek Cossacks never felt estranged enough from the empire to engage in large-scale rebellion, and the state never made forceful movements to abolish their autonomy as it had with the Zaporozhian and Don Cossacks. The Russian technique to establish a greater degree of control in the North Caucasus was to augment the old Terek Cossacks, to encourage immigration and to transfer new Cossacks there, but probably less because of a perceived need to populate the region with "their" men or to dilute the weight of the Old Believers, and more simply because of the insatiable demand for more colonists and fighters.[51]

What about "Cossack" identity—that is, historical or estate identity as a Cossack? As we have already seen, Terek Cossacks connected their history to the Don, to Yermak, to the famous Cossack rebels of the seventeenth and eighteenth centuries. And many Terek Cossacks came from other Cossack groups, especially from the Don and the Volga. There can be little doubt that connection to a larger sense of cossackdom was extremely important to many Terek Cossacks.

On the other hand, the Cossack estate in the North Caucasus did not provide for much coherence. As we have seen in Chapter 8, Terek Cossacks were not unified into the Caucasus Line host until 1832 and received a systematic legal statute only in 1845. Their service obligations—that which they did to make them "Cossack"—varied widely. And what did "Cossack" mean when state peasant villages and anemic military colonies were transformed into Cossack stanitsas literally overnight? The older Terek Cossack communities never saw them as equals, in any sense.[52]

In the North Caucasus, the reality—and I would claim the most important source of identity—was more locally grounded than any larger sense of cossackdom, at least up to the mid-nineteenth century. The Caucasus Military

Line was divided into numerous relatively small regiments and hosts, which rarely went on campaigns or to a battle en masse. They were usually scattered about at various defense lines and theaters of war. About the only time they fought together in large groups was when they defended their villages against mountaineer attacks.

So they looked more to their regiments—or their villages, or their part of their villages, even—for a sense of identity. In other words, they often did not get along very well with each other. The one attempt in 1745 to merge hosts failed after the Terek-Semeinoe and the Greben hosts continually quarreled about service requirements and leadership. They were redivided ten years later.[53]

The Greben Cossacks looked down on all new Cossacks as a lesser breed and seemed to have the best-developed local identity. This was reinforced by the fact that they were largely Old Believers. They reportedly viewed the Georgian Cossacks in their regiment as "sluggish foreigners" who were enrolled as Cossacks by mistake. They despised former peasant, Ukrainian Cossacks as fit only for the knout or the oxcart; supposedly they even had a hard time believing that the Ukrainian Zaporozhian host ever existed. In turn, the Ukrainians saw the Grebentsy as "Asians with Tatar beliefs." Georgian Cossacks did not intermarry with other Cossacks, their wives neither spoke nor understood Russian, and they did not intermingle much with their Greben Cossack neighbors. They told a story about how they fell into Cossack service only because their leaders squandered their annual tax payment on the way to Stavropol' and then asked to be admitted into the Cossack estate as a substitute.[54]

There were also many Cossacks who came from the mountains or were products of mixed marriages, who looked to the native cultures of the North Caucasus for at least part of their identities. Along the lower Terek, the influence was Chechen, Kumyk, and Tatar. Along the middle and upper Terek, it was Ossetian and Kabardian. Some of those who deserted were attempting to return to their homelands. The majority who did not desert looked to the south nonetheless, for their clothes, weapons, horses, food, and many other aspects of their material culture.

How did Terek Cossacks see themselves? As a local expert reported from his experience with the Mozdok Cossacks, "in most cases they call themselves simply 'Cossacks' not understanding the significance of the word...'Are you a Russian?' a traveler asks a Cossack. 'No,' he answers, 'I'm a Cossack.'"[55] But what exactly that meant is very difficult to establish, especially since most first-person Cossack sources come from the unrepresentative, literate, noble Cossacks. No doubt it meant different things to different people: a state-servant settler; a carrier of the true religion, Old Belief, ready, perhaps, to flee from religious persecution; a warrior; a rebel; a Mozdok Cossack, not a Greben Cossack; a Greben Cossack from Chervlennaia, and not Nikolaevskaia; a

Cossack, not a state peasant; a native in Russian service. The frontier identities of the Terek Cossacks were as diverse as the people themselves and many, no doubt, combined identities. Their societies were quite different from that which existed in the heartland of Russia and their loyalties were by no means simply to tsar and empire.

The history of Russian imperial expansion written from the perspective of the center rightly emphasizes the monochrome of territorial conquest—borders are, after all, rather stark. From the perspective of the frontier we see, rather, a pointillist riot of colors, which does not, of course, change the borders. But the diverse colors do make the achievement of empire building seem considerably less "total." Was this, though, a strength or a weakness? One of the reasons why the Russian empire grew relentlessly, incorporating so many different cultures, was because it often tolerated an incredible degree of diversity and—the word comes as a surprise—liberty, nowhere more so than in the North Caucasus. We should not forget that the Cossack system populated a turbulent frontier in a rather short period of time. The privileges and liberties granted to the estate allowed Russia to stake and defend its claim in the North Caucasus, no small feat. It was the regular army that really won the war against the mountain people, not the Cossacks, but it was the Cossacks, and the peasants who followed them, who won the land. That aspect of Russian imperialism—its ability to populate inhospitable frontiers with a minimum of state expense—was often stunningly successful.

But what kind of growth was this? The strength in territory was undermined by a weak attachment to the institutions, economy, and culture that supposedly defined Russia. It is hard to imagine Texas Rangers fleeing to Mexico, French soldiers joining up with Algerians, or American cavalrymen turning to Apaches for weapons. The undergoverned state has become almost a cliché of Russian history; the experience of the Terek Cossacks suggests that it was also an underassimilated empire. This becomes all-too-obvious today as we watch first republics and then regions devolve away from the center of Russian power. From the perspective of the nineteenth—and late twentieth—century, one must conclude that the tree of empire had some very shallow roots in spots. But then again, who could have imagined trees growing on such barren soil in the first place?

Notes

1. For a recent example of this type of Cossack history see A. M. and B. M. Gdenko, *Za drugi svoia ili vsë o kazachestve* (Moscow: Mezhdunarodnyi fond slavianskoi pis'mennosti i kultury, 1993), 185-238.

2. K. F. Gan, *Opyt'' ob''iasneniia Kavkazskikh geograficheskikh nazvanii* (Tiflis: Tipografiia kantseliarii Namestnika Ego Imperatorskago Velichestva na Kavkaze, 1909), 73, 82, 90, 104; Ramazan Traho, "Circassians," *Central Asian Survey* 10, no. 1/2 (1991): 62.

3. T. M., "Korespondentsiia 'Illiustrirovannoi Gazety' s Kavkaza," *Illiustrirovannaia gazeta*, 12 January 1867, 26-27; V. K. Shenk, ed., *Kazach'i voiska* (St. Petersburg: Imperatorskaia glavnaia kvartira, 1912; repr. Aktsionernoe obshchestvo "Dobral'," 1992), 171-89.

4. I. D. Popko, *Terskie kazaki so starodavnikh vremen* (St. Petersburg: Tipografiia Departamenta udelov, 1880), 277-78.

5. N. V. Galushkin, *Sobstvennyi Ego Imperatorskago Konvoi* (San Francisco: Izdatel'stvo B. V. Charkovskago, 1961), 10-11; Popko, *Terskie kazaki*, 276-77, 396-97; G. A. Tkachëv, ed., *Grebenskie, Terskie i Kizliarskie kazaki* (Vladikavkaz: Elektropechatnia tipografii Terskago oblastnago pravleniia, 1911), 102-05.

6. A. Tsimmerman, "Pis'mo iz st. Sunzhenskoi," *Kavkaz*, 9 January 1852, 5-7; P. Semenov, "Stanitsa Sleptsovskaia, Terskoi oblasti, Vladikavkazskago okruga," *Sbornik materialov dlia opsianiia mestnostei i plemen Kavkaza* 5 (1886): 172-74; Lekar Pereverzev, "Stanitsa Sleptsovskaia," *Kavkaz*, 8 January 1861, 15-16; P. Stepanov, "Beglye ocherki Kabardy," *Kavkaz*, 19 October 1861, 442-44.

7. Thomas M. Barrett, "Lines of Uncertainty: The Frontiers of the North Caucasus," *Slavic Review* 53, no. 3 (Fall 1995): 600-01; Zemliak, "Priberezh'e Kaspiiskago moria," *Terskiia vedomosti*, 12 February 1887, 3-4.

For stimulating insight on the iconization of "conquering victims" of the American frontier, see Richard White, "Frederick Jackson Turner and Buffalo Bill," in *The Frontier in American Popular Culture*, ed. James R. Grossman (Berkeley: University of California Press, 1994), 27-35.

8. "Starinnyia istoricheskiia pesni, sokhraniushiiasiu v grebenskikh kazakov," *Kavkaz*, 18 October 1852, 266; "Pesni Terskikh kazakov," *Terskiia vedomosti*, 30 September 1868, 162-63; 28 October 1868, 177-78; 16 December 1868, 208; G. Maliavkin, "Kak poshlo na Rusi kazachestva (kazach'e predanie)," *Terskiia vedomosti*, 1 January 1992, 2; P. A. Vostrikov, "Stanitsa Naurskaia, Terskoi oblasti," *Sbornik materialov dlia opisaniia mestnostei i plemen Kavkaza* 33 (1904): section 2, 103; V. A. Vodarskii, "Pesni, zapisannyia v Chervlennoi i Starogladkovskoi stanitsakh Terskoi oblasti v 1901 godu," *Sbornik materialov dlia opsianiia mestnostei i plemen Kavkaza* 39 (1908): 57-80; I. Mikhailov, "Pover'ia i predrazsudki rybakov pribrezhnyi Kaspiiskago moria," *Kavkaz*, 25 April 1853, 126; Tkachëv, *Grebenskie, Terskie i Kizliarskie kazaki*, 151-55.

9. Rossiiskii Gosudarstvennyi Voenno-Istoricheskii Arkhiv [RGVIA], f. 1058, op. 2, d. 1304, ll. 1-7; G. P. Gubanov, "Khutorskaia zhizn' v Terskoi oblasti," *Sbornik materialov dlia opisaniia mestnostei i plemen Kavkaza* 33 (1904): section 2, 37; N. Samarin, "Dorozhnyi zametki," *Severnaia pchela*, 133 (1862), 550-55; Fedor Chernozubov, "Ocherki Terskoi stariny. Pobegy k nepokornym gortsam," *Russkii arkhiv*, no. 1 (1912): 68-78; Vostrikov, "Stanitsa Naurskaia," section 2, 122-27; D. D. Pagirev, "Alfavitnyi ukazatel' k piativerstoi karte Kavkazskago kraia, izdaniia Kavkazskago voenno-topograficheskago otdela," *Zapiski Kavkazskago otdela Imperatorskago russkago geograficheskago obshchestva* 38 (1913): 13.

10. RGVIA, f. 14877, op. 1, d. 1397. ll. 1-2.

11. G. Prozritelev, ed., *Iz proshlago Severnago Kavkaza. Vospominaniia starago kavkaztsa otstavnago vakhtera Mefodiia Stepanovicha Soloduna* (Stavropol': Tipografiia gubernskago pravleniia, 1914), 18; G. A. Tkachëv, *Stanitsa Chervlennaia. Istoricheskii*

ocherk (Vladikavkaz: Elektropechatnia tipografii Terskago oblastnago pravleniia, 1912), 168-70; V. A. Alferov and S. A. Chekmenev, *Stepnaia vol'nitsa* (Stavropol': Stavropol'skaia knizhnoe izdatel'stvo, 1978), 144 (unfortunately Alferov and Chekmenev did not cite their source); Chernozubov, "Ocherki terskoi stariny," 70-71; RGVIA, f. 1058, op. 2, d. 1041, ll. 4-60.

12. Alferov and Chekmenev, *Stepnaia vol'nitsa*, 144; *Dvizhenie gortsev severovostochnogo Kavkaza v 20-50 gg. XIX veka. Sbornik dokumentov* (Makhachkala: Dagknigoizdat, 1959), 356-57, 486.

13. RGVIA, f. 38, op. 7, d. 374, ll. 1-25.

14. Tkachëv, *Stanitsa Chervlennaia*, 171, 174-75; RGVIA, f. 1058, op. 2, d. 1102, ll. 10-12; d. 1125a, l. 2; d. 1372, ll. 1-6; A. Anoev, "Iz kavkazskikh vospominanii," *Istoricheskii vestnik* 105, no. 9 (1906): 840; N. Samarin, "Dorozhnyia zametki," *Severnaia pchela*, no. 134 (1862): 550-55.

15. RGVIA, f. 1058, op. 2, d. 1102, ll. 1-24; d. 1125a, ll. 1-12; d. 1127, l. 3; d. 1200, ll. 1-15; f. 14877, op. 1, d. 96, ll. 7-8

16. RGVIA, f. 1058, op. 2, d. 1057, ll. 1-3; M. O. Kosven, *Etnografiia i istoriia Kavkaza* (Moscow: Izdatel'stvo vostochnoi literatury, 1961), 254-58; Tkachëv, *Stanitsa Chervlennaia*, 70-71, 81-85, 90-93; RGVIA, f. 1058, op. 2, d. 1116a, ll. 1-2.

17. RGVIA, f. 38, op. 7, d. 93, ll. 1-3.

18. *Akty sobrannye Kavkazskoi arkheograficheksoi komissieiu [AKAK]*, 12: 1398, *Dvizhenie gortsev*, 471, 498; Georgii Paradov, "Raskaz ochevidtsa o Shamile i ego sovremenniakh," *Sbornik materialov dlia opsianiia mestnostei i plemen Kavkaza*, no. 32 (1903): section 1, 18; Iu. Zagorskii, "Vosem' mesiatsev v plenu u gortsev," *Kavkazskii sbornik* 19 (1898): 221-27; Chernozubov, "Ocherki," 64-68; RGVIA, f. 1058, op. 2, d. 1150, ll. 86-89, 93-95; f. VUA, d. 6539, ll. 2-13; A. N. Genko, "Arabskaia karta Chechni epokha Shamilia," *Zapiski Institut vostokovedeniia Akademiia nauk SSSR* 2, no. 1 (1933): 28. These deserters were not only Cossacks but also soldiers from the regular army.

19. Tkachëv, *Stanitsa Chervlennaia*, 168-70; V. A. Potto, *Kavkazskaia voina v otdel'nykh ocherkakh, epizodakh, legendakh i biografiiakh* (St. Petersburg: Tipografiia R. Golike, 1885), 2: part 1, 86-87; RGVIA, f. 1058, op. 2, d. 869, ll. 1-15; d. 1040, ll. 30, 59-60; d. 1070, ll. 1-30; d. 1372, ll. 1-6; d. 1445, ll. 1-9; f. 38, op. 7, d. 128, ll. 18-19; Chernozubov, "Ocherki," 70-71; *Kavkaz*, 6 June 1857, 206; Tkachëv, *Grebenskie, Terskie i Kizliarskie kazaki*, 114-15.

20. John F. Baddeley, *The Russian Conquest of the Caucasus* (London: Longmans, Green and Co., 1908), 397; Friedrich Wagner, *Schamyl and Circassia*, trans. Kenneth R. H. Mackenzie (London: G. Routledge and Co., 1854), 88; Baron August von Haxthausen, *The Tribes of the Caucasus*, trans. J. E. Taylor (London: Chapman and Hall, 1855), 98; A. L. Zisserman, *Dvadtsat' piat' let na Kavkaze (1842-1867)* (St. Petersburg: Tipografiia A. S. Suvorina, 1879), 1: 329; Mikhail Semevskii, "Aleksandr Aleksandrovich Bestuzhev (Marlinskii). 1798-1837," *Otechestvennyia zapiski* 131, no. 7 (1860): 99-100; Lauren G. Leighton, *Alexander Bestuzhev-Marlinsky* (New York: Twayne Publishers, 1975), 35; Alexander Pushkin, *A Journey to Arzrum*, trans. Birgitta Ingermanson (Ann Arbor: Ardis, 1974), 30-31.

21. Z. Sosiev, "Stanitsa Chernoiarskaia," *Terskii sbornik*, no. 5 (1903): 36-38.

22. RGVIA, f. VUA, d. 6572, ll. 1-2; f. 1058, op. 1, d. 539, ll. 2-39; op. 2, d. 706, ll. 1-

6; Khorunzhii Eloev, "Stanitsa Georgievskaia. Istoriko-ekonomicheskii ocherk," *Terskii sbornik*, no. 5 (1903): 77-80; I. L. Omel'chenko, *Terskoe kazachestvo* (Vladikavkaz: Ir, 1991), 94-95.

23. RGVIA, f. 38, op. 7, d. 128, ll. 1-19.

24. Kosven, *Etnografiia i istoriia Kavkaza*, 254-58.

25. RGVIA, f. 14877, op. 1, d. 96, ll. 7-8; Tkachëv, *Grebenskie, Terskie i Kizliarskie kazaki*, 109-14; Tkachëv, *Stanitsa Chervlennaia*, 179-80. One of the most notorious converts was Shamil's wife Shuanet, originally a Mozdok Armenian who was taken captive in 1845. She remained devoted to him, even after Shamil was taken captive and resettled to Russia. After Shamil died, Shuanet moved to Turkey where she lived for the rest of her life, maintained by a pension from the sultan. See G. N. Prozritelev, "Shamil' v Stavropole," *Sbornik svedenii o Severnom Kavkaze* 9 (1914): 1-4.

Of course Russia also had its trophy captive-converts. The most famous was Shamil's son, Jamāl al-Dīn, who was taken captive in 1839 at the age of eight, raised at court, and apparently Russified and Westernized. Russia swapped him back for two Georgian princesses in 1856 and then followed the decivilization drama as he supposedly "began to become melancholy and wither" and finally died from despair in the wild and savage mountains. See S. Piotrovskii, "Poezdka v gory," *Kavkaz*, 11 September 1858, 363-64; G. Prozritelev, ed., *Iz proshlago Severnago Kavkaza. Vospominaniia starago kavkaztsa otstavnago vakhtera Mefodiia Stepanovicha Soloduna* (St. Petersburg: Tipografiia Gubernskago pravleniia, 1914), 16.

26. P. Stepanov, "Beglye ocherki Kabardy," *Kavkaz*, 19 October 1861, 442-44; I. Abozin, "Vozrazhenie," *Voennyi sbornik* 26, no. 8 (1862): 486-87; Sosiev, "Stanitsa Chernoiarskaia," 48-52.

27. P. Iudin, "Mozdokskie Kalmyki," *Zapiski Terskago obshchestva liubitelei kazach'ei stariny*, no. 12 (1914): 29-31; "Statisticheskiia izvestiia o Kavkazskoi oblasti i Zemle voiska Chernomorskago," *Zhurnal Ministerstva vnutrennykh del* 3, no. 5 (1830): 141; Abozin, "Vozrazhenie," 487; Iosif Debu, *O Kavkazskoi linii i prisoedinennom k nei Chernomorskom voiske* (St. Petersburg: Tipografiia Karla Kraiia, 1829), 63-64.

28. Iu. Shidlovskii, "Zapiski o Kizliare," *Zhurnal Ministerstva vnutrennikh del*, no. 4 (1843): 182; Zemliak, "Priberezh'e Kaspiiskago moria," *Terskiia vedomosti*, 12 February 1887, 3-4; G. N. Prozritelev, *Drevnie khristianskie pamiatniki na Severnom Kavkaze* (Stavropol': Tipografiia naslednikov Berk, 1906), 4, 6-7; P. Khitsunov, "O chakhirinskom kreste," *Kavkaz*, 13 April 1846, 59; "Raznyia izvestiia i zametki," *Vladikavkazskiia eparkhial'nyia vedomosti*, no. 7 (1896): 130-32; Mary L. Henze, "The Religion of the Central Caucasus: An Analysis from Nineteenth Century Travellers' Accounts," *Central Asian Survey* 1, no. 4 (1983): 45-58; John F. Baddeley, *The Rugged Flanks of the Caucasus* (Oxford: Oxford University Press, 1940; repr., New York: Arno Press, 1972), 1: 133; B. A. Kaloev, *Osetiny* (Moscow: Izdatel'stvo "Nauka." Glavnaia redaktsiia vostochnoi literatury, 1971), 249.

29. K. Samoilov, "Zametki o Chechne," *Panteon* 23, no. 9 (1855): section 3, 60-65; N. Samarin, "Dorozhnyia zametki," *Severnaia pchela*, no. 134 (1862): 556; Moritz Wagner, *Travels in Persia, Georgia and Koordistan; With Sketches of the Cossacks and the Caucasus* (London: Hurst and Blackett, 1856), 205. One of the main eighteenth-century exports from the North Caucasus to Russia was treacle, a medicinal compound used to treat poison cases. See A. I. Iukht, "Torgovye sviazi Rossii so stranami vostoka v 20-40kh godakh XVIII v.," in

V. I. Buganov, ed., *Istoricheskaia geografiia Rossii XVIII v.* (Moscow: Akademiia nauk SSSR, Institut istorii SSSR, 1981), 99.

30. "Materialy dlia statistiki Kizliarskago polka Terskago kazach'iago voiska," *Voennyi sbornik*, no. 12 (1869): 223-25; D...r Kozlovskii, "Zametki iz puteshestviia po Kavkazskoi linii," *Kavkaz*, 5 August-17 August 1865, 309-10; L. N. Tolstoi, *Kazaki* (Leningrad: Izdatel'stvo "Detskaia literatura," 1969), 153.

31. For more on the language of the Terek Cossacks, which was filled with Tatar, Turkish, Chechen, Kalmyk, and Ossetian words, see E. Butovaia, "Stanitsa Borozdinskaia, Terskoi oblasti, Kizliarskago okruga," *Sbornik materialov dlia opisaniia mestnostei i plemen Kavkaza* 7 (1889): 52; P. A. Vostrikov, "Stanitsa Naurskaia, Terskoi oblasti," *Sbornik materialov dlia opisaniia mestnostei i plemen Kavkaza* 33 (1904): section 2, 199; N. A. Karaulov, "Govor grebenskikh kazakov," *Sbornik materialov dlia opisaniia mestnostei i plemen Kavkaza* 37 (1907): section 3, 103-09.

32. Robert O. Crummey, *The Old Believers and the World of Antichrist: The Vyg Community and the Russian State 1694-1855* (Madison: University of Wisconsin Press, 1970), iii. For a brief, popular sketch of the history of Cossack Old Believer communities, see I. Iu. Selishchev, *Kazaki i Rossiia* (Moscow: VKhNRTs, 1992).

33. G. Mikhailovskii, "Svedeniia o raskole i raskol'nikakh v predelakh Kavkazskoi eparkhii," *Kavkazskiia eparkhial'nyia vedomosti* 3, 10 (16 May 1875): 324-37; Popko, *Terskie kazaki*, 129-44; N. P. Gritsenko, "Iz istorii staroobriadchestva na Tereke v XVIII-XIX vekakh," *Voprosy istorii Checheno-Ingushetii (dorevoliutsionnyi period)* 11 (1977): 71-75.

34. Popko, *Terskie kazaki*, 144-50; "Materiialy dlia statistiki Kizliarskago polka Terskago kazach'iago voiska," *Voennyi sbornik* no. 12 (Dec. 1869): 212.

35. G. Mikhailovskii, "Istoricheskiia svedeniia o raskole sredi terskikh (grebenskikh) kazakov vo vtoroi polovine XVIII stoletiia," *Kavkazskiia eparkhial'nyia vedomosti* 5, 2 (16 Jan. 1877): 60-77; 5, 3 (1 Feb. 1877): 94-101.

Fedor Stepanov was an extreme example of the easy ability to cross frontiers and change identity in the region. He was a Nogai Tatar who was captured by Kalmyks at age ten, then sold to a Kizliar merchant who converted him to Orthodoxy. Tatars later took him captive again and sold him at Bendery, south of Kishinev, where he reconverted to Islam. After six years, Ukrainian Cossacks stole Stepanov and took him to Mogilev where he once again became Christian. Later he took monastic oaths, moved to Russia, joined up with Don Cossack Old Believers in Kharkov and on the Volga, then moved to Astrakhan where he met an elderly Old Believer who advised him to move to the Terek where there was a great demand for Old Believer preachers. He became the senior priest of a skete, converted Cossacks to Old Belief, but then five years later changed his calling again when he moved to Kizliar, declared himself an Orthodox wanderer, and was married by an Orthodox priest. Stepanov periodically slipped away to Cossack villages to preach and his wife became suspicious when she saw his books and monastic dress. In 1756 she denounced him as a heretic and Stepanov was taken to a monastery in Astrakhan where he converted once again to Orthodoxy and lived out the rest of his life. See Popko, *Terskie kazaki*, 154-57; Mikhailovskii, "Istoricheskiia svedeniia," 62-66.

36. On Catherine's actions towards Old Believers, see N. M. Nikol'skii, *Istoriia russkoi tserkvi*, 4th ed. (Moscow: Politizdat, 1988), 242-45. The monasteries of Irgiz, in Saratov

krai, provided many priests and monks for the Terek Old Believers, who also were important conduits between the Moscow and Novgorod Old Believer communities and the frontier Old Believers. See also Bishop Nestrov, "Upravlenie Platona (Liubarskago), arkhiepiskopa Astrakhanskago i Kavkazskago, Kavkazskoiu pastroiu s 1800 po 1805 g.," *Kavkazskiia eparkhial'nyia vedomosti*, 1 February 1879, 123; Trifon Vasilikhin, "Ocherk staroobriadchestva v stanitse Kalinovskoi Terskoi oblasti, s 1840 do 1880 g.," *Kavkazskiia eparkhial'nyia vedomosti*, 1 January 1881, unofficial section, 26-29.

37. A. P. Pronshtein, ed., *Don i stepnoe Predkavkaz'e v XVIII-pervaia polovina XIX v.* (Rostov-on-Don: Izdatel'stvo Rostovskogo universiteta, 1977), 66; Ag...l Ar...v, "O srazhenii proiskhodivshem na reke Kalalakh v Aprele 1774 goda," *Kavkaz*, 21 October 1853, 339-40; P. G. Butkov, *Materialy dlia novoi istorii Kavkaza s 1722 po 1803 god* (St. Petersburg: Tipografiia Imperatorskoi akademii nauk, 1869), 1: 332-33; Popko, *Terskie kazaki*, 101-04; Aleksandr Rigel'man, *Istoriia ili povestvovanie o Donskikh kazakakh* (Moscow: Universitetskaia tipografiia, 1846), 140-41; I. I. Dmitrenko, "Materialy k istorii Terskago kazach'iago voiska," *Terskii sbornik*, no. 4 (1897): 72-79; *AKAK*, 1: 87-88.

Some Nekrasov Cossacks returned to the Soviet Union in the 1920s, some in 1962, others emigrated to the United States in 1963, and the rest perpetuated their interesting traditional Cossack subculture in Turkey. See Paul Avrich, *Russian Rebels 1600-1800* (New York: W. W. Norton & Co., 1972), 159, 164-65, 168-70 for general background and *Kazaki-Nekrasovtsy na chuzhbine i v Rossii*, Melodiia, S20 25931 000 and the liner notes by V. N. Medvedeva for a fascinating presentation of the music and the folklore of these understudied Cossacks.

Michał Czajkowski, the Polish nobleman and Romantic writer who became Sadik Pasha after he moved to Turkey in 1841 and converted to Islam in 1850, concocted plans to use Nekrasov Cossacks to help foment an uprising in Ukraine and then in the Crimean War against Russia. The latter actually came to fruition—his regiment of 1,400, including Nekrasovites, according to Ivan Rudnytsky, "played a fairly important role in the 1854 campaign." See Rudnytsky, "Michał Czajkowski's Cossack Project During the Crimean War: An Analysis of Ideas," in *Essays in Modern Ukrainian History* (Edmonton: Canadian Institute of Ukrainian Studies, 1987), 173-86.

38. Popko, *Terskie kazaki*, 161-62; Archpriest Ioann Popov, "Moi zaniatiia v arkhivakh," *Sbornik Obshchestva liubitelei kazach'ei stariny*, no. 1 (1912): 18-21; G. Mikhailovskii, "Istoricheskiia svedeniia o raskole sredi terskikh (grebenskikh) kazakov vo vtoroi polovine XVIII stoletiia," *Kavkazskiia eparkhial'nyia vedomosti* 5, no. 3 (1877): 99-100; Gritsenko, "Iz istoriia staroobriadchestva," 76-77; RGVIA, f. 405, op. 6, d. 1562, l. 1.

39. "Statisticheskiia izvestiia o Kavkazskoi oblasti i zemle voiska Chernomorskago," *Zhurnal Ministerstva vnutrennykh del* 3, no. 5 (1830): 141-45; N. I. Voronov, ed., *Sbornik statisticheskikh svedenii o Kavkaze* (Tiflis: Kavkazskii otdel Imperatorskago russkago geograficheskago obshchestva, 1869), 1: section 2, 14-17; "Vospominaniia o Grebenskikh kazakakh i Kavkazskoi linii," *Kavkaz*, 7 October 1856, 316-17; "Istoricheskiia svedeniia," 34-35; Voiskovoe khoziaistvennoe pravlenie, *Statisticheskiia monografii po izsledovaniiu stanichnago byta Terskago kazach'iago voiska* (Vladikavkaz; Tipografiia Terskago oblastnago pravleniia, 1881), 161-68; I. Slivitskii, "Ocherki Kavkaza i Zakavkaz'ia. Kazatskii khutor i staroobriadcheskie skity v Ishorakh," *Kavkaz*, 4 December 1848, 195-96; RGVIA, f. 1058, op. 1, d. 320, l. 7. For a 1847 regimental breakdown of the number of Old Believers, see RGVIA, f. 1058, op. 1, d. 319, ll. 175, 219-23, 229, 232, 243-51, 261-64. For a village by

village breakdown, see RGVIA, f. 1058, d. 1, op. 339, ll. 133-40, 148-55, 157-64, 175-83, 188-93, 210-16.

40. F. S. Grebenets, "Novogladkovskaia stanitsa v eia proshlom i nastoiashchem," *Sbornik materialov dlia opisaniia mestnostei i plemen Kavkaza* 44 (1915): 103-04; Trifon Vasilikhin, "Ocherk staroobriadchestva v stanitse Kalinovskoi Terskoi oblasti, s 1840 do 1880 g.," *Kavkazskiia eparkhial'nyia vedomosti*, 1 February 1881, unofficial section, 105; Voiskovoe khoziaistvennoe pravlenie, *Statisticheskiia monografii po izsledovaniiu stanichnago byta Terskago kazach'iago voiska* (Vladikavkaz: Tipografiia Terskago oblastnago pravleniia, 1881), 161-68, 234-36, 240-51, 369-71, 404-09; "Otryvki iz pisem s Kavkaza," *Voennyi sbornik* 43, no. 6 (1865): 302-03; V. Kikot, "Opisanie st. Umakhan-iurtovskoi, Terksoi oblasti, Kizliarskago otdela," *Sbornik materialov dlia opisaniia mestnostei i plemen Kavkaza* 16 (1893): 68-69, 80; Tkachëv, *Stanitsa Chervlennaia*, 24-26.

41. Voiskovoe khoziaistvennoe pravlenie, *Statisticheskiia monografii*, 235; Slivitskii, "Ocherki Kavkaza," 195-96; Vasilikhin, "Ocherk staroobriadchestva," 133-34; Reshetov, "Staroobriadcheskii skit v stanitse Kalinovskoi," *Sbornik materialov dlia opisaniia mestnostei i plemen Kavkaza* 16 (1893): 134-40.

42. Tkachëv, *Stanitsa Chervlennaia*, 145-47.

43. On "the town of Ignat" see K. V. Chistov, *Russkie narodnye sotsial'no-utopicheskie legendy XVII-XIX vv.* (Moscow: Izdatel'stvo "Nauka," 1967), 295-305. There were also rumors of Nekrasov Cossacks living in Svanetiia in the nineteenth century and a Molokan migration to Ararat where they hoped to live in paradise while the world below came to an end. See Kosven, *Etnografiia i istoriia*, 25 and Nikol'skii, *Istoriia russkoi tserkvi*, 316-17.

44. Crummey, *The Old Believers*, 214-18; Selishchev, *Kazaki i Rossiia*, 109.

45. Chistov, *Russkie narodnye sotsial'no-utopicheskie legendy*, 261-65; V. A. Lipinskaia, *Starozhily i pereselentsy Russkie na Altae XVIII-nachalo XX veka* (Moscow: "Nauka," 1996), 29-47; I. V. Poberezhnikov, "Podlozhnye ukazy i protest kazakov-staroobriadtsev iuzhnogo urala v seredine XIX v.," in *Kazaki urala i sibiri v XVII-XX vv.*, N. A. Minenko, ed. (Ekaterinburg: UrO RAN, Institut istorii i arkheologii, 1993), 109-10.

46. Chernozubov, "Ocherki Terskoi stariny," no. 10 (1911): 249-61; no. 6 (1912): 218-25; RGVIA, f. 1058, op. 2, d. 1112b, ll. 46-50, 72-76; d. 1118, ll. 1-38; d. 1122, ll. 1-52; d, 1126, ll. 1-11; d. 1139a, ll. 1-17; d. 1150, ll. 1-36; d. 1156, ll. 1-6, 14, 58, 60; d. 1157, 2-18; d. 1181, 1-7, 36-45; d. 1606, ll. 1-2; d. 1610, l. 1; Vasilikhin, "Ocherk staroobriadchestva," 1 January 1881, 30-34.

47. RGVIA, f. 1058, op. 2, d. 1284, ll. 1-8.

48. Rossiiskii Gosudarstvennyi Istoricheskii Arkhiv [RGIA], f. 1268, op. 7, d. 55, ll. 2-4.

49. Isabel de Madariaga, *Catherine the Great: A Short History* (New Haven: Yale University Press, 1990), 63.

50. On the importance of the North Caucasus in the creation of Russian national identity see Thomas M. Barrett, "The Remaking of the Lion of Dagestan: Shamil in Captivity," *The Russian Review* 53, no. 3 (1994): 353-66; Thomas M. Barrett, "Eastern Threats, Eastern Dreams: Imperialism and the Orient in the Journalism of the Left of the 1860s," *Central Asian Survey* 13, no. 4 (1994): 479-90; and Thomas M. Barrett, "Southern Living (in Captivity): The Caucasus in Russian Popular Culture," *Journal of Popular Culture* 31, no. 4 (1998): 75-93.

51. Gunther E. Rothenberg, *The Military Border in Croatia 1740-1881* (Chicago: University of Chicago Press, 1966).

52. RGIA, f. 1268, op. 4, d. 386, ll. 2-6; f. 1268, op. 5, d. 378, l. 2; P. Nitsik, "Byvshiia voennyia poseleniia na Voenno-Gruzinskoi doroge," *Terskiia vedomosti*, 25 January 1887, 3-4; P. Iudin, "Mozdokskie kalmyki," *Zapiski Terskago obshchestva liubitelei kazach'ei stariny* 12 (December 1914): 29-31; I. L. Omel'chenko, *Terskoe kazachestvo* (Vladikavkaz: Ir, 1991), 94-95; Voiskovoe khoziaistvennoe pravlenie, *Statisticheskiia monografii*, 373-74.

53. I. I. Dmitrenko, "Materialy dlia istorii Terskago kazach'iago voiska," *Terskii sbornik* 4 (1897): 85-90; Popko, *Terskie kazaki*, 188-89; P. L. Iudin, "Iz-za vlasti," *Zapiski Terskago obshchestva liubitelei kazach'ei stariny* 9 (September 1914): 39-42.

54. Voiskovoe khoziaistvennoe pravlenie, *Statisticheskiia monografii*, 369-71, 373-75; Abozin, "Vozrazhenie," 487.

55. Vostrikov, "Stanitsa Naurskaia," section 2, 199.

10

Epilogue:
The Changing World of
the Terek Cossacks

In April 1851, a twenty-two-year old Lev Tolstoi accompanied his brother Nikolai to the North Caucasus. The latter was returning to service and the budding writer seized the opportunity to spend a few years observing the war, the region, and the people. Twelve years later Lev published his impressions of the Terek Cossacks in a novel, *The Cossacks*, set in the village of "Novomlinsk"—Chervlennaia in disguise—"the metropolis of the Greben Cossacks."[1]

The young nobleman was struck by how different this world was from the one he left behind in central Russia. His novelist's eye for detail produced one of the best descriptions ever written of this branch of the Terek Cossacks. Besides noting the general tone of military life, Tolstoi accurately recorded the regional peculiarities of the Cossacks—their Chechen customs, Circassian dress, mountain weapons, Kabardian horses, and Tatar tongue; their grape arbors, thin forests, and manure burning in the stoves. He praised the Cossack woman, who was "powerfully developed both physically and morally, and though to all appearances in subjection, possesses—as is usually the case in the East—incomparably greater influence and weight in family affairs than her Western sister." He marveled at Cossacks' affiliation with the Chechens and their alienation from Russians and Ukrainians:

A Cossack is less inclined to hate the Chechen brave who killed his brother, than the Russian soldier billeted on him for the defense of his village but who has fouled his hut by smoking in it. He respects the enemy mountaineer, but despises the soldier, who in his eyes is an alien and an oppressor. In fact, the Cossack regards the Russian peasant as a foreign, wild, despicable creature, of whom he sees specimen enough in the traders and Ukrainian immigrants whom he contemptuously calls fullers. For the

Cossack, to be smartly dressed means to be dressed like a Circassian.[2]

Tolstoi also understood that the unique way of life of the Terek Cossacks was coming to an end. A deep nostalgia pervades *The Cossacks*, especially in the character of Eroshka, an elderly Greben Cossack who remembered the days when a tsaritsa (i.e. Catherine the Great) sat on the throne. Eroshka represents the old type of Terek Cossack, who had *kunak*s in the mountains, smuggled *burka*s across the Terek, and spent as much time thieving as fighting, plundering Chechens and Russians alike. Tolstoi based his character on a retired Cossack Epishka, whom Nikolai Tolstoi wrote about in 1857. He was, "the last type of the old Greben Cossacks," as he put it, who "was a fine fellow, a thief, and a swindler, who stole herds, sold people, and lassoed Chechens." The elder Tolstoi wrote that "even his service was not what we call 'service' these days" and pointed to his role as a mediator between the Russians and the Chechens.[3]

Such old-style Terek Cossacks disappeared as the foundation of their special culture crumbled. As Russian troops pushed Chechens away from the Terek and then away from the Sunzha beginning in the 1820s, and with the war in the northeast Caucasus winding down in the 1850s, there was less possibility and less need for mediation. That displacement of mountain people and mountain culture—although never complete—helped to reorient North Caucasian Cossack society.

The Russian trader, who Lev Tolstoi mentioned above, was another such herald of change. When the state withdrew the tax privileges granted to North Caucasian Armenians in 1836, their special role in maintaining the frontier economy began to weaken.[4] More Russian traders gradually arrived, pulling the local economy into the Russian orbit. The regional economic power shifted to the north and west as floods, market forces, and state fiscal policy ruined the viticulture-based economy of the lower Terek Cossacks. Merchants flocked to the boomtown of Stavropol' and Kizliar stagnated. Economic integration promoted Russification, as a colonel in the Caucasus grenadier artillery brigade realized in 1855: "Whoever visits the Caucasus, upon arriving at Stavropol', Piatigorsk, Kislovodsk, Vladikavkaz, Groznyi, etc., sees towns, lively trade, and Russian life."[5] The cultural bias is as significant as the towns left off of his list.

Stavropol' surpassed Kizliar as the most populous town in the North Caucasus in the 1840s. Between 1825 and 1856, Stavropol' nearly quintupled its population (from 3,603 to 17,625), while Kizliar barely grew at all, from 9,106 to 10,075. Already in 1841, the chief of the Caucasus *oblast'* reported that,

> the town of Kizliar, older than the other towns of the Caucasus *oblast'*, at the present time is in sorry shape. Everywhere you can see the decline of its previous prosperity and the poverty of the great part of its residents who previously were

very well-to-do.

On the other hand, for the rest of the century, merchants and peasant-settlers from the interior of Russia and Ukraine streamed to Stavropol' and to the northwest Caucasus in general.[6]

Stavropol' flourished from its rich steppe which supported both a cattle industry and a bountiful peasant agriculture. Grain, wool, leather, and other animal products flowed to the west through Rostov-on-Don, Taganrog, and the recently founded Azov port-town of Eisk. The later was founded in 1848; by 1852 it had a population of 9,043.[7]

Once the North Caucasus entered the industrial world with the building of the Vladikavkaz railroad, the local economy was integrated more powerfully into Russia and the lands of the Terek Cossacks became further marginalized. The first link between Rostov-on-Don and Vladikavkaz was completed in 1875, then various spurs and extensions were added in the next two decades, but they never reached Mozdok or Kizliar. Literally off the map, the old Terek Cossack towns now were lonely and soggy remnants of a previous era when being cut off from Russia meant being a part of the frontier culture of the North Caucasus.[8]

This next period in Terek Cossack history lies outside the scope of the present study. Everything that made this frontier such a unique part of Russia changed. The many hues of ethnic complexity became considerably paler, with mountain people moving away and a horde of Russians and Ukrainians moving in. The Christian-Muslim religious divide grew. Labor became plentiful. Frontier exchange ceased to be necessary. Genders became balanced. Cossack participation in the system of raiding and retribution weakened. The lure of desertion faded. With the end of the war, the local military service of the Terek Cossacks became anachronistic. And the North Caucasus began to transform from a frontier of the Russian empire into a region of Russia.

Tolstoi's Eroshka probably understood all of this. He certainly knew that he saw the end of an era, as he mourned the "golden days" and warned off young Cossacks from his old hobby of mounting raids on Nogai horses. "Times have changed," he lamented, "and you aren't the people. Shitty [*dermo*] Cossacks you are. Besides, look at all the Russians that have come down on us!"[9]

Notes

1. L. N. Tolstoi, *Kazaki* (Moscow: "Khudozhestvennaia literatura," 1981): 159.

2. Tolstoi, *Kazaki*, 158. Translation based party on Rosemary Edmonds in Leo Tolsoy, *The Cossacks*, trans. Rosemary Edmonds (Middlesex: Penguin Books, 1960), 179-80.

3. Tolstoi, *Kazaki*, 200; N. N. T. [N. N. Tolstoi], "Okhota na Kavkaze," *Sovremennik* 61, no. 1 (1857): 177.

4. Iu. Shidlovskii, "Zapiski o Kizliare," *Zhurnal Ministerstva vnutrennikh del*, no. 4 (1843): 194-95.

5. Cited in L. V. Kupriianova, *Goroda Severnogo Kavkaza vo vtoroi polovine XIX veka* (Moscow: Izdatel'stvo "Nauka," 1981), 38.

6. Quote in N. P. Gritsenko, *Sotsial'no-ekonomicheskoe razvitie priterechnykh raionov v XVIII-pervoi polovine XIX vv.* (Groznyi: Izdatel'stvo "Groznenskii Rabochii," 1961), 77-78; A. V. Fadeev, *Ocherki ekonomicheskogo razvitiia stepnogo predkavkaz'ia v doreformennyi period* (Moscow: Izdatel'stvo Akademii nauk SSSR, 1957), 234-35; Kupriianova, *Goroda Severnogo Kavkaza*, 39; A. L. Narochnitskii, ed., *Istoriia narodov Severnogo Kavkaza (konets XVIII v.-1917 g.)* (Moscow: "Nauka," 1988), 299-313.

7. Kupriianova, *Goroda Severnogo Kavkaza*, 39-50.

8. Kupriianova, *Goroda Severnogo Kavkaza*, 63-65.

9. Tolstoi, *Kazaki*, 207; Tolstoy, *The Cossacks*, 234.

Appendix:
Governmental Structure

Civil Government

1708   Kazan province formed; includes North Caucasus

1718   Astrakhan province formed out of southern part of Kazan province; includes North Caucasus

1786   Formation of Caucasus governor-generalship (*namestnichestvo*)

1802   Caucasus province formed

1822   Caucasus province becomes Caucasus *oblast'*

1847   Stavropol' province formed from Caucasus *oblast'*

Host and Regiment Formation

1720   Greben host subordinated to Astrakhan governor

1721   Greben host subordinated to War College

1722   Agrakhan host formed

1736   Agrakhan host disbanded and Terek-Kizliar and Terek-Semeinoe hosts formed

1746   Greben and Terek-Semeinoe hosts merged as Greben host

1755   Greben and Terek-Semeinoe host redivided

1770   Mozdok regiment formed

1776   Astrakhan Cossack host formed comprising Greben, Terek-Kizliar, Terek-Semeinoe, and the resettled Volga hosts and Mozdok and Astrakhan regiments

1786   Greben, Terek-Kizliar, Terek-Semeinoe, and Volga hosts and Mozdok regiment separated from the Astrakhan host and together with Khoper regiment receive the name of "settled Caucasus Line Cossacks"

1799   Volga host renamed Volga regiment

1824   Mountain regiment formed

1832   Caucasus Line host formed comprising Greben, Terek, Kizliar, Mozdok, Volga, Mountain regiments

1836   Terek and Kizliar regiments merged as Semeino-Kizliar regiment

1837   First and Second Little Russian regiments settled along the Georgian Military Highway

1839   Vladikavkaz regiment formed out of Second Little Russian regiment

1842   First Little Russian regiment joined to Vladikavkaz regiment, which enters the Caucasus Line host

1845   Sunzha and Second Volga regiments formed

1852   Second Sunzha regiment formed

1860   Terek Cossack host formed out of First and Second Volga, Mountain, First and Second Vladikavkaz, Mozdok, First and Second Sunzha, Greben, and Kizliar regiments along with two mounted artillery batteries and the Life-Guard Terek Cossack squadron of His Imperial Majesty's Personal Convoy

Bibliography

Archives

Rossiiskii Gosudarstvennyi Istoricheskii Arkhiv (RGIA), Russian State Historical Archive, St. Petersburg

Fond 1268 Kavkazskii komitet

Rossiiskii Gosudarstvennyi Voenno-Istoricheskii Arkhiv (RGVIA), Russian State Military-History Archive, Moscow

Fond 38 Departament general'nogo shtaba

Fond 405 Departament voennykh poselenii

Fond 644 Shtab komandiushchego voiskami Terskoi oblasti

Fond 1058, op. 1 Voiskovoe pravlenie Kavkazskogo lineinogo kazach'ego voiska

Fond 1058, op. 2 Voiskovoe dezhurstvo Kavkazskogo lineinogo kazach'ego voiska

Fond 14877 Glavnyi sviashchennik Kavkazskoi armii

Fond VUA Voenno uchenyi arkhiv

Newspapers

Kavkaz

Kavkazskiia eparkhial'nyia vedomosti

Stavropol'skiia gubernskiia vedomosti

Terskiia vedomosti

Tiflisskiia vedomosti

Vladikavkazskiia eparkhial'nyia vedomosoti

Nineteenth- and Early-Twentieth-Century
Journals of the Caucasus

Dagestanskii sbornik

Izvestiia Kavkazskago otdela Imperatorskago russkago geograficheskago obshchestva

Kavkazskii kalendar'

Kavkazskii sbornik

Kavkazskii vestnik

Kavkaztsy ili podvigi i zhizn' zamechatel'nykh lits, deistvovavshikh na Kavkaze

Kubanskii sbornik

Sbornik materialov dlia opisaniia mestnostei i plemen Kavkaza

Sbornik Obshchestva liubitelei kazach'ei stariny

Sbornik svedenii o Kavkazskikh gortsakh

Sbornik svedenii o Severnom Kavkaze

Terskii sbornik

Trudy Kavkazskago obshchestva sel'skago khoziaistva

Trudy Stavropol'skoi uchenoi arkhivnoi komissii

Zapiski Kavkazskago obshchestva sel'skago khoziaistva

Zapiski Kavkazskago otdela Imperatorskago geograficheskago obshchestva

Zapiski Terskago obshchestva liubitelei kazach'ei stariny

Document Collections

Akty istoricheskie, sobrannye i izdannye Arkheograficheskoiu komissieiu. Vol. 4. St. Petersburg: Tipografiia 2-go otdeleniia Sobstvennoi e.i.v. kantseliarii, 1842.

Akty sobrannye Kavkazskoi arkheograficheskoi komissieiu. Tiflis: Tipografiia Kantseliarii glavnonachal'stvuiushchego grazhdanskoi chast'iu na Kavkaze, 1870-1905. [*AKAK*]

Bliev, M. M., comp. *Russko-osetinskie otnosheniia v XVIII v. Sbornik dokumentov.* Vol.1. Ordzhonikidze: Ir, 1976.

"Donskie dela." *Russkaia istoricheskaia biblioteka* 18 (1898); 26 (1909); 29 (1913); 34 (1917).

Gadzhiev, V. G., ed. *Russko-dagestanskie otnosheniia v XVIII-nachale XIX v. Sbornik dokumentov.* Moscow: "Nauka," 1988.

Kosven, M. O., and Kh. Khashaev, eds. *Istoriia, geografiia i etnografiia Dagestana XVIII-XIX vv: Arkhivnye materialy.* Moscow: Izdatel'stvo vostochnoi literatury, 1958.

Kumykov, T. Kh., E. N. Kusheva, N. A. Smirnov, and U. A. Uligov, eds. *Kabardino-russkie otnosheniia v XVI-XVIII vv.* 2 Vols. Moscow: Izdatel'stvo Akademii nauk SSSR, 1957.

Mavrodin, V. V., ed. *Krest'ianskaia voina v Rossii v 1773-1775 godakh. Vosstanie Pugacheva.* Leningrad: Izdatel'stvo Leningradskogo universiteta, 1970.

Polnoe sobranie zakonov Rossiiskoi imperii s 1649 goda. 45 vols. in 48. St. Petersburg: Tipografiia II otdeleniia sobstvennoi Ego Imperatorskago Velichestva kantseliarii, 1839-1843; 2nd series, 1825 to 1881. 55 vols. St. Petersburg: Tipografiia II otdeleniia sobstvennoi Ego Imperatorskago Velichestva kantseliarii, 1830-1884. [*PSZ*]

Predtechenskii, A. V., ed. *Krest'ianskoe dvizhenie v Rossii v 1826-1849 gg. Sbornik dokumentov.* Moscow: Sotsekgiz, 1961.

Shikhsaidov, A. P., T. M. Aitberov, and G. M.-P. Orazaev, eds. *Dagestanskie istoricheskie sochineniia.* Moscow: "Nauka," Izdatel'skaia firma "Vostochnaia literatura," 1993.

Tsentarkhiv. *Pugachevshchina.* Edited by M. N. Pokrovskii. Moscow-Leningrad: Gosudarstvennoe izdatel'stvo, 1929.

Books and Articles

A...i, V. "Tri pis'ma o Piatigorske. Pis'mo pervoe." *Kavkaz*, 13 September 1847, 145-47.

Abaev, V. I. *Istoriko-etimologicheskii slovar' Osetinskogo iazyka*. Vols. 1, 2, 4. Moscow-Leningrad: Izdatel'stvo Akademii nauk SSSR, 1958, 1973, 1989.

Abozin, I. "Vozrazhenie." *Voennyi sbornik* 26, 8 (1862): 486-92.

Adel'-Gerai, Mirza. "Andreeva-derevnia." *Illiustratsiia* 181 (10 August 1861): 81-82.

Afanas'ev, M. "Selenie Kostek, Khasav-Iurtovskago okruga, Terskoi oblasti." *Sbornik materialov dlia opisaniia mestnostei i plemen Kavkaza* 16 (1893): 85-100.

Afanas'ev, N. "Stanitsa Terskaia, Sunzhenskago otdela, Terskoi oblasti." *Sbornik materialov dlia opisaniia mestnostei i plemen Kavkaza* 16 (1893): 101-33.

Ag...l Ar...v. "O Kizliarskoi torgovle otpusknymi i privoznymi tovarami s 1751 po 1755 i o provoze za granitsy serebrianoi monety v 1767-1768 godakh." *Izvestiia Kavkazskago otdela Imperatorskago russkago geograficheskago obshchestva* 5, 4 (1878): supplement, 65-66.

Agafonov, Oleg. *Kazach'i voiska Rossiiskoi imperii*. Moscow: AOZT, "Epokha," Izdatel'stvo "Russkaia kniga"; Kaliningrad: GIPP "Iantarnyi skaz," 1995.

Akhmadov, Ia. Z. "Iz istorii Checheno-Russkikh otnoshenii." *Voprosy istorii Dagestana* 2 (1975): 295-300.

Akhverdov, A. I. "Opisanie Dagestana. 1804 g." In *Istoriia, geografiia i etnografiia Dagestana XVIII-XIX vv*. Moscow: Izdatel'stvo vostochnoi literatury, 1958.

Alferov, V. A., and S. A. Chekmenev. *Stepnaia vol'nitsa*. Stavropol': Stavropol'skoe knizhnoe izdatel'stvo, 1978.

Anoev, A. "Iz Kavkazskikh vospominanii." *Istoricheskii vestnik* 105, 9 (September 1906): 820-51.

Arkhipov, A. I. "Neskol'ko svedenii o sovremennom sostoianii sel'skago khoziaistva na Kavkaze." *Moskvitianin* 6 (November 1851): 121-68.

B...o, Aleksandr. "Pis'mo iz Georgievsk." *Kavkaz*, 26 May 1857, 187.

Baddeley, John F. *The Rugged Flanks of the Caucasus*. 2d ed. Oxford: Oxford University

Press, 1940; repr., New York: Arno Press, 1972.

———. *The Russian Conquest of the Caucasus*. London: Longmans, Green and Co., 1908.

Barrett, Thomas M. "Eastern Threats, Eastern Dreams: Imperialism and the Orient in the Journalism of the Left of the 1860s," *Central Asian Survey* 13, no. 4 (1994): 479-90.

———. "Lines of Uncertainty: The Frontiers of the North Caucasus." *Slavic Review* 54, no. 3 (Fall 1995): 578-601.

———. "The Remaking of the Lion of Dagestan: Shamil in Captivity," *The Russian Review* 53, no. 3 (1994): 353-66.

———. "Southern Living (In Captivity): The Caucasus Theme in Russian Popular Culture," *Journal of Popular Culture* 31, no.4 (Spring 1998): 75-93.

Bartolomeia, I. A. "Poezdka v vol'nuiu Svanetiiu." *Zapiski Kavkazskago otdela Imperatorskago geograficheskago obshchestva* 3 (1855): 147-237.

"Bazarnyia tseny v g. Stavropole, s 4-go po 25-e Dekabria 1857 goda." *Izvestiia Kavkazskago otdela Imperatorskago russkago geograficheskago obshchestva* 5, 4 (1878): supplement, 323-324.

"Bazarnyia tseny v gor. Stavropole, s 19-e po 26-e dekabria 1856 g." *Izvestiia Kavkazskago otdela Imperatorskago russkago geograficheskago obshchestva* 5, 4 (1878): supplement, 257.

Belevy. *Puteshestviia cherez Rossiiu v raznyia Aziiatskiia zemli*. Translated by Mikhailo Popov. St. Petersburg: Imperatorskaia akademiia nauk, 1776.

Bentkovskii, I. V. *Grebentsy*. Moscow: Russkaia topolitografiia, 1889.

———. "Materialy dlia istorii kolonizatsii Severnogo Kavkaza." *Stavropol'skiia gubernskiia vedomosti*, 1883, 1-4.

———. *Reka Kuma i neobkhodimost' uluchshit' eia ekonomicheskoe znachenie*. Stavropol': n.p., 1882.

Berezin, I. N. *Puteshestvie po Dagestanu i Zakavkaz'iu*. 2d ed. Kazan: Universitetskaia tipografiia, 1850.

Berozov, B. P. *Istoricheskie etiudy (iz istorii vozniknoveniia Osetinskikh sel i kazach'ikh stanits)*. Vladikavkaz: Izdatel'stvo Severo-Osetinskogo gosudarstvennogo universiteta im. K. L. Khetagurova, 1992.

Berzhe, A. P. *Chechnia i Chechentsy.* Tiflis: Kavkazskii otdel Imperatorskago russkago geograficheskago obshchestva, 1859.

―――. *Kratkii obzor gorskikh plemen na Kavkaze.* Tiflis: Tipografiia Kantseliarii namestnika kavkazskago, 1858.

―――., comp. "Pugachev na Kavkaze v 1772 godu." *Russkaia starina* 37 (January 1883): 167-70.

Biriukov, I. A. "Iz istorii Volzhskago kazach'iago voiska." *Zapiski Terskago obshchestva liubitelei kazach'ei stariny* no. 1 (January 1914): 21-54.

―――. "Neskol'ko glav iz istorii Volzhskago kazach'iago voiska." *Sbornik Obshchestva liubitelei kazach'ei stariny* 4 (1912): 3-26.

Biriul'kin, A. "Kazaki." *Terskiia vedomosti,* 19 February 1874, 3.

Blanch, Lesley. *The Sabres of Paradise.* London: John Murray, 1960; repr., London: Quartet Books, 1978.

Bliev, M. M. and V. V. Degoev. *Kavkazskaia voina.* Moscow: "Roset," 1994.

Bobylev, Fedot. "Torgovlia Derbentskoiu marenoiu." *Kavkaz,* 17 February 1863, 87-88.

Bogoslavskii, V. S. *Piatigorskiia i s nimi smezhnyia mineral'nyia vody.* St. Petersburg: Tipografiia A. S. Suvorina, 1883.

Botsvadze, T. D. *Sotsial'no-ekonomicheskie otnosheniia v Kabarde v pervoi polovine XIX veka.* Tbilisi: Izdatel'stvo "Metsniereba," 1965.

Bronevskii, S. M. *Noveishie geograficheskie i istoricheskie izvestiia o Kavkaze.* Moscow: Tipografiia S. Selivanovskogo, 1823.

Brower, Daniel R. and Edward J. Lazzerini, eds. *Russia's Orient: Imperial Borderlands and Peoples, 1700-1917.* Bloomington: Indiana University Press, 1997.

Broxup, Marie Bennigsen, ed. *The North Caucasus Barrier.* New York: St. Martin's Press, 1992.

Bubnov, A. "Selo Raguli, Stavropol'skoi gubernii, Novogrigor'evskago uezda." *Sbornik materialov dlia opisaniia mestnostei i plemen Kavkaza* 16 (1893): 222-66.

Buganov, V. I., ed. *Istoricheskaia geografiia Rossii XVIII v.* Moscow: Akademiia nauk SSSR, Institut istoriia SSSR, 1981.

Butkov, P. G. *Materialy dlia novoi istorii Kavkaza s 1722 po 1803 god.* 3 vols. St. Petersburg: Tipografiia Imperatorskoi akademii nauk, 1869.

Butovaia, E. "Stanitsa Borozdinskaia, Terskoi oblasti, Kizliarskago okruga." *Sbornik materialov dlia opisaniia mestnostei i plemen Kavkaza* 7 (1889): 3-156.

———, and M. Lysenko. "Stanitsa Ishcherskaia." *Sbornik materialov dlia opisaniia mestnostei i plemen Kavkaza* 16 (1893): 37-56.

Chekmenev, S. A., ed. *Nekotorye voprosy sotsial'no-ekonomicheskogo razvitiia iugo-vostochnoi Rossii.* Stavropol': Ministerstvo prosveshcheniia RSFSR. Stavropol'skii gosudarstvennyi pedagogicheskii institut, 1970.

Chernozubov, F. G. "General-Maior P. S. Verzilin, pervyi nakaznyi ataman Kavkazskago lineinago voiska." *Zapiski Terskago obshchestva liubitelei kazach'ei stariny* no. 3 (March 1914): 5-8.

———. "Ocherki Terskoi stariny." *Russkii arkhiv* no. 3 (1912): 452-66.

———. "Ocherki Terskoi stariny. (1832-1837) Nabegi khishchnikov." *Zapiski Terskago obshchestva liubitelei kazach'ei stariny* 7 (July 1914): 5-18.

———. "Ocherki Terskoi stariny. (1850) S okaziei." *Zapiski Terskago obshchestva liubitelei kazach'ei stariny* 8 (August 1914): 61-66.

———. "Ocherki Terskoi stariny. Pobegy k nepokornym gortsam." *Russkii arkhiv* no. 1 (1912): 64-79.

———. "Ocherki Terskoi stariny. Pobegy v gory." *Russkii arkhiv* no. 10 (1911): 249-61.

Chistov, K. V. *Russkie narodnye sotsial'no-utopicheskie legendy XVII-XIX vv.* Moscow: Izdatel'stvo "Nauka," 1967.

Chistovich, Ia. "Kizliar i ego meditsynskaia topografiia za 100 let do nastoiashchago vremeni." *Voenno-meditsinskii zhurnal* 78 (1860): section 3, 1-40, 75-114.

Chuzhbinskii, A. "Aul za Terekom." *Panteon* 22, 8 (1855): section 3, 1-24.

Crummey, Robert O. *The Old Believers and the World of Antichrist: The Vyg Community and the Russian State 1694-1855.* Madison: University of Wisconsin Press, 1970.

D...v, I. "Ocherki Piatigorska i ego okrestnostei. Iarmarka." *Kavkaz*, 15 May 1848, 77-79.

Dal', V. I. "Poslovitsy Russkago naroda." *Chteniia v Imperatorskom obshchestvo* 4 (October-December 1861): 289-698.

Debu, Iosif. *O Kavkazskoi linii i prisoedinennom k nei Chernomorskom voiske*. St. Petersburg: Tipografiia Karla Kraiia, 1829.

———. "O nachal'nom ustanovlenii i rasprostranenii Kavkazskoi linii." *Otechestvennyia zapiski* 18, 48 (1824): 268-93; 19, 51 (1824): 48-74.

Deichman, A. I. "Neskol'ko slov o Kavkaze v sel'sko-khoziaistvennom otnoshenii." *Zapiski Kavkazskago obshchestvo sel'skago khoziaistva* 2 (1856): 1-28, 45-63, 93-103.

Deniskin, V. I. "Razvitie zemledeliia u Terskikh kazakov i izmenenie prirodnykh uslovii. (K postanovke problemy)." *Arkheologo-etnograficheskii sbornik* 4 (1976): 270-75.

Dmitrenko, I. I. "Materialy k istorii Terskago kazach'iago voiska." *Terskii sbornik* 4 (1897): 53-126.

Domanskii, A. "Korrespondentsiia iz Mozdoka." *Zapiski Kavkazskago obshchestva sel'skago khoziaistva* 9, 6 (1863): 87-90.

———. "Sel'skokhoziaistvennyia zametki iz nadterechnago kraia." *Kavkaz*, 30 August-11 September 1864, 382-84.

Dubrovin, N. F. *Pugachev i ego soobshchniki*. St. Petersburg: Tipografiia I. N. Skorokhodova, 1884.

Dumas, Alexandre. *Adventures in Caucasia*. Edited by A. E. Murch. Translated by A. E. Murch. Westport, Conn.: Greenwood Press, 1962.

"Dvizhenie menovoi torgovli s gortsami, v Stavropol'skoi gubernii, v 1849 godu." *Kavkaz*, 11 March 1850, 78-79.

"Dvizhenie torgovli v Iiule i Avguste mesiatsakh mezhdu gorskimi narodami i zhiteliami Kavkazskoi oblasti." *Kavkaz*, 12 October 1846, 163.

Dzagurov, G. A. *Osetinskie (Digorskie) narodnye izrecheniia*. Moscow: Glavnaia redaktsiia vostochnoi literatury, 1980.

Dziubenko, P. "Vinodelie na Kavkaze." *Russkaia mysl'* 7, 8 (August 1886): section 2, 113-121.

E...v, N. *Astrakhan' i Astrakhanskaia guberniia.* Moscow: Tipografiia V. Got'e, 1852.

Eliseev, A. "Kazatskaia vol'nitsa XIX veka i Russkaia kolonizatsiia." *Ekonomicheskii zhurnal* 3, 3 (1886): 36-46.

Eloev, Khorunzhii. "Stanitsa Georgievskaia. Istoriko-ekonomicheskii ocherk." *Terskii sbornik* 5 (1903): 76-94.

Erikson, E. V. "Chumnyia epidemii na Kavkaze v proshlom." *Kavkazskii vestnik* 9 (1900): section 2, 52-73.

"Eristovskii kanal." *Terskiia vedomosti,* 2 April 1870, 3.

Ermolov, A. P. *Zapiski A. P. Ermolova 1798-1826.* Moscow: "Vysshaia shkola," 1991.

Evetskii, Orest. "Sredstva, upotrebliaemyia Tatarami protiv zubnoi boli i likhoradki." *Tiflisskiia vedomosti,* March 1832, 144.

Evliia Chelebi [Evliya Çelebi], *Kniga puteshestviia.* Vol. 2, eds. A. D. Zheltiakov, and A. P. Prigor'eva. Moscow: Izdatel'stvo "Nauka," 1979.

Fadeev, A. V. *Ocherki ekonomicheskogo razvitiia stepnogo predkavkaz'ia v doreformennyi period.* Moscow: Izdatel'stvo Akademii nauk SSSR, 1957.

―――, ed. *Ocherki istorii Balkarskogo naroda (s drevneishikh vremen do 1917 goda).* Nal'chik: Kabardino-Balkarskoe knizhnoe izdatel'stvo, 1961.

―――. *Rossiia i Kavkaz pervoi treti XIX v.* Moscow: Izdatel'stvo Akademii nauk, 1960.

Falk, I. P. "Zapiski puteshestviia akademika Falka." In *Polnoe uchenykh puteshestvii po Rossii.* St. Petersburg: Imperatorskaia akademiia nauk, 1824.

Fedorova, R. V. "Primenenie sporovo-pyl'tevogo analiza v arkheologicheskikh issledovaniiakh prikaspiia i predkavkaz'ia." *Sovetskaia arkheologiia* 1 (1959): 286-90.

Forsyth, James. *A History of the Peoples of Siberia.* Cambridge: Cambridge University Press, 1992.

Gadzhi-Ali. "Skazanie ochevidtsa o Shamile." *Sbornik svedenii o Kavkazskikh gortsakh* 7 (1873): section 1, 1-76.

Gadzhiev, V. G. "Arkhiv Kizliarskogo komendanta." *Izvestiia Severo-Kavkazskogo nauchnogo tsentra vysshei shkoly.* Obshchestvennyi nauk 2 (1978): 10.

Gadzhieva, S. Sh. *Kumyki: Istoriko-etnograficheskoe issledovanie*. Moscow: Izdatel'stvo Akademii nauk SSSR, 1961.

Galushko, Iu. *Kazach'i voiska Rossii*. Moscow: Informatsionno-izdatel'skoe agenstvo "Russkii mir," 1993.

Gammer, Moshe. *Muslim Resistance to the Tsar: Shamil and the Conquest of Chechnia and Daghestan*. London: Frank Cass, 1994.

Gan, K. F. "Opyt ob"iasneniia Kavkazskikh geograficheskikh nazvanii." *Sbornik materialov dlia opisaniia mestnostei i plemen Kavkaza* 40 (1909): section 3, 1-164.

Gardanov, V. K. *Obshchestvennyi stroi Adygskikh narodov*. Izdatel'stvo "Nauka," Glavnaia redaktsiia vostochnoi literatury, 1967.

Gatagova, L. S. *Pravitel'stvennaia politika i narodnoe obrazovanie na Kavkaze v XIX v*. Moscow: Izdatel'skii tsentr "Rossiia molodaia," 1993.

Gavrilov, P. A. "Ustroistvo pozemel'nago byta gorskikh plemen Severnogo Kavkaza." *Sbornik svedenii o kavkazskikh gortsakh* 2 (1869): section 7, 1-78.

Geevskii, V. *Vozdelyvanie i upotreblenie kukuruzy*. Tiflis: Tipografiia Glavnago upravleniia namestnika kavkazskago, 1864.

Genko, A. N. "Arabskaia karta Chechni epokhi Shamilia." *Zapiski Institut vostokovedeniia Akademiia nauk SSSR* 2, 1 (1933): 21-36.

Gerasimov, I. P. *Kavkaz*. Moscow: Izdatel'stvo "Nauka," 1966.

Gersevanov, M. N. *Ocherk gidrografii Kavkazskago kraia*. St. Petersburg: Tipografiia Ministerstva putei soobshcheniia, 1886.

Gil'denshtedt, I. A. [Johann Anton Güldenstädt] *Geograficheskoe i statisticheskoe opisanie Gruzii i Kavkaza*. St. Petersburg: Imperatorskaia akademiia nauk, 1809.

Gnilovskoi, V. G. "Proshloe stavropolia po gorodskim planam." In *Landshafty i ekonomicheskaia geografiia Severnogo Kavkaza*. Stavropol': Ministerstvo prosveshcheniia RSFSR. Stavropol'skii gosudarstvennyi pedagogicheskii institut, 1977.

Golikova, N. B. *Ocherki po istorii gorodov Rossii kontsa XVII-nachala XVIII v*. Moscow: Izdatel'stvo Moskovskogo universiteta, 1982.

Golovchanskii, S. F. "Kniaz' Georgii Romanovich Eristov i kanaly—Eristovskii i

Kursko-mar'inskii." *Zapiski Terskago obshchestva liubitelei kazach'ei stariny* 12 (December 1914): 5-15.

———. "Pervaia voennaia ekspeditsiia protiv Chechentsev v 1758 godu." *Zapiski Terskago obshchestva liubitelei kazach'ei stariny* no. 11 (November 1914): 65-106.

———. "Stanitsa Prokhladnaia, Terskoi oblasti, Piatigorskago okruga." *Sbornik materialov dlia opisaniia mestnostei i plemen Kavkaza* 15 (1893): 1-36.

Gord...v, Gr. "Puteshestviia. Poezdka iz Pol'shi za Kavkaz." *Tiflisskiia vedomosti*, 20 February 1830, [not paginated].

"Goroda Stavropol'skoi gubernii." *Izvestiia Kavkazskago otdela Imperatorskago russkago geograficheskago obshchestva* 5, 4 (1878): supplement, 14-17.

"Goroda Stavropol'skoi gubernii." *Stavropol'skiia gubernskiia vedomosti*, 25 February 1850, 90-93; 20 May 1850, 241-44.

Grebenets, F. S. "Novogladkovskaia stanitsa v eia proshlom i nastoiashchem." *Sbornik materialov dlia opisaniia mestnostei i plemen Kavkaza* 44 (1915): 77-116.

———. "Pamiatniki Grebenskoi stariny." *Terskiia vedomosti*, 2 February 1900, 2.

Gren, A. "Bibliograficheskii spisok kart, kartin, sochinenii i statei otnosiashchikhsia k Terskoi oblasti." *Terskii sbornik* 2 (1892): section 2, 1-28.

Griboedov, A. S. *Polnoe sobranie sochinenii.* Vol. 3. Petrograd: Akademiia Nauk, 1917.

Gritsenko, N. P. *Goroda severo-vostochnogo Kavkaza i proizvoditel'nye sily kraia v-seredina XIX veka.* Rostov-on-Don: Izdatel'stvo Rostovskogo universiteta, 1984.

———. "Iz istorii staroobriadchestva na Tereke v XVIII-XIX vekakh." In *Voprosy istorii Checheno-Ingushetii (dorevoliutsionnyi period).* 11 vols. Groznyi: Checheno-Ingushskii ordena "Znak pocheta" institut istorii, sotsiologii i filologii pri Sovete ministrov ChIASSR, 1977.

———. *Sotsial'no-ekonomicheskoe razvitie priterechnykh raionov v XVIII-pervoi polovine XIX vv.* Groznyi: Izdatel'stvo gazety "Groznenskii Rabochii," 1961.

Gromov, V. P. "Rol' migratsii i estestvennogo prirosta naseleniia v zaselenii stepnogo predkavkaz'ia v pervoi polovine XIX veka." *Izvestiia Severo-kavkazskogo nauchnogo tsentra vysshei shkoly.* Obshchestvennye nauki 2 (1985): 76-80.

Grossman, James R., ed. *The Frontier in American Popular Culture*. Berkeley: University of California Press and Chicago: The Newberry Library, 1994.

Gubanov, G. P. "Khutorskaia zhizn' v Terskoi oblasti." *Sbornik materialov dlia opisaniia mestnostei i plemen kavkaza* 33 (1904): section 2, 35-101.

Gukasiants, L. "Selenie Karabagly." *Zapiski Terskago obshchestva liubitelei kazach'ei stariny* no. 6 (June 1914): 55-61.

Haxthausen, Baron August von. *The Tribes of the Caucasus*. Translated by J. E. Taylor. London: Chapman and Hall, 1855.

Henze, Mary L. "The Religion of the Central Caucasus: An Analysis from Nineteenth Century Travellers' Accounts." *Central Asian Survey* 1, 4 (April 1983): 45-58.

———. "Thirty Cows for an Eye: The Traditional Economy of the Central Caucasus—An Analysis from Nineteenth Century Travellers' Accounts." *Central Asian Survey* 4, 3 (1985): 115-29.

Istomina, E. G. "Volzhskii vodnyi put' vo vtoroi polovine XVIII-nachale XIX vv." In *Istoricheskaia geografiia Rossii XVII v.* Vol. 1. Moscow, 1981.

"Istoricheskiia svedeniia o Grebenskom kazach'em polku." *Sbornik Obshchestva liubitelei kazach'ei stariny* 4 (1912): 27-54.

Istoricheskoe obozrenie piatidesiatiletnei deiatel'nosti Ministerstva gosudarstvennykh imuschshestv 1837-1887. Vol. 2. St. Petersburg: Tipografiia Ia. I. Libermana, 1888.

"Istoricheskoe svedenie. (Raport komanduiushchago Kizliarskim polkom podp. Alpatova 31 Iiulia 1854 goda no. 4530))." *Sbornik Obshchestva liubitelei kazach'ei stariny* 2 (1912): 3-19.

Iudin, P. L. "Byla-li Andreevka kolybel'iu Tertsev'?" *Zapiski Terskago obshchestva liubitelei kazach'ei stariny* no. 10 (October 1914): 35-42.

———. "Iz-za vlasti. (Ocherk iz proshlago soedinennago Grebenskogo kazachestva.)" *Zapiski Terskago obshchestva liubitelei kazach'ei stariny* no. 9 (September 1914): 37-62.

———. "Mozdokskie Kalmyki." *Zapiski Terskago obshchestva liubitelei kazach'ei stariny* 12 (December 1914): 23-31.

———. "Pugachev—Terets." *Voenno-istoricheskii sbornik* 3, 1 (1913): 21-24.

————. "S Khopera na Kavkaze." *Zapiski Terskago obshchestva liubitelei kazach'ei stariny* no. 11 (November 1914): 5-63.

————. "Sostav kazach'ikh voisk na Kavkaze v 1767 g." *Zapiski Terskago obshchestva liubitelei kazach'ei stariny* no. 4 (April 1914): 5-19.

Iukht, A. I. "Torgovye sviazi Rossii so stranami vostoka v 20-40-kh godakh XVIII v." In *Istoricheskaia geografiia Rossii XVIII v.*, ed. V. I. Buganov. Moscow: Akademiia nauk SSSR, Institut istoriia SSSR, 1981.

Ivanov, S. "O sblizhenii gortsev s Russkimi na Kavkaze." *Voennyi sbornik* 7 (1859): 541-49.

"Iz otcheta Derbentskogo voennogo gubernatora o sostoianii Derbentskoi gubernii za 1850-1851 gg." *Voprosy istorii Dagestana.* 2 (1975): 269-75.

"Iz proshlago Dagestanskoi oblasti (po mestnym arkhivnym dannym)." *Dagestanskii sbornik* 2 (1904): 196-248.

Iziumov, Arkadii. "Stanitsa Aleksandriiskaia." *Terskiia vedomosti*, 30 July 1873, 3.

"Izvlechenie iz otcheta o menovoi torgovle s gorskimi narodami na Kavkaze, chrez posredstvo menovykh dvorov, za 1846 god." *Kavkaz*, 15 March 1847, 42-43.

K. "Pis'mo iz Piatigorska." *Kavkaz*, 13 June 1853, 175-76.

K., Kh. I. "Khoziaistvennyia zametki." *Kavkaz*, 18 January 1850, 18-20; 21 January 1850, 23-24.

K...skii. "Petrovskoe." *Kavkaz*, 15 September 1856, 288-89.

Kaloev, B. A. "Iz istorii Russko-Chechenskikh ekonomicheskikh i kul'turnykh sviazei." *Sovetskaia etnografiia* 1 (January-February 1961): 41-53.

————. *Mozdokskie Osetiny.* Moscow: Akademiia nauk SSSR; Institut etnografii im. N. N. Miklukho-Maklaia, 1951.

————. *Osetiny.* Izdatel'stvo "Nauka," Glavnaiaredaktsiia vostochnoi literatury, 1971.

————. *Skotovodstvo narodov Severnogo Kavkaza.* Moscow: "Nauka," 1993.

————. *Zemledelie narodov Severnogo Kavkaza.* Moscow: "Nauka," 1981.

————. "Zemledelie u gorskikh narodov Severnogo Kavkaza." *Sovetskaia etnografiia* 3

(May-June 1973): 43-53.

Kantariia, M. V. *Ekologicheskie aspekty traditsionnoi khoziaistvennoi kul'tury narodov Severnogo Kavkaza*. Tbilisi: "Metsniereba," 1989.

Kanukov, I. "Shaloputstvo v Kavkazskoi eparkhii." *Terskiia vedomosti*, 5 February 1877, 2-3.

Karaulov, M. A. "Govor Grebenskikh kazakov. Slova, zaimstvovannyia s Turetsko-Tatarskikh narechii." *Sbornik materialov dlia opisaniia mestnostei i plemen kavkaza* 37 (1907): section 3, 103-109.

———. *Terskoe kazachestvo v proshlom i nastoiashchem*. Vladikavkaz: Voiskovoi shtab Terskago kazach'ego voiska, 1912.

Kaznacheeva, T. P., ed. "Cherty obshchnosti zemledel'cheskoi kul'tury i ekologicheskikh predstavlenii narodov Severnogo Kavkaza." In *Problemy agrarnoi istorii narodov Severnogo Kavkaza v dorevoliutsionnyi period*. Stavropol': Stavropol'skii gosudarstvennyi pedagogicheskii institut, 1981.

Khashaev, Kh. M. *Obshchestvennyi stroi Dagestana v XIX veka*. Moscow: Izdatel'stvo Akademii nauk SSSR, 1961.

Khitsunov, P. "O Chakhirinskom kreste." *Kavkaz*, 13 April 1846, 59.

———. "O mestonakhozhdenii i razvalinakh goroda Madzhar, Stavropolskoi gubernii, v Piatigorskom uezde." *Kavkaz*, 2 April 1849, 51-52.

———. "Snosheniia Rossii s severnomiu chastiiu Kavkaza." *Kavkaz*, 20 April 1846, 62-64.

Khodarkovsky, Michael. *Where Two Worlds Met: The Russian State and the Kalmyk Nomads, 1600-1771*. Ithaca: Cornell University Press, 1992.

Kikot, V. "Opisanie st. Umakhan-Iurtovskoi, Terskoi oblasti, Kizliarskago otdela." *Sbornik materialov dlia opisaniia mestnostei i plemen Kavkaza* 16 (1893): 68-84.

"Kizliarskii Krestovozdvizhenskii monastyr'." *Izvestiia Kavkazskago otdela Imperatorskago russkago geograficheskago obshchestva* 5, 4 (1878): supplement, 24.

Kolodeev, Kh. "O rasteniiakh dlia zhivoi izgorodi na Kavkaze." *Kavkaz*, 14 February 1853, 51-52.

Konashevich. "Ekaterinograd." *Kavkaz*, 3 August 1861, 323.

Kosven, M. O. *Etnografiia i istoriia Kavkaza*. Moscow: Izdatel'stvo vostochnoi literatury, 1961.

Kotov, F. A. "Khozhdenie na vostok F. A. Kotova v pervoi chetverti XVII veka." *Izvestiia Otdeleniia russkago iazyka i slovesnosti Imperatorskoi akademii nauk* 12, 1 (1907): 77-78.

Kozachkovskii, V. *Razboi na Kavkaze. Ocherki*. Vladikavkaz: Elektropechatnaia Sergeia Kazarova, 1913.

Kozlovskii, D. "Zametki iz puteshestviia po Kavkazskoi linii." *Kavkaz*, 22 July-4 August 1865, 291-92; 23 July-6 August 1865, 295-96; 1 August-12 August 1865, 304; 5 August-17 August 1865, 309-10.

Krasovich, Nikolai. "Navodenie v Kizliare." *Kavkaz*, 31 August 1855, 291.

"Kratkaia zapiska o gorskikh narodakh." *Severnyi arkhiv* 22, 3 (1826): 21-32.

Kriukov. "Putevyia zametki." *Izvestiia Kavkazskago otdela Imperatorskago russkago geograficheskago obshchestva* 5, 4 (1878): supplement, 62-67.

Kriukov, Mikhail. "Goroda Stavropol'skoi gubernii." *Stavropol'skiia gubernskiia vedomosti*, 8 April 1850, 168-72.

————. "Putevyia zametki." *Kavkaz*, 8 October 1852, 248-50.

Krupnov, E. I. "Za ekonomicheskoe vozrozhdenie raionov prikaspiiskoi nizmennosti." *Sovetskaia arkheologiia* 3 (1963): 3-13.

Kuchiev, A. G., ed. *Gorod Mozdok*. Vladikavkaz: RIPP im. Gassieva, 1995.

Kumykov, T. Kh. *Vovlechenie Severnogo Kavkaza vo vserossiiskii rynok v XIX v.* Nal'chik: Kabardino-Balkarskoe knizhnoe izdatel'stvo, 1962.

Kupriianova, L. V. *Goroda Severnogo Kavkaza vo vtoroi polovine XIX veka*. Moscow: Izdatel'stvo "Nauka," 1981.

Kusheva, E. N. *Narody Severnogo Kavkaza i ikh sviazi s Rossiei vtoraia polovina XVI-30-e gody XVII veka*. Moscow: Izdatel'stvo Akademii nauk SSSR, 1963.

Kusov, Genrii. *Poiski kraeveda*. Ordzhonikidze: Izdatel'stvo "Ir," 1975.

Kuznetsov, V. A. *Ocherki istorii Alan*. Vladikavkaz: "Ir," 1992.

Kvezereli-Kopadze, N. I. "The Problem of Year-Round Traffic Through the Pass of the Cross on the Georgian Military Highway." *Soviet Geography* 15, 3 (Mar. 1974): 163-74.

Land, Frid. "Mestnost' i klimat stanitsy Aleksandrovskoi, lezhashchei mezhdu Stavropolem i Georgievskom." *Voenno-meditsinskii zhurnal* 63 (1854): section 7, 30-79.

Laudaev, U. "Chechenskoe plemia." *Sbornik svedenii o kavkazskikh gortsakh* 6 (1872): 1-62.

Lavrov, L. I. *Epigraficheskie pamiatniki Severnogo Kavkaza.* Vol. 1. Moscow: Izdatel'stvo "Nauka," 1966.

———. *Istoriko-etnograficheskie ocherki Kavkaza.* Leningrad: Izdatel'stvo "Nauka," 1978.

"Legenda o Kizliare." *Terskiia vedomosti*, 3 January 1891, 4.

Lerkhe, Ioann-Iakub. "Prodolzhenie izvestiia o vtorom puteshestvii doktora i kollezhskago sovetnika Lerkha, v Persiiu, s 1746 do 1747 goda." *Novyia ezhemesiachnyia sochineniia* 63 (1791): 58-79.

Lipinskaia, V. A. *Starozhily i pereselentsy Russkie na Altae XVIII-nachalo XX veka.* Moscow: "Nauka," 1996.

Litvinov, A. A. "Ob izmeneniiakh techeniia r. Tereka i beregov Kaspiiskago moria s 1841 po 1863 god." *Zapiski Kavkazskago otdela Imperatorskago russkago geograficheskago obshchestva* 6 (1861): section 4, 83-86.

Liuventseev, M. "Razskaz Mozdokskago Armianina." *Kavkaz*, 23 August 1850, 261-63.

Lola, A. M. "The Formation of Future Types of Rural Places in the Kuban Stavropol' Plain." *Soviet Geography* 9, 8 (October 1968): 689-98.

Longworth, Philip. *The Cossacks.* New York: Holt, Rinehart and Winston, 1970.

Lystsov, V. P. *Persidskii pokhod Petra I.* Moscow: Izdatel'stvo Moskovskogo universiteta, 1951.

M. "Tatarskoe plemia na Kavkaze." *Kavkaz*, 19 November 1859, 509-10.

M., A. "Religioznye obriady Osetin, Ingush i ikh soplemennikov, pri raznykh sluchaiakh. II. Prazdniki." *Kavkaz*, 13 July 1846, 110-12.

Maksimov, E. *Terskoe kazach'e voisko. Istoriko-statisticheskii ocherk.* Vladikavkaz:

Tipografiia Oblastnago pravleniia Terskoi oblasti, 1890.

Maliavkin, G. "Stanitsa Chervlenaia." *Etnograficheskoe obozrenie* 1 (1891): 113-36; 2 (1891): 29-41; 3 (1891): 50-68.

Malinin, K. N. *Terskie kazaki.* Moscow: Tipografiia T-va I. D. Sytina, 1908.

Marggraf, O. V. *Ocherk kustarnykh promyslov Severnogo Kavkaza s opisaniem tekhniki proizvodstva.* Moscow: Tipografiia S. V. Gur'ianova, 1882.

Markov, Aleksandr. *Petr Pervyi i Astrakhan'.* Astrakhan: Izdatel'stvo "Forzats," 1994.

"Materialy dlia istorii Severnago Kavkaza 1787-1792." *Kavkazskii sbornik* 18 (1897): 382-506.

"Materialy dlia izucheniia sekty Shaloputov." *Kavkazskiia eparkhial'nyia vedomosti* 3, 16 (16 August 1875): 523-26.

"Materiialy dlia statistiki Kizliarskago polka Terskago kazach'iago voiska." *Voennyi sbornik* no. 12 (December 1869): 207-47.

McNeal, Robert H. *Tsar and Cossack, 1855-1914.* New York: St. Martin's Press, 1987.

Mikhailovskii, G. "Istoricheskiia svedeniia o raskole sredi Terskikh (Grebenskikh) kazakov vo vtoroi polovine XVIII stoletiia." *Kavkazskiia eparkhial'nyia vedomosti* 5, 2 (16 January 1877): 60-67; 5, 3 (1 February 1877): 94-97.

———. "Svedeniia o raskole i raskol'nikakh v predelakh Kavkazskoi eparkhii." *Kavkazskiia eparkhial'nyia vedomosti* 3, 10 (16 May 1875): 324-37.

Minenko, N. A., ed. *Kazaki Urala i Sibiri v XVII-XX vv.* Ekaterinburg: UrO RAN, Institut istorii i arkheologii, 1993.

Mokhir, M. "Aksai (ili Tashkichu)." *Sbornik materialov dlia opisaniia mestnostei i plemen Kavkaza* 16 (1893): 30-36.

———. "Stanitsa Naurskaia, Groznenskago okruga." *Sbornik materialov dlia opisaniia mestnostei i plemen kavkaza* 15 (1893): 141-44.

Mordvinov, N. S. "Mnenie admirala Mordvinova o sposobakh, koimi Rossii udobnee mozhno priviazat' k sebe postepenno Kavkazskikh zhitelei." *Chteniia v Imperatorskom obshchestve istorii i drevnosti rossiiskikh pri Moskovskom universitete* 4 (October-December 1858): section 5, 109-112.

Morokhovets, E. A. *Krest'ianskaia reforma 1861 g.* Moscow: Sotseksiz, 1937.

Murzaev, E. M. *Toponimika i geografiia.* Moscow: Nauka, 1995.

N., N. "Stavropol'." *Kavkaz,* 3 August 1861, 323.

N., N. *Zapiski vo vremia poezdki iz Astrakhani na Kavkaze i v Gruziiu v 1827 godu.* Moscow: Tipografiia S. Selivanovskago, 1829.

Nadezhdin, P. P. *Kavkazskii krai: Priroda i liudi.* 3d ed. Tula: Tipografiia Vlad. Nik. Sokolova, 1901.

————, comp. *Priroda i liudi na Kavkaze i za Kavkazom.* St. Petersburg, 1869.

Narochnitskii, A. L., ed. *Istoriia narodov Severnogo Kavkaza (konets XVIII v.-1917 g.)* Moscow: "Nauka," 1988.

"Nakaz Astrakhanskago kazach'iago polka." *Sbornik Imperatorskago russkago istoricheskago obshchestva* 115 (1903): 453-56.

Nechaev, S. D. "Otryvki iz putevykh zapisok o iugo-vostochnoi Rossii." *Moskovskii telegraf* 7 (1826): section 1, 26-41.

Nemchirov, A. P. "O razvedenii mareny v Stavropol'skoi gubernii i o dvoiakom sposobe upotrebleniia mareny." *Izvestiia Kavkazskago otdela Imperatorskago russkago geograficheskago obshchestva* 5, 4 (1878): supplement, 25-26.

"Neskol'ko slov o nastoiashchem polozhenii Grebenskikh kazakov." *Terskiia vedomosti,* 10 June 1868, 94.

Nestrov, Episkop. "Upravlenie Platona (Liubarskago), arkhiepiskopa Astrakhanskago i Kavkazskago, Kavkazskoiu pastroiu s 1800 po 1805 g." *Kavkazskiia eparkhial'nyia vedomosti* 3 (1 February 1879): 117-32.

Nikol'skii, N. M. *Istoriia Russkoi tserkvi.* 4th ed. Moscow: Politizdat, 1988.

Nitsik, P. "Byvshiia voennyia poseleniia na voenno-gruzinskoi doroge." *Terskiia vedomosti,* 15 January 1887, 2-3; 25 January 1887, 3-4; 5 February 1887, 3-4; 22 February 1887, 3-4; 5 March 1887, 2; 29 March 1887, 3-4.

Nogmov, Shora. *Istoriia Adykheiskago naroda.* 3d ed. Piatigorsk: Tipografiia I. P. Afanas'eva, 1891.

"O Bragunskom vladenii." *Izvestiia Kavkazskago otdela Imperatorskago russkago geograficheskago obshchestva* 5, 4 (1878): supplement, 318-323.

"O khishchnicheskikh deistviiakh Cherkes i Chechentsev v nashikh predelakh." *Kavkaz*, 31 March 1857, 119-20.

"O khode torgovli na iarmarkakh Stavropol'skoi gub. i Chernomorii, v 1847 i 1848 godakh." *Kavkaz*, 31 July 1848, 123-24.

"O khode torgovli na iarmarke, v slobode Aleksandrovske, Piatigorskago uezda." *Kavkaz*, 21 August 1848, 135.

"O prodazhnykh tsenakh soli na 1850 god po Zakavkazskomu kraiu, Stavropol'skoi gubernii i Chernomorskoi beregovoi linii." *Izvestiia Kavkazskago otdela Imperatorskago russkago geograficheskago obshchestva* 5, 4 (1878): supplement, 20-21.

"O rozyske krest'iane." *Stavropol'skiia gubernskiia vedomosti*, 1 January 1850, 1.

"O vinodelii v Rossii." *Zhurnal Ministerstva vnutrennykh del* 3, 4 (1839): 107-22; 3, 5 (1830): 149-71.

"O zavedenii v gorode Stavropole obraztsovykh plantatsii mareny." *Izvestiia Kavkazskago otdela Imperatorskago russkago geograficheskago obshchestva* 5, 4 (1878): supplement, 59-60.

O., A. "Rubka lesa." *Voennyi sbornik* 16 (1860): section 2, 97-122.

"Ob uspekhakh sel'skago khoziaistva v Kizliarskom uezde." *Izvestiia Kavkazskago otdela Imperatorskago russkago geograficheskago obshchestva* 5, 4 (1878): supplement, 224-225.

"Obzor irreguliarnykh voisk v Rossiiskoi imperii." *Voennyi sbornik* 22, 12 (1861): section 2, 329-348.

"Ocherk voennoi zhizni Kavkazskikh lineinykh kazakov." *Russkii invalid*, 9 January 1849, 21.

Omel'chenko, I. L. *Terskoe kazachestvo*. Vladikavkaz: Ir, 1991.

"Opisanie Kavkazskago shelkovodstva." *Sbornik materialov dlia opisaniia mestnostei i plemen Kavkaza* 11 (1891): section 2, 1-155.

O'Rourke, Shane. "Women in a Warrior Society: Don Cossack Women, 1860-1914." In

Women in Russia and Ukraine, ed. Rosalind Marsh, 45-54. Cambridge: Cambridge University Press, 1996.

"Otryvki iz pisem s Kavkaza." *Voennyi sbornik* 43, 6 (June 1865): 299-320.

Pagirev, D. D. "Alfavitnyi ukazatel' k piativerstnoi karte Kavkazskago kraia, izdaniia Kavkazskago voenno-topograficheskago otdela." *Zapiski Kavkazskago otdela Imperatorskago russkago geograficheskago obshchestva* 30 (1913): iii-xii, 1-307.

Paradov, Georgii. "Raskaz ochevidtsa o Shamile i ego sovremennikakh." *Sbornik materialov dlia opisaniia mestnostei i plemen Kavkaza* 32 (1903): section 1, 10-24.

"Pavel Vasil'evich Shvetsov, maior Gruzinskago grenaderskago polka." *Russkii invalid*, 25 June 1816, 598-99.

Pavlov, A. [M.]. *Kratkoe obozrenie Kavkazskoi gubernii uezdnago goroda Kizliara.* Moscow: Tipografiia Avgusta Semena, 1822.

————. *O Aziiatskikh narodakh, obitaiushchikh v iuzhnoi Rossii.* St. Petersburg: Tipografiia Kh. Gintsa, 1841.

————. *O Nogaitsakh kochuiushchikh po Kizliarskoi stepi.* St. Petersburg: Tipografiia Vneshnei torgovli, 1842.

Pereverzev, Lekar. "Stanitsa Sleptsovskaia." *Kavkaz*, 8 January 1861, 15-16.

"Pesni Terskikh kazakov." *Terskiia vedomosti*, 30 September 1868, 162-63; 28 October 1868, 177-78; 16 December 1868, 208.

"Piatigorsk." *Kavkaz*, 11 March 1852, 78.

Piotrovskii, B. B., ed. *Istoriia narodov Severnogo Kavkaza s drevneishikh vremen do kontsa XVIII v.* Moscow: "Nauka," 1988.

Piotrovskii, S. "Poezdka v gory." *Kavkaz*, 7 September 1858, 359-60; 11 September 1858, 363-64.

Pisarev, S. *Trekhsotletie Terskago kazach'iago voiska. 1577-1877.* Vladikavkaz: Tipografiia Terskago oblastnago pravleniia, 1881.

"Pis'mo k redaktoru iz Dagestana." *Kavkaz*, 19 January 1846, 9.

Pliushch, A. "Stanitsa Urukhskaia. Istoriko-ekonomicheskii ocherk." *Terskii sbornik* 5 (1903):

95-107.

"Podvig kazaka Vasil'ia Doktorova." *Kavkaztsy ili podvigi i zhizn' zamechatel'nykh lits, deistvovavshikh na Kavkaze* no. 6 (1857): 22-23.

"Poezdka v Gruziiu." *Moskovskii telegraf* 15 (August 1833): 327-67.

"Pokhodnoi zhurnal Petra Velikago. 1722." *Pokhodnye i putevye zhurnaly imp. Petra I-go* (1855): 64.

Polievktov, M. A. *Ekonomicheskie i politicheskie razvedki Moskovskogo gosudarstva XVII v. na Kavkaze.* Tiflis: Nauchno-issledovatel'skii institut kavkazovedeniia Akademii nauk SSSR, 1932.

Polyevktov, M. "The Ways of Communication Between Russia and Georgia in the Sixteenth and Seventeenth Centuries." *Journal of Modern History* 2, 3 (September 1930): 367-77.

Ponomarëv, F. P. "Materialy dlia istorii Terskago kazach'iago voiska s 1559 po 1880 god." *Voennyi sbornik* 23, 10 (October 1880): 350-67; 23, 12 (December 1880): 335-54.

———. "Materialy po istorii Terskago kazach'iago voiska. 2-i Malorossiiskii polk." *Terskii sbornik* 6 (1903): 149-232.

———. "O maslianitse v Kizliarskom kazach'em polku." *Terskiia vedomosti*, 7 May 1870, 2-3.

———. "O zemledel'cheskikh zaniatiiakh zhitelei Kizliarskago kazach'iago polka." *Zapiski Kavkazskago obshchestva sel'skago khoziaistva* 15, 4 (1869): 127-43.

Popko, I. *Terskie kazaki s starodavnikh vremen. Istoricheskii ocherk.* St. Petersburg: Tipografiia Departamenta udelov, 1880.

Popov, Archpriest Ioann. "Moi zaniatiia v arkhivakh." *Sbornik Obshchestva liubitelei kazach'ei stariny* 1 (1912): 15-28.

Popov, I. M. "Ichkeriia." *Sbornik svedenii o kavkazskikh gortsakh* 4 (1870): section 1, part 5, 1-23.

Potto, V. A. *Dva veka Terskago kazachestva (1577-1801).* 2 Vols. Vladikavkaz: Elektropechatnia tipografiia Terskago oblastnago pravleniia, 1912.

———. *Kavkazskaia voina v otdel'nykh ocherkakh, epizodakh, legendakh i biografiaakh.* St. Petersburg: Tipografiia R. Golike, 1885-1891.

———, ed. *Pamiatniki vremen utverzhdeniia Russkogo vladychestva na Kavkaze*. Tiflis: Tipografiia Shtaba kavkazskogo voennogo okruga, 1906.

Pronshtein, A. P., ed. *Don i stepnoe predkavkaz'e XVIII-pervaia polovina XIX v.* Rostov-on-Don: Izdatel'stvo Rostovskogo universiteta, 1977.

Prozritelev, G. N. *Drevnie Khristianskie pamiatniki na Severnom Kavkaze*. Stavropol': Tipografiia naslednikov Berk, 1906.

———. "Istochnik Karabin. K istorii goroda Stavropolia." *Sbornik svedenii o Severnom Kavkaze* 11 (1914): 1-11.

———. "Iz istorii goroda Stavropolia." *Trudy Stavropol'skoi uchenoi arkhivnoi komissii* no. 7 (1915): section 5, 1-31.

———, comp. "Iz proshlogo Severnogo Kavkaza. Materialy dlia istorii g. Stavropolia i Stavropol'skoi gub." *Trudy Stavropol'skoi uchenoi arkhivnoi komissii* 2 (1910): section 4, 1-63.

———, ed. *Iz proshlago Severnago Kavkaza. Vospominaniia starago Kavkaztsa otstavnago vakhtera Mefodiia Stepanovicha Soloduna*. Stavropol': Tipografiia Gubernskago pravleniia, 1914.

———. "Kavkazskoe oruzhie." *Trudy Stavropol'skoi uchenoi arkhivnoi komissii* 7 (1915): section 10, 1-18.

———. "Napadenie gortsev na Mozdok, v 1843 g." *Trudy Stavropol'skoi uchenoi arkhivnoi komissii* 2 (1910): section 1, part 13, 1-5.

———. "Pervyia Russkiia poseleniia na Severnom Kavkaze i v nyneshnei Stavropol'skoi gubernii." *Trudy Stavropol'skoi uchenoi arkhivnoi komissii* 5 (1913): section 1, 1-18.

———. "Shamil' v Stavropole." *Sbornik svedenii o Severnom Kavkaze* 9 (1914): 1-11.

———. *Stavropol'skaia guberniia v istoricheskom, khoziaistvennom i bytovom otnoshenii.* 2 vols. Stavropol': Tipografiia "Proletarii," 1925.

———. "Vedomost' o kolichestve zemel', sostoiashchikh v pomeshchich'ikh vladeniiakh v Kavkazskoi oblasti v 1842 godu." *Trudy Stavropol'skoi uchenoi arkhivnoi komissii* 2 (1910): section 1, 1-3.

Pushkin, Alexander. *A Journey to Arzrum*. Translated by Birgitta Ingemanson. Ann Arbor:

Ardis, 1974.

Rakovich, D. V. *Proshloe Vladikavkaza*. Groznyi: Izdatel'stvo "Groznyi rabochii," 1911.

Rebrov, A. F. "Zima 1844-1845 goda na stepiakh pri-Kumskikh na Kavkaze." *Zhurnal sel'skago khoziaistva i ovtsevodstva* 3 (1845): 287-92.

Reshetov. "Staroobriadcheski skit v stanitse Kalinovskoi." *Sbornik materialov dlia opisaniia mestnostei i plemen kavkaza* 16 (1893): 134-40.

Rigel'man, Aleksandr. *Istoriia ili povestvovanie o Donskikh kazakakh*. Moscow: Universitetskaia tipografiia, 1846.

Rodionov, I. A. *Tikhii Don*. St. Petersburg: Petropolis, 1994.

Rogozhin, T. "Nechto iz verovanii, poverii i obychaev zhitelei st. Chervlennoi, Kizliarskago otdela, Terskoi oblasti." *Sbornik materialov dlia opisaniia mestnostei i plemen Kavkaza* 16 (1893): 57-67.

Romanovskii, D. I. *Kavkaz i Kavkazskaia voina*. St. Petersburg: Tipografiia Tovarishchestva "Obshchestvennaia pol'za," 1860.

"Rospis' gorodam i drugim zamechatel'nym mestam Kavkazskago kraia." *Kavkazskii kalendar'* (1855): 121-39.

"Rospis sluzhilym liudiam po oblasti Kazanskago dvortsa na 7146 (1637) god." *Izvestiia Obshchestva arkheologii, istorii i etnografii pri Imperatorskom Kazanskom universitete* 28, 4-5 (1912): 456-67.

Rovinskii, I. V. "Khoziaistvennoe opisanie Astrakhanskoi i Kavkazskoi gubernii, po grazhdanskomu i estestvennomu ikh sostoianiiu, v otnoshenii k zemledeliiu, promyshlennosti i domovodstvu." *Trudy Stavropol'skoi uchenoi arkhivnoi komissii* no. 2 (1910): section 4, 36-63.

Rozenberg, L. K. "Nekotoryia svoeobraznyia i maloponiatnyia slova, voshedshiia v govor naseleniia stanits Severnogo Kavkaza." *Sbornik materialov dlia opisaniia mestnostei i plemen Kavkaza* no. 38 (1908): section 2, 37-48.

Rzhevuskii, A., comp. *Tertsy. Sbornik istoricheskikh, bytovykh i geograf-ichesko-statisticheskikh svedenii*. Vladikavkaz: Tipografiia oblastnago pravleniia Terskoi oblasti, 1888.

S., M. *Rukovodstvo k poznaniiu Kavkaza*. St. Petersburg: Tipografiia Morskago kadetskago korpusa, 1847.

S...v, I. "Otkrytie remeslennoi shkoly v stanitse Naurskoi, Mozdokskago polka, vo vremia proezdka po voisku nakaznago atamana." *Terskiia vedomosti*, 10 June 1868, 94-95.

Safonov, I. "Mozdok." *Kavkaz*, 27 July 1861, 312-13.

Samoilov, K. "Zametki o Chechne." *Panteon* 23, 9 (September 1855): section 3, 43-86; 23, 10 (October 1855): section 2, 29-64.

Semenov, N. "Drugoe predanie o Kizliare." *Terskiia vedomosti*, 10 January 1891, 4.

―――. "Pis'mo k redaktoru." *Terskiia vedomosti*, 26 April 1887, 3-4.

―――. "Zametka." *Terskii sbornik* 1 (1890): section 2, 171-176.

Semenov, P. "Neskol'ko stranichek iz zhizni kazakov st. Sleptsovskoi, Sunzhenskago otdela, Terskoi oblasti." *Sbornik materialov dlia opisaniia mestnostei i plemen kavkaza* 1893 (16): 162-210.

―――. "Stanitsa Sleptsovskaia, Terskoi oblasti, Vladikavkazskago okruga." *Sbornik materialov dlia opisaniia mestnostei i plemen Kavkaza* 5 (1886): 172-208.

Semevskii, Mikhail. "Aleksandr Aleksandrovich Bestuzhev (Marlinskii). 1798-1837." *Otechestvennyia zapiski* 131, 7 (July 1860): 43-100.

Semilutskii, A. "Kratkii istoriko-statisticheskii obzor seleniia Bezopasnago, Stavropol'skoi gubernii." *Sbornik materialov dlia opisaniia mestnostei i plemen kavkaza* 16 (1893): 211-21.

Shabanov, I. "Predokhranitel'nyia mery, prinimaemyia protiv razlivov Tereka." *Kavkaz*, 17 March 1863, 137-38; 24 March 1863, 151-52; 28 March 1863, 155-58.

Shamrai, V. S., comp. "Istoricheskaia spravka k voprosu o iasyriakh na Severnom Kavkaze i v Kubanskoi oblasti i dokumenty, otnosiashchietsia k etomu voprosu." *Kubanskii sbornik* 12 (1907): 167-256.

―――. "Kratkii ocherk menovykh (torgovykh) snoshenii po Chernomorskoi kordonnoi i beregovoi linii s zakubanskimi gorskimi narodami." *Kubanskii sbornik* 8 (1902): 351-522.

Sharafutdinova, R. Sh. "Eschë odin 'nizam' Shamilia." *Pis'mennye pamiatniki vostoka* (1975): 168-71.

Shavkhelishvili, A. I. "K voprosu o pereselenii Checheno-Ingushskikh plemen s gor na ravninu." *Izvestiia Checheno-Ingushskogo respublikanskogo kraevedcheskogo muzeia* 10 (1961): 112-29.

Shatskii, P. A. "Izmeneniia struktury posevnykh ploshchadei predkavkaz'ia na protiazhenii XIX veka." *Istoriia gorskikh i kochevnykh narodov severnogo kavkaza* 3 (1978): 87-101.

————, and V. N. Murav'ev. *Stavropol': istoricheskii ocherk.* Stavropol', 1977.

Shcherbina, F. "Beglye i krepostnye v Chernomorii." *Kievskaia starina* 6 (June 1883): 233-48.

Shenk, V. K. *Kazach'i voiska.* St. Petersburg: Imperatorskaia glavnaia kvartira, 1912; repr., n.p.: Aktsionernoe obshchestvo "Dobral'," 1992.

Shidlovskii, Iu. "Zapiski o Kizliare." *Zhurnal Ministerstva vnutrennikh del* 4 (1843): 161-208.

Shipov, Nikolai. *Istoriia moei zhizni. Razskaz byvshago krepostnago krest'ianina.* St. Petersburg: Tipografiia V. S. Balasheva, 1881.

Shvetsov, V. *Ocherk o Kavkazskikh gorskikh plemenakh.* Moscow: Universitetskaia tipografiia, 1856.

Sitovskii, N. *Obzor dvadtsatipiatiletnei deiatel'nosti Kavkazskago obshchestva sel'skago khoziaistva (1850-1875).* Tiflis: Tipografiia Glavnago upravleniia namestnika kavkazskago, 1875.

Sivkov, K. V. "O proektakh okonchaniia Kavkazskoi voiny v seredine XIX v." *Istoriia SSSR* 3 (May-June 1958): 191-96.

Slatta, Richard. *Gauchos & the Vanishing Frontier.* Lincoln: University of Nebraska Press, 1983; repr. 1992.

Slivitskii, I. "Ocherk Kavkaza i Zakavkaz'ia. Bugry." *Kavkaz,* 18 September 1848, 145-47.

————. "Ocherki Kavkaza i Zakavkaz'ia. Kazatskii khutor i staroobriadcheskie skity v Ishorakh." *Kavkaz,* 27 November 1848, 190-92; 4 December 1848, 195-96.

"Smeta i taksa na otpusk iz kazennykh dach Stavropl'skoi gubernii lesnykh materialov na 1850-1851 gody." *Izvestiia Kavkazskago otdela Imperatorskago russkago geograficheskago obshchestva* 5, 4 (1878): supplement, 30-31.

Soimonov, F. I. *Opisanie Kaspiiskago moria i chinennykh na onom Rossiiskikh zavoevani i, iako chast' istorii gosudaria imperatora Petra Veligako*. St. Petersburg: Imperatorskaia Akademiia Nauk, 1763.

Solov'ev, S. M. "Rasskazy iz Russkoi istorii XVIII veka. Sto svadeb v Astrakhani." In *Chteniia i rasskazy po istorii Rossii*. Moscow: Izdatel'stvo "Pravda," 1989.

Sosiev, A. "Stanitsa Ekaterinogradskaia. Istoriko-statisticheskii ocherk." *Terskii sbornik 5* (1903): 1-29.

"Sredniia tseny v Dekabre mesiatse 1853 goda v g. Stavropole na produkty i s''estnye pripasy." *Izvestiia Kavkazskago otdela Imperatorskago russkago geograficheskago obshchestva* 5, 4 (1878): supplement, 90.

"Statisticheskie svedeniia o Kavkazskoi oblasti i Zemle voiska Chernomorskago." *Zhurnal Ministerstva vnutrennykh del* 2, 3 (1830): 183-206; 3, 4 (1830): 123-48; 3, 5 (1830): 111-48.

Stepanov, P. "Beglye ocherki Kabardy." *Kavkaz*, 19 October 1861, 442-44.

Steven. "Kratkaia vypiska iz puteshestviia g. kollezhskago sovetnika Stevena po Kavkazskomu kraiu v 1810 godu." *Severnaia pochta* 59 (1811): no page numbers.

Stökl, Gunter. *Die Entstehung des Kosakentums*. Munich: Isar Verlag, 1953.

Streis, Ia. Ia. [J. J. Struys]. *Tri Puteshestviia*. Moscow: Ogiz-Sotsekgiz, 1935.

Studenetskaia, E. N. *Odezhda narodov Severnogo Kavkaza XVIII-XX vv*. Moscow: "Nauka," 1989.

Sunderland, Willard. "Russians into Iakuts? 'Going Native' and Problems of Russian National Identity in the Siberian North, 1870s-1914." *Slavic Review* 55, 4 (1996): 806-25.

"Svedenie o iarmarke, byvshei Stavropol'skago uezda v selenii Medvezh'em, 20-go Sentiabria 1850 goda." *Kavkaz*, 20 December 1850, 399.

"Svedenie o iarmarke, byvshei v gorode Georgievske v den' pokrova Presviatyia Bogoroditsy, t.e. 1 Oktiabria 1850 goda." *Kavkaz*, 23 December 1850, 404.

"Svedenie o iarmarke, byvshei v gorode Georgievske v den' Sv. Nikolaia, 9 Maia 1850 g.." *Kavkaz*, 20 December 1850, 399.

T., N. N. [N. N. Tolstoi]. "Okhota na Kavkaze." *Sovremennik* 61, 1 (1857): 169-232.

Terskii oblastnyi statisticheskii komitet. *Sbornik svedenii o Terskoi oblasti.* Ed. N. Blagoveshchenskii. Vladikavkaz: Tipografiia Terskago oblastnago pravleniia, 1878.

Tkachëv, G. A. "Bitva 14 Maia 1614 g. pod Astrakhan'iu i eia znachenie v istorii Rossii." *Zapiski Terskago obshchestva liubitelei kazach'ei stariny* no. 7 (July 1914): 21-30.

————, comp. *Grebenskie, Terskie i Kizliarskiekazaki. (Kniga dlia chteniia v stanichnykh i polkovykh shkolakh, bibliotekakh i komandakh).* Vladikavkaz: Elektropechatnia tipografii Terskago oblastnogo pravleniia, 1911.

————. *Stanitsa Chervlennaia. Istoricheskii ocherk.* Vladikavkaz: Elektropechatnia tipografii Terskago oblastnogo pravleniia, 1912.

Tolstoi, L. N. *Kazaki.* Leningrad: Izdatel'stvo "Detskaia literatura," 1969.

Toropov, N. *Opyt'' meditsinskoi geografii Kavkaza.* St. Petersburg: Tipografiia Iakova Treia, 1864.

Totoev, F. V. "Razvitie rabstva i rabotorgovli v Chechne (vtoraia polovina XVIII veka-40-e gody XIX veka)." *Izvestiia Checheno-Ingushskogo nauchno-issledovatel'skogo instituta istorii, iazyka, literatury i ekonomiki pri Sovete ministrov Checheno-Ingushskoi ASSR,* seriia istoriia 8, 1 (1969): 185-96.

Traho, Ramazan. "Circassians." *Central Asian Survey* 10, 1/2 (1991): 1-64.

Tul'chinskim, N. P. "Poemy, legendy, pesni, skazki i poslovitsy gorskikh Tatar nal'chikskago okruga Terskoi oblasti." *Terskii sbornik* 6 (1903): 248-334.

Tvalchrelidze, A., *Stavropolskaia guberniia v statisticheskom, geograficheskom, istoricheskom i sel'sko-khoziaistvennom otnosheniiakh.* Stavropol': Tipografiia M. N. Khoritskogo, 1897.

Umanets, A. A. "Kizliarskii chastnyi karantin." *Zhurnal Ministerstva vnutrennikh del* 18 (1847): 74-84.

Urusov, S. M. "Stanitsa Ekaterinogradskaia, Terskoi oblasti, Mozdokskago otdela." *Sbornik materialov dlia opisaniia mestnostei i plemen Kavkaza* 33 (1904): 1-34.

Usner, Jr., Daniel H. *Indians, Settlers, & Slaves in a Frontier Exchange Economy: The Lower Mississippi Valley Before 1783.* Chapel Hill: University of North Carolina Press, for the Institute of Early American History and Culture, 1992.

V., S. P. P. "Vinogradnyia zavedeniia v Kizliare." *Kavkaz,* 12 October 1846, 164.

V...v, A. "Kratkii ocherk Stavropol'skii gubernii v promyshlennom i torgovom otnosheniiakh." *Kavkaz*, 15 May 1848, 79-80; 22 May 1848, 82-84; 5 June 1848, 90-92.

Varadinov, N. *Istoriia Ministerstva vnutrennikh del*. St. Petersburg: Tipografiia Ministerstva vnutrennikh del, 1858.

Vasil'ev, D. "Zagadka starogo Kizliara (Kizliar do 1735 goda)." In *Voprosy istorii Dagestana (dosovetskii period)*. Vol. 2. Makhachkala: Dagestanskii filial Akademii nauk SSSR. Institut istorii, iazyka i literatury im. G. Tsadasy, 1974.

Vasilikhin, Trifon. "Ocherk staroobriadchestva v stanitse Kalinovskoi Terskoi oblasti, s 1840 do 1880 g." *Kavkazskiia eparkhial'nyia vedomosti* 1 (1 January 1881): otdel neofitsial'nyi, 26-35; 2 (16 January 1881): otdel neofitsial'nyi, 44-56; 3 (1 February 1881): otdel neofitsial'nyi, 100-07.

Vavilov, N. I., "Gornoe zemledelie Severnogo Kavkaza i perspektivy ego razvitiia." *Izvestiia. Akademiia nauk SSSR*. Seriia biologicheskaia 5 (1957): 590-600.

"Vedomost' o karantinakh i zastavakh v Kavkazskoi oblasti sushchestvuiushchikh." *Trudy Stavropol'skoi uchenoi arkhivnoi komissii* 2 (1910): section 1, 1-4.

"Vedomost' o nedel'nykh bazarnykh tsenakh, sushchestvovavshikh v gorode Stavropole s 24 Sentiabria, po 1 Oktiabria 1850 goda." *Izvestiia Kavkazskago otdela Imperatorskago russkago geograficheskago obshchestva* 5, 4 (1878): supplement, 33-34.

Verstennikov, V. "Maslianitsa v Ekaterinograde." *Kavkaz*, 16 April 1849, 61-62.

Vertepov, G. A. "Khoziaistvennoe polozhenie nizov'ev reki Tereka." *Terskii sbornik* 6 (1903): 13-53.

Vinogradov, V. B., and T. S. Magomadova. "Gde stoiali Sunzhenskie gorodki?" *Voprosy istorii* 7 (1972).

Vodarskii, V. A. "Pesni, zapisannyia v Chervlennoi i Starogladkovskoi stanitsakh Terskoi oblasti v 1901 godu." *Sbornik materialov dlia opisaniia mestnostei i plemen Kavkaza* 39 (1908): 57-80.

Voiskovoe khoziaistvennoe pravlenie. *Statisticheskiia monografii po izsledovaniiu stanichnago byta Terskago kazach'iago voisko*. Vladikavkaz: Tipografiia Terskago oblastnago pravleniia, 1881.

Volkonskii, N. A. "Voina na vostochnom Kavkaze s 1824 po 1834 g. v sviazi s miuridizmom."

Kavkazskii sbornik 10 (1886): 1-224.

Volkova, N. G. "Madzhary (iz istorii gorodov Severnogo Kavkaza)." *Kavkazskii etnograficheskii sbornik* 5 (1972): 41-66.

Voronov, N. I., ed. and comp. *Sbornik statisticheskikh svedenii o Kavkaze*. Vol. 1. Tiflis: Kavkazskii otdel Imperatorskago russkago geograficheskago obshchestva, 1869.

Vostrikov, P. "Pover'ia, primety i suevernye obychai Naurtsev." *Sbornik materialov dlia opisaniia mestnostei i plemen Kavkaza* 37 (1907): section 2, 1-93.

————, P. A. "Stanitsa Naurskaia, Terskoi oblasti." *Sbornik materialov dlia opisaniia mestnostei i plemen kavkaza* 33 (1904): section 2, 102-309.

Vrotskii, N. A. "Groznyi. Chechnia kak khlebnyi oazis. Kanalizatsiia eia." *Terskiia vedomosti*, 22 January 1874, 2-3.

"Vzgliad na Kavkazskuiu liniiu." *Severnyi arkhiv* 2 (January 1822): 163-83.

Wagner, Friedrich. *Schamyl and Circassia*. Translated by Kenneth R. H. Mackenzie. London: G. Routledge and Co., 1854.

Wagner, Moritz. *Travels in Persia, Georgia and Koordistan; With Sketches of the Cossacks and the Caucasus*. London: Hurst and Blackett, 1856.

Z...v. "Puteshestviia. Poezdka iz Mozdoky." *Tiflisskiia vedomosti*, 10 July 1830, [not paginated]; 12 July 1830, [not paginated].

Zagorskii, Iv. "Vosem' mesiatsev v plenu u gortsev." *Kavkazskii sbornik* 19 (1898): 221-47.

"Zametki k istorii vinodeliia i vinogradarstva v Kizliare." *Trudy Kavkazskago obshchestva sel'skago khoziaistva* 30, 4 (1885): 329-36; 5 (1885): 349-58.

Zasedateleva, L. B. "Evoliutsiiia obshchiny u Terskikh kazakov v XVI-XIX vv." *Sovetskaia etnografiia* no. 1 (January-February 1969): 25-36.

————. "K istorii formirovaniia Terskogo kazachestva." *Vestnik Moskovskogo universiteta* no. 3 (1969): 53-65.

————. *Terskie kazaki*. Moscow: Izdatel'stvo Moskovskogo universiteta, 1974.

Zatonskii, Konstantin. "K voprosu o Terskom raskole." *Stavropol'skiia eparkhial'nyia vedomosti* 19 (1 October 1890): 357-61.

Zemliak. "Iz istorii vozniknoveniia v. Kizliara." *Terskiia vedomosti*, 10 February 1891, 3.

————. "Priberezh'e Kaspiiskago moria." *Terskiia vedomosti*, 4 January 1887, 2; 12 February 1887, 3-4; 8 October 1887, 3-4.

Zobov, Mikhail. "Iz stanitsy." *Terskiia vedomosti*, 8 January 1875, 2.

Zubov, Platon. *Kartina Kavkazskago kraia, prinadlezhashchago Rossii, i sopredel'nykh onomu zemel'*. St. Petersburg: Tipografiia Konrada Vingebera, 1834.

Index